Linguistic Variability and
Intellectual Development

MIAMI LINGUISTICS SERIES

MIAMI LINGUISTICS SERIES NO. 9

LINGUISTIC VARIABILITY & INTELLECTUAL DEVELOPMENT

By

Wilhelm von Humboldt

Translated by George C. Buck and Frithjof A. Raven†

UNIVERSITY OF MIAMI PRESS

Coral Gables, Florida

Originally published in 1836 by the Royal Academy of Sciences of Berlin under the title *Über die Verschiedenheit des menschlichen Sprachbaues und ihren Einfluss auf die geistige Entwickelung des Menschengeschlechts.*

Copyright © 1971 by
University of Miami Press

Library of Congress Catalog Card Number 75-81614

ISBN 0-87024-133-8

Manufactured in Great Britain

Contents

Publisher's Note

ALTHOUGH THIS EDITION of Wilhelm von Humboldt's *Linguistic Variability and Intellectual Development* is based entirely on the original German edition, the translators and the publisher have attempted to clarify certain aspects of this work for the modern-day reader. One step in this direction has been the addition of numerous translator's notes; although these are interspersed throughout with von Humboldt's original notes, they are all introduced by the phrase "Translator's note." Another such step has been the attempt to provide initials for every individual mentioned in the text or notes. The purpose of this, of course, is to aid the reader in identifying these individuals. Unfortunately, we ourselves have been unable to identify with any certainty Basile (quite possibly this could be Giambatista Basile) or Castorena, and, as a result, these names appear without initials. Finally, we have also attempted to compile a complete Bibliography of all works cited in the notes by von Humboldt and by our translators. These works are arranged in alphabetical order and are also numbered in chronological order. In the notes, each work is referred to by its number, which appears in brackets. For the reader to ascertain what work is being cited, he simply has to turn to the appropriate number in the Bibiliography. We have tried to provide complete publication data for all of the bibliographic entries, but in some cases this was not entirely possible.

In a slight reorganization of this edition, we have combined several of the original edition's first six chapters; it should be noted that this edition contains 22 chapters and the original edition 25, but no material has been omitted. The footnotes, in addition, have been numbered consecutively within each chapter and have been put into a Notes section in the end matter, preceding the Bibliography.

As Professor Buck quite rightly points out in his "Foreword," in von

Humboldt's time language investigation was lacking both a uniform terminology and a system for the representation of linguistic symbols. Because we have found it difficult to ascertain exactly what type of symbol von Humboldt is using at any given moment, we, like von Humboldt, have set all of the linguistic examples in italics, regardless of whether these examples represent a phoneme, a simple letter of the alphabet, or some other linguistic unit.

Translator's Foreword

THE BEGINNINGS OF any endeavor present formidable problems, some of which become insignificant in the light of subsequent progress. In the past century, language investigation has developed a solid body of tested techniques, as well as a terminology that is for the most part internationally accepted. Neither of these assertions can be made about von Humboldt's time. His groping about for what are now familiar terms is often painful, but his constant philosophizing about matters which either can now be factually ascertained or should be rejected out of hand since they do not admit of proof would certainly be anathema to the modern linguist. And yet it is always a fascinating experience to observe at firsthand the operations of a great mind maneuvering in uncharted waters. Von Humboldt's contribution to our linguistic knowledge is a substantial one and deserves a wider audience than it has as yet been granted.

In 1836, von Humboldt's *Über die Kawisprache auf der Insel Java* was published posthumously in Berlin. As Alexander von Humboldt's Preface to the first volume indicates, this was intended to be a three-volume work consisting of an extensive and far-ranging introduction on linguistic variability and intellectual development (Volume I); an in-depth study of the Kawi language (Volume II); and an examination of all of the other known Malayan and South Sea languages (Volume III). However, the second and third volumes never appeared. We are presenting here a translation of the "Introduction" (Volume I), which has been taken, with very few emendations, from a 1935 facsimile printing of the first edition. Von Humboldt himself supervised the printing of chapters 3–10 prior to his death. Extracts from this work were first printed in French in 1832 and were taken from a letter by von Humboldt to E. Jacquet: "Extraits d'une lettre de Monsieur le Baron Guillaume de Humboldt à E. Jacquet sur les alphabets de Polynésie asiatique," in *Nouveau Journal*

Asiatique, Series 2, Vol. IX (June 1832), pp. 484–508. As I have mentioned, the first German edition followed in 1836.

To Frithjof Raven must go most of the credit for the rough translation and linguistic commentary of three-fourths of this book. At his unexpected demise, I was asked by the publisher and the translator's wife, Peggy, to revise and complete the manuscript. This I have done to the best of my ability, grateful for the opportunity to help salvage a literary legacy. Any faults must be mine alone.

Von Humboldt's style is not a simple one for modern ears nor is his thought always clear. For the most part I have let stand all of Professor Raven's linguistic terms in deference to his long experience in that field. Otherwise I have felt free to make whatever changes seemed required either by the text itself or by modern usage. A translation in the style of the early nineteenth century did not seem called for in a scientific work. Under the assumption that its new-found readers would be primarily interested in the meaning and priority of ideas, I set as my goals clarity and grace to the maximal degree within my power. Despair was my constant companion until the final word offered consolation.

George C. Buck

Seattle, Washington
January 1970

Preface

by Alexander von Humboldt

I HAVE A sad and serious duty to fulfill. As this work is about to be released for publication, I have a few words to say concerning its arrangement and division into sections. I would betray the publisher's unwarranted confidence if, in the course of my individual comments, I were to touch upon more than the external format and dared to follow him who has gone to his eternal reward over the pathway traversed by him into the limitless realm of language.

While the work appears to be in its final draft, individual parts would certainly have undergone further revision and supplementation. For the introduction [presented here], which traces the influence of language on the intellectual development of mankind, there were many additions planned; although these were suggested in lively conversation, they were never written down. My brother supervised only the printing of the first book [the introduction], and we owe the careful reading of the entire manuscript and the publication of the entire work in its present form to the diligence and scientific training of a young scholar who has repaid an honorable trust with many years of devoted loyalty. Dr. J. Buschmann, Curator of the Royal [Prussian] Library, who was recommended to the deceased by his dear friend, Professor F. Bopp, was especially suited to offer such assistance because of the versatility of his knowledge and because of his enthusiasm for the languages of Southeast Asia and of the New World.

The second book, with which the following part will begin, presents the grammatical structure of the Kawi language, developed from the heroic poem *Brata Yuddha*, in continuous comparison with all of the other known Malayan and South Sea languages. In the third book, the character of each of these idioms is determined individually, especially that of the Madecassian, Tagalic, Tongic, Tahitian, and New Zealandic. Strangely

enough, the relationships among the peoples of that great island world
and their common emanations transmitted through various analogies lead
the scholar in a few details back to the firmly established soil of Sanskrit.
Since my brother received a new and important communication from Mr.
J. Crawfurd in London shortly before his death, he made additions to
several passages in the first book concerning languages that are discussed
in the following books.

Among the foreign scholars whose communications enriched this work,
Mr. J. Crawfurd, the talented author of the *History of the Indian Archipelago*
and the *Embassy to the Court of Ava,* deserves first mention. From his
extensive collection of writings in the Malayan languages, he offered to my
revered brother for his use three handwritten Javanese dictionaries and a
handwritten Javanese grammar, as well as a copy of the Kawi poem
mentioned above. In view of the inadequacy of all public aids, it would
have been impossible without that offering for my brother to master the
Javanese and Kawi languages in their peculiarities. Mr. J. Crawfurd,
whose personal acquaintance I was happy to enjoy first in Paris, will
certainly accept this expression of gratitude from both brothers, which
goes to him with the same good wishes with which he offered the above
mentioned important materials.

In matters concerning the philosophy of linguistics or the corpus of the
Sanskrit language in particular, my brother conferred continuously until
his death with a man who was bound to him by the bonds of a long-
standing friendship and mutual respect, and who by his acumen and
indefatigable activity exerted a continuously increasing influence on the
direction of general, comparative linguistics. Professor F. Bopp received
from the departed each completed section with the request that he subject
it to a rigorous critique. At this point a frank expression of gratitude is
due to the intellectually stimulating influence of such a friend.

Intellectual power and strength of character enabled him whose loss we
mourn to penetrate more deeply into the structure of a greater number of
languages than may ever have been comprehended by a single mind. His
studies were aided by the favorable aspect of external conditions, and
even his frequent changes of residence or his public life did not interrupt
them. We may rejoice in seeing the final, or should I say ultimate, results of
these investigations concerning the entire field of linguistics unfolded in
the following pages. It would require traversing almost the complete
circle of my brother's scholarly associations, which he made during his
travels in Germany, England, France, Italy, and Spain, were all of the
individuals to be enumerated who were of use to him in those general
investigations and in the establishment of this great linguistic collection,

which together with his manuscripts and in accordance with his last will were incorporated into the Royal Library for public use.

Many of his general views as they gradually presented themselves to him were given for examination to intelligent and linguistically trained men with whom the deceased was in literary correspondence: A. W. von Schlegel, G. Herrmann, to whom the translation of the *Aeschylean Agamemnon* (read in the middle of the war's battles) had brought my brother close, S. de Sacy, F. H. W. Gesenius, E. Burnouf, F. Thiersch, C. Lassen, S. du Ponceau in Philadelphia, J. Pickering in Salem, F. Rosen in London, P. von Bohlen in Königsberg, A. F. Stenzler in Breslau, A. F. Pott in Halle, R. Lepsius in Rome, F. Neumann in Munich, J. G. L. Kosegarten, the Egyptian traveller G. Parthey, J. F. Champollion, J. P. Abel Rémusat, H. J. von Klaproth, and F. E. Schulz, who met his death in the Orient on a prestigious venture. The following pages bear witness to my brother's debt to the profound scholar of all classical antiquity, our friend A. Boeckh, and especially to his fortunate investigations on general metrics and the influence of Hellenic root variation.

Among those who assisted my brother with the languages which are analyzed individually in the work, I mention briefly for Javanese Baron G. A. G. van der Capellen, former Governor-General of the Dutch possessions in India [1819–1826], H. E. Minto, the Earl of Minto [Governor of Madras], from whom my brother received a casting of the great Javanese inscription made famous by T. S. Raffles, the linguistically gifted R. van Eysinga, and Mr. J. F. C. Gericke of Batavia; for the Malayan language the instructive correspondence with Sir A. Johnston, Dr. W. Marsden, and the knowledgeable Mr. E. Jacquet of Paris; for the Madecassian and the languages of the South Sea Islands, Rev. J. J. Freeman, missionary to Antananarivo on Madagascar, Professor E. Meyen in Berlin, Dr. K. E. Meinicke of Prenzlow, A. Lesson in Paris, and A. von Chamisso, who with rejuvenated eagerness investigated the languages of the Sandwich Islands which he himself had had the good fortune to visit.

Just as the languages of the Asiatic Island Empire have been treated in the work which we are now publishing, my late brother has also analyzed, according to the same principles and even more extensively, the American languages whose study has occupied him very seriously for many years now. Many of these studies are appropriate for publication, and I hope that J. Buschmann, who has lived in a little-known part of New Spain and with whom my brother intended to edit a series of writings on the languages of this part of the world, will soon find the time to carry out that extensive plan with the aid of the material already gathered. The material in the present South Asiatic work which points toward the profusion of American languages creates the most ardent wish to see important aids for the knowledge of the idioms of the new continent used by the friends of philosophical linguistics. According to the plan of the deceased, a Mexican-Latin dictionary together with a book of grammar should initiate the new undertaking.

I cannot think of the Royal Library, which has recently been so much enriched by the grace of the royal personage, without simultaneously—as if from a debt of legacy—expressing my most heartfelt gratitude to Mr. F. W. Wilken, Privy Governmental Counselor and equally respected as Head Librarian and researcher in historical and linguistic areas, for the obliging kindness with which he offered everything that was requisite for the elaboration and publication of this linguistic study. The facile and continuous use of this public collection was favored by its close proximity to the attractive country estate [Tegel Castle], where the departed, solitary and surrounded by the spirit of ancient art, lived only for his serious studies and for his family, to whom he clung until the hour of his death with a gentle, loving heart.

"It is," according to a statement of F. Schiller, one of the noblest souls of our age, "a general prejudice to esteem the worth of an individual in terms of the subject matter with which he occupies himself, not according to the manner in which he treats it." But where the subject matter produces the form and lends shape to it, where grace of idiom unfolds from the underlying concept as from the tenderest bud of the intellect, there the dichotomy, shown up by this prejudice, will readily be expunged. The present work expands the range of ideas to an extraordinary degree and simultaneously instructs us through the corpus of language how to interpret the intellectual destiny of peoples. If my hopes do not deceive me, it will permeate the reader with an elevating belief in and respect for humanity. It cannot help but put forth the conviction that a certain magnitude in the treatment of an object originates not from intellectual foundations alone, but preferably from greatness of character, from an unfettered mind never restricted by contemporaneous trivia, and from the unplumbed depths of the emotions.

Berlin

March 1836

Transliteration of Foreign Alphabets

AFTER MANY ATTEMPTS at this subject I do not consider it practical to use the same method of transliteration everywhere; rather, I believe that the reader is better accommodated if on the whole I follow the best traditions in these matters and yet permit myself those deviations which are appropriate for the material and for my purposes. Thus, in this present work I have always kept in mind that I am dealing chiefly with Javanese and Sanskrit writing and with a subject treated largely by English writers. My intention therefore has been to represent the foreign alphabets in such a manner that the reader may definitely recognize the original foreign orthography in them through the use of a few rules derived from the orthography of those languages.

I have not altered the orthography nor burdened down with symbols words which have been incorporated completely into our own books such as "Java," "Sanskrit," "Pandit," and others. As a rule, I cite the Sanskrit names and words in their basic form, and only as an exception do I cite them in the nominative.

SANSKRIT ALPHABET

The long vowels and diphthongs *e* and *o* are designated by a circumflex; the *r* vowel (ऋ) by a dot under the *r* and an added *i* (*ṛi*); the mute palatal, nonaspirated surd (च) by *ch*; the mute palatal, nonaspirated sonant (ज) by *j*; the lingual consonants by the corresponding dentals with a dot placed below them; the first semivowel (य) by *y*; the final semivowel (व) by *w*; the palatal sibilant (श) *s* with a *spiritus lenis* placed directly above it (*ś*); the lingual sibilant (ष) by *sh*; and all of the aspirated consonants by the unaspirated ones with an added *h*. The *anusvâra* and all nasal consonants, excepting the dentals *n* and *m*, are designated by an *n* with a dot below it (*ṇ*). A further distinction between these sounds is not necessary since the reader knows which Sanskrit sign is to be substituted for *ṇ* in accordance with the alphabetic character immediately following.

The *visarga* [*visarjaniya*] is transliterated by an *h* with a dot below it (*ḥ*). However, it scarcely occurs since, when it appears in Sanskrit words in the nominative case, this case ending is more correctly indicated by *s*.

The Barmanic [Burmese] Language

I write the first six of the vowels, the long and short *a*, *i*, and *u*, as in Sanskrit; I write the seventh as *e*, the eighth as *ei*, the ninth as *au*, the tenth as *âu*, and the triphthong consisting of *a*, *i*, and *u* as *ô*.

The voiced and voiceless nonaspirated stop phonemes of the five classes of consonants are transliterated precisely as in Sanskrit.

With respect to the voiced and voiceless aspirate stops, the change is made merely by writing the *h* in front of, instead of after, the consonant as in transliterating Sanskrit, i.e., *hk*, *hch*, *ht*, and so forth. This reversal, which is not unnatural per se since the consonant does not merely assume the aspiration but is expelled with aspiration, serves no further purpose than to distinguish these characters from the thirtieth Burmese consonant. The latter has the sound of the English phoneme *th*, and hence I should not like to designate it otherwise.

The nasals of the three first classes—in addition to the *anusvāra*—could be indicated in Sanskrit by the same sign, since their use complies with definite rules. In Burmese, however, this is not the case. I therefore indicate the guttural by the Spanish palatalized *n* (*n con tilde*: *ñ*), the palatal by *ng*, those of the three remaining classes as in Sanskrit, and the *anusvāra* by an *n* with a dot above it (*ṅ*).

The four semivowels are written as in Sanskrit, and the consonant following is transliterated by *th*. This sound pertains to the sibilants in Burmese whose script has not adopted any sibilant from the Sanskrit alphabet. In the spoken tongue, however, the lingual (English *sh*) is encountered. The latter is indicated scripturally by an *h* appended to the three first semivowels and to the *th*. Moreover, I prefix this *h* to these letters so that *hy*, *hr*, *hl*, and *hth* express the phonetic value of English *sh* in pronunciation. However, this pronunciation does not appear constant with respect to *l*, for G. H. Hough writes the word *hlyâ* ['tongue'] in the spoken language as *shyâ*, in contrast to *hlê*. The thirty-first Burmese consonant I transliterate by *h*, as in Sanskrit.

The heavy [principal] accent is designated, as is the case in the Burmese dialect itself, by a colon placed at the end of the words (:); the simple dot

(.), by which the light [secondary] accentuation is marked, is not placed under the final letter as is true in Burmese script, but behind it and about halfway up (*a·*).

REMARKS RELATIVE TO OTHER LANGUAGES

With respect to the other languages, which I cannot mention in detail at this point, I use the orthography adopted by the main writers on each of them. The spelling therefore follows that of their mother tongue. Hence, for the North American, several Asiatic, and the majority of South Sea dialects this pattern is English; for the Chinese and Madagascan languages this model is French; and for the Tagalic[1] dialects, as well as for those of "New Spain" and South America, the reader must follow the pattern inherent in the Spanish phonetic system.

The Objective of the Present Treatise

THE DISTRIBUTION OF human beings into races and tribes and the variation in their languages and dialects are certainly closely related, but both of these result primarily from the productivity of human intellectual power in all its forms. It is in the creation of human intellectual power that they find their recognition and their explanation to the extent that research is able to penetrate the relationship between them. This revelation of human intellectual power about the earth during the course of millennia, varying in type and degree, constitutes the ultimate goal of all intellectual activity; it is, moreover, the ultimate idea which the history of the world must clearly strive to produce.

This expansion of the intellectual life is the sole possession that the individual, to the extent that he participates, may regard as indestructible. And in a nation it represents that entity from which, in turn, great individualities unfailingly develop. Comparative linguistics, or the precise investigation of the diversity through which innumerable peoples resolve the problem of linguistic structure imposed upon them as human beings, fails to attract serious interest unless its relationship to the pattern of national intellectual power is made clear. But the insight into the actual nature of a nation and into the internal relationships of an individual language, as well as its relationship to linguistic requirements in general, depends entirely upon consideration of the total intellectual individuality. For this alone, dictated by nature and its milieu, furnishes the articulation for the character of the nation. Upon its heritage alone, consisting of an accumulation of deeds, institutions, and productive ideas, is based the nation's character and rests its dignity and the power to continue itself diachronically down to posterity. Language [human speech] on the other hand is the organ of the internal being,[1] this self that progressively achieves internal cognition and enunciation. All of its tiniest rootlets are anchored

firmly in the national intellectual potential. The more appropriately the
latter reacts upon it, the more principled and richer its development. As
language in its intricacies is but an effect of the national linguistic sense,
those problems concerning the complex structuring of languages (from
which also stem their most important variables) cannot be solved adequately if one does not subscribe to this viewpoint. Material cannot, of
course, be sought there for that which is inherently restricted to historical
treatment by comparative linguistics. Nevertheless, an insight into the
original concatenation of facts and a comprehension of language as an
internally cohesive organism may be obtained. These, in turn, aid in a
correct appraisal of individual factors.

Observation of the connection between linguistic variation and the
distribution of tribes on the one hand, and the production of human
intellectual power on the other, as a relationship developing progressively
in varying degree and in new configurations, is the theme with which this
treatise will be concerned, insofar as these two phenomena are capable of
clarifying each other.

Linguistic Variability and
Intellectual Development

CHAPTER ONE

The Course of Human Development

A PENETRATING LOOK at the contemporary status of political, artistic, and scientific education reveals a protracted chain of mutually interacting and determinative causes and effects proceeding through many centuries. However, in pursuing the foregoing factors, it soon becomes evident that two different elements prevail which unfortunately cannot be investigated equally. For, whereas one portion of the progressive causal chain may be sufficiently clarified in terms of another, obstacles are now and again encountered that resist further attempts toward solution, as can be substantiated by every effort to compile a cultural history of the human race.

One can trace these obstacles to that intellectual power whose nature cannot be completely elucidated and whose effects preclude prediction. This power merges with its own product and that of its environment, yet shapes and modifies the product together with the environment according to its own inherent peculiarity. The universal history of the world could take its inception from any great individual of an era, revealing the frame of reference extant at the time and tracing the manner in which previous centuries gradually built it up. The way in which it produced its so clearly defined and basically supported activity with respect to that which constitutes its actual stamp may be detected, although it will be presented to a lesser degree than it is sensed; moreover, it cannot be derived from something other. This is the natural and ubiquitously recurring phenomenon of human activity. Originally, everything included therein is innate: perception, sensation, thought, decision, speech, and deed. Yet as this innate feature contacts the external ambient, it operates progressively and determines by its inherent configuration other activity, either internal or external. In the course of time, media develop to check what was originally hastily produced. Consequently, of the heritage of

elapsed centuries, progressively less is lost to posterity. This is now the area
wherein research may pursue the phenomenon stepwise. However, it is at
the same time transected by the operation of new and incalculable forces.
Without correct isolation and evaluation of these two elements, of which
the material constituting the one can be so potent that it hazards total
suppression of the other, no true estimation of the noblest factor is possible.
This has been proved by the history of all ages.

The deeper we descend into the past, the more the accumulation of
material transmitted from one generation to the next melts away. Then
another phenomenon is encountered which, to some extent, shifts the
investigation into a new field. The established individuals, familiar to us
by their external situations, appear more rarely and indistinctly. Their
destinies, their very names fluctuate. Indeed, it becomes uncertain
whether what has been ascribed to them was exclusively their effort, or
whether their names merely became the reference point for the works of
numerous individuals. They become lost in a category of shadow figures.
This is, for instance, the case in Greece with Orpheus and Homer, in
India with Manu, Wyàsa, and Wàlmiki, and with other celebrated names
of antiquity. But the definite individuality recedes even more as we progress farther into the past. A language so rounded off and polished as
Homeric Greek must have long been sung and resung in the undulations
of poetry—indeed throughout ages of which no records have been preserved. This is revealed even more distinctly in the original form of
languages per se.

Language is deeply entwined in the intellectual development of
humanity itself, it accompanies the latter upon every step of its localized
progression or regression; moreover, the pertinent cultural level in each
case is recognizable in it. There is, however, an epoch in which we only
discern it, and wherein it does not merely accompany intellectual development but occupies its place completely. Language wells from a depth of
human existence which prohibits regarding it generally as a labor and as a
creation of peoples. It possesses an evident spontaneity—even if in its
inherent nature it is simultaneously inexplicable. Considered from this
approach, it is no product born of activity (there is no dynamistic evolve-
ment), but an involuntary emanation of the intellect; hence it is not a
labor of nations, but rather a gift fallen to them as a result of their innate
destiny. They make use of it without knowing how they produced it.

Apart from this, languages must have evolved along with the flourishing
tribes from the respective intellectual peculiarities of the latter, which
imposed numerous restrictions on them. It is no empty play on words to
represent *language* as originating spontaneously and divinely free, whereas

languages are depicted as bound to, and dependent on, the nations to which they pertain,[1] for in such case they have entered into a definitely restricted area (see chapters 3, 4, and 19). When speech and song [poetry] first flowed freely, language developed in accordance with the measure of enthusiasm, in conjunction with the freedom and intensity of the collaborating intellectual powers involved.[2] This enthusiasm could, however, only emanate from all individuals simultaneously; each individual had to be supported by his neighbor in this effort, since enthusiasm receives new impetus only from the assurance that it is being understood.[3] There is thus disclosed herein, even if obscurely, a glance into a time when individuals are lost in the masses of peoples and when language itself is the product of the intellectual creative power.

In every survey of world history there is a factor of progress, to which allusion is made here also. It is, however, by no means my intent to establish a teleological system or a completeness converging at infinity; in fact, I find myself upon an entirely different course. Peoples luxuriate vegetatively as do plants, propagating their kind over the surface of the earth and enjoying a happy and active life. This process continues without interruption for each extinguishing life and without consideration for its effect on future centuries. The fate determined by nature, that everything which breathes shall fulfill its destiny to its last gasp, and the objective of a charitable benevolence, which dictates that every creature enjoy his life, are attained. Indeed, each new generation traverses the same happy or sorrowful existence of successful or impeded activity. Wherever the human being appears, however, he acts as a human, associates with others, makes arrangements, and enacts laws; where this cultural phenomenon has occurred less successfully, migratory individuals or groups have introduced their more successful features. Thus with the origin of man is also implanted the germ of civilization, which grows with the progressive development of man's existence. We can perceive this humanization in increasing progressions. Indeed, this feature is based partially on its very true nature, and partially on the extent to which it has already flourished, resulting in the fact that its further improvement may scarcely be disturbed.

In the two points brought out here lies a systematization which cannot be overlooked. It will prevail also in others, but it will not confront us in this manner. It may not be presumed, however, if seeking it out threatens to lead us astray in the investigation of factual data. That factor which concerns us here can be subordinated to this systematization least of all. The phenomenon of the intellectual power of the human being in its varying configuration is not bound to progress with respect to time and to collections of data.[4] Its origin is as inexplicable as its effect is calculable. Furthermore, the acme in this generic bracket is not exactly the most recent to appear. Hence, if it be desired to pursue here the traces left by the cultural achievements of creative nature, ideas must not be interpolated into it, but it must be taken as found. In all its creations it produces a certain number of forms, in which are expressed the realization of each generic type and the perfection of its idea. We cannot ask why there are not more or other forms. The only pertinent reply would be, of course, that others simply do not exist. According to this viewpoint, however, everything existing in both intellectual and corporeal form may be regarded as the effect of a basic force, developing according to limiting conditions unknown to us.

It we do not wish to renounce all discoveries of a relationship obtaining among the phenomena associated with the human race, we must revert to some independent and original cause, which is not in itself determined or transitory. This leads us naturally to a life principle, developing freely in its totality, a principle moreover whose individual facets are not inherently dissociated from one another even though their external manifestations occur in isolation. This aspect of a life principle is entirely different from a view of its objectives inasmuch as it is not directed toward a set goal but emanates from a cause recognized as unfathomable. It alone seems to the present author a feasible explanation of the differing reaction patterns of the human intellect. For, if I may be permitted to make such distinctions, the customary demands of mankind are satisfactorily met by forces of nature and by the mechanical continuation of human activity. But the appearance of a greater individuality in individuals and in peoples, practically inexplicable by any derivation, interferes suddenly and without warning with the course more obviously determined by cause and effect.[5] This same viewpoint is now equally applicable to the principal ranges of effectiveness of human intellectual power, specifically to the realm of language, which I should like to dwell on. The variability of language can be regarded as the striving with which the power of speech, a universal human endowment, erupts more or less successfully depending on whether it is aided or hindered by the people's innate intellectual power.

For, if languages are considered a purposeful intellectual endeavor, it becomes obvious that this objective may be attained to a lesser or greater degree. Indeed, the various ways in which this inequality of proficiency will manifest itself are revealed early. Greater proficiency may be discerned fundamentally in the vigor and plenitude of the intellectual power affecting language. It is further evident in the particular fitness of this power as it affects distinctiveness of concepts, or in the depth of its penetration into the nature of a concept, highlighting its most distinctive characteristic. It is no less distinguishable in the industry and creative strength of the imagination, as well as in the harmony and rhythm of all of the elements of language, to which belong the facility and versatility of the vocal organs and the acuity and refinement of the ear. Furthermore, we must take into consideration the nature of the transmitted material and the historical midpoint at which a nation, acted upon by antiquity and realizing its own inherent potential, finds itself in an era of a significant linguistic transformation.[6] There are also problems in languages which may be judged only by the effort expended on them, rather than by the results of same. For languages are not always successful in developing their latent directions completely, no matter how distinctly the presence of these directions is indicated. To this area pertains, for example, the entire problem of inflection and agglutination, concerning which a great deal of misunderstanding has prevailed and still persists. The fact that some nations of more fortunate talents and under more favorable circumstances possess more excellent languages than do others derives from the very nature of the matter. However, we are also led to the more deeply rooted cause already mentioned: the creation of language is an innate necessity of humanity. It is not a mere external vehicle, designed to sustain social intercourse, but an indispensable factor for the development of human intellectual powers, culminating in the formulation of philosophical doctrine. The latter can be achieved only when man, working with his fellow man, sharpens his thinking. If we regard each language as an experiment, which we can hardly avoid doing, and then take all languages together as a series, contributing to the fulfillment of this need, then it can probably be assumed that the power to create speech does not reside in man until, individually or collectively, he has produced whatever satisfies most completely the necessary requirements.[7] Therefore, within the scope of this assumption, a stepwise progression of the principle underlying the structural character of languages may be discovered even among apparently unrelated languages and language groups. But in this case, this relationship between externally disconnected phenomena must repose in a common internal cause, which can only be the development of the acting force. Language is one of the forms of expression of the universal human intellectual power, and it is continuously dynamic. Differently expressed, we see in language man's striving to wrest reality from the idea of linguistic perfection. To pursue this striving, and to represent it in its simplest, ultimate solution, is the occupation of the comparative linguist.[8]

The study of languages has no need for this viewpoint, which perhaps appears too hypothetical, as a foundation. Yet it can and must utilize it as a stimulant to attempt to ascertain whether such a stepwise progressive approximation to perfection in its structure can be discovered. There could be, after all, a series of languages of simpler and more composite organization which, after comparison, might reveal in their structures a growing approximation of the ideal linguistic development. Even in the case of complex forms, the nucleus of these languages would logically have to bear the imprint of their particular drive for perfection, an imprint that would have to be more clearly discernible in these complex forms than in others. Progress in such languages would be noted above all in the discreteness and the perfected articulation of their sounds, in the dependent syllable formation, in the separation of their subformations, and in the structure of their simplest words. It would be evidenced further in the treatment of words as complete phonetic morphemes, which sought to obtain true word unity corresponding to the unity of concept. Finally, it would be found in the appropriate separation of that which should appear independent in language and that which should appear with the independent unit, as form.[9] For this purpose, a method is required to distinguish loosely joined linguistic material from that which has become symbolically fused. In this consideration of languages, however, I shall single out the changes which can be derived from their original forms in accordance with the destiny of the language. The circuit of the primeval forms appears to be closed and, in the position in which we now find the development of human powers, not repeatable. For no matter how innate language is in its entirety, it still possesses at the same time an independent external existence, exerting a power against man himself. The origin of such primordial forms would hence presume a differentiation of peoples excellently endowed with rather keen intellects which can now no longer be conceived, unless a definite epoch in human history, as well as in the individual man, was allotted to the emergence of new languages.

CHAPTER TWO

Effect of Exceptional Intellectual Power: Civilization, Culture, and Education

THE TRULY CREATIVE principle operating in the recondite and secret course of mankind's development is the power of the intellect which sallies forth from its inner depth and plenitude to intervene in the events of the world; although in sharp contrast to it, the visible development is obviously linked by a cause and effect relationship to the hidden one, which I touched on above. It is the eminent intellectual peculiarity, broadening the concept of human intellectuality, that emerges unexpectedly and, insofar as its most abstruse features are concerned, inexplicably. It is distinguished particularly by the fact that its products do not become mere foundations upon which one may continue to build, but bear within themselves the creative spark of life. These products propagate life because they proceed from its fullness; the energy producing them works at peak intensity in truly creative fashion, though it is naïvely unaware of its own action. It has not hit upon something new simply by accident, nor merely continued with an old procedure. The plastic art of Egypt originated in this manner. It succeeded in constructing the human figure organically and thereby first impressed the stamp of genuine art on its works. In this respect, although with otherwise close kinship, Hindu (Indian) poesy and philosophy and classical antiquity bear a differing character. The latter, moreover, is marked by the Grecian and Roman manner of thinking and representation. Likewise, the principal basis of modern culture originated later from Roman poetry and from the intellectual life in the European Occident, which developed suddenly with the decline of the Roman tongue, and which has now become independent. Where such phenomena did not occur or were stifled by adverse conditions, even the noblest culture was unable to achieve greatness again, once its natural course was impeded. This is illustrated by the Greek language and by many residua of Greek art dating from the centuries that Greece, through no fault of its own, was held captive by barbarism. The venerable form of the language then becomes fragmental and admixed with foreign elements, and its true organic structure disintegrates. The forces besetting it are incapable of redirecting it upon a new course of development with the breath of new life. Circumstances which explain all such phenomena can be ascertained.

The human being always relates to existing material. For every idea whose discovery or execution imparts a new impetus to human endeavor, it can be shown by sagacious and meticulous research how it was previously present and grew little by little in the human mentality. But, whenever the stimulating breath of genius is absent in individuals or in peoples, the subdued hue of such glowing coals never bursts into bright flames. No matter how little the nature of these creative forces actually permits seeing through them, it is still apparent that they have the capacity to control the appropriate material from within, to transform it into ideas or to subordinate it to ideas. Even in his most primitive state, man transcends the instant of present time and does not tarry in the realm of mere sensual pleasure. Among the crudest hordes of barbarians are found love of adornment and finery, dancing, music, and song. There may also be detected inklings of a divine future, together with the hopes based upon it, including traditions and legends that usually revert to the origin of man and his native soil. The more intensely and brightly the intellectual power, operating automatically in accordance with its principles and intuitive faculties, casts its light into this realm of the past and future, with which man surrounds his immediate existence, the more purely and richly does his culture take shape. Thus originate science and art. The goal of mankind's progress is, therefore, always the fusion of that which is spontaneously created from within the individual with the given external circumstances. Both the individual creativity and the culture are, moreover, comprehended in their purity and perfection, and they are interdependent, as the urgencies of their natures demand.

Although we have represented intellectual individuality as something excellent and distinguished, it must—even where it has attained its loftiest level—still be regarded as a restriction of nature in general, a course the individual is compelled to pursue. This follows because every idiosyncrasy can exist only by virtue of a predominant and hence exclusive principle. But precisely by such constriction is the force heightened and intensified, and the associated exclusion may be guided by a principle of totality until several such peculiarities are again unified. Upon the foregoing is based essentially every more elevated association of human beings in amity, love, or sublime collaborative effort dedicated to the well-being of the fatherland and humanity.

Without pursuing further this line of thought as to how the restriction of individuality discovers for the human being the only way to approach ever more closely the unattainable totality, it will suffice at this point merely to draw attention to the power which actually constitutes man as such and is simultaneously the simple definition of his being, in its contact with the environment. It is revealed in the vegetative aspect of human life, which develops mechanically along a prescribed course. It is also seen in individual phenomena and in new configurations which expand this concept. Thus, for example, the invention of algebra was such a new configuration of the mathematical direction of the human mind. Similar examples may be found in every science and in every art. Such evidence in language will be sought out at a later point.

These configurations are not, however, limited merely to patterns of thought and representation, but are encountered quite excellently in character development. For, what proceeds from the totality of human power must not rest, lest it revert completely to its primitive state. The feelings and thoughts of the inner man, together with the environment under his influence, must make it evident that they are exposing the whole of human nature in expanded form, while remaining subjected to those extensive individual efforts. The most general effect, raising the human race to its most dignified position, originates at this point. But it is language, the focal point at which the most varied individualities are united by expressions of external ambitions and inner perception, that enjoys the closest and liveliest mutual relationship with character. The most forceful and the most gently receptive, the most incisive and the most fruitful human minds pour into language their power and their tenderness, their depth of spirit; it, in turn, sends forth from its womb related echoes that are destined to propagate identical moods. The more character becomes refined and ennobled, the more it smoothes and unifies the individual aspects of the spirit and imparts to them, just as in the plastic arts, a configuration, comprehensible in its unity but in each case forming an ever purer contour from within. This configuration is suited to represent and promote language by its subtle harmony. But the effects of character development are incomparably more difficult to compute than are those of mere intellectual progress, since they are based for the most part on the mysterious influences by which one generation is linked to the succeeding one.

There are, thus, in the course of development of the human race

progress mutations which are attained only because an unusual power unexpectedly soars upward to them. These are cases for which we must
replace the usual explanation that the effect is produced by the assumption of an equivalent force. All intellectual advance can proceed only from
the manifestation of innate power. To this extent it always has a concealed, inexplicable basis, attributable to its automatic nature. However,
when this innate power suddenly exceeds, in its creativity, the con-
straints placed upon it by its previous course, all possibility of explanation
ceases. I hope I have made the foregoing statements clear to the point of
conviction, for they are important. Moreover, it now follows automatically
that, where intensified examples of the same effort can be discerned, no
gradual progression may be assumed, unless the facts require it irrefutably,
since every significant increase pertains to a particular creative power. The
structure of the Chinese and of the Sanskrit languages may serve as an
example. Probably a gradual progression from the one to the other could
be conceived. However, if one truly senses the essence of language at all,
and of these two in particular, when one has advanced to the point of
fusion of concept with the phoneme[1] in both, there is disclosed in the
latter the principle of their differing organic structures. In abandoning the
possibility of gradual development of the one from the other, one will
assign to each its own foundation in the spirit of their respective races.
Hence they will be evaluated solely in terms of the general drives governing linguistic evolution, and only in the ideal sense will they be considered
as stages in the succession of linguistic structure. By neglecting the meticulous separation herein established of the escalating creative progress of
human intellectual power, which must be calculated and may not be
foreseen, we ban the operation of genius completely from the history of the
world, a factor that is revealed at given moments in peoples as well as in
individuals. One runs into the danger also of improperly evaluating the
varying conditions of human society. Thus features are frequently
ascribed to civilization and culture which could not possibly have resulted
from them, but which were effected by a power to which they themselves
owe their existence.

With respect to languages a very general concept prevails: we must
impute to them all their merits and every expansion of their scope, just as
if it were but a question of the difference between culture and uncultured
idioms. If we consult history, such a power of civilization and culture over
language cannot be at all confirmed. Java obviously received a civilization
and culture higher than its own from India, and both, moreover, to a
significant degree. However, its indigenous tongue did not as a consequence change its more primitive form, even though it was less adapted

· ·

to the requirements of logical thought. Instead, it plundered what was requisite from the far more refined Sanskrit and forced it into its own mold.[2] Even India itself, though civilized ever so early and without foreign communication, did not receive its language in this way. It welled rather from its deep-seated linguistic principle, produced by a genuine linguistic sensitivity, just as its civilization itself flowed from the genius inherent in its populace. For this reason language and civilization are not always in a like ratio to one another. Peru was easily the most civilized country in America, no matter what aspect of language and civilization under the Incas is considered. Certainly, however, no linguistic scholar of the general Peruvian language,[3] which the Peruvians attempted to spread through war and conquests, will concede a preferential position to it compared to the remaining dialects of the New World. It is, according to the author's convictions, significantly inferior to the Mexican. Allegedly rude and uncultured languages may possess conspicuous excellences in their structures fundamentally. It would not, therefore, be impossible that they might excel in this respect over more highly cultured tongues. Even comparison of the Burmese language, in which Pali has undeniably acquired a portion of Hindu culture, with that of Delaware (not to mention the Mexican) would scarcely permit any doubt to persist concerning the superiority of the latter.

The matter is, however, too important not to discuss in greater detail and from the approach of its innate foundations. Insofar as civilization and culture impart to nations previously unknown ideas from foreign sources or develop them from their inherent stock, the foregoing viewpoint is undeniably correct in at least one other respect. The need for a concept and its resultant elucidation must always precede the word, which is merely the expression of the complete clarity of a concept. If we cling unilaterally to this viewpoint, however, and if we believe it possible to disclose the advantages of one language over another by this criterion alone, we will fall into an error deleterious to the true evaluation of language. To want to judge the extent of a people's ideas in a definite epoch merely by perusing their dictionary is already highly doubtful. Without criticizing the pointlessness of attempting this in view of the incomplete lexicographical compilations of so many non-European nations, it must be instantly apparent that a great number of ideas, especially nonsensual ones, to which the foregoing contentions refer, may be expressed by metaphors unfamiliar to us or by circumlocutions. There reposes, however, both in the concepts and in the language of every people, no matter how uncultured, a totality that corresponds to the scope of unrestricted human cultural capacity. This factor is by far the most decisive one involved. From it all details which humanity comprehends may be drawn without outside aid; and, without fail, whatever we encounter within language itself certainly cannot be termed foreign to the language in question. A factual proof of this is furnished by those languages of uncultivated nations, such as those of the Philippines and the American Indians for example, which were long worked over by missionaries. We find very abstract concepts in them, designated without addition of foreign expressions. It would certainly be interesting to know how the indigenous peoples comprehend these terms. Inasmuch as they are constructed of elements of their own languages, they must be connected to them by some analogous meaning. However, this viewpoint leads us astray because it conceives of language too much as an area to be expanded from without as if by conquest, and hence misconstrues its true nature and its most essential peculiarity.

It is not a question of how many concepts a language designates with its native words. This procedure takes place automatically when the language pursues the true course originally traced for it by nature. Furthermore, this is not the aspect from which a language must first be evaluated. Its actual and fundamental effectiveness in the human being relates to his reflection and to the creative power inherent in reflective thought. Hence, in a much deeper sense, language is immanent and constitutive. It may be asked whether and to what extent it promotes the clarity and correct arrangement of concepts or places difficulties in their path. Or to what degree does a language preserve the inherent semantic lucidity of the concepts conveyed to it from prevailing world opinion? How does the euphony of its sounds, whether soothing or elevating, react upon human sensitivity and attitude? Therein, and in numerous other similar dispositions of the total way of thinking, lies that factor which constitutes its true advantages and determines its influence upon intellectual development. This, however, is based on the totality of its original endowments, its organic structure, and its individual forms. Civilization and culture, even though relatively late, do not drift aimlessly by the foregoing. By using expanded and more refined ideas to express itself, language gains in clarity and precision. The plasticity of a language is clarified by an enriched imaginative pattern, and its euphony increases in quality in response to the heightened demands of a more practised ear. However, this entire course of progressive linguistic culture may only advance within the limits prescribed by its original linguistic predisposition. A nation can exploit a defective language as an implement for creating an idea beyond the range of its original intiative. It cannot, however, cancel out its inherent limitations, which are present from the outset. To this extent even the highest state of development remains imperfect. No matter what future generations may add to a language externally, such material is assimilated and modified in accordance with its principles.[4]

From the standpoint of the intimate evaluation of the intellect, civilization and culture cannot be regarded as the apex to which the human mind can aspire. In most recent times both have flourished to the highest degree and to maximum universality. One would scarcely want to contend with the same certainty that the inherent phenomenon of human nature, as we see it in several epochs in antiquity, has recurred with equal power and frequency, or even in fact to an intensified degree, and one would want to contend even less that this was precisely the case in those nations to which the spread of civilization and a certain culture owes the most.

Civilization is the humanization of peoples in their external accoutrements and customs and in their innermost sentiments. Culture adds science and art to this refinement of the social state. However, when in our language we speak of "refined education," something simultaneously more elevated and intimate is meant. It is the type of mental disposition, originating from the perception of intellectual and moral aspiration, that harmoniously permeates the sensibilities and character.

Civilization can emerge from the innermost depths of a people, wherein it bears witness to that indefinable elevation of the spirit. Conversely, however, whenever it is transplanted into a nation from foreign sources, it spreads more rapidly and perhaps penetrates more deeply all institutions of the state. But it does not react with equal energy upon intellect and character. It is an admirable prerogative of our most recent era to transport civilization to the remotest parts of the earth, to associate this effort with every enterprise, using every means at our disposal. The governing principle of universal humanity at work here denotes a level of progress to which only our age has ascended. All great inventions, furthermore, of recent centuries aspire in unison to bring about this state of civilization. The Greeks and Romans were far less effective in their colonies in this respect. To be sure, this may be traced to the lack of so many external media of international communication and to the state of civilization itself.[5] However, they also lacked the inherent principle from which alone true living is able to mature.

The Greeks and the Romans possessed a clear concept of lofty and noble human individuality that was interwoven deeply into the pattern of their perception and intellectual disposition. However, the idea of merely respecting a person as a human being never enjoyed any value in their thought pattern. Even less value did they impute to the sentiments of the resultant human rights and duties. This important segment of universal good breeding remained foreign to them in the course of their ultra-nationalistic development. Even in their colonies they probably did not mix much with the natives, but rather compelled the latter to move beyond their boundaries. Then, too, their colonials developed differently in the altered environments.[6] Thus there arose—as manifested by Greater Greece, Sicily, and Iberia[7]—new ethnic configurations with respect to character, political opinions, and scientific development. The Hindus understood very well how to stimulate and make fruitful the inherent powers of the peoples with whom they became associated. The Indian Archipelago[8] and especially Java furnish us a remarkable proof of this contention. For there, when we confront Hindu cultural heritage, we generally observe how the indigenous spirit seized upon it and subsequently continued to build upon it. Along with their more highly developed external comforts, their greater wealth of media that permitted increased enjoyment of life's gifts, and their art and science, the Hindu settlers brought to foreign soil a breath of life whose soul-giving power has first taken shape on their native shores. The individual social aspirations were not as isolated in the case of the ancients as is true with us. They were far less able to impart what they possessed without the soul which had created it. Because this situation differs radically in our case, and because a power reposing in our own civilization drives us even further forward in this direction, the peoples receive under our influence a far more uniform configuration. As a result, the development of the original peculiarities of colonial peoples is often nipped in the bud, even where such development might have occurred.

CHAPTER THREE

Cooperation of Individuals and Nations

IN THIS SURVEY of the intellectual development of the human race, we have so far considered it in its course through the succession of generations and, in so doing, have designated the four chief determinative features. These are: the quiet life of peoples in accordance with the natural conditions of their existence on the face of the earth; the migratory and warlike activities, carried out intentionally or forced upon a people by enemy pressure; the sequence of intellectual mutations that are reciprocally linked as cause and effect; and, finally, the intellectual phenomena which can only be explained by the power revealed in them. There still remains the consideration of how the foregoing development of the human race, which contains the reason for its progress in each given instance, is effected in each individual generation.

The effectiveness of the individual is always finite and interrupted. However, at least in appearance, and to a certain extent in reality too, the individual in this respect moves in the same direction as does the entire race, since his effectiveness (as a determined and a determinative entity) is inseparably associated with past and future time. But, after more thorough perception, we see that the direction of the individual compared to that of the entire race is still divergent. Hence, to the extent that world history concerns the inner man, it consists of both of the directions under scrutiny. These directions intersect but, at the same time, are closely linked to each other. The divergence is directly visible in the fact that the destinies of the race, independent of the evanescence of successive generations, proceed inseparably apace. Though changing, insofar as we can see, those destinies progress as a whole to a heightened state of excellence. Conversely, the individual is eliminated from all participation in those destinies, but he does not consider himself at the end of his career. The realization of his exclusion comes to an individual in the midst of his most significant activity, and thereafter he regards his career as divorced from the course of those destinies. Even in his life as a whole, he feels an antithesis between self-education and that world configuration through which each individual in his circle engages in reality.

The organizational make-up of human nature guarantees that this antithesis does not become noxious to the development of the race or to the training of the individual. Self-instruction can only proceed apace with the world configuration. Above and beyond his lifetime, heartfelt needs, images of phantasy, family ties, and striving for fame, joyous prospects for the future germination of the seeds sown unite man with the destinies he is abandoning. As a result of this antithesis, and constituting its very basis moreover, an internal disposition of the spirit arises in which repose the most powerful and most sacred emotions. This feature of man operates more effectively to the extent that the individual does not consider himself alone, but rather considers all his fellow men likewise destined to undergo a solitary self-education that extends throughout their life spans. Consequently, all ties which unite kindred spirits gain a different and more elevated significance. Nuances, important for all human development, arise from the various degrees to which that disposition, the ego, is raised, and from its more or less exclusive dominion. It seeks isolation from reality, even while tied to it. India furnishes a remarkable example of the level of purity to which it may become refined, but at the same time of the abrupt contrasts to which it may degenerate. Moreover, ancient India can be explained principally from this standpoint.

This attunement of the soul exerts a particular influence upon the language. Language assumes a differing configuration in a people which gladly pursues the solitary paths of abstract reflection, as it does, moreover, in nations which require intermediary comprehension chiefly for external pursuits. Symbolism is comprehended quite differently by the former, and entire areas of linguistic structure remain uncultivated in the latter. For language must first be introduced via an obscure and undeveloped emotion into those spheres in which it is to cast its light. How the discontinuous terrestrial existence of individuals is connected to the continuous development of the race in a region perhaps unknown to us remains an impenetrable mystery. However, the awareness of this impenetrability effects an important consideration in the intimate rearing of the individual, because it awakens in him a respectful modesty in the face of something unknown which persists after all cognitional matter has vanished. It is comparable to the impression of night in which a solitary and diffused coruscation of objects unfamiliar to us replaces everything ordinarily visible.

The continuity of the destinies of the race and the sharp cleavage between the individual generations resulting from the different values that each generation finds in antiquity also exert an important effect. The subsequent generations are confronted by a situation largely resembling a stage—an image that is quite pertinent, moreover, owing to the progressive improvement of the media preserving the intellectual heritage of the past—upon which a richer and more brightly illuminated drama unfolds its plot. The entraining stream of events diverts generations—apparently by chance—into darker and more stringently fateful periods of life, or into brighter periods that are easier to live through. For those actually living, this distinction between the generations is of lesser magnitude than it appears to be when viewed as history. Many points of reference are lacking. In each moment only a portion of development is experienced. We engage the present with enjoyment and activity, and the prerogatives of contemporary existence lead us past its obstacles. Like a cloud emerging from fog and mist, an epoch assumes a completely bounded aspect only when viewed in perspective from afar. Purely in the effect that each age exerts on the following does that influence handed down by our progenitors become distinct. Our modern education, for example, is based to a large extent on the contrast between ourselves and classical antiquity. It would be difficult and distressing to state what would remain of it were we to divorce ourselves from everything pertaining to this antiquity.[1] However, if we investigate the condition of the peoples who made up this era in all their historical details, we find that they do not correspond actually to the image which we bear of them in our minds. What exerts the powerful effect upon us is our conception thereof, which wells from their greatest and purest efforts, a feature emphasizing more their spirit than the reality of their organizations. This is a feature, moreover, which leaves contrasting features unconsidered, which places no requirements on those features not in agreement with the accepted interpretation. We are not led by any arbitrariness to such a conception of their peculiarity. The ancients are entitled to it, and it would not be possible for any other age. The deep feeling that we have for their nature alone confers upon us the capability of elevating ourselves to their level. Since reality in their case always blended easily with idea and phantasy, and since these in turn reacted on the former, we justifiably transpose them exclusively into this region. For in accordance with their spirit, as evidenced in their writings, their artistic creations, and their efforts underscored by a wealth of deeds, they describe the sphere accorded to humanity in perfect purity, totality, and harmony, even if reality did not correspond entirely to their image of it. In this way, they bequeathed to us a seemingly ideal image in the guise of an ennobled human nature. As between sunny and clouded skies, their superiority over us rests not so much in their configurations of life itself as in the wonderful brilliance that radiated from and upon them.

Even if we were to assume that earlier peoples had a great influence on the Greeks, there is not a shred of evidence that they themselves ever looked up to any foreign models. Within their own culture, however, they did have something similar in the epics of Homer and his successors. Just as the Greeks appear natural to us and in the depths of their structure inexplicable, just as they are for us models to be imitated, and a great source of intellectual enrichment, by the same token that dark period [Homeric], with its unique antecedents shining forth prominently, played a similar role for the Greeks. But the Greeks did not have an effect on the Romans similar to the effect they have on us. For the Romans, the Greeks were simply a contemporaneous nation of greater culture which possessed a literature dating back to earlier times.

From our point of view, India reverts to a too remote and obscure past to enable us to pass judgment upon its antiquity. In an older time at least, it did influence the Occident, but this was at most by its opinions, inventions, and legends, and not by the peculiar form of its intellectual product, since the effect of the latter could not have been obliterated without a trace. In my treatise on the Kawi language (Book 1, pp. 1, 2) I had occasion to treat in greater detail how important the intellectual influence of peoples upon one another is. Their own antiquity must have had the same effect on the Hindus as did that of the Greeks. This relationship between past and present is much more distinct, however, in China, owing to the influence and the philosophical lore of the works in the old style, in contrast to later works.

Since languages, or at least their elements (a difference not to be unheeded), are handed down from one age to the following, and since we may speak of newly initiated languages only by completely transcending the realm of our experience, the relationship of the past to the present penetrates to the very roots of their cultural development. Even in the case of fully developed languages, the question as to which position an age is accorded by the place it occupies in the series we know becomes extremely important because language is at once a way of comprehending the total process of thinking and feeling. And in representing a people from ancient times, languages cannot have an effect on a later people without also becoming an influential factor in their language. Thus, our present-day languages would have assumed a different conformation in many respects if, instead of classical antiquity, the Hindu had reacted so continuously and thoroughly upon us.

The individual human being is always to be considered both as part of a unit such as his nation, or the stock to which it belongs, and as part of the entire human race. Regardless of which aspect we look at, his life is necessarily allied with gregariousness. As we have seen above, this is true whether his life is judged from external or internal considerations. The helplessness of man in his vegetative existence on earth drives him to associate with others to make possible joint enterprises. These, however, require mutual comprehension through language. Even in the most solitary seclusion of the spirit, intellectual training is possible only through mutual understanding, and language must be directed to an understanding being. The articulated sound [phoneme] issues from the breast to awaken in another individual an accord through aural perception. Simultaneously, the human being thereby discovers that there exist about him beings with identical inner needs. He becomes additionally aware that such individuals are capable of appreciating sympathetically the multitudinous longings lodged in his mental reaction patterns. The premonitive suspicion of the existence of a totality and the striving toward it arise directly from the sensation of individuality. These become intensified, moreover, to the same extent that this sensation becomes more acute, inasmuch as every individual bears in himself the total nature of the human being, but merely along an individualized course of development. We do not have even the faintest idea of another person as an individual consciousness differing from our own. However, the striving mentioned and the germ of unquenchable longing, implanted in us by the concept of humanity itself, prevent the conviction that the individuality separated from ourselves is at best only a phenomenon of the limited existence of intellectual beings from becoming extinct.

The relation of the individual to a whole, which intensifies his power and stimulation, is too important a point in the intellectual economy of the human race, if I may be permitted this expression, not to make definite allusion to it at this juncture. The amalgamation of nations and of racial stocks, invariably and immediately producing their separation, depends on historical events, predominantly on the character of their dwellings and migrations. However, if one wishes to detach all influence of intimate (or even instinctive) coincidence or repulsion therefrom, without desiring precisely to justify this attitude personally, every nation still can and must be considered as a human individuality pursuing a peculiar innate career, even when separated from its external attachments. The more it is understood that the effectiveness of individuals, regardless of status, is capable of permanent impact only to the extent that they are borne to loftier levels by their national spirit and in turn impart new impetus to it from this standpoint, the more obvious becomes the necessity to seek the basic explanation of our present-day cultural level in these national intellectual individualities. History offers them to us in clearly defined outline wherever it has handed down to us data valid for the evaluation of the inherent culture of peoples. Civilization and culture gradually cancel out the harsh contrasts between peoples, and the striving toward a more general and moral form of a deeply penetrating, nobler culture becomes even more successful. Progress in science and in art, ever striving toward more general ideals and unfettered by nationalistic bias, also concurs with the foregoing statement. But whenever people seek these goals, they achieve them in a different spirit. The variety of ways in which human peculiarity is capable of being expressed without faulty one-sidedness converges at infinity, and, furthermore, the successful attainment of the goals generally sought after depends without reservation on this diversity. They require the complete, undivided unity of that power, never to be elucidated in its totality but functioning in its most acute individuality. Therefore, in order to engage fruitfully and powerfully in the general course of cultural development, it is requisite in a nation not only to rely on success in individual scientific efforts, but preferably to aim toward an objective consisting of the total exertion constituting the midpoint of the human being. This factor is most clearly and completely expressed in philosophy, creative writing, and art, whence it wells forth to engulf the entire conceptual pattern and disposition of the people involved.

To a limited extent and indirectly, every significant intellectual activity of the individual is also an integral part of the masses by virtue of the relationship between them which we have examined here. The existence of languages proves, however, that there are also intellectual creations that do not proceed from one individual to the remainder of the group, but instead erupt only from the simultaneous and spontaneous activity of all. In the area of languages, therefore, since they always have a national form, nations as such are really and directly creative.

Yet precautions must be taken against interpreting this viewpoint without considering its due limitation. Inasmuch as languages are inseparably interlaced with the innermost nature of man and far more automatically erupt from it than they are arbitrarily engendered by it, the intellectual peculiarity of peoples could equally well be termed its effect. The truth is that both emerge simultaneously and in reciprocal coincidence from unfathomable depths of the mind. We are not acquainted with any linguistic creation of such type from experience. Nor is an analogy for its evaluation tendered us anywhere. When we speak of primitive languages, we employ such a designation only because of our ignorance of their earlier constituents. A chain of related tongues has surged onward for millennia before attaining that point of development which we, because of our scanty knowledge, designate the oldest. But it is not merely the rudimentary formation of the truly primitive language that is inexplicable. We cannot even explain the origin of the secondary formations of subsequent languages whose parts we know very well how to analyze. All genetic origin in nature, principally, however, its organic and animate examples, escapes our observation. No matter how accurately we may explore the preliminary conditions, the gulf persists between the condition and the phenomenon which separates the something from the nothing. The same thing is also true at the instant of cessation. All human comprehension lies but midway between the two. In the realm of languages, an epoch of origin, dating from quite accessible periods of history, furnishes us with a striking example. We may pursue a diversified sequence of changes which the Latin language underwent during its decline and collapse. To these may be added the admixtures introduced by immigrant hordes. Yet, despite such knowledge, the origin of the living germ which develops again into newly florescent tongues is not well explained.[2] A new inner principle uniquely reassembled the disintegrating structure, but we, who always find ourselves merely in the field of its operation, perceive its transformations only via their mass impact. It may therefore seem preferable to leave this point completely untouched. But this is impossible if we want to sketch the development of the human intellect even in its boldest outlines, since the structure of languages, even of those that are isolated in all aspects of derivation or agglutination, is a fact which determines this trend most fundamentally and which is revealed in this collaboration of individuals in a manner otherwise not occurring. Thus we acknowledge that we are poised at a boundary beyond which neither historical nor free thought enables us to go, but we still must record the fact and its direct consequences.

The first and most natural of these is that the relationship of the individual to his nation rests precisely at the midpoint from which the total intellectual power determines all thinking, sensation, and volition. For language is related to everything contained in it, to the totality and to the individual. No part of it is or remains foreign to itself. It does not just passively receive impressions, but it selects from among the multiplicity of possible intellectual directions a single definite one and modifies internally every outside influence exerted upon it. Language cannot be regarded in any way as something externally divorced from its own intellectual peculiarity. Hence, even though it may appear different at first glance, it cannot actually be taught but must be awakened in the mind. It can only be tendered the thread by which it automatically develops. While languages are in the unambiguous sense of the word (see chapters 1 and 19) creations of nations, they still remain personal and independent creations of individuals. This follows because they can be produced in each individual, yet only in such a manner that each individual assumes a priori the comprehension of all people and that all people, furthermore, satisfy such expectation. Language may therefore be considered as a general philosophical vehicle, or as an association of ideas, since it combines both approaches. At any rate, it rests of necessity on the totality of human power. Nothing can be excluded from it, since it embraces everything.

In nations, both generally and in various epochs, this power differs individually in degree and in accordance with the possible course of evolution. The variation, however, must become evident in the result, that is, in the language. This power is primarily evident in the abundance of its external effect or its automatic, internal functioning. Therefore, examples are numerous, where, if the series of languages is pursued comparatively, the explanation of the structure of the one from the others proceeds with facility. However, languages are encountered which appear separated from the remaining ones by an actual abyss. Just as individuals by the power of their idiosyncrasies impart to the human intellect a new impetus in uncharted directions, nations may do the same for linguistic formation. However, between linguistic structure and success in all other types of intellectual activity, there prevails an undeniable relationship. This relationship, moreover, lies principally—and we shall consider it here from this aspect only—in the inspiring breath which structural linguistic power infuses, in the act of the transformation of the world, into ideas. Such is the nature of this infusion that it diffuses harmoniously through all parts of its dominion. If it may be deemed possible that a language originates in a nation exactly in this manner, as the word most meaningfully and intuitively evolves from the world view, most purely representing it anew and molding itself in such a way as to penetrate every nuance of thought easily and unobtrusively, then this language must—so long as it maintains its vital principle at all—evoke the selfsame power trained in the same direction with equal success in every individual. The ingress of such a language, or of one closely approaching it, into the history of the world must establish an important era in the course of human development, and precisely in the area of its loftiest and most marvelous productions. Definite intellectual courses and a definite impetus, propelling the mind along such a path, cannot be conceived before such languages have originated. They therefore constitute a true point of inflection in the internal history of the human race. If they must be regarded as the apex of linguistic structure, they are the initial stage of a soul-stirring culture rich in phantasy. Therefore, it is quite correct to contend that to this extent the work of nations must precede the work of individuals, although precisely what has been said here proves irrefutably how simultaneously the activity of both is intertwined in producing these creations.

CHAPTER FOUR

A More Detailed Consideration of Language

WE HAVE NOW arrived at the point in the primitive culture of the human race where we recognize languages as prerequisite for pursuing loftier human activity. Languages develop under equal conditions and together with intellectual power, and at the same time they constitute its stimulating, vital principle. The two factors do not proceed consecutively and separately with respect to each other, but are absolutely and inseparably the very same activity of the intellectual capacity. While a people produces freedom from within itself for the development of its language, at the same time it seeks and obtains the objective itself, which is something different and loftier. Moreover, in attaining this objective by way of poetic creativity and brooding meditation, a people reacts simultaneously upon the language itself. If the first crude and uncultured attempts at intellectual effort are designated by the term literature, language always proceeds in step with the latter, and the two are inseparably united.

The intellectual peculiarity and the linguistic conformation of a people are related by such an intimate fusion that, given the one, the other could be entirely derived from it. For intellectuality and language permit and promote only mutually agreeable formations. Language is, as it were, the external manifestation of the minds of peoples. Their language is their soul, and their soul is their language. It is impossible to conceive them ever sufficiently identical. How they in truth combine with each other in one and precisely the same source is incomprehensible to us and remains inexplicably concealed from our perception.

Without wishing to decide upon the priority of either the one or the other, we must consider as the real explanatory principle and as the true determinative cause of linguistic variability the intellectual power of nations, because it alone vitally and independently confronts us. Language, conversely, merely clings to it. For, to the extent that language reveals itself as creatively independent, it strays beyond the realm of phenomena into an ideal status. Historically, we are concerned in all instances only with the human being as a spokesman, but that is no reason to lose sight of the true relationship. In reality there is no such arbitrary distinction between intellectuality and language. If language correctly appears to us as something possessing divine characteristics, unlike other intellectual creations, the relationship between language and human intellectual power might be a different one if the latter did not confront us in the form of isolated phenomena, but instead were to transmit its very nature directly to us from its unfathomable depths, and we were capable of perceiving the interconnections within the human individuality, since language too transcends the estrangement inherent in individuals. It is particularly important for practical purposes not to stop just at any mediocre explanatory principle of languages but to ascend to the highest and ultimate one. It is equally important to consider as the focal point of the entire intellectual conformation, the axiomatic tenet, that the structure of languages in the human race varies because and to the extent that it is the intellectual idiosyncrasy of nations themselves.

However, if we delve into the problem pertaining to the nature of this variability of linguistic structure, as we cannot abstain from doing, we may no longer wish to apply the investigation of intellectual peculiarity solely to the quality of language. In early epochs to which the present observations transpose us, we know the nations involved via their languages alone. We do not even know exactly which people we must keep in mind with respect to each language. Thus Zend is really for us the language of a nation, and we can determine more about that nation and its people only by conjecture. Among all manifestations by which intellect and character are recognizable, language is truly the only suitable medium to reveal them both down to their very most secret nooks and crannies. If languages now are regarded as the explanatory basis of successive intellectual developments, they must be considered as having originated from intellectual peculiarity. However, in order to seek out the nature of this peculiarity in the structure of each individual representative and thus carry to completion the observations introduced here, we must now embark upon a more detailed examination of the nature of languages and the possibility of their retroactive differences. In this way, we will connect comparative linguistic research to its ultimate and most exalted point of reference.

CHAPTER FIVE

Morphology of Languages

A PARTICULAR LINE of linguistic research is required for the successful pursuit of the course plotted in the foregoing exposition. Language must be regarded not as a dead product of the past but as a living creation. It must be abstracted from all that it effects as a designation of comprehended ideas. Furthermore, we must revert to a more meticulous examination of its origins and its interaction with intellectual activity. The varied progress of recent decades in linguistic study facilitates a survey of the entire field. It is now possible to move closer to the objective of stating the individual approaches through which hordes of people, subdivided, isolated, and yet ethnically coalescing, were successful in pursuing the business of perfecting speech production. Herein, moreover, rests the cause of the variation in human linguistic structure, as well as the effect of that variation on the development of the intellect, that is, the entire object of our present preoccupation.

At the very first step upon this course of research, however, an important obstacle rises before us. Language presents us infinite details in words, rules, analogies, and exceptions of all kinds. As a result, we encounter no little embarrassment as to how we are to reconcile this confusing, chaotic mass, despite its initial arrangement, with a uniform image of human intellectual power. Even if we possess all of the necessary lexical and grammatical details of two important linguistic stocks or families, such as the Sanskritic and Semitic for example, we are only but slightly advanced in our efforts to reduce the character of each to such simple outlines that a fruitful comparison and determination of their proper places in the general business of linguistic creation, appropriate to their relationship to the intellectual power of nations, are made possible. The foregoing requires a special searching out of the common sources of the individual peculiarities—the condensation of the scattered features into an organic whole. This is the only way in which we can gain control of the details. Therefore, to compare fruitfully differing languages with respect to their characteristic structure, careful research of the form [morphology] of each of them must be conducted. In this way it will be possible to ascertain the manner in which each solves the principal problems confronting all linguistic production. Since this expression of form is used in a variety of meanings in linguistic investigations, I believe it incumbent upon me to delineate in greater detail the sense in which it is to be interpreted here. This appears so much the more requisite inasmuch as we are not speaking of language per se, but of the individual examples that are pertinent in determining in a delimiting manner what is to be understood by an individual language in contrast to the linguistic family on the one hand or to a dialect on the other. Finally, what is the significance of one language taken alone, which, during its course of evolution, has undergone essential modifications?

Properly conceived of, language is something persistent and in every instant transitory. Even its maintenance by writing is only an incomplete, mummified preservation, necessary if one is again to render perceptible the living speech concerned. In itself language is not work (*ergon*) but an activity (*energeia*). Its true definition may therefore only be genetic. It is after all the continual intellectual effort to make the articulated sound capable of expressing thought. In a rigorous sense, this is the definition of speech in each given case. Essentially, however, only the totality of this speaking can be regarded as the language. For in the jumbled chaos of words and rules, which we generally call a language, only the isolated entity produced by speech is present, and, furthermore, this is never complete. In addition this entity requires new study if we are to perceive in it the nature of the living language and thereby divulge its true image. The most elevated and finest features of a language cannot be recognized from these diverse and separate elements. They can be perceived only in connected discourse, which proves so much the more that the real language lies in the act of its physical production. It alone must be kept in mind as the fundamental factor in all investigations, designed to penetrate into the living existentiality of language. Breaking it down into words and rules is but a lifeless tour de force based on scientific dismemberment.

To designate languages as an intellectual activity is completely correct simply because the existence of the intellect can only be conceived as activity. The structural dissection of languages indispensable to their study even requires us to regard them as a process progressing via definite media toward definite objectives; hence we must consider languages to

such an extent as truly national structures. We have already been warned
of possible misinterpretation in this instance (see chapters 1, 3, and 4);
therefore, these statements cannot be prejudicial to the truth.

In the foregoing exposition (chapter 3), I have called attention to the
fact that we find ourselves in our linguistic study transported to an
historical midpoint, and that neither a nation nor a language among those
known to us may be termed original. Since each has received material
transmitted by earlier generations from a prehistoric antiquity unknown
to us, the intellectual activity producing the ideas according to the
explanation already advanced is constantly directed toward something
already given; this activity is not purely creative but rather modifies the
heritage.

This effort operates in a constant and uniform manner. For it is the
same intellectual power, differing only within definite narrow limits, that
performs this work. Its purpose is comprehension.[1] Thus nobody may
speak to another person in a manner different from that in which the latter,
under identical conditions, would have spoken to him. Furthermore, the
material handed down is not only the same, but also, in view of its
identical origin, it has a closely related intellectual bent. The form of the
language is determined by the constant and uniform feature reposing in
this effort of the intellect. This feature is aimed at elevating the articulated
sound to the level of expressing ideas, it is conceived as perfectly as
possible in its context, and it is presented systematically.

In this definition, the form appears to be a scientifically produced
abstraction. But it would definitely be incorrect to contemplate it in its
essence merely as such a nonexistential, conceptual entity. Rather, it is in
fact the absolutely individual urge through which a nation imparts validity
to ideas and perceptions in language. Only because we are never given the
opportunity of witnessing this urge in the undivided totality of its striving
but only in its individual effects in each case, does it remain possible for us
to summarize the uniformity of its effectiveness in a lifeless, general concept. In itself the foregoing urge is unified and viable.

The difficulty of the most important and refined linguistic investigations
very frequently lies in the fact that something flowing forth from the total
impression of language is certainly perceived by the clearest and most
convincing emotion. Yet attempts fail to present it in sufficient completeness and to delimit it within the scope of definite concepts. Here, too, it is
necessary to struggle with this difficulty. The characteristic form of a
language depends on each of its smallest elements. Each is determined by
the language in some way or other, no matter how imperceptible this may
be in an isolated detail. On the other hand, it is scarcely possible to find

elements for which it could be claimed that the form was a decisive part of them, taken individually. Therefore, if any given language is perused thoroughly, much is found that could be conceived differently without damage to the nature of its morphology. To perceive the latter rigorously differentiated in such case, we are per force referred to the total impression. Now here the converse immediately arises. The clear-cut individuality obviously confronts us, forces itself incontrovertibly upon our senses. In this respect languages may most aptly be compared with human physiognomies. The individuality is undeniably there, yet similarities are evident. However, no measurement and no description of the components in detail and in their interconnection are capable of summarizing the individual nature in a single concept. It is based on the totality, and yet on the individual interpretation as well. Hence, every physiognomy certainly appears different to each individual. Since language, no matter in what configuration it be taken up, is always an intellectual exhalation of a national-individual life, both aspects must be fulfilled in it. No matter how much is attached to or incorporated in it, or to what extent it may be detailed or dissected, an unknown quantum always remains. It is precisely this factor, which eludes treatment, that includes the unity and spirit of a living entity. Thus, in terms of this quality of languages, the representation of the morphology of any given example can never be accomplished completely. Nevertheless, this objective can be achieved in all cases to a certain degree, and this is satisfactory for an overall consideration of the whole. For this reason, however, the course which the comparative linguist must follow in order to ferret out and divulge the mysteries of language is no less plotted by this concept. By neglecting this approach, he will infallibly overlook numerous points of research; he will, moreover, be compelled to leave much that is explicable unexplained and will interpret as isolated material that is actually connected by living association.

It is already self-evident from the foregoing exposition that by the expression "morphology of language" I do not mean merely its so-called grammatical pattern. The distinction which we are prone to make between the grammar and the dictionary is useful only in learning languages. It can neither prescribe limits nor stipulate rules for true linguistic research. The concept of linguistic morphology extends beyond the rules of word order [syntax], even transcending those of word formation [lexical structure]. The preceding statement is valid with respect to the latter to the extent that it refers to the application of certain general logical categories of activity, passivity, substance, attributes, and so forth to roots and primary words.[2] This concept is actually quite applicable to the structure of primary words per se and, indeed, must be applied to them to the maximum possible degree if the true nature of language is to be recognized.

Admittedly, a material stands in contrast to morphology. However, to find the material of linguistic morphology, the bounds of language must be transcended.[3] Within the limits of language only something in comparison with something else may be respectively regarded as material: for example, the primary word in relationship to the declension. In other respects, however, what is here material is again recognized as form. A language can also borrow words from a foreign tongue and actually treat them as material.[4] But then these words are such with respect to the borrowing idiom and not per se. Considered absolutely, there cannot be any deformed material within the language, inasmuch as everything in it is directed toward a definite objective—the expression of ideas. Furthermore, this task begins with its first element, the articulated sound, which after all becomes articulated by morphological processes. In any case, the real material of a language is on the one hand the phonetic sound [phoneme], and on the other hand the totality of meaningful impressions and independent intellectual motions which precede the construction of the concept with the aid of speech [i.e., language].[5]

It is, therefore, self-evident that the actual character of the sounds involved must be accorded special attention in order for us to get an idea of the form of a language. The exploratory research on the morphology of a language commences with the alphabet, and through all of the component parts of the morphology this is treated as its most especial foundation.[6] In any case, nothing factual and individual in nature is excluded by this concept of morphology. Conversely, everything that is in any way to be historically established, as well as the most individualized features, is comprehended and included in this concept of morphology. If the course outlined here is pursued, even all the details will be incorporated in the research; otherwise they hazard being overlooked. Admittedly, this procedure involves a troublesome and tedious fundamental investigation, often proceeding into the range of the infinitesimal or picayune. However, it is upon nothing but inherently petty details that the total impression of languages is based. Furthermore, nothing is as incompatible with their study as the desire merely to seek out the features which are gross, predominant, and intellectual. Exact investigation of every grammatical subtlety and of the breakdown of words into their elements is absolutely needful in order to preclude errors in all evaluations made of languages. It is automatically to be understood that a detail may be accepted as an isolated fact in the concept of the morphology of language only if a method of linguistic structure can be discovered.[7] Through the representation of the form, the specific course that the language and the nation to which it belongs have embarked upon for the expression of ideas will be recognized. One must be in a position to survey the way in which a language relates to other languages with respect both to the definite objectives prescribed for it and to its counteraction upon the intellectual activity of the nation. Language is in its very nature a comprehension of the speech elements in an intellectual unity, elements which in contrast to it are to be regarded as raw material. For in every language reposes such a unity, and by means of this all-embracing unity a nation makes the language handed down to it by its forefathers its own. This very same unity must therefore be found in our investigation, for only when the ascent from these scattered elements to the unity is achieved do we get a concept of the language itself. Without such a procedure the danger obviously arises of our not even understanding the appertaining elements in their true peculiarity and still less in their actual relationship.

It should be noted that the identity, as well as the relationship of languages, must rest upon the identity and the relationship of their forms [morphemes], since the effect can only be equal to the cause. The morphology therefore determines alone to which others a language belongs as a cognate tongue. This finds application immediately to the Kawi dialect, which, no matter how many Sanskrit words it may have absorbed, still does not cease to be a Malayan tongue.[8] The forms [morphemes] of several languages may combine in a still more general form, and in fact the morphemes of all do this, to the extent that we start in all cases merely from the most general features. That is to say, we begin with the circumstances and associations requisite for the designation of concepts and the images needed for proper syntax; with the identity of vocal organs, whose scope and nature permit but a definite number of articulated sounds; and finally with the relationships which prevail between individual consonantal and vocalic sounds and certain sensory impressions, whence uniformity of designation, without cognate relationship, originates. For in language the individualization within general conformity is so marvelous that we may state with equal correctness that the entire human race possesses but a single language and each human possesses a particular one.[9] However, among the linguistic similarities united by more intimate analogies, those arising from a cognate relationship between nations stand out most distinctly. How great and of what quality such a similarity must be to justify the assumption of cognate relationship where historical evidence does not immediately substantiate such bonds is here external to the field of investigation. We shall occupy ourselves at this juncture with application to cognate tongues of the concept just developed of the morphology of language. It follows naturally from the foregoing that the morphology of the individual cognate languages must be reencountered in that of the entire linguistic family. Nothing may be contained in them that is not in harmony with the general morphology. As a rule, we will find in the morphology each of its idiosyncrasies alluded to in some way or other. In every family of languages there will be also one language containing the original morphology more purely and more completely.[10] For here we are speaking only of dialect variants, deriving from each other, where an actually given material (the latter term always taken and used as above defined) is transmitted from one people to another in a definite sequence— which may rarely be verified exactly—and modified by the recipients. This metamorphosis itself, however, can but remain a closely related change in all instances; this is owing to the similar conceptual patterns and ideological bents of the intellectual powers effecting the transformation, as well as to the uniformity of speech organs and hereditary phonetic habits and to the many coincidental, external historical effects.

CHAPTER SIX

Nature and Properties of Language

SINCE THE variation in languages is based upon their morphology, and since the latter is most closely associated with the intellectual capacities of nations together with the forces permeating them at the instant of their creation or of a new formulation, we must now develop this concept in detail.

The discrete principles of morphology come to light when we reflect on language in general and when we dissect individual idioms. They include the phonetic form (*Lautform*) and the usage to which the phonetic form is put to designate objects and to associate ideas. Usage is founded upon the requirements that thinking imposes upon language, whence the general laws governing language originate. This component is identical in all human beings as such in its original direction to the point of the peculiarity of their natural endowments or subsequent developments. In contrast, the phonetic form is the actual constitutive and guiding principle respective to the variability of languages, both inherently and in the retarding force which it opposes to the innate speech tendency involved. As a component of the complete human organism related intimately to its inherent intellectual power, it is associated naturally with the total foundation of the nation. However, the manner and reasons underlying this association are cloaked in an obscurity scarcely permitting any clarification. The individual morphology of every language is derived from these two intellectually interdependent principles. They constitute the points which linguistic derivation in its dissection must accept to investigate the present in their relationships. The most indispensable factor is that, with respect to this undertaking, a proper and worthy consideration of language, respective to the depths of its origins and the extent of its scope, be used as a basis of operation. For the present, then, we shall be content to examine these parameters.

At this point, I shall discuss the process of language in its broadest sense. I shall consider it not merely in its relationship to speech and the stock of its word components as its direct product, but also in its relationship to the human capacity for thought and perception. The entire course of operation, starting from its emanation from the intellect to its counteraction upon the latter, comes into consideration.

Language is the structural organ of ideas. Intellectual activity—completely intellectual, completely innate, and to a certain extent passing without a trace—becomes externalized in speech and perceptible to the senses. It and the language, therefore, are a unit and are indivisible from one another. Intellectual activity is inherently tied to the necessity of entering into a combination with the phoneme (*Sprachlaut*). Otherwise thought cannot attain distinctness, the image cannot become a concept. The indissoluble bond connecting thought, vocal apparatus, and hearing [auditory perception] to language reposes invariably in the original arrangement of human nature, a factor that defies further clarification. The coincidence of the sound with the idea thus becomes clear. Just as the idea, comparable to a flash of lightning, collects the total power of imagination into a single point and excludes everything that is simultaneous, the phonetic sound resounds in abrupt sharpness and unity. Just as the thought engages the entire disposition, the phonetic sound is endowed with a penetrating power that arouses the whole nervous system. This feature, distinguishing it from all other sensory impressions, is visibly based upon the fact that the ear is receptive to the impression of a motion, especially to the sound of a true action produced by the voice (which is not always the case for the remaining senses). Furthermore, this action proceeds from the interior of a living creature, consists of the articulated sound of a thinking person, and is received as an unarticulated one by a sensitive fellow human being.[1]

Inasmuch as thought in its most typically human relationships is a longing to escape from darkness into light, from limitation into infinity, sound streams from the depths of the breast to the external ambient. There it finds in the air, this most subtle and motile of all elements whose apparent incorporeality significantly corresponds to the intellect, a marvelously appropriate intermediary substance. The incisive sharpness of the phoneme is indispensable to our understanding of physical and other objects, for objects in external nature, as well as in the internally excited activity, exert a compulsion upon man, penetrating his being with a mass of characteristics. He, however, strives to compare, distinguish, and combine. Furthermore, he aims at the formation of an ever more comprehensive unity. He demands, therefore, to be able to comprehend objects in terms of a definite unity and requires the unit of sound to represent them appropriately. The sound, however, does not displace any of the other impressions which the objects are capable of producing upon the external or internal senses, but instead becomes their bearer. Moreover, it adds, in its individual association with the object, a new designative impression according to the manner in which the individual sensitivity of the speaker conceives it. The sharpness of the sound permits an indeterminable number of modifications, absolutely distinct from each other in conception and not mixing together in combination. This is not true to the same extent of any other sensory effect. Inasmuch as intellectual striving does not merely occupy human understanding but stimulates the entire human being, it is especially promoted by the sound of the human voice. For, as living sound, it proceeds, as does respiration itself, from the breast; it accompanies—even without speech—pain and joy, aversion and avidity, breathing life from which it streams forth into the mind which receives it. In this respect it resembles language. The latter reproduces the evoked sensation simultaneously with the object represented. Thus it connects man with the universe or, to express it differently, associates his independent activity with his sensory receptivity. To the phoneme, finally, is appropriate the erect posture of humans, which is denied to animals and by which man is, so to speak, called upright. For speech does not want to resound dully along the ground; it desires to pour forth freely from the lips toward the person at whom it is directed, accompanied by the facial expression of the speaker, as well as by the gestures of his hand; speech thus wishes to be associated with everything that designates the humanity of man.[2]

After this provisional consideration of the suitability of the sound to the operations of the intellect, we may now proceed to examine in greater detail the relationship of cogitation to language. Subjective activity in thought produces an object, for no idea may be considered a mere receptive contemplation of an already present object. The activity of the senses must be synthetically combined with the intimate operation of the intellect, and from this association the idea is liberated. With respect to the subjective force involved, it then becomes the object, which is perceived anew, and which then reverts to the subjective force. For this purpose language is indispensable, for when in its intellectual striving it makes its way past the lips, its product wends its way back to the speaker's own ear.[3] The concept is thus shifted over into a state of objectivity, without losing its subjectivity. Only language is capable of this. Without this feature, that is, without this continuous regression of objectivity to the subject, in which language collaborates, the formulation of concepts (and consequently all true thinking) is impossible. Apart from the communication between one human and another, speech is a necessary condition for reflection in solitude. As a phenomenon, however, language develops only in social intercourse,[4] and humans understand themselves only by having tested the comprehensibility of their words on others. For objectivity is increased whenever a word coined by oneself resounds from a stranger's lips. However, subjectivity suffers no loss, since humans always feel a bond with their fellows; indeed, it is intensified, since the idea transformed into speech no longer pertains exclusively to a single subject. By being transmitted to others, it becomes associated with the common heritage of the entire human race, each of whose members possesses an innate quality demanding fulfillment from the other members. The broader and more active this social intercourse in its effect upon a language, the more the language profits, other conditions remaining constant. What language makes necessary in the simple act of production of ideas is incessantly repeated in the intellectual life of man. Communication through language furnishes him conviction and stimulation. The power to think requires something equal to yet differentiated from itself. It is fired up by its equivalent; from its counterpart it acquires a touchstone for its innermost products. Although the basis for the perception of truth reposes in man's inner recesses, his intellectual striving toward truth is always surrounded by the danger of deception. With an immediate and clear sense only for his varying limitations, he is forced to regard truth as something external to himself. One of the most powerful media to approach veracity, and to measure one's remoteness from it, is the social exchange of ideas. All speech, starting from the very simplest, consists of an association of the individual perception with the common denominator of human nature.

The situation is no different as far as understanding is concerned. Nothing can be present in the mind (*Seele*) that has not originated from one's own activity. Moreover understanding and speaking are but different effects of the selfsame power of speech. Conversation is never comparable to the transmission of information (*Stoff*). In the person comprehending as well as in the speaker, the subject matter must be developed by the individual's own innate power. What the listener receives is merely the harmonious vocal stimulus. It is, therefore, natural for man to enunciate immediately what he has just comprehended. In this way language is native to every human being in its entire scope; this signifies that everyone possesses a drive, controlled by a modified regulatory power, that is directed toward bringing forth little by little his entire language and understanding it when produced, as the internal or external occasion requires.

Comprehension, as we understand it, could not be based upon automatic internal responses, and social discourse would have to be something other than the mere arousing of the auditory capabilities of the hearer, if the unity of human nature did not lie in the variation of the individuals—splitting itself up as it were into distinct individualities. The comprehension of words is something completely different from the understanding of unarticulated sounds and includes much more than the mere reciprocal production of sounds and of the indicated object. The word can also be taken as an indivisible entity, just as we recognize the significance of a written word group without being sure of its alphabetic composition. It might be possible that the soul of the child operates in this way during the very beginnings of comprehension.[5] Whenever animal sensory capacity, as well as the human power of speech, is excited (and it is probable that even in children there is no instant when this—no matter how feebly attested—would not be the case), the word is perceived as articulated. Now, however, the factor which articulation adds to the simple evocation of its meaning (an evocation which naturally takes place more completely as a result of the articulation) is that it represents the word with no intermediate by its morphology, that is, through its form as a part of an infinite whole, of a language. Because of articulation, therefore, even in individual words the possibility is present of constructing from the elements of language a number of other words actually running to an indeterminately high number, according to definite feelings and rules, and to establish thereby a relationship between all words, corresponding to the relationship of the concepts. The spirit would not, however, get any idea of this artificial mechanism, nor would it comprehend articulation any more than the blind man does colors, were there not a power residing in it that permits attainment of such a possibility. Indeed, language may be regarded not as a passive entity, capable of being surveyed in its entirety, nor as a something impartable bit by bit, but rather as an eternally productive medium; one for which, furthermore, the laws of its genetic processes are defined, but for which the scope and to some extent the manner of production remain completely undetermined. The speech learning of children is not an apportioning of words, a depositing in the files of memory, and a subsequent repetitive babbling through the lips, but a growth of speech capacity via maturation and practice. What one has heard does more than merely report information to oneself. It also prepares the mind to understand more easily what has not yet been heard and clarifies that which has been long-since heard though only half or not at all understood at the time. This is because the similarity between what has been heard long ago and what has just been perceived suddenly becomes obvious to the perceptive power, which has become more acute in the interim. This sharpens the urge and the capacity to channel material heard into the memory more rapidly, and it permits increasingly less thereof to pass by as mere sound. Progress hence accelerates in steadily increasing proportions, since the heightening of technique and the accumulation of information reciprocally intensify and expand. The fact that there is a development of the power to create speech taking place among children, rather than a mechanical learning, also proves that, since a certain period during one's life is allotted to the development of the most important human powers, all children speak and understand under the most varied circumstances at approximately the same age, varying only within a short time span. But how could the hearer gain control over himself simply by the growth of his own power over the spoken word, developing in isolated fashion within him, if the same essence were not in the speaker and the listener, separated individually and mutually appropriate, so that a signal, created out of the deepest and most personal nature, and as fine as the articulated sound, is a sufficient mediator to stimulate both of them identically?

Against this the objection could be raised that before they learn to speak children of every people, when displaced from their native linguistic ambient, will develop their speech proclivity in the foreign tongue. This incontrovertible fact, it could be averred, proves distinctly that speech is merely a reproduction of what has been heard and, without consideration of the uniformity or variability of the being, depends entirely upon social intercourse. In cases of this kind, it has been hard to observe with sufficient exactitude how difficult it was to overcome the inherited structure,[6] and how the latter nevertheless persisted unconquered in its most delicate nuances. Disregarding the foregoing, we can explain this phenomenon sufficiently by the fact that man is everywhere one with his kind, and development of speech capacity may proceed with the aid of any given individual. It does not for this reason evolve any the less from the intimate self; only because it simultaneously requires external stimulation must it prove analogous to that which it is experiencing, and it is capable of so doing via the coincident features of all human tongues. Even disregarding this, however, we can say that the power of geneology over languages lies clearly enough before our eyes in their distribution according to nations. In itself, this is easily comprehensible, inasmuch as descent acts so powerfully, in fact predominantly, on the entire individuality with which each particular language is most intimately associated. If language were not to enter by its very origin from the recesses of human nature into an actual association with physical descent, why would the parental idiom, for the educated and the uncultured as well, possess a so much greater power and intimacy than a foreign tongue? Does not one's native tongue capture the ear with a kind of sudden enchantment after a long absence, and does it not awaken nostalgia when heard on foreign soil? This certainly is based not upon its intellectual attributes, nor upon the idea or emotion expressed, but precisely upon its most inexplicable and most individual features, its phonemes and sounds. It seems to us as if we are perceiving a part of our very selves through our native tongue.

In a consideration of the factor produced by language, the manner of conception cannot be substantiated; it is as if it merely designated the objects perceived in themselves. Moreover, one would never exhaust the deep and full content of language by means of these objects. Just as no concept is possible without language, at the same time language cannot be an object for the soul, since, indeed, every external object attains complete substantiality only through the medium of a concept. However, the entire manner of subjective perception of objects is transmitted necessarily into the structure and into the usage of language. For the word originates precisely from this perception; it is an offprint not of the object per se, but of the image of the latter produced in the soul. Inasmuch as subjectivity is unavoidably admixed with all objective perception, it is possible—even independent of language—to regard every human individuality as a separate and unique viewpoint of the cosmos. However, the fact that it may be regarded thus is greatly enhanced by language, since the word, as will be shown subsequently, with an accretion of self-significance (*Selbstbedeutung*), becomes the object and obtains a new property. This property and that of a phoneme are necessarily analogous to that of the language as a whole; since a homogeneous subjectivity operates on the language of a nation, a unique cosmic viewpoint reposes in every tongue. Just as the individual sound intervenes between object and man, the entire language does so between him and nature acting upon him both externally and internally. He surrounds himself with an ambient of sounds in order to assimilate and process the world of objects. These expressions do not in any way exceed the measure of simple truth. Man lives principally, or even exclusively with objects, since his feelings and actions depend upon his concepts as language presents them to his attention. By the same act through which he spins out the thread of language he weaves himself into its tissues. Each tongue draws a circle about the people to whom it belongs, and it is possible to leave this circle only by simultaneously entering that of another people.[7] Learning a foreign language ought hence to be the conquest of a new standpoint in the previously prevailing cosmic attitude of the individual. In fact, it is so to a certain extent, inasmuch as every language contains the entire fabric of concepts and the conceptual approach of a portion of humanity. But this achievement is not complete, because one always carries over into a foreign tongue to a greater or lesser degree one's own cosmic viewpoint— indeed one's personal linguistic pattern.

Even the beginnings of language may not be conceived as restricted to such a scanty stock of words as is generally the case if, instead of seeking their origin in an original human gregarious sociability, we impute such inception to the need of mutual aid and relegate human kind to an imaginary natural status. Indeed, these are among the most erroneous viewpoints that can be formulated respecting language. Man is not so indigent, and had he sought merely an auxiliary aid, inarticulate sounds would have sufficed. Language is completely human even in its beginnings and extends unintentionally to all objects of accidental sentient percep- tion and internal treatment. Even the languages of so-called savages, which should approach more closely than others such a natural state, reveal a plentitude of multifarious expressions. Words well voluntarily from the breast without need or intent, and there has probably not been in any desert waste a migratory horde that did not possess its own songs. As an animal species, the human being is a singing creature, but he combines ideas with the musical sounds involved.

Language, however, not only transplants an indefinite quantity of material elements from nature into the soul [intellect]; it also supplies to it that which we perceive as form in the totality. Nature unfolds before us a multicolored and, according to all sensual impressions, a multishaped variety, bathed in luminous clarity. Our reflective thinking discovers in it a regulated pattern that is congenial to our intellectual form. Quite apart from the physical existence of objects, an external beauty clings to their outlines as a charm intended for man alone. This is a beauty, moreover, in which this regulated pattern and the sensory material join together in a persistently inexplicable bond because we are gripped and carried away by it. All this we find again in analogous accordances in language, and it is capable of representing it. For, when by its hand we pass over into a world of sounds, we do not abandon that actually surrounding us. The regulated pattern of language in its own structure is related to that of nature; and because it stimulates through this structure the activity of man's highest and most human powers, it brings him closer to an under- standing of the formal impression of nature. Such understanding can be considered only as a development, however inexplicable, of intellectual powers. By the rhythmical and musical form peculiar to sound by associa- tion, language enhances the impression of the beauty in nature by transposing it into another area; it operates, however, independent of this impression via the mere melody of speech upon the temper of the intellect.

Language, as the sum total of its creations, is in each case different from what is uttered. Prior to completing this section, we must take up a more detailed consideration of this variation. A language in its complete scope contains everything transformed into sounds by it. However, just as the thought material and the combinations thereof can never be exhausted, the quantity of material to be designated and associated is likewise infinite. In addition to the elements already formed, language consists above all of methods to carry out the labor of the intellect, for which it prescribes course and form. The elements once formulated certainly constitute to some degree a dead mass, but this mass bears in itself the virile germ of never-ending determinacy. Therefore, at every single point and in every single epoch, language, just as nature itself, appears to man—in contrast to everything already familiar and reasoned out—as an inexhaustible mine in which the intellect is capable of discovering still unfamiliar material, and in which the sensory apparatus may perceive emotional stimuli hitherto not felt. In every treatment of language by a truly great and new genius, this phenomenon is manifested in reality. Man needs it as inspiration in his continual intellectual striving and in the steady development of his intellectual biosis; he must know that, in addition to the region already mastered, there is an infinite mass to be further disentangled, and that the path to this remains unobstructed. Language, however, proceeds from its obscure, undisclosed depth simultaneously in two directions. It flows forth from the past containing untold and unknown wealth, which to some extent can still be recognized,[8] but then it veers off and becomes inaccessible, leaving behind only the sensation of its unfathomableness. Language possesses for us this infinite feature[9]—it has neither a beginning nor a discernible end, and upon it a brief past casts its light—in common with the entire existence of the human race. But in language one senses more distinctly and in a more lively way how the distant past is related to the emotion of the present, since language has traversed the sensory mechanism of earlier generations and preserved their inspiration. These previous generations have been preserved for us, moreover, in the selfsame sounds of our mother tongue, which become for us the expression of our emotions and are related to us both on a national and a family scale.[10]

This partially fixed and partially fluid factor in language produces a singular relationship between it and the speaking generation. There is produced in it a stock of words and a system of rules, via which in the course of millennia it grows to an independent power. In the foregoing exposition our attention was drawn to the fact that the concept taken up by language becomes to some extent an object to the soul and to such extent exerts upon it a power alien to it. But, we have regarded the object as having originated preeminently from the subject, that is, the effect as having derived from that entity upon which it reacts. Now the converse viewpoint appears, according to which language is indeed an alien object, its effect having proceeded in fact from something other than that upon which it reacts. For language must necessarily belong to two individuals (see pp. 36, 37), and it is truly a property of the entire human race. To the extent that it preserves for the intellect the slumbering idea in written form, it fashions a peculiar existence for itself. To be sure, it can persist only in the brief span of each thought process, but in its totality it is independent of this process. The two mutually opposing viewpoints, one which sees language as alien and the other which sees it pertaining to the soul, one which sees language as independent of the soul and the other which sees it dependent upon it, are really combined in language and constitute the idiosyncrasy of its nature. This conflict of ideas, moreover, must not be solved so that language becomes in part alien and independent and in part neither. Language is objectively reactive and independent precisely to the extent that it is subjectively reacted upon and dependent. For language has nowhere—not even in writing—a permanent abode; its dead component, so to speak, must ever be reproduced anew in thought, must be alive in speech or comprehension, and must consequently pass over to the subject in its entirety. It is inherent, however, in the act of this generation for language to be transformed into the object also; in this way it experiences in every case the entire effect of the individual. This effect, however, is bound by that which the individual is effecting and has effected. The true solution of the foregoing antithesis reposes in the unity of human nature. What stems from that is the factor in which the concepts of subject and object, of dependence and independence merge with each other, which is in reality native to me. Language belongs to me because I bring it forth as I do; and since the reason for this lies both in the current speech and in that previously spoken by all races of man (to the extent that speech communication—without interruption—may have persisted among them), it remains language itself by which I am still restricted. However, what restricts and determines me in it, has come to me from human nature intimately related to me. Hence, the alien component in it is such only for my transiently individual nature, but not for my originally true nature.

It becomes clear how slight actually the power of the individual is compared to the might of language, if we consider how upon each generation of a people all those features which language has accrued in all previous centuries act as bonds, and how only the power of individual generations makes contact with language. Moreover even this contact of an individual generation is not pure, since the maturing and declining generations live admixed side by side. Only by the unusual plasticity of language, that is, the possibility of integrating its forms in an extremely variable manner without deleterious effect upon general understanding, and by the power which all living intellectualism exerts upon its dead heritage, is the equilibrium restored to some extent. Yet it is always the language which makes one feel most virile, makes one feel that he is an efflux of the entire human race. Because everyone meanwhile reacts upon it individually and incessantly, each generation nevertheless produces a change in its language which often escapes notice.[11] This change does not always rest in the words and forms themselves, but occasionally only in their modified usage; and where writing and literature are lacking, this latter is more difficult to perceive. The reaction of the individual upon language becomes more obvious if one considers that the individuality of a language (as the word is generally understood) is only such by comparison, and that its true individuality reposes in the given speaker at any time. This must be considered if the concepts are to be sharply defined.[12] Only in the individual does language attain its final distinctness. Nobody conceives in a given word exactly what his neighbor does, and the ever so slight variation skitters through the entire language like concentric ripples over the water. All understanding is simultaneously a noncomprehension, all agreement in ideas and emotions is at the same time a divergence. In the manner in which language is modified by each individual there is revealed, in contrast to its previously expounded potency, a power of man over it. It can be construed as a physiological effect (if we want to apply the expression to intellectual power); the power emanating from man is purely dynamic. In the influence exerted upon him lies the principled structure of language and of its forms, whereas in the reaction proceeding from him reposes a principle of freedom. For in man a certain something may arise whose reason no rational process is capable of isolating from preceding conditions; furthermore, we would misconstrue the nature of language and thus injure the historical veracity of its origin and transformation, were we to exclude the possibility of such inexplicable phenomena from it. However, even if the freedom involved be indeterminable and inexplicable, perhaps its boundaries within a certain space conceded to it alone might be found. Linguistic investigation must recognize and respect this phenomenon of freedom, but it must also meticulously trace its limits.

CHAPTER SEVEN

The Phonetic System of Languages

DRIVEN BY AN inner urge, man extorts the articulated sound, the basis and essence of all speech, from his anatomic apparatus; animals would be capable of the like were they endowed with the same spiritual urge. The initial and most indispensable element of language is based so completely and exclusively in the human intellect that its permeation is sufficient, and also requisite, for transforming animal sound into articulate speech. For the intent and capacity for meaningfulness—the latter certainly not in a general sense but in the specific meaning of representing a thought— alone constitute the articulated sound. Moreover, nothing else can be cited to designate its difference on the one hand from animal cries and on the other from musical notes. It cannot be described qualitatively[1] but solely according to its production. This is not owing to lack of capability on our part but is characteristic of articulate sound in its peculiar nature, since this phenomenon is nothing but the intentional process of the soul to utter it and contains only the minimal physical substance requisite for perception.

This entity, the audible sound, may even to some extent be separated from its body and thereby permit the articulation to become still more distinct. The foregoing may be observed in the case of deaf mutes. All communication with them via the ear is precluded; however, they learn to understand speech by observing the motion of the speech organs of the speaker and through written material, whose nature is completely constituted by articulation. Indeed, they themselves speak when the position and movements of their speech organs are appropriately guided. This can happen only as a result of an articulatory capacity that is inherent even in them, because, through the association of their thought processes with their speech apparatus and from observing the movements of the speaker's speech organs, they learn to divine the remaining factor, his thoughts.

The tone which we hear is revealed to them by the position and motion of the organs and by the appertaining script; they perceive the pertinent articulation minus its accompanying sound through the eye and through the strained effort to speak themselves. Hence a remarkable dissection of the articulated sound takes place in them. They really understand the language, since they read and write alphabetically and even learn to speak; they do not merely recognize ideas through stimulation by signs and pictures. They learn to speak not only because they possess reason as do other humans, but actually because they, too, possess speech capacity, a coincidence of their thought process with their speech apparatus. Finally, they possess the urge to cause both factors to interact, factors, moreover, that are essentially based in human nature, even if crippled in one aspect. The differences between them and us is that their speech implements cannot be awakened to imitate the example furnished by a completely articulated sound, and hence the expression of their activity must be learned through an artificial, roundabout process contrary to nature. In them it is also revealed how closely the written word is associated to language, even when auditory instrumentality is absent.

Articulation is based on the power of the intellect to compel the speech apparatus to treat sound in a manner that corresponds to the operation of the mind. The way in which such formulation and articulation meet, as if in an associative medium, is that the areas of both are broken down into their basic components. The agglutination of these components then forms integral entities, which in turn strive to become components of new complete entities. Furthermore, the process of thinking inevitably reduces multiplicity to unity. The characteristics of the articulated sound are, therefore, sharply perceived unity and the capability of entering into a definite relationship with all other articulated sounds.[2] The separation of the sound from all the impure allophones is indispensable for clarity and harmonious sound. But the sound also flows directly from the intention of making it an element of speech. It stands there in all its purity whenever speech is genuinely vivid, frees itself from confused animal cries, and emerges as the product of purely human impulse and intent. Its adaptation into a system, by virtue of which every articulated sound is possessed of qualities enabling it to align all other sounds either as allies or in direct opposition to itself, is effected by the nature of the creation. For each individual sound is formed in relation to others, all of which are equally necessary to free and complete speech. Although we cannot state just how this happens, articulated sounds burst forth from each people in that relationship to one another that its language system requires. The variety of the speech organs and the spatial location in each of them, where the articulated sound is produced, form the main differences between systems. To these are joined the secondary characteristics such as aspiration, sibilance, nasality, and so forth, which can be peculiar to each system without regard to differences in the organs. However, the foregoing speech properties constitute a threat to the distinctiveness of speech sounds. A strong proof of the predominance of correct linguistic sense is an alphabet that keeps a rein upon the enunciation of these sounds, so that they impinge upon the most sensitive ear in complete and nonadmixed purity. These secondary attributes must thereupon fuse with the basic articulation to produce a distinct modification of the principal sound and should be banished absolutely in any other undisciplined occurrence.[3]

Articulated consonants cannot be enunciated unless accompanied by a current of air imparting sound. In accordance with the point of production and the aperture through which it flows, this exhalation of air produces just as definitely differing sounds occurring in a mutually fixed sequence as those contained in the consonantal series.[4] The syllable is produced by this twofold sonic process. However, it does not contain two or more sounds, as our orthography would seem to indicate, but only a single one uttered in a definite way. The division of the simple syllable into a consonant and vowel, to the extent that we may conceive the two as independent, is but an artificial one. In nature, consonant and vowel are mutually determinate to the extent that they constitute for the ear a completely indissoluble unit. Hence, if writing is to designate this natural quality, it would be more correct not to treat the vowels as independent characters,[5] but merely as modifications of consonants, as several Asiatic alphabets do. To be precise, vowels cannot be pronounced alone either. The air current producing them requires an impetus which makes them audible;[6] and even if this does not produce a distinct initial consonant, still an aspiration—no matter how faint it may be—is necessary. Some languages indicate this as prior to every initial vowel.[7] This aspiration may actually be intensified to engender a truly guttural consonant, and language is capable of indicating the various stages in this induration[8] by special characters. The vowel requires the same distinctiveness as the consonant, and the syllable must bear the distinctiveness of both. In the vocalic system, however, it is difficult to substantiate this feature, although it is necessary for perfection of the language. The vowel combines not merely with a preceding but also with a following sound, which may be a pure consonant or a mere aspiration such as the Sanskrit *visarga* and in some cases the Arabic final *elif*. There, however, the purity of the sound is more difficult for the ear to perceive than is true for initial position, especially when no actual consonant but only a secondary quality[9] of the articulated sounds associates with the vowel. Hence, the orthography of some peoples appears deficient when judged from this standpoint. By the two series of mutually determinative but audibly and, in the abstract, definitely differentiated consonants and vowels there originates not only a new multifariousness of conditions in the alphabet, but also an antithesis of the two series with respect to each other, of which language makes extensive use.

For every alphabet, therefore, a twofold feature can be distinguished in the sum of articulated sounds through which the alphabet reacts more or less beneficiently upon the language. This factor is the absolute wealth of sounds in the language and their relative status with respect both to each other and to the completeness and principled structure of a consummate phonetic system. According to its schematic character, such a system contains the same number of classes of alphabetic symbols as it does articulated sounds that sequentially relate with each other or contrast owing to their differences—that is, the antithesis or relationship taken with respect to all the relationships in which they can occur. When analyzing an individual language, we ask ourselves first whether the diversification of its sounds completely or deficiently covers the points of the scheme which the relationship or the antithesis indicates; we then ask whether the wealth of phonetic values, which can hardly be overlooked, is uniformly distributed in all its components in accordance with a general blueprint of the entire phonetic system corresponding to the speech sensitivity of the people in question, or whether some categories are deficiently developed while others are excessively developed. The true principled organization, which Sanskrit approaches very closely, would require that every sound, articulated in varying ways according to the point of origin, be conveyed through all classes, and consequently through all phonetic modifications which the ear is accustomed to distinguishing in languages. It becomes readily evident that this whole aspect of language is primarily a matter of a fortunate organization of the ear and the speech apparatus. It is, however, by no means unimportant how sonorous or phonetically deficient, how verbose or taciturn a people may be with respect to its natural disposition or sensory perceptivity. For the pleasure received from the articulated sound yields the speakers of a language a wealth of combinations. A certain free and hence more noble pleasure in the production of even a nonarticulated sound cannot be denied in all cases. To be sure, necessity frequently unleashes it, particularly in the event of repugnant sensations; in other instances, when it entices, warns, or summons aid, it is intentional. However, it also flows forth without need or intent from the joyful sensation of existence, and not merely from unchecked desire but from a delicate delight in the artistic resonance of the cadences. This is the poetic factor, a flickering spark gleaming in the obscurity of animal stupor. These varying types of sounds are very unequally distributed among the more or less silent and sonorous genera of animals, and relatively few have been accorded the more elevated and gladsome type. It would be instructive for language—but will perhaps remain forever unfathomed—if we knew whence this differentiation derives. That birds alone possess the capacity of song might perhaps be explained by the fact that they live more freely than other animals in the ambient of tonality and its purer regions, were not so many other avian genera, like many earthbound animals, restricted to a few monotones.

In language, however, it is not the wealth of sounds that is decisive. It is rather a matter of chaste limitation of the sounds requisite to speech and to their appropriate balance. Linguistic sense must therefore contain something else, some feature which we are incapable of clarifying in detail, an instinctive presentiment of the entire system which the language needs in its individual structure. What is actually repeated in the entire generation of language occurs here also. Language can be compared to a prodigious fabric in which every part is related to the adjoining one and all of them persist in a more or less distinctly discernible association. Man touches in speaking only an isolated portion of this fabric, with the relationships that serve as his point of departure being immaterial. However, he does so instinctively, as if all the components, with which that individual portion must necessarily agree, were simultaneously present.

The individual articulations constitute the foundation for all phonetic combinations of language. The boundaries within which the foregoing phonemic entities are enclosed are, at the same time, more narrowly defined by phonetic shifts that are peculiar to most tongues and which are based on particular laws and speech habits. Both the consonantal and the vocalic series are involved. Some languages differ from each other additionally by the fact that they preferentially or for varying purposes exploit one or the other of the series mentioned. The essential utility of this transformation is that, while the absolute linguistic wealth and phonetic multiplicity are increased, the primitive stem may still be recognized in the transformed element. Language is thus put in a position of moving with greater freedom without losing the thread that is necessary for seeking out the relationship between concepts and the intelligibility. For these factors follow the modification of the sounds, or precede such change, and establish linguistic laws in the process. As a result, language profits by a more lively clarity. Deficient conversion of sounds impedes the recognition of the designated concepts with respect to the sounds, a difficulty which would be even more perceptible in Chinese if the analogy of orthography did not frequently assume the place of sound analogy in derivation and compounding. The sound transformation, however, is subject to a twofold principle whose components often support each other but which in other cases prove mutually antithetical. One of these is a merely organic factor that originates from the speech apparatus and its concerted operation, depends on the facility or difficulty of pronunciation, and hence follows the natural relationship of the sounds. The other factor is given by the intellectual principle of the language, impedes the organs from succumbing to their inclination toward inertia, and holds them firmly to sound combinations which would not be inherently natural to them. To a certain extent both principles are in harmony with each other. The intellectual factor must for the promotion of easier and more fluent pronunciation yield to the other insofar as possible. Indeed, occasionally to get from one sound to the next, if such a combination is deemed necessary by the designation, other transitions, merely organic in nature, are brought into play. In a certain regard, however, both principles are so antithetical that, if the intellectual factor slackens in its effectiveness, the organic one becomes preponderant, just as principle chemical affinities prevail in the animal body upon extinction of life.[10] The collaboration and the antagonism of these principles produce both in the form of languages appearing original to us and in their resultant development a multiplicity of phenomena that precise grammatical analysis discovers and enumerates.

The phonetic transformation here being discussed occurs principally in two or, if you will, three stages of linguistic structure: in the roots, in the words derived from them, and in the further development of the latter into the various general forms that are included in the nature of the language. The portrayal of a language must begin with the peculiar system that each tongue assumes in this regard. For this is equivalent to the stream bed in which its current flows from age to age; its general directions are thereby determined, and its most individual phenomena can be traced to this foundation by a persevering analysis.

By the term "words" we mean the signs of individual concepts. The syllable forms a sound unit, but it only becomes a word when there is some significance attached to it; this often requires a combination of several such units. Therefore, in the word two units, the sound and the idea, coalesce. Words thus become the true elements of speech; syllables lacking significance actually cannot be so designated. If language is conceived as a second world, formed objectively in accordance with man's impressions of the real one, then words are the sole objects therein for which the character of individuality is maintained in the form. Speech proceeds in uninterrupted constancy, but the speaker has in mind only the totality of the idea to be designated, before reflection on language intrudes. It is impossible to imagine language as originating from the designation of objects by words and from there making the transition to agglutination. In reality speech is not composed of words which have preceded it; rather, words proceed from the totality of speech. However, they are already perceived without actual reflection even in the crudest and most uncultured speaking, since word formation is a necessity of speaking. The peripheral scope of the word is the boundary to which language is independently structured. The simple word is the complete flower bursting from the bud, and in the word belongs the complete product of language itself. For the sentence and speech, language determines only the regulating form and relinquishes the individual configuration to the arbitrary option of the speaker. Words often seem isolated in speech itself. Their true discovery in the continuum of speech is accessible only to the acuteness of an already well-developed linguistic sense; this is one area in which the advantages and shortcomings of individual languages become visible.

Since words are always juxtaposed to ideas, it is natural that related ideas are designated by related sounds. If the derivation of ideas is more or less distinctly perceived in the intellect, a derivation of the sounds must correspond in such a way that the relationship of ideas and sounds corresponds. The phonetic relationship, which should not become identical with the sound, can only become evident by the fact that a portion of the word undergoes a change subject to definite laws, while another portion remains totally unchanged or suffers but a slight identifiable modification. The fixed portions of words and morphemes are termed root factors, and when they are represented as separate entities they are the roots of the language itself. In some languages these roots appear only rarely in their bare form in connected discourse, in others they appear not at all. In fact, if the concepts are distinguished precisely, the latter is always the case. For as these roots enter into speech patterns, they assume even in concept a category that corresponds to their connection; therefore, they no longer contain the bare and formless root idea. On the other hand, they cannot be regarded in all languages as a product of mere reflection and as the ultimate result of word analysis—that is, simply as a grammatical labor. In languages with a great variety of sounds and expressions, and which possess definite derivational laws, the radical sounds must stand out clearly in the phantasy and memory of its speakers as the original designative entities, and in their recurrence in so many gradations of the concepts, they must stand out as the entities of general designation. If, as such, they become deeply impressed upon the intellect, they are also easily woven into connected discourse unchanged and consequently are a part of the true morphology (*Wortform*) of the language. They can, however, even during the primeval period of development have been in current use for formative purposes in this way, so that they really preceded the derivations and became fragments of a later expanded and thoroughly transformed language. In this way we can explain how, for example, in Sanskrit, if we consult the documents familiar to us, we find only certain roots ordinarily inserted into speech. In such matters chance naturally plays a governing part; and if the Hindu grammarians stated that every one of their alleged roots could thus be utilized, this is probably not a fact excerpted from the language but rather a law formulated by them arbitrarily. They appear on the whole, in the case of linguistic forms, not merely to have collected those used but to have carried every form through all roots; and this system of generalization is to be noted in other portions of Sanskrit grammar as well.[11] Enumeration of roots occupied the Sanskrit grammarians especially, and the complete compilation of them is indisputably their work.[12] There are, however, languages which truly have no roots in the sense assumed here, because they lack laws governing derivation and phonetic changes affecting simpler phonetic combinations.[13] In such cases, as in Chinese, roots and words coincide because the latter cannot be broken down or expanded into any other forms; the language merely possesses roots.[14] It would be conceivable that from such languages others might have originated by the addition of phonetic changes to the words, so that the bare roots of a new language would consist of the stock of words of an older language completely or partially lost from speech. However, I cite this merely as a possibility; that such a process actually occurred in any language could only be proved historically.

In going back to the simple stage, we have here separated the words from the roots; we can, however, distinguish the words from the actual grammatical forms by ascending to a more complex level. Words, in order to be incorporated into speech, must intimate differing conditions, and the designation of these conditions may take place in the words in such a way that a third, expanded phonetic form [morpheme] as a rule originates. If the morphemic distinction alluded to here is sharp and exact in a language, the words cannot fail to designate these conditions, and to the extent that the conditions are designated by phonetic difference, the words cannot enter unchanged into speech but become at best parts of other words bearing these phonetic signs. Now where this is the case in a language, these words are termed basic words; the language then possesses a phonetic form consisting of three expanding stages. This is the state in which a phonetic system develops to its greatest extent.

Aside from the refinement of the speech and auditory apparatuses and the inclination to impart to the sound the greatest multiplicity and most complete development, the advantages of a language with respect to its phonetic system are based especially on the relationship of the latter to significance. To portray external objects that simultaneously impinge on all the senses and the internal stimulation of the mind merely by impressions upon the ear is to a great extent an inexplicable operation as far as the detail is concerned. That there is a connection between the sound and its significance appears certain, but the character of this connection can rarely be stated completely; often it may only be divined, and much more frequently it cannot be guessed at all. If one stops with the simple words, since compounds do not enter into the discussion at all, a threefold reason becomes apparent for combining certain sounds with certain ideas. This, however, does not solve the problem, particularly in the area of application. Accordingly, a threefold designation of the concepts can be distinguished.

1. The first is the directly imitative concept, in which the tone that a resounding object brings forth is reproduced to the extent that articulated sounds are capable of reproducing unarticulated ones. This designation is pictographic so to speak. Just as the picture represents the manner in which an object appears to the eye, language depicts the manner in which it is perceived by the ear. As imitation always encounters unarticulated tones, articulation is, so to speak, contradictory to this designation; and depending on whether the nature of these tones asserts itself too intensively or too little in this disagreement, either too much of the nonarticulated is residual, or it becomes blurred to the point of being unrecognizable. For this reason, this designation—wherever it appears with any intensity—cannot be absolved from a certain crudity and is little pronounced in the progressive development of the language.

2. The second is the indirectly imitative designation, which shares in a property that is common to the sound and the object. Although the concept of the symbol in language goes much farther, this latter may be termed the symbolic designation. It selects sounds to designate the objects which, inherently and in comparison with others, produce for the ear an impression similar to that of the object upon the soul. For example, "stand," "steady," and "stare" give the impression of fixity; the Sanskrit *lî*, "melt" or "disperse," suggests melting away; and "not," "gnaw," and "envy" imply a fine and sharp severance. In this way objects that produce similar impressions obtain words with predominantly the same

sounds, such as *waft*, 'wind,' *welkin*, 'wish'; in all of these the restless motion confusedly passing before the senses is expressed by the letter *w*, hardened from the letter *u*, which is inherently dull and hollow sounding. This type of designation, which is based upon the significance of each individual letter, has indisputably exerted upon the primitive word designation a great and perhaps definitive influence. Its necessary consequence has been a certain equality of designation throughout all languages of the human race, since the impressions of objects everywhere had to assume more or less the same relationship to the sounds. Much of this kind of material can still be recognized in languages today. However, if we desire to formulate therefrom a constitutive principle and verify this type of designation as generally valid for languages, instead of limiting it to mere historical derivation or labelling it a decision-making principle subject to grave doubt, we expose ourselves to great dangers and in every respect are following a slippery path. Disregarding other reasons, we cannot tell with any certainty what was either the original sound or the original meaning of words in languages. Yet this is the crux of the matter. Very often a letter [15] replaces another only as a result of organic or accidental change, as *n* for *l* or *d* for *r*, but we cannot always discern where this was the case. Therefore, inasmuch as the same result may be attributed to various causes, great arbitrariness cannot be excluded from this type of explanation.

3. The third is designation based on phonetic similarity in accordance with the relationship of the concepts to be designated. Words whose meanings closely approach one another become endowed with similar sounds; however, in contrast to the designative bracket just considered, emphasis in this instance is not upon the character inherent in these sounds themselves. This manner of designation, to elucidate it properly, presumes whole words of a certain scope in the phonetic system and can thus be applied extensively only in such a system. It is, however, the most fruitful of all the designations and the one which most distinctly represents all of the relationships of what has been intellectually created in a linguistic context. This designation, wherein the analogy of concepts and sounds—each in their own domain—is pursued so that both keep pace with each other, may be termed analogical.

In the entire range of language designation, two categories are to be distinguished from each other: the individual objects or concepts, and those general relationships which may be associated with many of the former, partly for designating new objects or ideas and partly for connecting speech elements. The general relationships pertain largely to the conformation of thought itself, and, because they may be derived from an original principle, they establish closed systems. In these systems, the isolated factors—both with respect to one another and with respect to the thought form encompassing the whole—are determined by intellectual necessity. Now, if in a language an extensive phonetic system permitting a multiplicity of possibilities is added, the concepts of this category and the sounds can be carried through in a progressively concomitant analogy. For these associations, the symbolic and analogical designations, of the three types enumerated previously, are especially applicable, and they can actually be clearly recognized in a number of languages. If, for example, in Arabic the construction of collective nouns is achieved by the very common method of inserting a lengthened vowel, the comprehended quantity is represented symbolically by the length of the sound [phoneme]. This may be regarded, however, as a refinement resulting from a more highly developed sense of articulation. Some ruder languages indicate similar phenomena by an actual pause between the syllables of the word, or by a technique which closely approaches the realm of gestures, so that the allusion becomes even more corporeally imitative.[16] Of similar nature is the direct repetition of the same syllable for multiple allusion, especially for that of plurality and to indicate past time. It is remarkable to see in Sanskrit—and to some extent in the Malayan linguistic family as well— how refined languages exploit reduplication of syllables; they weave them into their phonetic system, modify them by laws of euphony, and thereby remove from them the ruder, symbolically imitative tinkling of syllables. The designation of intransitive verbs is very refined and meaningful in Arabic, owing to the use of the weaker but simultaneously acutely penetrating *i* in contrast to the *a* of the active, and in several languages of the Malayan family, owing to the insertion of the deep-sounding nasal articulated more or less in the back of the mouth. In such case, the nasal must be preceded by a vowel, and the choice of this vowel follows the analogy of designation. With the exception of a few cases where this vowel assimilates to the following syllable owing to the power exerted by the sound over the significance, the deep back vowel *u* emanating from the depths of the speech organs introduces the nasal *m*. Hence, the inserted syllable *um* constitutes the mark of the intransitive characteristic.

In this highly intellectual region of linguistic structure, still another, more elevated principle develops in a special way. This is the pure and (if the expression be permitted) naked sense of articulation. Just as the effort to impart meaning to the sound creates the nature of the articulated sound, whose essence consists exclusively of this intention, the same effort operates in the direction of a definite meaning. This definiteness increases as the area to be designated effectively penetrates the intellect, since the soul itself establishes this area, even though it does not always come over the threshold of consciousness in its totality. Thus speech structure in this case can be conducted more purely by the endeavor to distinguish to the finest degree by selection and gradation of the sounds the similar and dissimilar features of the concepts involved. The purer and clearer the intellectual viewpoint of the area to be designated, the more this viewpoint feels itself compelled to be guided by this principle. Its final victory in this aspect of its business is the complete and visible dominion thereof. If we regard the refinement of the speech organs and of the ear, as well as the sense of euphony, as the first advantage, in the intensity and purity of this sense of articulation reposes a second and important advantage of speech-constructing nations.[17] Here everything depends on the fact that the meaning must truly permeate the sound, and that, simultaneously, to the linguistically perceptive ear nothing but the meaning must be contained in the sound, or, to turn the thought around, the sound must appear precisely and solely determined for the meaning. This naturally presumes a very sharp delineation of all relationships, as well as an equal precision for the sounds. The more definite and incorporeal the sounds are, the more sharply they are set off from each other. Through the predominance of the sense of articulation, both the receptivity and the automatic activity of the language-creating force within us are not merely intensified but also kept in the only proper channel. Since this force, as I have already remarked (see p. 48), always affects every detail in language in such a way that the entire fabric to which the individual item belongs seems instinctively present, this instinct for total presence is effective and is perceptible in proportion to the intensity and purity of the sense of articulation.

The phonetic form is the expression which the language produces for the concept. However, the form can also be regarded as a receptacle which the language constructs and whose shape it also assumes so to speak. The creation, if it is to be actual and complete, can be valid only with respect to the original linguistic invention. This depends upon a condition with which we are not acquainted but which we must assume as a necessary hypothesis. The application of an already available phonetic form to the more intimate objectives of the language, however, can be deemed possible in the medial period of linguistic structural development. Through internal revelation and the favorable operation of external circumstances, a people could impart form to the inherited language which would so greatly alter it that it would as a result become an entirely different and new one. There can be a reasonable doubt that this is possible for languages of completely differing form. Conversely, it is undeniable that languages are guided by the more lucid insight of the intimate morphology of language to construct more varied and more sharply delineated nuances, and that for this purpose they utilize their available phonetic form in an expanding or refining manner. Thus, in linguistic families a comparison of the individual related languages informs us which has advanced in this way beyond the others. Several such cases are encountered in Arabic, if we compare it with the Hebrew; and it will be an interesting investigation, reserved for my treatise on the Kawi language of Java, to determine if and in what way the languages of the South Sea Islands may be regarded as the basic form from which the Malayan of the Indian Archipelago and of Madagascar merely represents a further development.

The whole phenomenon is explained completely from the natural course of speech production. As its very nature demonstrates, language is present in the soul in its totality. Every detail in it behaves in such a way that it corresponds to another detail still indistinct and either to a whole consisting of the sum of the phenomena involved and the principles of the intellect or to a possible whole yet to be created. The actual development occurs gradually, and the new increment is constructed analogically according to principles already existing. Not only must we start from these principles in all linguistic elucidation, but we may do this with complete assurance inasmuch as they issue forth clearly from an historical analysis of languages. What has already been established to a certain extent in the phonetic pattern violently seizes the new formation and does not permit it to pursue an essentially different path. The various types of verb in the Malayan languages are indicated by syllables which are prefixed to the basic word. There has obviously not always been such a multiplicity and such a fine distinction between these syllables as we find in the writings of the Tagalic grammarians. However, those syllables which have been added little by little always appear in the same position. We find a similar occurrence in those cases where the Arabic attempts to designate differences left undistinguished by the older Semitic. The solution here is to exploit auxiliary verbs for the construction of some tenses rather than to give the word a configuration by agglutination of syllables that is not in accordance with the linguistic family.

It therefore becomes easily explicable that it is chiefly the phonetic pattern which establishes the difference between languages. This lies in their very nature inasmuch as the actual, corporeal sound alone constitutes the language; moreover, the sound permits a far greater multiplicity of variations than does the innate speech form, which necessarily proceeds with greater uniformity. The powerful influence of the sound arises, however, in part from that which it exerts on the innate form itself. For, if one always conceives of the structure of language as a concerted action of intellectual endeavor to designate the material required by the innate linguistic purpose of the utterance of the corresponding articulated sound, the physical factor already produced, as well as the principle upon which its multiplicity reposes, must readily gain superiority over the idea that is seeking to become clear by new configuration.

At all events, linguistic structure must be regarded as a production in which the innate idea must overcome a difficulty in order to manifest itself. This difficulty is the sound [phoneme], and the triumph over the obstacle is not always successful. It is often easier to yield in the realm of ideas and to apply the same sound or the same phonetic form for different items, as is done in those languages which form the future and subjunctive identically owing to the incertitude inherent in both (see Chapter 11). Certainly in such a case there is always a weakness in the sound-producing ideas involved, for the truly potent linguistic sense always overcomes the difficulty triumphantly. But the phonetic form utilizes its weakness and to some extent masters the new configuration. Instances are found in all languages where it becomes clear that the innate striving—in which we have to seek out the true language—has been more or less diverted from its original course in the acceptance of the sound. We have already discussed those languages in which the speech apparatus unilaterally makes its nature effective by displacing the true basic sounds bearing the meaning of the word (see pp. 48, 49 above). It is worthwhile noting how the linguistic sense operating internally often accepts this for a long time, but then, in an individual case, suddenly forces its way through and, without yielding to phonetic inclination, holds unswervingly to a single vowel. In other cases a new form, demanded by the linguistic sense, is created, but at that very instant it is modified by the phonetic inclination, which, so to speak, reaches a conciliatory agreement with the vowel. For the most part, however, essentially differing phonetic forms exert a definitive effect on the entire attainment of the innate linguistic objectives. In Chinese, for example, no modification of words guiding the connection of speech elements could arise because the phonetic structure holding the syllables rigidly apart became firmly established, thus counteracting their modification and juncture. The original cause of these impediments may be of a quite opposite nature. In Chinese it appears to lie more in the lack of inclination on the part of the populace to impart to the sound richly imaginative variety which promotes harmony. Where this is absent and where the intellect does not see the possibility of clothing the various trends of thought with appropriate phonetic nuances, it fosters to a lesser extent a fine distinction between these relationships. For the inclination to construct a multiplicity of fine and sharply contrasting articulations and the striving of reason to create for language as many and definitely separate forms as it needs, in order to fetter fleeting thought in its infinite ramifications, always stimulate each other. Originally, in the invisible movements of the intellect, one may not conceive the designating power and that necessary for designation in any way as separate, insofar as the phoneme and what the innate linguistic purpose requires are concerned. The general linguistic capacity unites and comprehends both. However, the way in which the idea as word contacts the external ambient, and the way in which the force of an already formed material approaches man, through the tradition of an extant language which man must ever and again automatically produce within himself, permit the dichotomy to arise. This dichotomy justifies and compels us to consider the creation of language from these two variant aspects. In the Semitic languages, the conjunction of the organic differentiation of a rich multiplicity of sounds and of a fine sense of articulation, motivated in part by the type of these sounds, explains why these languages possess a far more artistic and ingenious phonetic form and why they even distinguish principal grammatical concepts with clarity and definiteness. In these languages, however, the linguistic sense has by following in one direction neglected the other. Since it has not pursued with proper decisiveness the true, natural purpose of the language, it has turned for attainment of an advantage to meaningful and multifariously processed phonetic form. The natural structure of the languages led it to this end. The root words, disyllabic in structure as a rule, found the space to modify their phonemes internally, and this modification required vowels especially. Since the latter are obviously finer and more incorporeal than the consonants, they aroused and tuned the innate sense of articulation to greater refinement.[18]

There is another way in which we can conceive of a preponderance of the phonetic form, taken per se, determining the character of languages. The aggregate of all the media which language exploits to attain its objectives can be termed its technical structure; this can be subdivided, in turn, into the phonetic and intellectual components. The author understands in terms of the former the structure of words and forms insofar as they concern the sound or are motivated by it. This phonetic component is richer when the individual forms possess a broader and more sonorous scope; this is the case, for example, whenever it supplies differentiating forms by expression for the same concept or the same relationship. The intellectual aspect comprehends what is to be designated and distinguished in language. To it pertains, for example, the degree to which a language encompasses designation of gender, of the dual, and of tenses by all the possible combinations of the concept of time with the course of action, and so forth.

In this aspect language appears as an implement designed for a purpose. However, as this implement obviously stimulates the purely intellectual as well as the noblest sensory powers by means of the order of ideas, the clarity, and the acuteness expressed therein, as well as by the euphony and rhythm, the organic speech structure can assimilate the language and, regardless of its purposes, can also capture the enthusiasm of nations and, in fact, does so. The technical character thus outgrows the requisites for attainment of the purpose. And it can likewise be thought that languages in this respect transcend the need rather than lag behind it. If the English, Persian, and actual Malayan tongues are compared with the Sanskrit and Tagalic idioms, such a difference in the scope and wealth of the technical linguistic structure is perceived. Yet the direct linguistic objective, the reproduction of the idea, does not in the case of the former three suffer; all three of them attain it indubitably, but this is owing in part to their eloquent and poetic versatility. With respect to the preponderant role of the technical character in language and as a whole, I shall reserve discussion for a later point in this treatise. Here I wished only to mention that the phonetic factor may preponderate over the intellectual. And, no matter what the superiorities of the phonetic system might be, such a disparity always weakens the language-producing force since that which in itself is unified and vital, keeps intact even in its effect the harmony reposing in its nature. Where moderation is not completely abandoned, the wealth in the phonetic stock of languages can be compared to coloration in painting. The impressions of both produce a similar sensation. The concept also reacts otherwise if it appears in great bareness like a mere outline than if it seems more colored, if the expression be permitted, by the language.

CHAPTER EIGHT

Internal Linguistic Morphology and Structure

ALL THE ADVANTAGES of highly artistic and musical phonetic forms, though combined with the most lively sense of articulation, remain incapable of furnishing the intellect with worthy, agreeable languages, if the radiant clarity of the ideas does not penetrate the language with its light and warmth. That portion of language which is most intimately and purely intellectual is actually the most significant. It is that portion which dictates the way in which linguistic production makes use of the phonetic form, and it is responsible for the fact that language is capable of lending expression to everything which, as the result of progressive conceptual effort, the greatest minds of the most recent generations strive to entrust to it. This quality, native to language, depends upon the agreement and the collaboration of the laws revealed in it with each other and with the principles of observation, thinking, and sensation in general. The intellectual capacity, however, has its existence solely in its activity. It is the power which explodes with all its force along a clearly channeled course. Therefore, the foregoing laws are nothing other than the channels in which the intellectual activity moves during the process of linguistic production or, to use another analogy, nothing but the forms in which the intellectual activity stamps out the sounds. There is no power of the soul which would not be active in this process. Nothing in the intimate nature of man is so deep, so fine, and so inclusive that it would not pass over into the realm of language and be recognizable in it. The intellectual advantages of language rest therefore exclusively in the well-ordered, solid, and clear intellectual organization of peoples in the era of its construction or reconstruction, and they are its image, indeed its direct offprint.

It may appear as if all languages would have to be identical to each other in their intellectual process. For the phonetic pattern, an infinite multifariousness is comprehensible; since the mental and physical individuality originates from so many different causes, the possibility of its gradations cannot be estimated. However, that which rests solely upon one's own intellectual activity, as the intellectual component of language does, seems to have to be the same for all people in view of the identity of objective and of means. To be sure, this linguistic component does maintain a great uniformity, but for several reasons a significant variation arises from it. On the one hand, it is produced by the numerous gradations in which the speech-producing power is more or less effective, both absolutely and with respect to the relationship of the activities occurring within it. On the other hand, there are forces involved whose creations cannot be measured by reason and in accordance with mere ideas. Phantasy and emotion bring forth individual configurations in which the individual character of the nation stands out; and, as in all individual matters, the multifariousness of the manner in which the very same thing can be represented proceeds to infinity.

But even in the mere ideal portion, which depends on mental associations, are found differences that almost always emanate from incorrect or deficient combinations. To recognize this, it is necessary only to stop and consider the actual grammatical laws. For example, the various forms which in accordance with the requirements of speech must be designated separately in the structure of the verb should be enumerated in the same way in all languages since they can be found by simple derivation of concepts. However, if Sanskrit is compared with Greek in this respect, it is striking that in the former the concept of mood not only remained obviously undeveloped but in the production of the language itself was not even truly felt nor clearly distinguished from the tense. It is therefore not properly associated with the concept of time and not at all developed with respect to time.[1] The same is true for the infinitive, which, in addition, has been drawn over into the area of the substantive, with the result that its verbal nature is completely misconstrued. Although a predilection for Sanskrit is certainly justifiable, it must be admitted that in this respect it lags behind the more recent language. The nature of the speech favors inaccuracies of this type by understanding how to render them harmless with regard to the essential attainment of its objectives. It permits one form to displace another,[2] or conveniently takes recourse to paraphrasing wherever it is deficient in neat and concise expression. In spite of this, such imperfections are not any the less erroneous, particularly when they occur in the purely intellectual component of the language. I have already remarked that at times the blame for this phenomenon can be ascribed to the phonetic pattern which, once accustomed to certain structures, misleads the intellect into drawing new concepts that require new types of structures into its established structural procedure. This is not always the case, however. What I have just stated regarding the treatment of the mood and the infinitive in Sanskrit could not be explained probably in any way by the phonetic pattern. At least I have been incapable of discovering anything of this kind in it. Its wealth of media is also adequate to lend sufficient expression to the designation. The cause is a more intimate one. The ideal structure of the verb—its inner organism completely separated into its differing parts—did not develop with sufficient clarity before the formative intellect of the nation developed. This deficiency is all the more marvelous, however, because no language represents the true nature of the verb so accurately and so imaginatively as Sanskrit. There is a pure synthesis of essence and idea. Sanskrit knows only verbs of motion which always suggest definite individual conditions. The root words cannot be regarded at all as verbs, nor even as verbal concepts. The cause of such a deficient development or incorrect idea of a linguistic concept may be sought more or less externally in the phonetic pattern or internally in the ideal conception. Thus the error always lies in a deficient power of the productive speech capacity. A ball hurled with the requisite force cannot be deflected from its trajectory by opposing obstacles, and conceptual material, grasped and processed with appropriate intensity, develops with uniform perfection throughout its finest ramifications, and can be isolated only by the sharpest cleavage.

Just as the designation of the concepts and the designation of the laws of syntax appear to be the most pertinent points to be considered in the phonetic pattern, they are equally important with respect to the innate, intellectual component of language. With both designations the question arises whether the expression sought refers entirely to individual objects or whether relationships are to be represented which, while being applicable to a good number of individual objects, gather these objects together under a general concept, so that actually there are three cases to be distinguished. The designation of concepts to which the first two belong constituted word structure in the case of the phonetic pattern. In this instance it constitutes the ideological structure, for every concept must be contained by its own characteristics or by its relation to others, while the sense of articulation finds the designating sounds. This is the case even for external, corporeal objects which can be frankly perceived by the senses. Even for them the word is not the equivalent of the object hovering before the senses, but is rather the conception thereof by the speech production at the very moment it creates the word. This is an excellent source of the variety of expressions for identical objects; if in Sanskrit, for example, the elephant is termed sometimes the "double drinker," sometimes the "two-toothed one," and sometimes "the one provided with but a single hand," there are thereby just as many different concepts designated, even if the same object is meant in each case. For language never represents the objects, but always the concepts independently constructed by the intellect in the course of speech production. It is about this construction that we are speaking, insofar as it must be regarded as quite innate, preceding so to speak the sense of articulation. Admittedly, this distinction holds only for linguistic analysis and cannot be regarded as present in nature.

From another viewpoint, the latter two of the three cases distinguished above are closer to each other. The general relationships to be designated with respect to the individual objects and the grammatical word inflections are based for the most part on the general forms of perception and on the logical arrangement of the concepts. Hence there reposes in these two cases an observable system with which the system resulting from every particular language can be compared. If this is done, the following two points emerge: the correct isolation of the material to be designated, and the ideal designation selected for every such concept. For precisely what has been expounded above comes true here. However, since we are always concerned with the designation of nonsensual concepts, indeed often with mere relationships, the concept for the language must often, if not always, be taken figuratively; and in the combination of the simplest concepts are revealed the actual depths of the linguistic sense, which dominates the entire language from its very foundation. Person, consequently the pronoun, and space relationships play the most important part in the establishment of the concepts; often we are unable to prove how the concepts are related to one another and how in an even simpler perception they are united to one another. In these relationships are revealed what language, as such, most peculiarly and more or less instinctively establishes intellectually. Here least of all should space be left to individual variation, and the difference between languages in this respect should rest simply on the fact that in some a more fruitful usage of the relationship is made, and the designation drawn from the depths of the linguistic sense is clarified and made more accessible to the consciousness.

The designation of the individual internal and external objects penetrates more deeply into the sensual perception, phantasy, and emotion, and, through the collaboration of the foregoing, into the character absolutely, since here nature is combined with man, who in part combines actual material substance with his fashioning intellect. In this area, therefore, the national peculiarity shines forth especially. For man approaches external nature with comprehension and independently develops his intimate sensations according to the manner in which his intellectual powers are graded in various relationships. This is just as pronounced in speech production to the extent that it innately constructs concepts in anticipation of the word. The great boundary line here is whether a people puts more objective reality or more subjective intimacy into its language. Although either of these becomes more distinctly developed only gradually in the progressive structure, its seed unmistakably reposes in the primary structure. The phonetic pattern also bears its stamp. For the more clarity the linguistic sense requires in the presentation of intellectual objects, and the more pure and incorporeally described definiteness it demands for intellectual concepts, the more sharply are revealed the articulated sounds, since in the intimacy of the soul what we reflectively separate is indivisibly one, and the more sonorously do the syllables arrange themselves to form words. This distinction between a clear and fixed objectivity and a deeply exercised subjectivity becomes striking upon careful comparison of Greek and German. This influence of the national peculiarity in language is noticed in two ways: in the structure of the individual concepts and in the relative wealth of the language in concepts of a given type. In some instances, phantasy and emotion, guided by sensory observation, play a part in the individual designation; this part is played in other instances by reason with its fine distinctions, and in still others by the intellect with its bold associations. Consequently, the uniform coloration, applied to the expressions for the most multifarious objects, is also evident in the national conception of nature. Not less distinct is the preponderance of the expressions pertaining to a single intellectual direction. Such a situation is discernible, for example, in Sanskrit in the predominating number of religious-philosophical words, a feature in which perhaps no other language can compare. It must be added that these concepts for the major part are constructed in the barest condition possible and only from their simple, primitive elements; consequently, the deeply abstractive sense of that nation is even more brilliantly underscored. The language for this reason bears the same impression inherently that is found in the entire literature and intellectual activity of Indian antiquity, indeed in the external way of life and morality. The language, literature, and disposition attest unanimously that internally the direction was upon the primary causes and the final goal of human existence, whereas externally the designating trait was the state to which existence was exclusively dedicated, that is, reflection and striving toward the godhead and priesthood. These were the prevailing characteristics of the nationality. Secondary features in the language, literature, and disposition were the minute speculation about this goal that often threatened to dissolve into nothingness, and the mania to be able to transcend the limits of human power by adventurous practices. It would, however, be one-sided to think that the national peculiarity of the intellect and of the character was revealed only in the conceptual structure. It exerts an equally great influence on the word order and is immediately recognizable in it. Furthermore, it is understandable how this internal ardor, of whatever intensity or type, erupts into the expression of a complete thought and a stream of sensations in such a manner that its unique qualities are immediately apparent. In this respect Sanskrit and Greek lead to attractive and instructive comparisons. However, the peculiarities in this portion of the language are pronounced only to a minimal extent in individual forms and definite laws, and linguistic analysis hence encounters here a more troublesome task. On the other hand, the type of syntactic structure of entire series of ideas is associated precisely with what we were discussing farther back, that is, with the structure of the grammatical forms. For poverty and indefiniteness of forms prohibit an idea from sweeping over a broad range of speech and necessitate a simple, periodic sentence structure which finds but a few resting points sufficient. Even where a wealth of finely distinguished and sharply designated grammatical forms is present, an intimate, lively impulse toward longer, more meaningfully involved, and more inspired sentence structure must be included if the word order is to flourish to a state of perfection. This impulse must have been less energetically effective in the epoch in which Sanskrit attained the form of its written productions known to us, since otherwise, as the genius of the Greek tongue succeeded in doing, it would have anticipated to some extent the possibility of doing that which we now rarely find revealed in its word order.

Much in the periodic structure and in the word order cannot be traced to laws but depends on the individual speaker or writer. Language then has the merit of granting freedom and unlimited means for a variety of expressions, even if it often offers only the possibility of producing them at any given instant. Without changing the language in its sounds and in its morphology and laws, time, aided by burgeoning ideas, increased power of thought, and more penetrating perception, often introduces new elements into language. In such case, a different meaning is inserted into the same framework; under the same impression something different is tendered, and according to the same principles of association a differently graduated progression of ideas is indicated. This is the constant product of the literature of a people. In the foregoing, however, this fruit is borne especially by poetry and philosophy. The development of the remaining sciences furnishes language a single material or separates and defines more firmly what is available. Poetry and philosophy, however, touch in a quite different sense the most intimate features in man himself and, therefore, react even more intensively and structurally upon the language that is so intimately a part of man. Those languages in which a poetic and philosophical spirit has predominated in at least one epoch are most capable of perfection in the course of their development. This is doubly true when this predominance has originated from its own inner urging rather than from foreign imitation. At times in entire linguistic families and peoples, as in the Sanskrit and Semitic, the poetic spirit is so lively that its appearance in an earlier dialect of the group arises anew in a later one. Whether the wealth of sensory perception in languages is also capable of accretion in this manner would be difficult to determine. However, that intellectual concepts and the sounds designating them, drawn from intimate perception, impart in progressive usage a deeper and more soulful content is revealed by experience in all languages which have developed over the centuries. Highly intelligent writers impart to words this increased content, and an alertly receptive nation assimilates it and propagates it. In contrast, metaphors, which to the youthful mind of ancient times seemed to have wonderfully seized upon the imagination—as shown by the traces that languages preserve of them—become so worn in daily use that they are scarcely perceived any longer. In this simultaneous progress and recession, languages exert an influence that is commensurate with their progressive development, and which is appropriate to them in the great intellectual economy of the human race.

CHAPTER NINE

The Relationship of Phonemic Quantity to Intellectual Concept

THE ASSOCIATION OF the phonetic pattern with the inherent linguistic principles produces the perfection of languages. The peak of this perfection is based on the fact that this association, active in all of the operations of the speech-producing intellect, achieves pure permeation. From the first element, the creation of language is a synthetic process; it is such a process in the most genuine meaning of the word: synthesis creates something that is not present per se in any of the associated constituents. This goal is attained, however, only when the entire configuration of the phonetic pattern and that of the innate structure fuse firmly and simultaneously. The resulting beneficent result is the complete propriety of the one element to the other so that neither overshoots the other, so to speak. If this objective is reached, the inherent linguistic development will not follow a one-sided course where it is lost to phonetic pattern production, and the phonetic unit [phoneme] will not predominate over the precise requirements of the idea through luxuriant voluptuousness. Rather, the phonetic unit will be guided toward euphony and rhythm by the intimate stirring of the soul preparatory to the creation of language. Moreover, through both of the foregoing factors, it will furnish a counterbalance to the mere tinkling sound of syllables, and it will discover a new trail which will allow the sound, if thought actually breathes soul into the sound, to return to the thought an inspiring principle from its nature. The firm association of the two main constitutive components of language is expressed especially in the sensual and highly imaginative existence which flourishes for language as a result of this association; one-sided rational domination, dryness, and sobriety are the unfailing consequences, when language expands and becomes more refined intellectually, if the cultural drive

of the phonetic stock no longer possesses the requisite intensity, or if at
the immediate outset its forces have operated unilaterally. This is observable in detail in those languages such as Arabic, in which some tenses
are constructed only by detached auxiliary verbs, and in which therefore
the idea of such forms has not been effectively accompanied by the impulse
of phonetic structure and formation. In some verbal forms, Sanskrit has
actually combined the verb "to be" with the verbal concept in the word unit.

Neither this example, however, nor others of a similar type which could
be readily enumerated, particularly from the field of word formation,
show the full meaning of the requirement stated here. The complete
synthesis we are talking about derives not from details but from the entire
nature and form of the language. It is the product of power at the instant
of speech production and designates exactly the degree of its intensity.
This situation resembles a poorly minted coin whose detail is perceptible
but which lacks the customary eye-catching lustre of precision milling. In
any case, language frequently reminds us, and to a great extent here, in
the most profound and inexplicable portions of its process, of art. The
sculptor or painter weds the idea with the material, and from his creation
it is apparent whether this combination in its innate quality radiates true
genius, or whether the isolated idea has been more or less copied labori-
ously and fretfully with chisel or brush. The latter condition is revealed
here more in the weakness of the total impression than in individual
deficiencies. The way in which the lesser success of the needed synthesis of
the external and internal linguistic structure is actually revealed in a
language will be outlined later by a few grammatical points. To pursue
the traces of such a shortcoming, however, into the extreme refinements of
linguistic structure is not only difficult but to a certain degree impossible.
Furthermore, it will be even less possible to demonstrate this deficiency in
all cases in words. Our feelings are not deceived in this matter, however,
for the erroneous factor is even more distinctly pronounced in the effects.
True synthesis results from an inspiration known only to high and
energetic power. In the case of incomplete synthesis, this inspiration was
lacking. Consequently, a language which has thus originated exerts a less
inspiring force in its use. This is apparent in its literature, which inclines
less toward those genres which require such inspiration and more toward
those which obviously belong in a lesser category. The lesser national
intellectual power, to which the blame for this deficiency is to be charged,
perpetuates this condition through the effect of an underdeveloped
language on subsequent generations, or rather the weakness becomes
manifest throughout the entire life of such a nation until—owing to some
stimulus—a modification of intellectual patterns originates.

CHAPTER TEN

The Linguistic Process: Etymology and Morphology

THE PURPOSE OF this introduction—to represent languages in the variability of their structure as the necessary foundation for the progressive development of the human intellect and to discuss the interactive effect of the one upon the other—has forced me to go into the nature of language as a whole. Maintaining that standpoint, I must pursue this course further. In the foregoing I have discussed only the general and fundamental characteristics of language and have done little to develop its definition in more detail. If one is seeking the nature of language in its phonetic and ideological patterns and in the correct and vigorous interpenetration of the two, an innumerable quantity of details that confuse the application of this knowledge remains to be determined. Inasmuch as my present intention is to plot a course for individual, historical, and comparative linguistics by preparatory observations, I must continue to elucidate the general factors and, at the same time, must draw together into a state of unity the particular features that emerge. The nature of language itself lends us a hand in reaching such a goal. Since it, in direct conjunction with intellectual power, is a complete organism, we can distinguish in it not only components but also laws of procedure, or, because I consistently like to select expressions which do not even apparently prejudice historical research, directions and endeavors. If we desire to contrast language with the organism of the human body, the above-mentioned directions and endeavors may be compared with physiological laws whose scientific consideration differs basically from the analytic description of the individual parts. Therefore, in the following it will not be a question of successive detail, as in our grammars—that is, a chronicle of phonetic systems, noun, pronoun, and so forth—but of the idiosyncracie of languages which permeate all those individual components and determine them in greater detail. This method will appear suitable and judicious for another reason. If my previously mentioned objective is to be achieved, the investigation must focus especially upon the variation in linguistic structure that cannot be traced to the uniformity of a linguistic family. The foregoing will have to be sought particularly in those cases where the language process is most closely connected to its finite endeavors. This leads us again, but in another respect, to the designation of concepts and to the association of ideas in a sentence. Both emanate from the intention of the perfection of the idea and from external comprehensibility. To a certain extent independent thereof, an artistically creative principle takes shape simultaneously in language, which quite definitely and innately belongs to it personally. For the concepts in language are conveyed by tones, and the harmony of all intellectual powers is combined thus with a musical element which, entering into language, does not sacrifice its nature but merely modifies it. The artistic beauty of language is therefore not bestowed upon it as an accidental adornment. Rather the opposite is true; it is a basically requisite consequence of its further essence and the infallible touchstone of its intimate and general perfection. For the intimate operation of the intellect does not sweep to its boldest heights until the sensation of beauty pervades it with clarity.

The language process is not, however, a factor by which an individual phenomenon comes to pass. It must offer the possibility of producing an indeterminable quantity of such phenomena under all the requirements established for it by ideas. For it confronts quite definitely a truly boundless area, the scope of everything conceivable. It must therefore make infinite use of finite media and is capable of so doing through the power that produces both ideas and language. Inherently, however, it is necessary that the language process exert its effect bilaterally, first proceeding from itself to the utterance, and then reverting to the power producing it. Both effects are modified in every individual language by the method observed in it, and they must therefore be taken collectively in their representation and evaluation.

We have already seen in the foregoing exposition that the invention of words in general consists merely of selecting analogous phonemes for analogous concepts in accordance with the relationship conceived in both areas and of casting these sounds into a more or less definite mold. In view of this, two things must be considered: the word form [morphology] and the word relationship. Further broken down, the latter is a threefold entity, consisting of the sound, the logic of the concepts involved, and the retroactive effect of the words upon the mind. As the word relationship is based on ideas, insofar as it is logical, we are first reminded here of that portion of the word stock in which words are recoined in accordance with concepts of general relationships into other words—concrete to abstract, individual to collective, and so forth. I separate this portion of the vocabulary at this point, however, since the characteristic modification of these words is quite closely associated to that modification which the same word assumes in various circumstances with respect to speech. In these cases, a portion of the meaning of the word always remaining constant is bound together with a changing one. The same situation takes place elsewhere in language. Very often a basic component of the word can be recognized in the concept common to the designation of various objects. The language process can promote or impede this recognition, can emphasize or obfuscate the basic concept and the relationship of its modifications to the concept. The designation of the concept by the sound is an association of things whose nature can in truth never be combined. However, the concept is just as incapable of being detached from the word as a human being is incapable of dispensing with his facial traits. The word is its individual construction, and if it wishes to abandon the latter, it can find itself again only in other words. In any case the soul must continuously attempt to make itself independent of the region of language, inasmuch as the word constitutes a restriction to its constantly increasing sensitivity and often threatens to stifle particular shades of thought by its nature, which is more material with respect to the sound and more general with respect to meaning. It must treat the word as a checkpoint of its internal activity rather than permit itself to be held captive within its limits. But whatever the soul preserves and attains by this means, it adds to the word. Thus, from its continuous effort and countereffort, and with appropriate vitality from the intellectual powers, an ever greater refinement and a growing spiritual enrichment of the language take place, and they intensify their demands on the language to the extent that they are better satisfied. As is apparent in all highly cultured languages, words contain a more comprehensive or a more deeply penetrating meaning to the degree to which idea and sensitivity surge to higher levels.

The coupling of the varying nature of the concept with the phoneme requires, if we disregard the corporeal sound of the latter and confront the image itself, the mediation of both by some third factor in which they can meet. This mediating factor is always of a sensory nature, as in the German word *Vernunft* reposes the notion of taking (*des Nehmens*), in *Verstand* that of standing (*des Stehens*), and in *Blüte* that of welling forth (*des Hervorquellens*). It pertains to the external or internal perception or activity. If the derivation of this factor permits discovery, one can trace it back, by always separating off the more concrete elements from it, either totally or depending on its individual character, to extension or intension, or to change in both, so that we arrive at the general spheres of space and time and the degree of perception. Now if the words of an individual language are thoroughly investigated in this way, it is possible—albeit with the exception of many individual points—to recognize the threads by which they are connected and to sketch the general method involved in an individualized manner, at least in its principal outlines. We then attempt to ascend from the concrete words to the root-like ideas and perceptions by which every language in its words imparts the phoneme together with the concept according to its native genius. This comparison of language with its ideal scope seems, conversely, to require descending from the concepts to the words, since only the concepts as the primary images may contain what is needed for an evaluation of the word designation according to its class and completeness. Pursuit of this course, however, is impeded by an internal obstacle, since the concepts (inasmuch as they are marked by individual words) can no longer merely represent something general but must be individualized. But, if we attempt to attain the purpose by establishing categories, there remains between the most restricted category and the concept to be individualized by the word an abyss never to be traversed. Thus, to what extent a language exhausts the number of concepts to be designated, and in what fixity of method it descends from the original concepts to the particular derivatives concerned, can never be stated with any degree of completeness, since the course of tracing the ramification of concepts cannot be carried out, and that of the words themselves, though showing what has been achieved, does not reveal what is required.

The word supply of a language cannot be regarded in any way as a finished mass. It is, without exclusive consideration for the consistent coinage of new words and word forms [morphemes] and as long as the language remains alive in the mouths of the populace, a continuous creation and recreation of the word-building capacity. This takes place first in the linguistic stock, to which the language owes its form, then in the learning of speech by children, and finally in daily speech usage. The unfailing presence of the word requisite in each instance in the latter usage is certainly not attributable merely to memory. No human memory would have sufficient range to achieve this if the spirit did not instinctively contain the key for the structure of words themselves. A foreign language is learned only by the fact that little by little, and even if it be only by practice, this key is mastered. This is accomplished only because of the sameness of basic speech structures and because the particular relationship of such structures prevailing between individual peoples. With respect to dead languages, matters are a bit different. Their linguistic stock is certainly in our direction a closed totality or corpus, which is susceptible only to more remote discovery by successful research. However, they may be studied successfully by acquisition of the principle that was formerly alive in them. They experience quite truthfully an actual, momentary resuscitation or reanimation. A language cannot under any conditions be investigated like a dead plant. Language and life are inseparable concepts, and learning them from these two aspects is always recreation. From the standpoint taken here, the unity of the word stock of every language is revealed most distinctly. It is a totality because a single power has created it, and this creation has been continued in an unbreakable concatenation. Its unity is based upon the connection between the mediating perceptions and the phonemes, guided by the relationship of concepts. It is this connection, therefore, which we must immediately consider.

The Hindu grammarians constructed their system, certainly too artificial but on the whole remarkably clever, on the assumption that the vocabulary present in their language could be explained entirely by its own material. They therefore regarded their language as an original one and thought they had excluded all possibility of the assimilation of foreign loan words in the course of time. Both assumptions were indisputably false. For, without consideration of all the historical reasons, or reasons to be found in the language itself, it is in no way probable that any truly original language could have survived in its primitive state to our times. Perhaps the Hindu grammarians were more concerned with their method of bringing the language into a systematic organization for convenience in learning it than they were with the historical correctness of this scheme. However, during the flowering of their intellectual culture, the speakers of Indic languages probably fared no better than other nations in this respect. Man always seeks the relationships, even for external phenomena, first in the realm of ideas; the historical phase is always last, and pure observation or experimentation do not come until much later in accordance with idealistic or imaginative systems. Man first attempts to dominate nature, starting with ideas. If we admit this, the assumption of the explicability of Sanskrit by itself alone attests to a correct and penetrating vision into the nature of language. For a truly original language, severed absolutely from foreign admixture, would actually have to preserve in itself such a demonstrable relationship of its total vocabulary. Furthermore, this was an enterprise worthy of respect simply for its boldness in concentrating with such perseverance and inflexibility on the word structure as the most remote and mysterious component of all languages.

The essence of the phonetic association of words is based on the fact that a moderate number of the root sounds underlying the entire vocabulary is used, by additions and modifications, for expression of increasingly more definite and more highly composite concepts. The recurrence of the same root sound, or the possibility of recognizing it according to definite rules, and the principles prevailing in the modifying augmentations or internal changes then determine the explicability of the language through itself, which can be termed a mechanical or technical procedure.

However, there is an important difference among words with respect to the intent of their creation. This difference which concerns the root words has, moreover, been very much neglected. The great majority of root words are, so to speak, of narrative or descriptive nature, designating motions, properties, and objects per se without reference to an assumed or felt personality. For others, in contrast, it is precisely the expression of the latter or the simple reference to it which constitutes the exclusive essence of the meaning. I believe that I have correctly shown in an earlier treatise[1] that personal pronouns must have been the original ones in every language, and that it is quite incorrect to regard the pronoun as the most recent part of speech in language. A narrow, grammatical conception of the representation of the noun by the pronoun has displaced the viewpoint on this question drawn from a more profound level of the language. The first factor is naturally the personality of the speaker himself, who is in constant and direct contact with nature, and who cannot possibly fail to express in language his own ego in contrast to it. The "thou," moreover, is an automatic counterpart of the "I"; and by a new contrast arises the third person which, however, since the sphere of the sentient and speaking personalities is now abandoned, is broadened to an inert entity. If every concrete property be disregarded, the person, specifically the "I," stands in an external relationship with space and in an internal one with perception. Thus prepositions and interjections are associated to the pronoun, for the former are relationships of space or of time considered as an extension toward a definite point not to be separated from their concept, while interjections are mere eruptions of life's emotions and sensations. It is even probable that the actual, simple pronouns have their origin in a spatial or emotional relationship.

The distinction made here is subtle, however, and must be understood precisely as delimited above. For, on the one hand, all words designating innate perceptions, as well as those relative to external objects, are constructed descriptively and generally objectively. The above distinction is based merely on the fact that the actual perceptive response of a given individuality constitutes the essence of the designation. On the other hand, there can be pronouns and prepositions in languages, and there really are such, which have been adapted from quite concrete adjectives. Grammatical person can be designated by something related to its concept, and the preposition in a similar way may be associated with a noun that is related to its concept, as *hinter* ('behind, in back of') is to *Rücken* ('back, dorsal portion of the body'), or as *vor* ('before, in front of') is to *Brust* ('breast, pectoral portion of the body'). Words which have really thus originated can become so unrecognizable in the course of time that it is difficult to decide whether they are derivations or original words. Even if individual cases may give rise to disputes, it cannot be denied that every language must have originally had words that were derived from the direct emotion and sensation of the personality involved. We owe F. Bopp great credit for having first distinguished this twofold category of root words and for having introduced this factor, previously disregarded, into lexical structure and morphology. Moreover, we will immediately see in the following in what an ingenious way, also first discovered by F. Bopp in Sanskrit forms, language combines both, each in a different valuation, for its purposes.

The objective and subjective roots of the language (if for brevity I may use this by no means exhaustive designation) do not share a completely identical nature with each other and therefore, taken precisely, cannot be regarded as basic sounds [phonemes] in the same way. The objective roots bear the appearance of analytic origin. The secondary phonemes have been detached, and the significance, in order that all the words classified in the rubric may be comprehended, has been expanded to a fluctuating scope; thus forms have been constructed which, in this configuration, can only be termed abstractions. The latter are therefore not words in the usual and literal meaning. The subjective roots were clearly coined by the language itself. Their concept permits no extension and is in all cases the expression of sharp individuality. The concept was indispensable to the speaker and was sufficient to a certain extent until the consummation of gradual expansion of the language. As will be seen shortly in detail, the concept indicates a primitive state of languages which, without historical proofs, may be assumed of the objective roots only with great reservation.

The term "roots" can be applied only to those basic sounds which are directly associated with the concept to be designated, without intervention of other sounds that are already significant in themselves. In this rigorous meaning of the term, roots do not need to belong to the actual language. Indeed, in languages whose morphology includes the joining of roots with secondary sounds this may scarcely be the case at all or only under certain conditions. The true language is only that which is revealed in speech, and linguistic invention cannot be conceived as proceeding downward along the same root which analysis pursues upward. If a root appears as a word in such a language, as in युध्, *yudh*, 'fight,' in Sanskrit, or as part of a compound, as in धर्मविद्, *dharmavid*, 'versed in justice,' these are exceptions which do not at all justify the presumption of a state in which, as in Chinese, the bare roots became incorporated in the speech. It is much more probable that as the root phonemes became increasingly familiar to the ear and to the consciousness of speakers, the more such individual cases of the use of bare roots arose. However, as we trace our way back analytically to the root sounds, we ask ourselves whether we have always been really successful in locating the simple forms. In Sanskrit several alleged roots are composite forms or are derived by reduplication. This has been brilliantly demonstrated by F. Bopp, and A. F. Pott's revelations in the important study already mentioned will certainly serve as the basis for further research on this subject. However, there is even some doubt about roots which really appear simple. I mean here especially those which deviate from the structure of simple root syllables or which surround the vowel only with consonantal phonemes that fuse with it to the point of difficult separation. Compounds may be also concealed in root syllables, and these may have become indistinguishable phonetically through contraction, loss of vowels, or other changes. I say this not to substitute empty conjectures for facts but rather in order not to preclude arbitrarily further penetration by historical research into insufficiently fathomed linguistic situations and because the problem here concerning the connection of languages to structural capacity requires seeking out all roots which the origin of linguistic structure may have followed.

Root phonemes become recognizable by their continuous recurrence in widely varying forms, but they should attain even greater clarity if a language has developed a concept of the verb in accordance with its nature. For, in spite of the fugacity and motility of this part of speech, which is never at rest so to speak, the selfsame root syllable is revealed in ever-changing secondary phonemes. The Hindu grammarians operated with a quite correct feeling for their language: they treated all roots as verbal roots and assigned each to a definite conjugation. However, in the very nature of linguistic development itself lies the fact that historically the concepts of motility and of properties will be the first to be designated. This is because only they in turn can immediately, and often in the same sequence of events, be the designators of the objects involved, insofar as simple words designate them. Motion and property, however, stand in close proximity to one another, and even more frequently a lively linguistic sense impetuously connects the latter to the former. That the Hindu grammarians perceived this basic distinction between motion and property on the one hand and words indicating independent things on the other is proved by their distinguishing between *krit* and *unâdi* suffixes. Words are derived directly from the root phonemes by both of them. The former, however, form only words in which the root idea itself is provided with general modifications that are applicable to several words simultaneously. True substances are very rarely found among them and only insofar as their designation is of this definite type. Conversely, the *unâdi* suffixes comprehend only terms applied to concrete objects, and in the words constructed by adding them the most obscure portion is precisely the suffix itself, which ought to contain the more general concept modifying the root phoneme. It cannot be denied that many of these constructions are forced and obviously nonhistorical. The intent of their origin is all too clearly recognized in the principle of relating all the words of the language without exception to assumed roots. Among these terms for concrete objects may be included foreign compounds adopted into the language on the one hand and compounds which have become unrecognizable on the other hand. There are indeed examples of such unrecognizable compounds among the *unâdi* words mentioned. This is naturally the most obscure part of all languages, and therefore it has recently been found preferable to establish a separate class of obscure and uncertain derivation made up to a large extent of the *unâdi* words.

The nature of the phonemic linkage is based upon the conspicuousness of the stem syllable which is more or less carefully preserved by the languages depending upon the degree of consistency in their organization. In languages endowed with a very highly developed structure, however, secondary phonemes of a general modifying type join with the stem phoneme, in its capacity as a concept individualizer. Usually in pronunciation each word has but one main accent, and the unstressed syllables drop with respect to the accented ones (see Chapter 13); in the same way, in simple, derived words the secondary phonemes occupy a smaller although very important bracket in correctly organized languages. They are the sharp signs or marks for our human reason, indicating where it must place the concept of the more perceptively specified stem syllable. This principle of perceptive subordination, which is connected to the rhythmic structure of words, appears to prevail formally throughout very purely organized languages without instigation in this direction by the words themselves. The effort of the Hindu grammarians to treat all the words of their language in accordance with the foregoing statement attests at least to a correct insight into the spirit of their tongue. Since the *unâdi* suffixes are not supposed to have been found among the earlier grammarians, it appears that these were not discovered until later. It is in fact revealed in most Sanskrit words for concrete objects that this structure consists of a short ending which drops off together with a predominant stem syllable. This can be reconciled very fittingly with what has been said previously concerning the possibility of compounds which have become indistinguishable. The same urge has acted upon the compound as upon the derivative, and in comparison with the more individual or otherwise definitely designating portion it has permitted the other one to drop little by little both in concept and in the phonemic component. For whenever we encounter obliterations and displacements of phonemes in languages, which are closely spaced and almost incredible in appearance during the course of time, and which contrast with a tenacious retention of quite individual and simple ones that are discernible through the course of centuries, this factor probably can be traced for the most part to the striving or the yielding of its innate linguistic sense, however motivated. Time does not obliterate per se but only to the extent that the linguistic sense previously permits a phoneme to drop from the language, whether intentionally or indifferently.

CHAPTER ELEVEN

Isolation, Inflection, and Agglutination
of Words

BEFORE WE TURN to the reciprocal relationships of words in connected discourse, I must mention a property of languages which pertains not only to these relationships but also to a portion of word structure itself. In the previous exposition (see pp. 71, 78) I have mentioned those words which are derived from the root by the addition of a general concept applicable to an entire class of words and which are additionally designated in accordance with their position in connected discourse. The effective or restrictive property of languages in this case is that which we are accustomed to comprehending by the expressions: isolation of the words, inflection, or agglutination. This property is the focal point about which the perfection of linguistic organization revolves. We must therefore consider it in such a way that we successively investigate the innate requirement from which it originates in the soul, how it is expressed in the phonetic treatment, and whether the aforesaid innate requirements are satisfied by this statement. In so doing, we must always follow the classification established above of the interacting activities in the language.

In all classes summarized here there lies in the innate designation of words a twofold factor whose nature must be carefully separated. Namely, there becomes associated to the act of the designation of the concept itself an additional and particular operation of the intellect which deflects the concept into a definite category of thought or speech. The complete sense of the word proceeds simultaneously from the foregoing conceptual expression and the latter modifying allusion. These two elements, however, lie in quite different spheres. The designation of the concept belongs to the increasingly more objective processes of the linguistic sense. Shifting it into a definite category of thought is a new act of linguistic self-assertion by which the individual case, the individual word, is referred to the totality of the possible cases in language or speech. Only by this operation, which is achieved in the greatest purity and depth and which is firmly incorporated into the language itself, is its independent activity, originating from the thought process and responding to the external impressions in pure receptivity, joined to the operation with the appropriate fusion and subordination.

Hence, there are naturally stages in which various languages satisfy this requisite, since in the innate speech structure no language can disregard it entirely. However, in those languages where this feature becomes externally designated, it is a matter of the profoundness and viability with which they actually ascend to the original categories of thought and in their relationship provide the categories validity. For these categories again form a connected whole whose systematic completeness more or less radiates throughout the languages concerned. The inclination for classification of concepts, for determination of the individual items by the category to which they belong, however, can also arise from a need to distinguish and designate, because we associate the categorical concept to the individual one. This inclination, therefore, inherently admits various stages in accordance with this or that purer origin triggered by the need of the intellect according to logical order. There are languages which regularly add the generic concept to the nomenclature of living creatures, and among these languages are those in which the designation of this generic concept has become an actual suffix, recognizable only by analysis. These cases are connected to what has been said above to the extent that in them a twofold principle, an objective one of designation and a subjective one of logical classification, is apparent. On the other hand, they digress entirely therefrom by the fact that in them only differing classes of actual objects, and not the forms of thought and speech, enter into the designation. Words thus constructed now become quite similar to those in which two elements form a composite concept. Conversely, what corresponds in the internal configuration to the idea of inflexion is distinguished precisely by the fact that only one element shifted into a definite category, instead of two elements, produces the twofold factor that is used as the point of departure in the determination of this concept. That this twofold factor, when analyzed, is not uniform, but is of a differing nature and appertains to various spheres, constitutes the characteristic attribute. Only thereby can purely organized languages attain the profound and solid combination of spontaneity and receptivity from which an infinity of conceptual associations proceeds, all of them bearing the stamp of a genuine form and completely satisfying the requirements of the language. In reality this does not preclude room being found in the words constructed in this way for differences originating merely from experience. However, in languages which with regard to this component of their structure proceed from the correct intellectual principle, these differences are more generally conceived and by the entire remaining process of the language are placed upon a higher level. Thus, for example, the concept of gender difference could not have arisen without actual observation, even if it automatically becomes associated more or less immediately through the general concepts of spontaneity and receptivity with the original differences of conceivable forces. This concept is in fact elevated to this height in languages which absorb it entirely and which designate it in a manner similar to the way they designate words which originate from the mere logical distinctions of ideas. Two concepts are not simply joined together. One is transferred mentally into a class whose concept inheres in many natural beings but which could be conceived of as a variety of alternately active forces, independent even of individual observation.

What has been perceived in the intellect during the speech-constructing periods of nations always gains prevalence in the corresponding phonemes. Therefore, just as the feeling of necessity initially arose to impart to the word a twofold expression in accordance with the needs of changing speech or with respect to its enduring meaning, there emerged from internal sources inflexion in languages. We, however, can only pursue the opposite path; we can penetrate intimate semantics only by analyzing the phonemes. Here we find where this property, which is in fact a twofold one—a designation of the concept and an indication of the category into which it is assigned—is developed. In this way, perhaps the twofold effort can be distinguished most definitely; it is an effort to impress the concept and, at the same time, to impart to it the distinguishing sign of the bracket in which it is to be imagined. The variousness of this intention, however, must issue from the treatment of the phonemes themselves.

Words only admit transformation in two ways: by internal change or by external increment. Both are impossible where the language incorporates all words rigidly in their root form without possibility of an increment and also allows no latitude for change medially. Where internal change is possible and is even promoted by the word structure, the differentiation of the indication of the designation—to retain these expressions—is easy and unerring by this method. For the intention to preserve the identity of the word, inherent in this procedure, and still to show it as differingly constituted is best achieved by medial transformation. Matters are quite different with respect to the external increment [agglutination]. Invariably it is composition in the broader sense, and no harm shall befall the simplicity of the word in this instance. Two concepts should not be linked to a third; one should be conceived of in a definite relationship. In this case, therefore, an obviously more artificial procedure is required which manifests itself in the phonemes by virtue of the vitality of the intellect's intention. The allusive portion of the word must appear with the phonetic clarity both invested in it and established on another line in opposition to the preponderance of the designating aspect. The original designating sense of the addition, if at all present, must disappear in the intention of using it only allusively, and the addition itself, united to the word, must be treated simply as a necessary and dependent portion of it, and not as inherently capable of independent existence. If the foregoing takes place, there originates, in addition to medial modification and compounding, a third lexical transformation by structural addition. In such case we have the true concept of a suffix. The continued effectiveness of the intellect upon the phoneme then automatically transforms the composition into attachment [agglutination]. An opposing principle reposes in these two factors. Composition is concerned with the maintenance of multiple stem syllables in their significant phonemes, whereas agglutination tends to destroy their inherent meaning. Via this contentious treatment the language attains its twofold objective, that is, by the preservation and the annihilation of the recognizability of the phonemes. Compounds become obscure only when, as we have seen in the foregoing discussion, the language, following a different feeling, treats them as agglutinations. I have, however, mentioned composition more because agglutination could have erroneously been confused with it than because it might actually belong in one and the same category with it. This is always only seemingly true. Moreover in no way may agglutination be considered mechanically, that is, as intentional association of basically separate entities and obliteration of the traces of composition by lexical unity. The word inflected by agglutination is just as much a unit as are the various parts of a budding flower. And what transpires here in language is of a purely organic nature. No matter how distinctly the pronoun adheres to the person of the verb, in genuinely inflected languages it is not attached to it.[1] The verb was not conceived as separated but existed as an individual form in the presence of the soul, and the phoneme also traversed the lips as one and indivisible. By the inscrutable spontaneity of language, the suffixes issue forth from the root. And this occurs as long as and to the extent that the creative capacity of the language is present. Not until this principle ceases to be operative can mechanical attachment come to pass. In order not to impair the true procedure and thus reduce language to a mere rational process, we must always keep in mind the conception of the process we have just discussed. However, we must not think that because this conception leads to the inexplicable it does not clarify anything, that the truth lies only in the absolute unity of what has been associated in thought and which is based in the origin and in the symbolic agreement of the innate idea with the external phoneme, and that for the remainder the conception veils the impenetrable in figurative expression. For even if the phonemes of the root often modify the suffix, they do not do this always, and it can be said only figuratively that the latter issues forth from the nucleus of the root. This can only signify that the intellect conceives them as inseparable and that the phoneme, pliant with respect to this connected thought, casts them also into a single mold for the ear. I have, therefore, preferred the presentation chosen above and will retain it in the following pages. Preserved from all admixture with a mechanical procedure, it cannot give rise to misapprehensions. For application to actual languages, however, analysis of agglutination and lexical unit is more fitting, because the language possesses technical media for both, and particularly because agglutination in certain categories of languages is not distinguished purely and absolutely but only to a degree from true compounding. The use of the expression "agglutination," which applies only to an increment in the case of genuinely inflectional languages, assures the correct interpretation of the organic process involved in comparison with that of mere attachment.[2]

Since the genuineness of the agglutination is revealed especially in the fusion of the suffix with the word, inflected languages possess at the same time effective media for constructing the lexical unit. The two trends, to impart to words by fixed connection of syllables in their interior an outwardly definite and distinct form on the one hand, and to separate agglutination from composition on the other, promote each other. Due to this association I have spoken here only of suffixes, increments at the end of the word, and not of affixes at all. The factor which can determine the unity of the word in phoneme and meaning can proceed only from the stem syllable, that is, from the designating part of the word, and its effectiveness in the phoneme can only extend principally that which follows. The syllables attached at the beginning always fuse to a lesser degree with the word, just as with respect to accentuation and metrical treatment the indifference of syllables lies especially in the prefixes and the true compulsion of the meter involves only the actual stressed syllable. This observation appears particularly important to me for the evaluation of those languages in which the incremental syllables are, as a rule, attached to the beginning of the word. They proceed more by compounding than by agglutination, and the feeling of truly successful inflexion remains foreign to them. Sanskrit, which so completely reproduces all nuances of the association of its tenderly allusive linguistic sense with the phoneme, establishes separate rules of euphony for the attachment of suffixed terminations and for that of prefixed prepositions. It treats the latter as elements of compound words.

The suffix indicates the relationship in which the word is to be taken. Thus, in this sense, it is in no way meaningless. The same is true for the internal transformation of words, and hence of inflection generally speaking. However, between the internal metamorphosis and the suffix exists the important difference that, with respect to the former, no other basic meaning can originally have been involved, whereas the incremental syllable likely possessed such a basic meaning. The internal transformation of words is therefore always symbolic, even if we cannot always grasp this phenomenon. An analogy with that which is to be expressed in both cases exists in the type of change made, as for example the transition from a front to a back phoneme or from a shorter to a longer one. This possibility prevails with respect to suffixes. They may just as well be original and exclusively symbolic, and this property may then merely repose in the phonemes. It is, however, by no means necessary that this always be thus; moreover, it is an incorrect interpretation, a misconstruing of the freedom and multiplicity of the paths which language follows in its constructions, if we desire to term inflectional those incremental syllables which never bore an independent meaning and which owe their existence in languages only to an intent directed toward inflection. If the intent of reason is conceived to be directly creative in languages, it is my innermost conviction that this is always a misconception. To the extent that the initial movement in language must always be sought in the intellect, everything in it and in the utterance of the articulated phoneme itself must be termed intentional. The manner in which it proceeds, however, is always a differing one, and its structures originate from the interaction of the external impressions and the internal emotion, in relation to the general purpose of language, which combines subjectivity with objectivity in the creation of an ideal world that is neither entirely internal nor entirely external. The factor which is in itself truly designative, and not merely symbolic nor merely indicated, loses this character when the requirement of the language demands it by the type of treatment involved as a whole. For an example of this, we need only to compare the independent pronoun with that suffixed to the persons of the verb. The linguistic sense distinguishes correctly between pronoun and person. Furthermore, it conceives of person not as the independent substance but as one of the relationships in which the basic idea of the inflected verb must necessarily appear. The linguistic sense, therefore, treats person simply as a part of the verb and permits time to deform and erode it. In this process the certainty persists, owing to confidence in the reliability of the linguistic sense, that the deformity of the phonemes will not impede recognition of the proper allusion. The disfigurement may really have taken place, or the agglutinated pronoun may have for the most part remained unchanged, but in any case the situation and the result are always the same. The symbolism does not rest here upon a direct analogy of the phonemes, but it proceeds from the attitude of the language infused into them in a rather artful manner. If it is indubitable that not merely in Sanskrit but in other languages as well the agglutinative syllables are taken more or less from the area of the above-mentioned roots referring directly to the speaker, then the symbolic element reposes in this fact itself. The relationship to the categories of thinking and speaking indicated by the agglutinative syllables can find no more meaningful expression than in phonemes or sounds which directly have the subject as the initial or terminal point of their meaning. Accordingly, to the foregoing the analogy of tonal elements may be associated, as F. Bopp has so elegantly shown in the Sanskrit nominative and accusative endings. In the pronoun of the third person, the sibilant *s* phoneme is imparted symbolically to the animate persons [those endowed with gender], whereas the duller sound of the nasal *m* is accorded to the genderless neuter obviously in the same manner. The same alternation of alphabetical characters of the endings distinguishes the subject actor, the nominative, from the accusative, the object of the action.

The original independent significance of suffixes is, therefore, no necessary hindrance with respect to the purity of genuine inflection. Words constructed with such inflectional syllables appear as concepts which are just as definite as those resulting from internal change but are of simple type and are cast in various molds. Hence, they fulfill the purpose of inflection. However, the significance requires certainly greater intensity of the inherent sense of inflection and a more decided dominance of the phonemes by the intellect, which in such case must overcome the deterioration of the grammatical structure in compound formations. A language such as Sanskrit, which utilizes chiefly such originally independent and significant inflectional syllables, reveals thereby the confidence which it places in the power of the intellect animating it.

The phonetic capacity and the phonemic patterns customary in nations contribute significantly to this component of language. The inclination to combine the elements of speech with one another—to associate phoneme with phoneme where their nature permits, to fuse one with another, and in general to change them in contact as their properties permit—facilitates the operation of inflectional sense directed toward uniformity, just as the more rigorous tendency to keep tones apart in some languages counteracts success in this direction. Now if the phonemic capacity promotes the inherent requirement, the original sense of articulation is animated. In this way the significant cleavage of phonemes comes to pass. By virtue of such cleavage, even an individual phoneme may become the carrier of a formal condition, a factor which is more decisive here than in any other part of the language, inasmuch as here an intellectual direction is to be indicated rather than a concept designated. Therefore, the acuteness of the capacity of articulation and the purity of the inflectional sense persist in a reciprocally intensifying association.

Between the lack of any indication of the categories of words, as is apparent in Chinese, and true inflection there can exist no third possibility that is compatible with pure organization of languages. The only conceivable intermediate possibility is the compound used as inflection; that, however, is an intended but not completely successful inflection, a more or less mechanical attachment and not a purely organic incorporation. This hybrid construction, which is not always easy to discern, has in recent times been termed agglutination. This attaching of determining, subordinate concepts arises from weakness in the innate organizing linguistic sense or from neglect of its true direction. However, it indicates an effort not only to provide phonetic validity for the conceptual categories but also to treat them in this process not as entirely equal with respect to the true designation of the concepts. Thus, when a language does not abandon such grammatical indication, it not only fails to establish purely the concepts involved but also falsifies them in their very essence. Such a language can therefore apparently, and up to a certain extent actually, possess a mass of grammatical forms, and yet nowhere does it truly achieve the expression of the true concept of such a form. It can, moreover, contain in isolated instances actual inflection via internal transformation of words, and time can apparently transform its true original compounds into inflections. Therefore it becomes difficult, and indeed in part remains impossible, to judge each individual case correctly. However, the factor which determines the entire matter is the compilation of all related cases. From the common treatment of these cases is then determined to what degree of strength or of weakness the inflectional trend of the innate linguistic sense exerted its power upon the structure of the phonemic quanta. The difference can be ascribed to degree alone, for these so-called agglutinating languages are not distinguished from the inflectional ones according to typology, as is true of those which reject all allusion by inflection, but only by the degree to which their obscure effort in the same direction is more or less unsuccessful.

Where brilliance and acuteness of the linguistic sense follow the proper course during the structural period—and with these characteristics it cannot be otherwise—an innate clarity permeates the entire linguistic structure, and the principal manifestations of its effectiveness stand in close connection with one another. Thus we have witnessed the unsoluble connection of the inflectional sense with the striving toward word unity and the capacity of articulation which significantly splits up phonemic patterns. The effect cannot be the same where only individual sparks spurt from the pure efforts of the intellect. The linguistic sense has pursued generally a single course deviating from the proper one, but it often attests of great acumen and at the same time of delicate feeling. (The author will return to a further discussion of the linguistic sense at a later point.) This sensitivity and shrewdness often exert their effects on the individual case, too. Thus, in those languages which cannot justifiably be designated as inflectional, the internal transformation of words, where such occurs, is mostly of the type that follows the innately indicated method more or less by a rough reproduction of the phoneme. For example, the plural and the preterite are designated by a material checking of the voice or by aspiration intensively ejected from the throat. The internal transformation reverts to the boundaries precisely where purely constructed languages, such as the Semitic, reveal the greatest sharpness of the sense of articulation by symbolic change of the vowel—not exactly in those areas mentioned but in other grammatical transformations, and almost abandoning the area of articulation. According to my experience, no language is completely agglutinative. In individual cases, moreover, it cannot often be decided how great or how small a share the sense of inflection has had in the apparent suffix. In all languages which in fact reveal inclination toward phonemic fusion, or which do not reject this feature rigidly, a unique inflectional tendency is visible. However, a reliable and certain judgment concerning the totality of the phenomenon cannot be delivered save according to the organization of the complete structure of such a language.

CHAPTER TWELVE

The Word Unit: The Incorporative Capacity of Language

EVERY PECULIARITY ORIGINATING from the intimate concept of language engages its entire organization. This is particularly true of inflection. It is most intimately related to two differing and apparently opposing segments, which, however, work together organically. These two components are word unity and the appropriate division of the sentence parts, which permit the proper articulation of the sentence. The relationship of inflection to word unity becomes automatically comprehensible, since its effort consists quite definitely in the construction of a unit, and it is therefore not satisfied with a mere totality. However, inflection also enhances the appropriate sentence articulation and its freedom of formation by providing the words in it with distinguishing marks to which the recognition of their relationship to the entire sentence can safely be entrusted. It thereby eliminates the anxiety produced by trying to hold the sentence together like an individual word and emboldens us to break it down into its component parts. But what is even more important, by means of its retrospective effect upon the forms of thought, insofar as the latter refer to the language, inflection arouses a more correct and explicit insight into the unit relationships in a sentence. For actually all three of the peculiarities of language mentioned here spring from the same source —from the vital concept of the relationship of speech to the language as a whole. Therefore, inflection, word unity, and proper sentence breakdown ought never to be separated in a consideration of language. Not until these other points have been included does inflection appear in its true, beneficently operating power.

Speech requires elements befitting the possibility of its limitless range of use, which is not to be measured at any given moment. This requirement, moreover, increases intensively and extensively the higher the level to which language ascends. For at its highest level language becomes a vehicle of the creation of ideas and of the totality of thought development itself. Its direction always proceeds in man toward this latter goal, even where its actual development meets with any arbitrary number of impediments. Therefore, it ever seeks the arrangement of linguistic elements containing the most vivid expression of the thought patterns. Hence inflection is especially suitable to speech, because the character of inflection is to consider concepts with simultaneous respect for their external as well as their internal connotations. This respect facilitates the progress of thought by the regularity of the selected course. With these linguistic elements, however, speech desires to attain innumerable combinations of the winged idea without being restricted in its infinite scope. Sentence structure underlies the expression of all these associations. Moreover, the free flight of ideas mentioned is possible only if the components of the simple sentence are connected or separated in accordance with the necessity arising from its nature and not more or less by arbitrary decision.

Development of ideas requires a twofold process: a conceptualization of the individual concepts involved and an association of them to produce a thought or idea. Both aspects of this process appear in speech. A concept is enclosed in phonemes which belong together and which cannot be separated without destroying the meaning, and signs identifying its relationship to the sentence structure are imparted to it. The word thus constructed is enunciated by the tongue, owing to the fact that this organ separates it from others to which it is joined. However, in this process, the simultaneous intricacy of all the words in the sentence is not abrogated. In this respect the word unit is revealed in the narrowest sense of the term; that is, it is revealed in the treatment of each word as an individual entity, which can come in contact with others to a varying degree without sacrificing its independence. We have seen previously, however, that within the sphere of the same concept—that is, within a single word—occasionally a united diversity is found. From this factor originates another category of word unit, which, to distinguish it from the above external type, may be called an intimate or internal one. Depending directly upon whether the diversity factor is uniform and merely combines to produce a composite whole, or whether it is nonuniform (designation and indication) and must represent the idea with a definite impression, the internal word unit has a narrower or broader meaning than the external word unit.

The word unit in the language has two sources. One is the innate linguistic sense relative to the requirements of idea development, the other is the phonemes. Inasmuch as all thinking consists of a process of separation and combination, the linguistic sense requirement—the representation of the various brackets of the unity of ideas symbolically in speech—must automatically be awakened and come to light in accordance with its mobility and the orderly principles in the language. On the other hand, the phoneme seeks to bring its various modifications coming into contact with one another into a relationship suitable to both the pronunciation and the ear. Often it merely levels out difficulties or follows organically established habits. The phoneme, however, goes further; it constructs rhythm segments and treats them as an entity for the ear.[1] However, both of these, the innate linguistic sense and the phoneme, cooperate by the fact that the latter accedes to the requirements of the former. As a result, the treatment of the phonetic unit becomes the symbol of the definite conceptual unit sought. The latter, resultantly made phonemic, suffuses speech as an intellectual principle. The melodically and rhythmically treated phonetic formation arouses by reverse action a closer association of the ordering forces of reason in the soul through creative and metaphorical phantasy. As a result, the intertwining of the forces, directed outwardly and inwardly according to the intellect and nature, produces a heightened life and a harmonious activity.

The designative media of the word unity in speech are the pause, change of alphabetical characters, and accent.[2]

The pause can serve only to indicate the external unity. Within the word, it would destroy its unity. In speech, however, a fleeting cessation of the voice at the end of words, perceptible only to the practised ear and designed to render the element of the idea identifiable, is natural. At the same time, the necessary aspect of the organized sentence, that is, the audible unity of the idea, stands in contrast to the striving for the designation of the unity of the concept. Languages in which a proper and delicate sense is manifested reveal both intentions and level out the foregoing contrast, often by intensifying it and sometimes by other means. I shall take the explanatory examples here in all cases from the Sanskrit language, because this idiom treats word unity more happily and exhaustively than any other, and also because it possesses an alphabet which, to a greater extent than our own, represents the exact pronunciation both audibly and graphically.[3] Sanskrit does not permit every character of the alphabet to terminate a word. It thus recognizes the individuality of the word and sanctions its separation in speech by the fact that it regulates the modifications of characters coming into contact in terminal and initial positions differently than it regulates those coming into contact in medial positions. At the same time, however, in Sanskrit more than in any other language of its linguistic family the complex interlacing of ideas follows the fusion of phonemes. Hence, at first glance the word unity appears destroyed by the ideological unity. When the final and initial vowels are transformed into a third, there undeniably originates as a result a phonemic unit composed of two words. Where final consonants change before initial vowels, it is probably not because the initial vowel—always accompanied by a slight aspiration—does not join up with the final consonant in the same sense in which the Sanskrit language regards the consonant as an indivisible unit with the vowel following it in the same syllable. Although this consonantal modification always destroys the indicated division between individual words, this slight disturbance can never truly obliterate this separation in the mind of the auditor. Indeed, it cannot even significantly weaken recognition thereof. On the one hand, the two principal methods for the modification of contiguous words—the fusion of vowels and the change of voiceless into voiced consonants before vowels—do not occur inside the same word. On the other hand, in Sanskrit the inner word unity is always so clear and definitely ordered that in all the phonemic intricacy of speech it can never be mistaken that independent phonetic units merely come into direct contact with one another. Furthermore, even if the phonemic complexity of speech supports the contention of fine sensitivity of the ear and the active emphasis upon the symbolic indication of the unity concept, it is still remarkable that other Indic languages, especially the Telingic to which no independently evolved high cultural status can be ascribed, possess this idiosyncracy, which is associated with the most intimate phonemic habits of a people and probably is not therefore a property that readily proceeds from one tongue to another.[4] The interlacing of all sounds in speech is inherently more natural in the uncultured state of language, inasmuch as the word must first be separated out from speech in general. In Sanskrit, however, this peculiarity became an innate and external beauty of speech which must not be the less esteemed simply because it could be dispensed with as a luxury not necessary to the concepts involved. There is obviously a reverse effect of the language upon the intellect producing the idea, differing from the individual expression. And for this factor none of its advantages, which individually may appear dispensable, is lost.

The intimate word unity can truly emerge only in languages which, by clothing the concept with its secondary determinations, expand the basic phoneme to polysyllabic status and within this framework permit multifarious modifications and changes of alphabetical characters. The linguistic sense oriented around the beauty of the phoneme treats this internal sphere of the word according to general and particular laws of euphony and harmony. However, the sense of articulation also collaborates, especially in these constructions, sometimes by modifying phonemes to a differing semantic significance and at other times by attracting phonemes which possess independent validity to its purview. In such cases they come to be used as mere signs of secondary determination, and their original objective meaning becomes symbolic. By subordination to a principal concept, the phoneme itself is often reduced to the status of a simple element. Therefore, even in the case of differing origin, the sound assumes a configuration similar to the purely symbolic one that is actually produced by the sense of articulation. The more animated and active the sense of articulation is in the process of the continuous coalescence of concept and phoneme, the more rapidly this operation proceeds.

Now a verbal structure arises through the medium of the factors at work in this operation which are simultaneously satisfying reason and aesthetic feeling; a precise analysis, starting with the word stem, must be concerned with accounting for every alphabetical character that is added, eliminated, or modified for reasons of semantics or phonemics. It can actually attain this objective to the extent that all analogies elucidating such change are brought into play. The scope and the multifariousness of this word structure are greatest and most satisfying for comprehension and for the ear where no uniform and definite pattern is impressed upon the original word forms [morphemes] and where attachments are used only for indication of the secondary determinations, especially with respect to the intimate and purely symbolic change of characters of the alphabet. The means, which at first appear cruder and less cultured if we mistake them for mechanical addition, undeniably exercise an advantage in this process over the inherently finer and more artistic means which through the power of their inflectional sense, are raised to a higher level. Disregarding the admirable and extensive intellectual system of inflection and articulation, we may trace the word structure in the Semitic languages extensively to the disyllabic root structure and to their disinclination toward compounding. Although the foregoing factors fail by far to achieve the variety, scope, and appropriateness that are requisite to the overall objectives of the language and which are achieved by Sanskrit, the Semitic nevertheless proves equal to the latter.

Sanskrit designates through the phoneme the various degrees of unity which the innate linguistic sense feels a need to differentiate. For this purpose it exploits chiefly a different treatment of the syllables and individual phonemes that combine in the same word as distinct conceptual elements by means of the alphabetical characters coming into contact. I have already indicated that the treatment differs depending upon whether contiguous words are involved or whether internal word structure is concerned. The language continues to follow the same course. If the rules for these two cases are considered as two great and mutually opposite classes, the language indicates the word unity in accordance with the following gradations, proceeding from the looser to the more fixed combination: (1) in compound words; (2) in words compounded by prefixes, principally verbs; (3) in words which are constructed by suffixes (*taddhita* suffixes) from basic words existing in the language; (4) in words (*kridanta* words) which are derived by suffixes from roots, that is, from words which actually lie external to the language; (5) in the grammatical declensional and conjugational forms.

The first two types of words follow on the whole the rules for attachment for separate words, and the last three follow those relative to agglutination in the medial position in words. Yet, as may readily be understood, individual exceptions exist. And for the entire graduation here established, no absolute variation of the rules for each class exists as a basis of distinction, but merely for a greater or lesser—though very definite—approximation. In the exceptions themselves, however, there is often betrayed in a meaningful way the intent of more fixed unification. Thus for separate words, if we disregard a single and only apparent exception, the final consonant of a preceding word never brings about a change in the initial letter [phoneme] of the consecutive one. On the other hand, this takes place in some compound words and in prefixes in such a way that it occasionally affects the second initial consonant, as when अग्नि, *agni*, 'fire,' is compounded with स्तोम, *stôma*, 'sacrifice,' to produce अग्निष्टोम, *agnishṭôma*, 'burnt offering.' By this remoteness from the rules of agglutination of separated words, the language obviously indicates its feeling for the requirement of word unity. Yet it cannot be denied that compound words in Sanskrit become all too identical to the separate words, owing to the further and more general treatment of their contacting final and initial phonemes and by the lack of juncture phonemes, which are always used by Greek in such a case. The accent, admittedly unknown to us, can scarcely have obliterated this. Where the first member of the compound preserves its grammatical inflection, the connection truly rests solely in the speech usage, which either always combines these words or never utilizes the last member alone. However, the lack of inflections designates the unity of these words more for the understanding without attaining any value for the ear as a result of the fusion of the phonemes. Where the basic form and case ending coincide in the phoneme, the language fails to designate definitely whether a word stands alone or constitutes a component of a compound. Therefore, a long Sanskrit compound is, according to the express grammatical indication, less an individual word than a series of non-inflected concatenated words. It is a correct linguistic feeling of Greek that it never permitted its compound nouns to degenerate in this fashion through inordinate length. Sanskrit, however, proves in turn by other peculiarities how meaningfully it is able to indicate the unity of these words at times. The foregoing may be illustrated by those cases where Sanskrit combines two or more substantives, no matter what genders are represented, into a genderless compound unit.

Among the classes of words which follow the rules for medial agglutination, the *kridanta* words and those grammatically inflected resemble each other most closely. If between them there are still traces of even more intimate connection, these are owing more to the difference of the case and verb endings. The *krit* suffixes behave entirely as the latter. This is because they directly treat the root, which they actually first introduce into the language, since the case endings—in this respect identical to the *taddhita* suffixes—associate to basic words already given by the language itself. The intimacy of phonemic fusion is properly most solid in the inflection of the verb, inasmuch as the verbal concept may be separated to the least extent from its secondary determinations in the mind.

I have here intended to show only how the laws of euphony digress according to the gradations of the internal word unity in the case of contiguous sounds. Precaution must be taken, however, to avoid interpreting this as something actually intentional. As I have already remarked, the word "intention" must be cautiously defined and understood when applied to languages. Insofar as this term is defined as stipulation or even an effort proceeding from human will toward a distinctly conceived goal, the idea of intention is foreign to languages. We cannot remind ourselves of this fact too often. Intention is always expressed only in an original, instinctive emotion. Such a feeling for the unity of concepts according to my conviction has certainly been imparted to the phoneme, and precisely because it is an emotion, it has not always been imparted consistently in all places or with equal consequence. To be sure, a number of the individual deviations from the laws of agglutination arise phonetically from the nature of the letters [phonemes] themselves. Since all grammatically formed words always occur in the same combination of initial and final letters with these elements, but since the same contact recurs only alternately and individually in separated and even in composite words, a particular pronunciation is naturally produced with ease in the separated words which fuses all elements more intimately. Therefore, the feeling of word unity in these cases may be considered as having originated from the foregoing but in a manner opposite to the process I have indicated above.

Still the influence of this innate feeling of unity remains the primitive one, since from it proceeds the fact that the grammatical agglutinations become incorporated into the word stem and do not, as in some languages, remain detached. For the phonetic effect, it is important that both the case endings and the suffixes begin only with certain consonants. Hence, only a definite number of compounds are possible. Their number is least with respect to case endings, greater for the *krit* suffixes and verb endings, and even more extensive for the *taddhita* suffixes.

In addition to the diversity of the principles of agglutination with respect to contiguous medial consonants, there is found in languages another phonemic treatment of the word which even more definitely designates its unity. This phonemic treatment permits its total structure to influence the modification of the individual phonemes, particularly the vowels. This takes place when an association of more or less important syllables exerts an influence upon the vowels already present in the word; when an inceptive increment of the word produces abbreviations or elisions thereof; when expanding syllables assimilate their vowel to those of the word, or vice versa; and when a special stress is accorded to a syllable by phonetic intensification or by phonetic change with respect to the ear. Where not purely phonetic, each of these cases may be regarded as directly symbolic for the innate word unity. In Sanskrit this phonetic treatment is evinced in multiple form and always with remarkable consideration for the clarity of the logical form and the beauty of the aesthetic configuration. Therefore, Sanskrit does not assimilate the stem syllable, whose fixity must be maintained, to the endings. However, it does allow lengthening of the stem vowel. From the regular recurrence of the latter in the language, the ear easily recognizes the original vowel. A remark of F. Bopp attests to his refined linguistic sense; he noted that this modification of the stem vowel is in Sanskrit not qualitative but quantitative.[5] The qualitative assimilation originates from carelessness of pronunciation or from the pleasure produced by uniformly sounding syllables. A more elevated and refined euphonic sensitivity is evident in the quantitative modification of the moric factor. In the former the significant stem vowel is sacrificed, whereas in the latter it is retained and lengthened, thus remaining intelligible to both the ear and the mind.

The granting to a syllable of a word in pronunciation a special weight prevailing over the entire word may be seen in Sanskrit in the features termed *guna* and *vriddhi*. These are two such artfully developed media, both of which are associated with the remaining phonemic pattern, that they have remained exclusively peculiar to Old Indic. None of the sister tongues preserves these phonetic changes with respect to the system and the spirit involved. Only individual or isolated fragments of them are recorded in a few derivative dialects of Indo-European. *Guna* and *vriddhi* produce for the phoneme *a* a lengthening, and for the vowels *i* and *u*, the diphthongs *ê* and *ô*; they change the vowel *r* into *ar*;[6] and they intensify *ê* and *ô* by renewed diphthongization to *ai* and *au*. If a vowel follows *ê* and *ai* or *ô* and *au* produced by *guna* and *vriddhi*, these diphthongs resolve into *ay* and *ây*, or *aw* and *âw*. As a result, a double series of quintuple phonetic changes originates which by definite laws of the language and by continuous reversion in use always lead back to the same protophoneme. The language thus becomes endowed with a multiplicity of euphonious phonemic associations without the slightest deleterious effect upon comprehension. In the *guna* and *vriddhi* phenomena, in each case one sound is substituted for another. Yet, *guna* and *vriddhi* cannot be regarded as mere vowel changes that are common in many other languages. The important distinction between the two lies in the fact that in the case of mere vowel change the vowel substituted for another is always in part at least foreign to the original one in the modified syllable. Therefore, the cause must be sought in efforts toward grammatical differentiation, in a principle of assimilation, or in any other causative factor. Consequently, the new sound may vary in terms of the differing conditions involved, whereas in the case of *guna* and *vriddhi* it always originates uniformly from the protophoneme of the modified syllable itself and pertains to it alone. According to F. Bopp's explanation, if the *guna* sound वेद्मि, *vêdmi*, is compared with that originating by assimilation, that is, with तेनिम, *tênima*, the inserted *ê* in the former morpheme originated from the *i* of the modified syllable, whereas in the latter it originated from that of the following one.

Guna and *vriddhi* are intensifications of the basic phoneme and, indeed, not simply with respect to the latter but with respect to each other as the comparative and superlative. Increasing in equal quantitative measure, they are intensifications of the simple vowel. In the length of enunciation and of the phoneme, this increase is unmistakably apparent to the ear. This increase, however, is also revealed, for example, in the meaning of the participle of the future passive, which is constructed by affixing the syllable *ya*. The simple idea there requires only *guna*, whereas the intensified one associated with necessity demands the *vriddhi*: स्तव्य, *stavya*, 'a praiseworthy person,' and स्ताव्य, *stâvya*, 'a necessarily and in all ways praiseworthy person.' The concept of intensification does not exhaust the particular nature of these phonetic changes. Here the *vriddhi* of *a* must be expected, but it belongs in this class only to a certain extent in terms of its grammatical usage and not at all in terms of its phonemic value. For all remaining vowels and diphthongs the characteristic feature of these intensifications lies in the fact that through them a transformation of the phoneme is produced by means of the combination of dissimilar vowels or diphthongs. The combination of *a* with the remaining vowels or diphthongs constitutes the basis of all *guna* and *vriddhi* phenomena. It may now be assumed that in the *guna* a short *a* occurs before the simple vowel, whereas in the *vriddhi* a long *a* occurs in the same context; or that a short *a* always occurs in the *guna* before the simple vowel, whereas in the *vriddhi* it comes before the vowel already strengthened by *guna*.[7] As far as I know, the origin of lengthened vowels by mere coalition of identical ones is not ascribed to the *vriddhi* concept by the Hindu grammarians with the sole exception of *a*. Now, since in *guna* and *vriddhi* a phoneme originates which always has a very differing effect on the ear, and since it has its basis exclusively in the protophoneme of the syllable, the *guna* and *vriddhi* phonemes proceed from the innate depth of the syllable itself in a manner distinctly perceptible to the ear but which cannot be described in words. Therefore, if *guna*, which so often changes the stem syllable of verbs, were a definite characteristic of certain grammatical forms, the latter according to the sensory phenomena could also be literally termed developments from the interior of the root. Moreover, this is true to a greater extent than is found in the Semitic dialects where mere symbolic vowel change occurs.[8] This is not at all the case, however, since the *guna* is only a secondary formation which Sanskrit adds to verb forms according to definite rules, beyond their true characteristics. It is by nature a purely phonetic phenomenon and, insofar as we are able to discern its causes, is explicable solely from the phonemes concerned and is not per se meaningful or symbolic. The only case in the language which must be excepted from the foregoing is the "gunation" of the gemination vowel in intensive verbs. This feature reveals so much the more the intensifying expression which the language in an otherwise unusual way intends to impart to these forms, since gemination customarily shortens the long vowel, whereas the *guna* here, though not otherwise, occurs with long, medial root vowels.

In contrast, the *guna* can be regarded in many cases as a symbol of the internal word unity, since these phonetic changes occurring by degrees in the vocalic sphere produce a less material, more definite, and more closely associated lexical fusion than do the changes noted in contiguous consonants. In this respect, they resemble somewhat the accent, because the same effect, the special weight of a predominant syllable, is produced by the accent in the tone level, whereas in *guna* and *vriddhi* it is the result of phonemic transformation. Therefore, if in certain cases they accompany the innate word unity, they still continue to be one of the various expressions which language, not always pursuing the same course, employs to indicate it. This may also be the reason why they are especially characteristic and peculiar to the highly polysyllabic, long forms of the tenth class of Sanskrit verbs and of the causative verbs related to it. Now if, on the other hand, they are admittedly to be found also in quite short verbs, it cannot be for this reason denied that they impede the disintegration of the syllables of long verbs and that they require the voice to hold them solidly together. In this respect it seems very significant that the *guna* predominates in classes of words having the most fixed unity, that is, in the *kridanta* words and verb endings, and in them generally affects the root syllable. In contrast, it never occurs in the stem syllable of declensional forms or in words constructed by the *taddhita* suffixes.

Vriddhi finds a twofold application. On the one hand, like the *guna*, it is purely phonetic and increases the *guna* necessarily or according to the arbitrary will of the speaker; on the other hand, it is meaningful and purely symbolic. In the former configuration, it affects especially final vowels, just as the long vowels among them accept gunation, a process not occurring otherwise. This arises from the fact that the lengthening of a final vowel encounters no restriction. This is the same principle which in Javanese permits the *a* incorporated in the consonant to terminate in an obscure back vowel *o*. The significance of the *vriddhi* is revealed particularly in the *taddhita* suffixes and appears to have its original abode in generic denominations and in collective and abstract nouns. In all these cases the original, simple, and concrete idea is expanded. However, the same expansion is carried over metaphorically to other cases, even if not with the same consistency. This may be the reason that adjectives formed by the addition of *taddhita* suffixes sometimes have *vriddhi*, while in other instances the vowel remains unchanged. The adjective can be considered as a concrete property, but equally as comprehending the entire mass of items in which it appears.

The presence or lack of *guna* in the verb produces in grammatically determined cases a contrast between gunated and nongunated derivative forms. Occasionally, but much more rarely, an identical contrast is produced by the necessary or arbitrary use of the *vriddhi* in opposition to *guna*. F. Bopp first explained this contrast deriving from the effect of the phonemic heaviness or lightness of the terminations of the root vowel in a manner which certainly seems entirely satisfactory on the whole, even if it requires overlooking a few exceptions. The phonemic heaviness hinders its lengthening, while phonemic lightness appears to elicit it. One or the other takes place each time the ending is affixed directly to the root or when it impinges upon a vowel capable of gunation along the way.

Where the effect of the inflectional syllable is impeded by an intervening vowel or consonant and where, consequently, the dependency of the root vowel upon it ceases, the use or nonuse of gunation, although it regularly occurs here in certain cases, cannot be explained in any way on the basis of the sounds. This difference in the root syllable, moreover, cannot be traced at all to any very general law in the language. The true explanation of the use or lack of gunation appears to me to be found in the history of the derivational forms of the verb. This, however, is still a very obscure area, and we are incapable of divining in it more than fragmentary detail. Perhaps there were in times past two types of derivation, owing to dialects or epochs, either with or without gunation. From their mixture arose the present configuration in the language. In fact, a few classes of roots appear to be traceable to such a conjecture. These roots, especially in the meaning mentioned, may be derived with or without gunation, or they are gunated throughout while the analogy of the language generally would require the contrast mentioned. The latter occurs only in isolated exceptions. The former, however, takes place in all verbs that are conjugated simultaneously in accordance with the first and sixth classes, as well as in those belonging to the first class whose multiform preterite is constructed quite uniformly according to the pattern of the sixth class with its preterite augment, save for the lacking *guna*. This entire sixth-class configuration, corresponding to the second aorist in Greek, might very possibly be nothing but a true augment preterite of a nongunated derivative form alongside of which a gunated one has subsisted (the contemporary augment preterite of first-class roots). It is very probable to me that in the true sense of the word there are but two, and not three, preterites in Sanskrit as we count them today. Hence, the formations of the allegedly third type, that is, of the multiform type, are merely secondary forms inherited from other linguistic epochs.

If, in this way, a twofold conjugation with and without *guna* is assumed in the language, the question arises whether gunation was displaced or assumed at that point where the ponderosity of the terminations produces a contrast. A decision must unhesitatingly be made in favor of the former. Phonetic changes such as *guna* and *vriddhi* cannot be grafted on to a language. According to J. Grimm's fortunate expression applied to German vowel gradation [*Umlaut*], they extend to the very basis of the idiom, and their origin can be explained from the obscure and long diphthongs which are encountered in other languages also. Euphonic sensitivity may have attenuated them and ordered them in accordance with a quantitatively determined relationship. The same inclination of the speech organs toward vowel lengthening may, however, have erupted in a rhythmical way in the case of a fortunately organized people. It is not necessary and scarcely advisable to conceive every excellent quality of a cultured language as having originated stepwise and gradually.

The difference between the crude natural sound and a cultivated tone is revealed more distinctly in another morpheme that contributes to the internal lexical structure; reduplication, the repetition of the initial syllable of a word or of the entire word, which is done either to intensify significance for multifarious expression or because it is a mere phonetic habit, is native to the languages of many uncultured people. In others, as in several of the Malayan family, reduplication betrays an influence on the phonetic sensitivity by the fact that it is not always the root vowel but occasionally a related one that is reiterated. In Sanskrit, however, the reduplication is in every case so fittingly modified to the internal word structure that five or six different configurations thereof, distributed throughout the language, can be enumerated. All of them, however, emanate from the twofold principle of adapting this initial syllable to the particular form of the word and promoting the internal word unity. Some are simultaneously designative for definite grammatical forms. The adaption is at times so ingenious that the syllable actually designed to be prefixed splits the word and becomes situated between its initial vowel and its final consonant. This is perhaps owing to the fact that the same forms also require prefixing the augment, and both of these prefixed syllables as such could not have been indicated in a distinguishable way in initially vocalic roots. Greek, in which augment and reduplication in these cases actually coalesce in the *augmentum temporale* [temporal augment], has developed similar forms to attain the same objective.[9] This is a remarkable example, revealing how in the case of an active and virile sense of articulation the phonetic development breaks its own particular and marvelous trails to accompany the innate organizational linguistic sense in all of its various directions, maintaining each distinguishable.

The intention of connecting the word securely with the prefix is expressed in Sanskrit in the consonant stems by the brevity of the reiterated vowel, even in opposition to a long root vowel, so that the prefix of the word is suppressed. The only two exceptions to this abbreviation in the language have a unique basis that outweighs the general reason: for the intensive verbs it is the indication of their intensification; for the multiformed preterite of the causative verbs it is the euphonically required balance between the reiterated and root vowels. For initially vocalic roots, the special weight of the phoneme falls upon the initial syllable, where the reduplication is manifested by the lengthening of the initial vowel, thereby promoting the close association of the remaining to the affixed syllables as we have seen in the case of gunation. Reduplication is in most cases a true designating mark of certain grammatical forms, or in any case a phonetic modification characteristically accompanying them. Only in a minor portion of the verbs (those of the third class) is it indigenous to them. Here also as in the case of gunation, however, we are led to suspect that in an earlier time the language derived verbs with and without reduplication and without undergoing a change in itself or in its meaning as a result. The augment preterite and the multiform preterite of some third-class verbs are distinguished simply by the presence or absence of reduplication. This appears for this phonetic pattern even more natural than gunation, for the amplification of the statement by the phoneme through reiteration can originally be the effect only of the liveliness of individual emotion. Therefore, even when it becomes more general and more principled, it can stimulate varying usage.

The augment, which in its indication of past time is related to the feature of reduplication, is treated in a similar manner, promoting word unity for initially vocalic roots, and therein reveals a remarkable contrast to the identical negative prefix.[10] For, since the *alpha privatum* attaches to these roots by simple insertion of an *n*, the augment fuses to its initial vowel and thus reveals its definitely greater intimacy of combination as a verb form. However, in this coalescence it skips the gunation thereby originating and is lengthened to the *vriddhi* state. The foregoing is obviously to be ascribed to a feeling for the internal word unity, which desires to impart to this initial vowel holding the word together as great a predominance as possible. To be sure, in another verb form, specifically in the reduplicated preterite, there is also encountered in some roots a nasal infix, that is, the insertion of an *n*. However, this case is found but quite rarely in the language, and agglutination is associated to a lengthening of the vocalic prefix.

In addition to those briefly touched upon, sonorous languages possess a number of other media, all of which express the feeling of necessity, imparting to the word an organic structure that combines inner repleteness and euphony. Without considering the changes the language produces by medial continguous phonemes in accordance with the general principles of the language, we may attribute to these in Sanskrit vowel lengthening, vowel change, shift of the vowel to semivowel, the expansion of the latter to the status of a syllable by a following semivowel, and to some extent the insertion of a nasal infix. In all these cases the final structure of the phoneme arises simultaneously from the character of the root and the nature of the grammatical agglutinations. Concomitantly, the independence and solidity, the relationship and the contrast, and the

phonetic weight of the individual phoneme are expressed either in original
harmony or in a conflict always nicely adjusted by the organizational
linguistic sense. The care directed toward the structure of the word
totality is betrayed even more distinctly in the law of compensation.
According to this principle, an intensification or weakening occurring in
one part of the word is responsible for an oppositely directed change in
another part to maintain equilibrium. In this latter development, the
qualitative character of the alphabetical symbols is disregarded. The
linguistic sense emphasizes only the incorporeal quantitative character
and treats the word metrically, as a rhythmical series. In this respect
Sanskrit contains remarkable forms, not readily found in other tongues.
The multiform preterite of the causative verbs (the seventh-class formation in F. Bopp's system), having both augment and reduplication,
furnishes a remarkable example of this in every respect. Since in the forms
of this tense pattern the reiterative and root syllables always follow
directly the augment, which is always short for initially consonantal
roots, the language tends to impart to the vowels of these two syllables a
definite metrical relationship. With few exceptions, where these two
syllables metrically resound in a pyrrhic (अजगदं, *ajagadam*, ‿‿‿‿, from
गद्, *gad*, 'talk') or spondaic (अदध्रांड, *adaḍhrâdam*, ‿—‿, from ध्राड्,
dhrâḍ, 'fall off,' 'decline,' 'wilt') manner, they either ascend iambically
(अडुदूषं, *adudûsham*, ‿‿—‿, from डष्, *dush*, 'to sin,' 'besmirch oneself'),
or descend trochaically, which is true in the majority of cases (अचीकलं,
achîkalam, ‿—‿‿, from कल्, *kal*, 'to hurl, swing or oscillate'), and for the
same roots rarely allow the language a choice between this double vocalic
measure. Now if we investigate the quantitative relationship of these forms
which at first glance appear very complex, it is found that the language in
this case pursues a very simple method. By producing a transformation
within the root syllable, it simply applies the principle of phonetic
compensation. After shortening the root syllable, it merely restores the
original equilibrium by lengthening the reiterative syllable. From
the foregoing originates the trochaic subsidence, which apparently gives the
language a particular pleasure. The change in the quantity of the root
syllable seems to exert a deleterious effect on the principle higher in
priority that is directed toward the maintenance of the stem syllables.

   Precise research reveals, however, that this is by no means the case.
These preterites are constructed not from the primitive but from the
causative root already grammatically changed. As a rule, therefore, the
reduced length is native only to the causative root. Where the language
in these constructions impinges upon a primitive length of the stem or even
upon a diphthong, it desists from this process. It leaves the root syllable

unchanged and does not lengthen the reiterative syllable either, which is short in accordance with the general rule. From this difficulty, which runs counter to the actually intended process for these forms, arises the upward, iambic lilt which constitutes the natural, unchanged quantity ratio. At the same time, the language notes the cases where the length of the syllable proceeds not from the nature of the vowel but from its position before two successive consonants. In these cases, it does not pile up two lengthening media, and thus even in the trochaic subsidence it does not leave the reiterative vowel unlengthened before two initial consonants of the root. It is noteworthy that the actual Malayan language reveals this care to maintain the unity of the word in grammatical agglutinations and to treat this feature as a euphonic phonetic totality by quantity shift of the root syllable. Owing to their syllabic repleteness and euphony, the Sanskrit forms cited are the most distinct examples of what a language is capable of developing from monosyllabic roots. To do this, however, it must combine a highly developed alphabet with a phonetic system that reproduces the refinement of the ear and the most delicate nuances of the symbols, to which are added agglutination and internal change in accordance with definite rules based on manifold and distinguished principles.[11]

CHAPTER THIRTEEN

Accentuation

ANOTHER TYPE OF word unity, common to all languages by nature but detectible only in dead languages where the fugacity of pronunciation is preserved for us by comprehensible signs, lies in the accent. In the syllable, three kinds of phonetic properties can be distinguished. These are the peculiar type of its phonemes, its moric measure, and its accent. The first two are determined by the nature of the syllable and constitute its corporeal configuration, so to speak. The tone (which the author takes to mean the speech tonality and not the metrical arsis), depends, however, on the freedom of the speaker, is a force imparted by him, and is equivalent to a foreign spirit breathed into the syllable. It hovers over speech like a principle more spiritual than the material language itself and is the direct expression of the value which the speaker desires to impress upon it and upon each of its component parts. Fundamentally, every syllable is capable of accentuation. If, however, among several only one is actually accentuated, the emphasis upon those directly accompanying it is canceled unless the speaker purposely stresses one among them. This cancellation produces a combination of those becoming unstressed and the stressed syllable. Both phenomena, the elimination of stress and syllabic combination, determine and restrict each other, and each directly entrains the other in its wake. Thus originate word accent and the word unity effected by it. No independent word can be conceived without an accent, and no word can have more than one main accent. Were two accents present, the word would disintegrate into two entities and hence would become two words. Conversely, there may certainly be secondary accents in a word, which originate either from the rhythmical quality of the word or from semantic nuances.[1]

More than any other part of the language, accentuation is subject to the influence both of the meaningfulness of speech and of the metric property of the phonemes involved. Originally and in its true configuration, it proceeds indisputably from the former. However, the more the mind of a nation is trained upon rhythmical and musical beauty, the more influence this accentuation requirement is accorded. Nonetheless, there is inherent in the accentuation drive, if I may be permitted to use this expression, far more than the significance that is directed merely toward comprehension. There is also expressed in accentuation the urge to designate far beyond mere necessity the intellectual intensity of the idea and of its components. This is more discernible in English than in any other language, for in English the accent very frequently overwhelms the tempo and in the process even changes the characteristic value of the syllables. It would be highly incorrect to ascribe this to a deficient sense of euphony. It is, in contrast, only the intellectual energy relative to the character of the nation, consisting of swift conceptual decision in some cases or of serious solemnity in others, which strives above all else to designate in pronunciation the element emphasized by the mind. From the association of this peculiarity with the laws of euphony, which is often conceived in great purity and sharpness, originates the English word structure, which is truly wonderful in its intention toward accentuation and pronunciation.[2] If the need for intensive and sharply shaded accentuation were not so deeply grounded in the English character, the demand for public eloquence would not suffice in explaining the great attention so evidently accorded this segment of the language in England. If all other portions of the language are more closely associated with the intellectual peculiarities of nations, accentuation, conversely, is bound up more intimately with character.

The association of words in speech also reveals cases where less weighty words are associated to more weighty ones by accent without coalescing into a unit. This is the state of enclitical relationship, that is, of the Greek ἔγκλισις. The lighter or less stressed word sacrifices its independence enclitically, but remains a separate element of speech. It loses its accent and falls into the accent range of the more important word. However, if this region is protracted by this increment to a degree antithetical to the principles of the language, the more important word, by assuming two accents, transforms its unstressed final syllable into an oxytone and as a result associates the less weightier to itself.[3] By this association, however, the natural word division should not be disturbed. The process of enclitic accentuation confirms this in several cases. When one enclitic word follows another, the latter in accordance with its accent does not fall into the area of the weightier word as does the former, but the former assumes the acute accent for the latter. The enclitic word is thus not skipped over but is treated with the respect due an independent word, and it associates another to itself. The particular idiosyncrasy of such an enclitic word even asserts its influence on the type of accentuation, a fact which further affirms what has been stated previously. Now, inasmuch as a circumflex accent cannot change into an acute, the entire enclitic process is interrupted when the first of two successive enclitic words becomes circumflexed. Then the second enclitic word retains its original accentuation.[4] I have cited these details, only to show how carefully nations which have guided their intellect toward a very elevated and refined development of their languages also indicate the various degrees of word unity in those cases where neither separation nor fusion is complete and definitive.

CHAPTER FOURTEEN

The Incorporative System of Languages: Syntactical Sentence Components

THE GRAMMATICALLY CONSTRUCTED word, which we have heretofore considered with respect both to the association of its elements and to its unity as a totality, is destined to become an element of the sentence. In the case of the sentence, the language must construct a second and more lofty unit—more lofty not merely because it is of greater scope but also because it depends more exclusively on the discipline of the innate linguistic sense owing to the fact that the phoneme can affect it only in a subsidiary way. Languages such as Sanskrit, which weave into the unity of the word its relationship through to the sentence, permit the latter to disintegrate into its components through which, according to its nature, it impinges upon comprehension. From these components, these languages build up their unity, so to speak. Languages such as Chinese, whose linguistic system contains very basic and unchanging words, do the same thing and almost more rigorously, since the words occur entirely isolated. However, in constructing the unity of the sentence, these languages come to the aid of comprehension in part through nonphonetic media, such as the position of words, and in part through the use of separated words. But, if these two media are taken together, there is another, oppositely directed medium which firmly holds the unity of the sentence for our understanding. This consists in treating the sentence with all of its necessary parts not as an entity constructed of words but truly as a single word.

If we start with the sentence, which is originally more correct since every statement (no matter how incomplete) really constitutes in the intention of the speaker a conclusive concept, languages which exploit the last medium mentioned above do not split up the unity of the sentence at all but rather strive in their development to bind all of its components more and more rigidly together. They visibly displace the boundaries of word unity by drawing the words into the area of sentence unity. A correct distinction between the two proceeds from truly inflected languages, since the Chinese method too feebly evinces the feeling of sentence unity in the language. And languages prove that inflection in its true spirit has completely permeated them only when they fully develop word unity on the one hand and keep it rigidly within its actual area on the other; that is, when the sentence is divided into all of its necessary parts, and when, from them, its unity in turn is again built up. Inflection, word unity, and sentence division are closely related to the extent that an incomplete development of one of these segments always proves definitely that none of them has predominated in its entirely pure and undimmed meaning in the speech structure. This triple process, the meticulous grammatical preparation of the word for association in the sentence, the entirely indirect and principally nonphonetic indication thereof, and the tight preservation of the entire sentence insofar as possible in a form pronounced as a unit, exhausts the manner in which languages combine words into sentences. In most languages, stronger or weaker traces of all three methods are found. However, where one of them definitely predominates and becomes the midpoint of the organization, it then guides the entire structure with a more or less rigid consistency. Sanskrit, Chinese, and, as I shall immediately elucidate, the Mexican language can be established as examples of the most intensive prevalence of each of them.

In order to bring about the union of the simple sentence into a single, phonetically bound form, the Mexican[1] language emphasizes the verb as the true midpoint of the sentence. Insofar as possible, it joins the governing and governed parts of the sentence to the verb and imparts to this union produced by a phonetic process the impression of a connected whole: *ni-naca-qua,* 'I eat meat.' This combination of the substantive with the verb could be regarded as a compound verb, equal to the Greek κρεοφαγέω. The language, however, obviously conceives it differently. For, if for any reason the substantive itself is not incorporated, the language replaces it with the pronoun of the third person, a distinct proof that both it and the verb simultaneously require the following structural scheme: *ni-c-qua in nacatl,* 'I eat it, the meat.' According to its form, the sentence should be concluded in the verb, with the subsequent apposition only determining it more closely. However, the verb cannot be conceived without these complementary secondary determinations in the Mexican manner of thinking. Therefore, if no definite object is present, the language combines with the verb its own indefinite pronoun used in a double form for both persons and things: *ni-tla-qua*, 'I eat something'; *ni-te-tla-maca*, 'I give someone something.' The language gives clearer evidence of its purpose in permitting these compounds to appear as a whole, for when a verb that comprehends the sentence itself or its schematic structure is transposed into a past tense and is thus provided with the augment *o*, this is placed at the beginning of the compounded structure. This indicates clearly that the foregoing secondary determinations always and necessarily belong to the verb, even though the augment is added only to indicate past action. Thus of the form *ni-nemi*, 'I live,' which as an intransitive verb cannot entrain any other pronouns, the perfect is *o-ni-nen*, 'I have lived'; of *maca*, 'to give,' it is *o-ni-c-te-maca-c*, 'I have given it to somebody.' It is even more important, however, that the language distinguishes very carefully between an absolute and an incorporative form for words used in this incorporation. Without this precaution the entire method would become awkward for our understanding, and therefore we must regard it as its basis. In the incorporated state, as in compound words, nouns dispense with the endings which are always present in the absolute state and which characterize them as nouns. 'Meat,' which we found incorporated above as *naca*, is in its absolute form *nacatl*.[2] Of the incorporated pronouns, none is used in the same form separately. The two indeterminant ones do not occur in an absolute state in the language, and those which govern a definite object have a form that differs more or less from their independent one. The method described, however, reveals automatically that there must be two incorporated forms, one for the pronoun when it is governing and another for when it is governed. To be sure, the independent personal pronouns can be placed ahead of the form depicted here for special emphasis. However, the incorporated ones referring to them are not omitted for this reason. The subject of the sentence expressed in a particular word is not incorporated, but its presence is shown in the form by the fact that in the third person of the form a governing pronoun indicating it is always lacking.

If the different manners in which the simple sentence may be presented to the mind are rapidly scanned, it is obvious that the rigorous incorporation system cannot be consistently carried out in all cases. Therefore, concepts in individual words must often be excerpted from the form which cannot encompass them all. In such a case, the language always follows a chosen course and evolves new remedial aids where it impinges upon difficulties. For example, when something is supposed to happen either for or against with respect to something else, and when the definite governed pronoun would thus be ambiguous since it would have to refer to two objects, the language constructs via an incremental ending a distinct class for such verbs and proceeds as usual for the remainder. The sentence scheme is now again complete in the combined pattern, with the indication of an accomplished action in the governed pronoun and the secondary reference to another pronoun in the ending. Now, in the certainty that both of these objects will be understood without providing an identification of their relationship, the language can let them follow externally: *chihua*, 'make' or 'do,' becomes *chihui-lia*, 'do for or against someone,' with change of the *a* into *i* according to the law of assimilation, and this can then become *ni-c-chihui-lia in no-piltzin ce calli*, 'I make it for the my son a house.'

The Mexican incorporation method attests of a proper feeling for sentence structure by the fact that it connects the designations of the relationships in the sentence to the verb, the point at which the sentence gathers a unity. It is thereby fundamentally and advantageously distinguished from Chinese, which lacks such specification and in which the verb is not even surely distinguishable by its position but often only materially by its meaning. However, with respect to the components of more complicated sentences that occur external to the verb, Mexican becomes completely identical to Chinese, for in transferring the entire indicating property to the verb, it leaves the noun completely uninflected. The Mexican method approaches that of Sanskrit to the extent that it actually expresses the thread connecting the sentence components. Otherwise, however, it stands in a remarkable antithesis to Sanskrit. Sanskrit designates in an entirely simple and natural manner every word as a constitutive part of the sentence. The Mexican incorporation process does not do this, but it does permit—where everything cannot be compressed into a unit—identifications to proceed from the midpoint of the sentence, which, like compass points, indicate the directions in which we must seek the relationship of the individual components to the sentence. We are not exempted from seeking and guessing; rather we are cast back into the opposite system of nonindication by this definite type of indication. Even if this method in this way has something in common with those of Sanskrit and Chinese, its nature would be misconstrued were we to regard it as a mixture of both or were we to think that the intimate linguistic sense did not possess the power to carry the indication system throughout all parts of the language. Rather, there is obviously a peculiar manner of conception in this Mexican sentence structure. The sentence is not to be constructed, is not to be gradually built up of components, but is to be expressed all at once in a form compressed to unity.

If we dared to descend into the primeval beginnings of language, we would surely find that man inwardly relates a complete meaning with every sound emitted as language: that is, for him it is a complete utterance. Man does not intentionally emit merely an isolated word, even though his statement according to our viewpoint may only contain such an entity. Therefore, the original relationship of the sentence to the word cannot be conceived of one in which an already inherently complete and detailed sentence is subsequently broken down into words by abstraction. If, as is most natural, linguistic structure is conceived as successive, it must be based upon an evolutionary system, as all things of natural origin are. The emotion expressing itself in sound contains everything in germinal form. However, in the sound itself, everything is not immediately apparent. The hidden portions of the sentence gradually become clearer and emerge in individual sounds only after the emotion has become more sharply defined, after the articulation has gained freedom and precision, and after the success of an attempted mutual understanding has elevated man's spirits. The Mexican process enjoys a certain similarity with this procedure. It immediately represents a combined totality, which is complete and sufficient. By the pronoun it designates what has not yet been determined individually as an indeterminate something, but subsequently it depicts this indeterminate residuum in detail. From this procedure it follows automatically that, even though the incorporated words lack endings which they possess in their independent state, this must not be conceived in the reality of linguistic invention as a rejection of the terminations in favor of incorporation but as an addition to the state of independence. My words must not be misunderstood if I say that for this reason the Mexican speech structure appears to me to lie closer to those primeval beginnings mentioned. The application of time concepts to the development of a human peculiarity such as language, which lies so entirely in the incalculable original capacity of the soul, always contains something very doubtful and precarious. Obviously the Mexican sentence structure is a very ingenious and often reworked composition which has retained only the general type of those primitive constructions. Furthermore, the regular separation of the various types of pronouns is reminiscent of a time when a clearer grammatical concept prevailed. These junctures to the verb [agglutinations] developed harmoniously and in a degree equal to the development of the word unit and the inflections of the verb itself. The distinction lies only in the fact that what in the primordial beginnings is an undeveloped bud is presented in the Mexican tongue as a composite whole, complete and indivisible. In contrast, the Chinese leaves it entirely up to the hearer to seek out the composition, which is scarcely indicated by any phonemes, while the more vital and bolder Sanskrit immediately presents to the eye the part in its relationship to the whole and indicates it distinctly, moreover.

The Malayan languages do not follow the incorporative system, but they do have a certain similarity to it owing to the fact that they express the directions which the sentence pursues by careful designation of the transitive, intransitive, or causative properties of the verb. They seek by this means to compensate for the lack of inflections serving the comprehension of the sentence. Some of them gather determinants of all types about the verb, thereby expressing to some extent whether it is singular or plural. This designation of the verb also indicates the relationship of the other sentence components to it. Moreover, in these Malayan dialects the verb is not absolutely noninflected. Inflections and a certain striving toward Sanskrit word unity cannot be denied with respect to the verb to the Mexican tongue, in which the tenses are designated by individual final phonemes and in part symbolically.

A somewhat lesser degree of incorporation is revealed in languages which do not allow the verb to absorb entire nouns into the framework of its inflections, but which express in the verb not merely the governing pronoun but also the governed. In these languages there are various shadings of incorporation, depending on whether this method has become more or less firmly established in a language and whether this indication is also required when the explicit object of the action follows independently. Where this type of verb inflection has attained its complete development with the pronoun, where it is incorporated into and interwoven with it and is significant in various directions, as in some North American Indian dialects and in Basque, there are a mass of verbal inflectional forms which are difficult to survey. With admirable care, however, the analogy of their structure is fixed so that comprehension is preserved by a thread of meaning proceeding through them. Since frequently in these forms the person of the pronoun recurs in various respects as acting and as the direct and indirect object of the action, and since these languages for the major part lack any kind of declensional inflections, there must be differing pronominal affixes in accordance with the phoneme, or possible misunderstanding must be prevented in some other way. As an excellent example of such a tongue we can cite the Massachusetts Indian dialect of New England, a branch of the great Delaware family of languages. With the same pronominal affixes, between which it does not make a phonemic distinction as does the Mexican, it determines in its complex conjugation all inflections. For this purpose, it makes use principally of the medium of prefixing in certain cases the passive person, so that when the rule has been grasped the generic type to which the person belongs may be recognized immediately by the initial phoneme of the form. However, as this medium does not suffice completely, the language unites other indicators to the word—especially a final phoneme; in this case, when the two first persons are passive, the third is designated as active. The practice of designating the differing significance of the pronoun by the place it occupies in the verb has always appeared very remarkable to me because it either presumes a definite manner of conception in the intellect of the people or leads to the conclusion that the totality of the conjugation was hazy in the linguistic sense of the people, and that this linguistic sense arbitrarily employed position as a means of differentiation. I feel the former is by far more probable. At first glance, it does in fact seem arbitrary that the first person, as a governed item, has a suffix added to it at the point where the second person is the active person, and, on the other hand, that it precedes the verb at the point where the third person appears in an active role, in view of the fact that we always say, *du greifst mich*, 'you seize me,' and *mich greift er*, 'me seizes he,' and not vice-versa. Still, one reason may lie in the fact that the two first persons exercise a greater degree of vividness in the people's imagination, and that the nature of these forms originated with the passive person being affected, which is not unnatural to conceive. Of the two first persons, the second person again seems to be superior; for the third person in its passive role is never prefixed, and the second person under the same condition never has another position. But where the second person in its active role occurs with the first-person passive, the second person still maintains its preferred position, while the language avoids any confusion in another way. The fact that the position of the pronoun in these forms remains identical in the idiom of the main branch of the Delaware tribe, the Lenni Lenape language, also speaks for this view. Also the dialect of the Mohicans (actually Muhhekaneew), familiar to us from J. F. Cooper's genial novel, does not appear to digress from this. Always, however, the fabric of this conjugation remains so ingenious that it is impossible to escape the idea that here, as we have already observed of language in general, the structure of each component was made with reference to an obscurely sensed whole. The grammars merely give paradigms and contain no structural breakdown, but I have been completely convinced of the regularity prevailing in the apparent chaos by a precise and extensive structural tabulation, constructed from J. Eliot's paradigms.[3] The paucity of aids does not always permit the analysis to penetrate all parts of each form. In particular, it does not allow the separation of what the grammarians consider merely euphonious characters [phonemes] from all the characteristic ones. However, the rules carry throughout the greater portion of the inflections. Where cases continue to remain dubious, the meaning of the form can be shown by the fact that for definite reasons it can be no other. In any case, it is unfortunate when the innate organization of a people in combination with external conditions guides linguistic structure along this course. The grammatical forms conjoin for understanding and sound into masses which are too great and unwieldy. Freedom of speech feels itself bound, because instead of putting together individual elements to express changing ideas in various relationships, it must extensively utilize absolutely stereotyped expressions; moreover, it must always use the entire expression even though it does not always need all of its components. At the same time the connections within these composite forms are too loose to permit fusion of its individual components into a state of true word unity.

Thus the compound suffers when organically incorrect division is undertaken. The reproach is made here for the entire incorporation process. To be sure, the Mexican language strengthens the word unity by the fact that it knits together fewer determinations by pronouns into the verb inflections; moreover, it never in this way indicates two definitely governed objects but places the designation of the indirect reference in the termination of the verb itself whenever a direct object coexists. On the other hand, it always connects what would be better left unconnected. In languages which betray a high sense of word unity, the indication of the governed pronoun has at times penetrated into the verb form; in Hebrew, for example, these governed pronouns are suffixed. However, in this case the language permits us to recognize what distinction it makes between these pronouns and those of the acting persons, and which pronouns essentially belong to the nature of the verb itself. It places the latter into the closest connection with the stem and attaches the former only loosely; indeed it occasionally separates the former completely from the verb and makes them independent.

Languages which in this way overlap the boundaries of word and sentence structure customarily lack declension. They generally have no cases, or, as in Basque, they do not always distinguish the nominative from the accusative in the phoneme. This may not be regarded as the cause of the insertion of the governed object; we may not assume that they desired thereby to prevent the indistinctness originating from the lack of declension. Rather, this lack is the result of the foregoing process.

The reason for this confusion between that which belongs to the part and that which belongs to the whole of the sentence lies in the fact that in the organization of the language the correct conception of the individual parts of speech was not clearly in mind. A clear concept would have produced both the declension of the noun and the restriction of the verb forms to their essential determinations. If instead of that, however, the language first took the approach which consists merely of holding closely together in the word that which belongs together in the construction, the development of the noun would naturally have appeared less necessary. The image of the noun as a part of the sentence was not dominant in the imagination of the populace, and it was subsequently evolved merely as an explanatory idea. Sanskrit has completely refrained from the inter-weaving of governed pronouns into the verb.

I have not as yet mentioned the conjunction of the pronoun in those cases where it is more naturally disjunctive—that is, the juncture of the possessive pronoun with the noun. This is because it is based primarily on something other than what is being discussed here. The Mexican language has a special abbreviation for the possessive pronoun, and the pronoun thus encompasses in two separated forms the two principal parts of the language. In Mexican, and not only in this tongue, this combina-tion has syntactic application, and a discussion of it therefore belongs precisely here. This language uses the attachment of the third-person pronoun to the noun as an indication of the genitive relationship by permitting the noun in the genitive case to follow. Mexicans say, for example, *sein Haus der Gärtner*, 'his house the gardener,' instead of *das Haus des Gärtners*, 'the house of the gardener.' It is evident that this is exactly the same as the process that is used in the case of a verb governing a termin-ally affixed substantive.

The junctions with the possessive pronoun are not merely much more frequent in Mexican than appears necessary, but with some concepts, such as those dealing with degree of relationship and the parts of the human body, this pronoun is indissolubly fused. Where no individual person is to be designated, the indefinite personal pronoun is added to the degree of relationship, whereas that of the first person plural is added to the members of the body. Therefore, they do not simply say *nantli*, 'the mother,' but usually say *te-nan*, 'somebody's mother,' and just as seldom do they say *maitl*, 'the hand,' but rather say *to-ma*, 'our hand.' In many other American Indian tongues this attachment of these ideas to the possessive pronoun proceeds to the apparent impossibility of separation. The reason is probably not obviously syntactical, but rather lies still deeper in the conceptual processes of the people. Where the intellect is still but little accustomed to abstraction, it compresses into unity what it often concatenates. Moreover, what reason is capable of separating only with difficulty or not at all, the language conjoins into a single word, wherever it inclines toward such attachments. Such words afterward become current as a stereotype coined once and for all, and the speakers no longer think of separating the component elements. Furthermore, the continuous reference of the thing to the person lies in the more original attitude of the human being and does not become restricted to those cases where it is really necessary until the cultural level rises. In all languages containing strong traces of this earlier status, the personal pronoun hence plays a more important part. With respect to this viewpoint, several other phenomena confirm my conclusions. In Mexican the possessive pronouns control the word to such an extent that its endings are generally changed, and these composite structures regularly have a plural ending peculiar to them. Such a transformation of the entire word proves visibly that it is regarded innately as a new individual concept and not merely as an opportunely occurring conjunction of two different ones in speech. In Hebrew we see the effect of the varying fixity of the conceptual association on the word juncture in particularly meaningful nuances. As already noted, the pronouns of the acting person of the verb become most closely associated to the stem, because the verb cannot be conceived without them. The solid union that results then pertains to the possessive pronoun, and the pronoun of the object of the verb becomes very loosely associated to the stem. According to purely logical reasoning, in both the latter cases the greater fixity should be on the side of the object governed by the verb, if it were desired to accord a distinction between them at all. Obviously this is required more by the transitive verb than the possessive pronoun in general is required by the noun. That the language here takes the opposite course can scarcely be traced to any reason other than that this relationship was most frequently conceived by the people as an individual unit.

If all cases in which whatever could construct an individual sentence is reduced to a single word form are ascribed to the system of incorporation, which we must do, strictly speaking, then examples thereof are encountered in languages where it is otherwise foreign. However, they generally occur in these languages in composite sentences and are used to avoid inserted clauses or parenthetical expressions. The way to connect incorporation in the simple sentence to the lack of declension of the noun is to trace it either to the absence of a relative pronoun and appropriate conjunctions or to lesser habitual use of these combinative media. In the Semitic languages the use of the *status constructus* is less striking even in these cases, since they are not disinclined to incorporation in any case. However, with respect to Sanskrit, I need only to remind the reader of the so-called participles terminating in *twâ* and *ya* and of the compounds, such as the *bahuvrihi* type, which include entire relative clauses in themselves. The latter have gone over into Greek only to a small extent. Greek generally makes a less frequent use of this type of incorporation, employing more often the medium of connective conjunctions. Greek even prefers to increase the intellectual labor by using constructions that are left unconnected. By two great contractions, Greek imposes a certain clumsiness on the periodic sentence structure, and Sanskrit is not always free of this either. This is the case specifically where languages are inclined to break up into sentences word forms which have been impressed into a unit. The reason for this dulling of the forms need not always lie in an enfeebled structural power of language, for the habit of a more correct and decisive division of ideas can dissolve what was meaningfully and animatedly resolved into a unit. In such case, the result is less appropriate to the expression of the supple ideological connection. Determination of the limit of what and how much can be combined into a single form requires a delicate and refined grammatical sense. Of all the nations, this was probably especially inherent in the Greeks. Moreover, in their idiom, which they consistently entwined with their lives through a rich and careful linguistic usage, it developed to a state of optimum refinement.

CHAPTER FIFTEEN

Congruence of Phonetic Patterns of Languages with Grammatical Requirements

GRAMMATICAL FORMATION ARISES from the principles of human thinking by language and is based upon the congruence of the phonetic forms with the latter. Such a congruence must be present in every language in some way or another. The difference lies only in degree, and the blame for deficient development may be attributed to insufficient vividness of the afore-mentioned laws in the soul or to deficient flexibility in the phonemic system. A lack in one of these factors, however, always affects the other immediately. Perfection of language requires that every word be identi-fied as a definite part of speech and include those properties which philo-sophical analysis of language recognizes therein. Thus, perfection of languages presupposes inflection per se. Hence, the question arises in what way the simplest part of perfected speech structure, the conversion of a word to the status of a part of speech by inflection, can be conceived as proceeding from the mind of a people. Reflective consciousness of the lan-guage cannot be presumed as its origin; nor would it include any creative power for phonemic development. Every advantage which a language pos-sesses in this truly vital component of its organization proceeds originally from a living, sensory view of life. However, because the highest power, devi-ating least from the truth, originates in the purest harmony of all intellectual capacity whose most ideal flower is language itself, that which has been drawn from its view of life automatically has a retroactive effect on the language. That is the way it is in this case also. The objects of external perception as well as of intimate sensation are represented in a twofold relationship: that is to say, they are represented in their particular qualitative properties, which distinguish them individually, and in their general concept, which is apparent to the appropriately active perception and which is also always revealed by something in the appearance and in the emotion involved. We might mention the flight of a bird, for example, as a definite motion produced by wing power; at the same time, however, we might conceive of it as a directly ephemeral activity only to be recorded mentally in this transitory state. Conditions proceed similarly in all other cases. A perception proceeding from the most lively and harmonious exertion of human powers exhausts everything in the material presented to view and does not confuse detail but clearly analyzes it. From recognition of the foregoing double relationship of objects, that is, from the feeling for their correct relationship and from the vividness of each individual impression produced, inflection originates automatically as the linguistic expression of what has been perceived and felt.

It is at the same time remarkable to perceive the differing route upon which intellectual attitude embarks with respect to sentence structure. It does not start from its ideal, it does not compose it with inordinate effort; rather, it gets to it unconsciously by imparting phonemic configuration to the clear-cut and completely absorbed impression of the object. Because this occurs correctly every time and always according to the same emotion, the idea becomes coordinated by the words thus constructed. In its true, innate nature, the intellectual accomplishment mentioned here is a direct efflux of the strength and purity of the original linguistic capacity reposing in human kind. Perception and emotion are, so to speak, only the manipulations by which it is drawn over into the range of external phenomenology. For this reason it is understandable that there is so much more contained in its final result than the latter considered by itself appears to offer. Taken rigorously, the incorporative method is by nature truly antithetical to inflection, because the latter proceeds from the individual whereas the former starts from the whole. It can only partially revert again to inflection through the triumphant influence of the innate linguistic sense. However, there is always betrayed in incorporation, owing to the lesser intensity of the linguistic sense, the fact that the objects are not presented in equal clarity with regard to the individual points of sensory contact to our perception. Arriving thus at a different procedure, the incorporative method attains a unique power and freshness in the association of ideas by the vigorous pursuit of this new course. The relationship of objects to their most general categorical concepts, to which the parts of speech correspond, is an ideal one, and its most general and purest symbolic expression is drawn from the personality which, at the same time, is manifested as its most natural designation. Thus what has been stated previously concerning the meaningful intertwining of the pronominal stems into the grammatical forms applies here too.

When inflection is truly developed in a language, the further evolution of the inflectional system proceeds by its own effort in accordance with a perfected grammatical approach. It has already been indicated above how the further development now and again creates new forms or penetrates structurally into existing ones not previously used, resulting in differing significance even in languages of the same group. In this respect I need only remind the reader of the Greek past perfect which originated from a merely variant form of a Sanskrit aorist.[1] Respecting the influence of phonemic formation upon this subsequent development, which must never be overlooked, we must not confuse whether the penetration into existing forms acts restrictively upon the differentiation of the multitudinous grammatical concepts or has only incompletely absorbed them. In an earlier period of the language, there could have been a preponderance of perceptive morphological creation in which a multiplicity of forms corresponded to one and the same grammatical concept, even in the case of the most correct linguistic approach. In these earlier periods, during which the innate creative spirit of man was completely absorbed by language, words were represented as objects in themselves, they seized upon the power of imagination by their sound, and they realized their particular nature predominantly in multiplicity. Not until later did the grammatical concept gradually gain power, obtaining control over words and subjecting them to its uniformity. In Greek, especially in the Homeric language, significant traces of that earlier condition have been preserved. On the whole, however, there is revealed precisely in this point the notable difference between Greek and Sanskrit. Whereas the former delimits the forms more exactly according to grammatical concepts and utilizes their multiplicity more carefully to denote finer gradations, Sanskrit tends to emphasize the technical media of designation, applying them more generously on the one hand but clinging to them better, more simply, and with less frequent exceptions on the other.

CHAPTER SIXTEEN

Structural Differences Between Languages

SINCE LANGUAGE, AS I have already remarked frequently, has only an ideal existence in the minds and hearts of men but never possesses a material existence even though engraved in stone or bronze, and since the power of tongues no longer spoken—to the extent that they may still be perceived by us—largely depends upon the strength of our intellectual power to revive them, there can be in language an instant of true static status that is only as great as that found in the incessantly burning ideas of men themselves. It lies in the nature of language to be a progressive development under the influence of the intellectual power of its speakers in every case. In this course of development, two periods arise naturally which must be distinguished. In one the creative phonemic drive of the language is still in a state of growth and vigorous activity; in the other, after complete structural development of at least the external linguistic form, an apparent cessation develops and a visible decrease in the foregoing creative intellectual drive follows. However, even during the period of decline, new life principles and successful innovations in the language may originate, a subject I will touch upon in greater detail subsequently.

In the course of development of languages, two mutually restrictive causes collaborate. These are the principle originally determining the direction of the language and the effect of the material already brought forth, whose power is always in an inverse ratio to the operative force of the principle. The existence of such a principle in every language cannot be doubted. Just as a people or human intellectual power absorbs linguistic elements, it must in turn combine them into a unit quite involuntarily and without becoming distinctly conscious of them, since without this operation neither a thinking process in the individual nor a mutual comprehension would be possible. Precisely the foregoing would have to be assumed, if it were possible to trace back the process involved in the origin of a language.

That unity, however, can only be one of an exclusively governing principle. If this principle approaches the general structural linguistic principle in man as far as the individualization of humans permits, and if it permeates the language in its complete and unimpaired force, it will filter through all stages of its evolutionary course in such a way that in place of a vanishing force there always recurs a new one appropriate to the procedure concerned. It is inherent in every intellectual development that the force actually does not die out, but only changes in its functions or substitutes one of its factors for another. However, if in the first principle something not necessary to the basic linguistic pattern becomes admixed, or if the principle does not truly permeate the phoneme, or if to some not purely organic material something else which is deformed becomes associated to produce an even greater deviation, a foreign force becomes opposed to the natural course of development. Then the language is unable to gain new strength by pursuit of its natural course, which every correct development of intellectual powers is able to do. In this case also, as in the designation of the multifarious association of ideas, language requires freedom. A characteristic of the purest and most successful linguistic structure is if, in the formation of words and junctures, it suffers no more restriction than necessary, if it combines freedom with governing principles and assures the freedom its existence by limitations. The right intellectual capacity must be in a natural state of harmony with the proper developmental course of language. Since the need to think arouses speech in man, the successful thought progress must also promote that which emerges purely from the concepts of language. If a nation endowed with such a language were to sink into a state of intellectual sluggishness and weakness for other reasons, it would always be able to work its way out of this condition via its language. Conversely, intellectual capacity must from its own resources find levers to produce its own improvement when a language digresses from the correct and natural developmental course. It will then react upon the language by means of media it creates, but not creatively since its creations can only be the result of its own existential drive. However, it can structurally interpolate, can impart meaning to its forms which it had not assigned them, and can permit an application to which it would not have lead.

Now, among the innumerable extant and dead languages a difference can be established which is important for the progressive culture of the human race. This distinction is between languages which have developed powerfully and consistently from a pure principle in legitimate freedom and those idioms which cannot boast of this advantage. The former are the successful fruits of the linguistic drive pullulating in multifarious effort in the human race. The latter have a diverging form in which two things coalesce. These are deficiencies of the intensity of the pure linguistic sense originally inherent in man, and a unilateral deformation originating from the circumstance that to a phonemic form [morpheme] not necessarily proceeding from the language others become associated, attracted by the deformity.

The above investigations furnish a guideline for researching this distinction in actual languages and presenting it in simple form, no matter to what extent the languages appear to be a confusing mass of detail at first. We have attempted to show what is involved in the case of the highest principles and thereby to establish points to which linguistic analysis may be elevated. Regardless to what extent this approach can be clarified and smoothed, the possibility of finding in each language the form from which the quality of its structure emanates will be present. Furthermore, from what has been developed we will be able to establish a measure of the advantages and deficiencies of each language.

If I have succeeded in portraying the inflectional method in its entirety, imparting by itself to the word true internal solidity for the intellect and the ear and simultaneously breaking down the various parts of the sentence which is requisite for the intricacy of thought, it is indubitable that it preserves exclusively in itself the pure principle of linguistic structure. Inasmuch as it takes every element of speech in its twofold value, that is, in its objective meaning and in its subjective reference to the concept and the language, and designates this twofold factor in its relative importance by appropriate phonetic forms, it increases the most original essences of language, articulation and symbolization, to their highest degree. Consequently, it can only be a question of ascertaining in which languages this method has been preserved most consistently, most completely, and with the greatest freedom. No language may have attained this apex, but a difference in degree was observed above between Sanskrit and the Semitic languages. In the latter inflection was found in its truest and most unmistakable form and was combined with the finest symbolization; nonetheless, it was not carried through all portions of the language and was limited by more or less accidental laws, by the disyllabic word form, by the vowels that are used exclusively for designating inflection, and by an apparent reticence to construct compounds. In the former we noted that the solidity of word unity carried through all parts of the language preserves inflection from any suspicion of agglutination, and that inflection operates in the language with maximum freedom.

Compared with the incorporative method and that consisting of loose affixation without true word unity, the inflectional method appears to be a genial one, proceeding from the true intuition of the language. Because intuitional languages appear anxious to unite detail into sentences or to present the sentence immediately as a unit, the inflectional method directly identifies the component of the association of ideas in each case. Moreover, in accordance with its nature it cannot separate in speech its relationship to this association of ideas. Feebleness of the speech-building drive in some cases, as in Chinese, does not allow the inflectional method to react with the phoneme; in other cases, such as in those languages which follow only an incorporative process, it is not permitted to predominate freely. The effect of the pure principle can also be impeded by unilateral deformation; this is the case in Malayan, for example, where an individual structural form, the determination of the verb by modifying prefixes, has become dominant to the point of neglecting all others.

But no matter how different the deviations from the pure principle may be, it will still always be possible to characterize every language according to the lack of referential designations in it, according to the effort to append them and to elevate them to declensions, and according to the expedient of branding as a word what speech ought to represent as a sentence. The nature of such a language will proceed from the mixture of these principles, but as a rule there will develop from their application an even more individualized form. For where the complete energy of the guiding force does not preserve the proper equilibrium, one part of the language readily but improperly attains a disproportionate development ahead of another. From this and other circumstances, striking, individual qualities may also originate in languages in which it is not possible otherwise to recognize the characteristic of being excellently suited for thought. Nobody can deny that the old style Chinese reveals a stirring dignity owing to the fact that important ideas impinge directly upon each other; it reveals a simple grandeur because, by discarding all useless secondary designations, it seems to take recourse in depicting pure thought via language. The actual Malayan tongue is not unjustly praised for its facility of expression and for the simplicity of its associations. The Semitic languages preserve an admirable artistry evinced in the fine distinction they make in the significance of many vowel gradations. Basque possesses in its lexical structure and in its speech associations a special power resulting from the brevity and boldness of its expression. The Delaware Indian tongue and other American Indian dialects combine in a single word a number of ideas for which we would require many words. All these examples, however, only prove that in whatever direction the human intellect proceeds unilaterally, it is always capable of producing something great, something which has a fruitful and stimulating reactive effect upon itself. These individual points do not decide the advantages of languages with respect to each other. The true advantage of a language is only its development from a guiding principle and with a factor of freedom, enabling it to maintain all intellectual capacities of man in a state of lively activity, to serve them as a sufficient vehicle of communication, and, by semantic repleteness and intellectual governing principles which it preserves, to exert always a stimulating effect. In this formal qualitative aptitude reposes everything developed from language that reacts beneficially upon the intellect. This aptitude is like a stream whose waves can propagate with the absolute assurance that the sources and springs by which the stream is fed will never fail. For the intellect hovers over language as over an unfathomable abyss from which it is capable of drawing material in proportion to what has already been exhausted from the source. This formal scale or measurement can be applied to languages only if we attempt to subject them to a general comparative investigation.

CHAPTER SEVENTEEN

The Character of Languages

ALTHOUGH WE HAVE now considered the grammatical and external structure of language, we have not as yet exhausted its nature. The actual and true character of language is based upon something much more subtle, more remote, and less accessible to analysis. There always remains, however, the necessary foundation, principally considered heretofore, in which the more subtle and refined element can take root. To represent this more distinctly, we must glance back for a moment on the general course of development of languages. In the morphological period, nations are occupied more with language itself than with its purpose, that is, than with what they are to designate. They struggle with the expression of ideas. This compulsion, combined with the inspiring stimulation of success, produces and maintains their creative power. Language originates, if a figure of speech may be permitted, in the same way that in physical nature one crystal crystallizes to the next. The structural development proceeds gradually, but according to a law. This initially more intensively prevailing direction upon language, the living product of the intellect, lies in the nature of things; it is revealed, however, in the languages themselves which, the more original they are, the more morphologically wealthy they are. The morphology obviously has some excess over and above the needs of the idea and therefore is moderated in the transformations which languages of the same family undergo under the influence of more mature intellectual development. When this evolution analogous to crystallization is terminated, the language is in a finished state, so to speak. The instrument is at hand, and it merely falls to the intellect to use it and to become immersed in it. This occurs in fact; and the language attains color and character by the varying manner in which the intellect expresses itself through speech.

We would be very much in error to presume the same distinction in nature that I have intentionally made here for the sake of clarity. The continuous operation of the intellect exerts in its usage a definite and persisting effect. Only it is more subtle, and occasionally at first glance it escapes notice. Also no period in the history of the human race or of a people can be considered exclusively and intentionally as one of linguistic development. Language is forged by speaking, and speech is the expression of an idea or of a sensation. The thinking and sensations of a people, through which, as I have just stated, its language achieves color and character, react upon it from its earliest beginnings. Conversely, it is certain that the further a language advances in its grammatical structure, the fewer become the cases requiring a new decision. Hence, the struggle with the ideological expressions becomes weaker; and the more the intellect exploits what has already been created, the more its creative drive, and hence its creative power, languishes. On the other hand, the mass of material phonemically produced grows. The latter, moreover, reacting upon the intellect and by virtue of its peculiar principles, impedes the free and independent effectiveness of the intellect. In these two points lies what in the distinctions mentioned above pertains not to the subjective conviction but to the actual essence of the matter. Still, in order to pursue the interweaving of the intellect with language more precisely, we must distinguish the grammatical and lexical structure as the fixed and external attribute of language from its innate character which, similar to a soul, resides in language and produces the effect which every language produces peculiarly upon us as soon as we begin to master it. This does not mean in any way that this effect is foreign to the external structure. The individual life of a language extends through all its fibers and permeates all phonemic elements. Attention should merely be drawn to the fact that the external realm of morphology is not the only area which the comparative linguist needs to investigate. Furthermore, he must realize that there is something lofty and primitive in language beyond the limits of recognition which remains to be divined. What has been said here can be attested by simple examples in languages that derive from a widely disseminated and highly ramified family. The organization of the lexical structure and word order in Sanskrit, Greek, and Latin is very similar and in many respects identical. However, everyone senses the difference in the individual nature of this organization; this is not simply a difference in the character but one which, having penetrated deep into the language itself, determines its actual structure. Therefore, I shall dwell upon this distinction between the principle from which the structure of the language develops and its actual character. Moreover, I flatter myself in the certainty that you will not consider this distinction as being too sharp, and that it will not be mistakenly interpreted as being merely subjective.

To consider the character of languages more exactly, insofar as we compare it with their organization, we must scrutinize the state of their structural perfection. The joyous wonderment derived from seeing language itself as an ever new production gradually diminishes. The activity of the nation is transferred more to its use, and the latter embarks with the peculiar spirit of the populace upon a career in which neither party can claim independence from the other, but in which each takes pleasure in the enthusiastic aid of the other. The admiration and pleasure now turn toward individual items felicitously expressed. Poems and songs, prayers, proverbs, and stories excite the ardent desire to preserve them from the transitoriness of fleeting conversation. They are preserved, changed, and imitated. They become the foundation of literature. This culture of the intellect and of the language proceeds gradually from the totality of the nation to individuals, and the language falls into the hands of poets and teachers to whom, little by little, the populace turns. As a result, the language achieves a twofold configuration from which two mutually supportive springs, power and purity, arise as long as this contrast maintains its proper proportions.

In addition to these structuralists, who are actively engaged in constructing the language by their efforts there are the actual grammarians who put the final touches on the perfection of the organization. It is not their business to create. It is impossible for them through their own efforts to popularize inflection or loss of initial or final phonemes in a language where these features are absent. However, they do eliminate, generalize, regularize, and fill out residual gaps. By their efforts the scheme of the conjugations and declensions in inflected languages can be justly derived, because they first compile the totality of the cases concerned and bring them to our view. In this area they exercise a regulative power, because they draw upon the infinite treasures presented by the language being perused. Since they actually first introduce the concept of such schemata into our consciousness, forms which have really lost all significance may again become meaningful merely by the position they occupy in the scheme. Such treatments of one and the same language may follow each other in different epochs. In all cases, however, if the language is to remain simultaneously popular and cultured, the uniformity of its flow from the populace to the writers and grammarians and from the latter back to the populace must proceed without interruption.

As long as the vital spirit of the people continues to react upon itself and upon its language, the latter becomes refined and enriched, and these characteristics in turn exert a stimulative effect upon the intellect. However, in the course of time, an epoch may arise in which the language outgrows the spirit or intellect, so to speak. In this state of sluggish relaxation, the language ceases to be self-creative and begins to carry on an increasingly empty sport with turns of phrases and forms which derived from truly intellectual usage. This is, then, a second debilitation of language, if the decline of its external structural drive is considered to be the first. At the second stage, the bloom of its character fades, but languages and nations may be aroused from this state and raised culturally by the genius of individual men of greatness.

Language develops its character especially in its literary periods and in the preparatory phase that culminates in them. For it then withdraws more from the mundaneness of material life and becomes elevated to pure conceptual development and free representation. It seems strange, however, that languages, with the exception of that factor imparted to them by their external organization, should be capable of possessing a peculiar character, since each is designed to serve as an implement for the most varied individualities. Without considering differences of sex and age, we can say that a nation probably includes all the nuances of human idiosyncracies. Even those individuals who start from the same point and who pursue the same occupation differ in their manner of comprehension and in the way they are reacted upon. This difference is even greater for language inasmuch as it enters into the most secret recesses of the mind and emotions. Everyone uses language for the expression of his particular idiosyncrasy, for it always proceeds from the individual and everyone utilizes it for himself alone. Nonetheless, it suffices for everyone insofar as words, though inadequate, still satisfy the urge to express one's innermost feelings. It cannot be claimed that language as a universal vehicle will equilibrate these differences. It probably does build bridges from one individual to another and mediates mutual understanding; on the other hand, it rather enlarges the difference, since by its elucidation, distinction, and refinement of ideas it makes us more clearly conscious of how it takes root in the original intellectual foundation. The possibility of a language serving such varied individualities as a medium of expression appears therefore to presume in language a complete lack of character. This, however, is not at all true. Language comprehends in fact the two contrasting properties: namely, it is divided up into an infinity as the sole language in one and the same nation; and at the same time these many variants are united into one language having a definite character which distinguishes it from the tongues of other nations. One notes how differently each individual absorbs and uses the same mother tongue, if everyday life does not reveal this distinctly to begin with, in the comparison of significant writers, each of whom creates his own language. The variation in the character of several languages becomes apparent at first glance, for example, in a comparison of Sanskrit, Greek, and Latin.

If we now investigate more exactly how language unites these two antithetical factors, we see that the possibility of serving the most differing individualities as a vehicle reposes in the innermost essence of its nature. Its element, the word, which we may retain for the sake of simplicity, does not impart as a substance something already produced, nor does it contain an already closed concept; it merely stimulates construction of these through independent power and in a definite way. Humans do not understand each other by the fact that they abandon themselves to symbols, nor by the fact that they determine to produce exactly and completely the same idea. Rather, they contact in each other the same link in the chain of their mental concepts and innate conceptual products; that is, they strike the same key of their intellectual instrument, whereupon in each individual corresponding ideas are triggered, although they are not the same. Only within these limitations and with these divergences do they zero in on the same word. In naming the most common object, a horse for example, all humans mean the same animal, but each person relegates a different concept to the word, more imaginary, more rational, or more animate than a physical object, or perhaps more inanimate. Thus, in the period of linguistic structure in some languages, a mass of expressions may originate for the same object. They indicate the many properties by which it was conceived and which were substituted for the object itself. Now, if in this way the link in the chain, or the key of the instrument, is touched, the totality vibrates; and that which issues forth from the soul as an idea harmonizes with everything surrounding the individual link. The image evoked variously by the word bears the imprint of the peculiarity of each individual, but it is designated by all of them by the same phoneme.

The individualities present within the same nation are included in the national uniformity, which in turn distinguishes each individual mental quirk from similar ones in other peoples. From this uniformity and from the stimulation native to each particular language originates the character of the language. Every language receives a definite individuality from the nation and reacts in a uniform manner upon it. The national character is supported and intensified by the common dwelling place and by common activities, and, indeed, to a certain degree it is produced by them. Actually, however, the national character is based on the uniformity of disposition, which is generally explained by the common origin of the people. In the common origin also rests the impenetrable secret of the varying association of the body with its intellectual power, an association that constitutes the essence of every human individuality. The only question that may arise is whether there could be any other way of explaining the uniformity of these natural endowments. In no case may language be excluded from this problem, for in it the union of the phoneme with its meaning constitutes a feature that is as inscrutable as that disposition. Concepts can be split up, words can be divided into components, to the extent we are capable of so doing, and still we get no closer to an explanation of the mystery of how ideas are actually combined into words. In their most original and primitive relationship to the essence of individuality, therefore, all nationalities and languages are directly equivalent to each other. However, language reacts more obviously and more intensively upon individuality, and the concept of a nation must be based especially upon language. Since the development of man's human nature depends upon the nature of language, the concept of the nation as a host of people constructing a language in a definite manner is directly manifest through language.

Language also possesses the power of alienating and incorporating, and by its own force it proclaims the national character, even in the case of varying origin. This fact distinguishes a family from a nation. In a family there is a truly recognizable relationship among its members, and the same family may flourish in two different nations. In the case of nations it may be dubious—and in widely disseminated races this is an important consideration—whether all those speaking the same languages are of common origin, or whether this uniformity has originated from a primordial natural endowment, combined with propagation over the same territorial area under the influence of uniformly operating causes. Regardless of what connection the development of languages may have with these causes beyond our power of investigation, it is still certain that the development of language first conveys national differences into the sphere of the intellect. By this development these national differences are brought to our consciousness, and from it they receive objects [words], more accessible to clear insight, through which they must find expression, and in which at the same time the differences themselves appear spun out in a finer and more definite manner. Owing to the fact that language intellectualizes man to the point attainable by him, he is withdrawn increasingly from the obscure region of undeveloped perception. As a result languages themselves, which are the tools of this development, obtain such a definite character that that of the nation can be better recognized in it than in the manners, customs, and deeds of the nation. This is the reason why peoples lacking a literature and whose speech usage we do not investigate with sufficient thoroughness often appear more uniform to us than they really are. We do not recognize these distinguishing traits because they are not conveyed to our mind by the medium which would make them evident to us.

If the character of languages is separated from the external form, in terms of which alone a given language can be conceived, and if both are compared, the character is found to consist in the manner in which the concept is combined with the phonemes. Taken in this sense, the character is, so to speak, the spirit which makes itself indigenous in the language and which animates it as if the language were a body produced from it. The character is a natural consequence of the protracted effect of the intellectual peculiarity of the nation. Because the latter always picks up the general meanings of words in the same individual way and accompanies them with the same collateral ideas and emotions, and because it produces ideological combinations along the same lines while using the freedom of syntax in the same relationships, in which the measure of its intellectual boldness relates to the capacity of its comprehension, it imparts a peculiar coloration and shading to language which fixes these peculiarities and thus reacts along the same track. From every language, therefore, conclusions can be drawn with respect to the national character. Even the languages of rude and uncultured peoples bear these traces and thereby often permit us to glance into the intellectual idiosyncracies which ought not to be expected at this level of deficient culture. The languages of the indigenous American tribes are rich in examples of this type; we find them in bold metaphors, in correct but unexpected combinations of ideas, in cases where inanimate objects are transposed by genial phantasy into the realm of animate beings, and so forth. Although these languages do not pay attention to the difference in gender, they do consider to a very extensive degree the distinction between living and lifeless objects, and their viewpoint in this case proceeds from grammatical treatment. When they group constellations, men, and animals together grammatically in the same class, it is obvious that they regard the former as independently moving beings endowed with personality and also apparently guiding human destiny from above. In this respect it is a pleasure leading to the most varied considerations to go through the dictionaries of the dialects of such peoples. Moreover, if we consider that the attempts at persevering analysis of the forms in such languages, which are evident in the foregoing, permit disclosure of their intellectual organization from which their structure originates, all dryness vanishes from linguistic study. In each of its components, the study of languages leads back to the innate intellectual configuration which throughout all the ages of man has been the bearer of the most profound viewpoints, the greatest wealth of ideas, and the noblest emotions.

In those cases where the characteristics of a people's peculiarity can be found only in the individual elements of its language, only rarely or never can a continuous and coherent image of that peculiarity be outlined. This is a difficult business at best and becomes truly possible only where nations have put down in a more or less extensive literature their opinion of the universe and have imprinted it on their language in connected discourse. For with reference to the validity of the individual elements of their speech and to the subtleties of its combinations, which cannot be entirely traced back to grammatical rules, discourse contains an enormous amount of material which can no longer be distinguished clearly when it is broken down into these elements. A word for the most part attains its full validity only in the combination in which it appears. This branch of linguistics therefore requires an exact critical treatment of the literary monuments present in a language, and masterfully prepared material is found in the philological treatments of the Greek and Latin writers. For even if the study of the whole language is the ultimate objective, we must start first from the literary monuments preserved in the language, attempting to edit and preserve them with maximum purity and fidelity and to use them as reliable sources of knowledge of antiquity. No matter how closely the analysis of language, the research of its relationship to others of the group, and the explanation of its structure by this process must remain bound to the treatment of linguistic monuments, there are two different directions of linguistic study, each of which requires different talents and produces different results. It would perhaps not be incorrect to differentiate in this way between linguistics and philology and to give to the latter the narrow meaning customarily associated with it; in recent years, however— especially in France and England—this term has been extended to include any occupation with any given language. It is certain that linguistic research, at least as discussed here, can be based only on philological treatment of literary monuments within the broad meaning just established. Because great men, who with conscientious faithfulness have glorified this field of scholarship in recent centuries, establish the linguistic usage of every writer down to the most minute phonemic modifications, language is revealed to be continuously under the dominant influence of intellectual individuality. Furthermore, it becomes possible to search out the individual points to which such influence is associated. At the same time we learn what pertains to the epoch, to the locality, and to the individual, and how the general language comprehends all these differences. Recognition of details, however, is always accompanied by the impression of a whole, without the phenomenon losing something of its peculiarity by analysis.

Not only does the original foundation of national peculiarity clearly react upon language, but every change of its innate direction occurring in time, every external event which elevates or suppresses the soul and the intellectual sweep of the nation, and above all the impulse imparted by its outstanding mentalities do also. As an eternal intermediary between the intellect and nature, language becomes reconstituted in accordance with every gradation of the intellect; however, traces thereof become ever more subtle and more difficult to discern in detail, and the factual state is revealed only in the total impression. No nation could animate and fructify the language of another with the spirit and intellect native to it without reconstructing it into a different one. What has already been observed relative to all individuality holds here also. Although among various languages each individual one, because it follows a uniquely defined course, excludes all others, several may still coincide in a common objective. Therefore, the character difference of languages need not necessarily consist in absolute advantages of the one over the other. Insight into the possibility of forming such a character requires a still more precise consideration of the way in which a nation must inherently treat its language in order to impress upon it such a cast of features.

If a language were used simply and exclusively for the everyday needs of life, its words would merely serve as representative symbols of the resolve or desire to be expressed. Under such conditions, there could no longer be any question of an inherent conception or interpretation permitting the possibility of variety. The material thing or action would in the imagination of both the speaker and his protagonist immediately and directly replace the word. Fortunately, such a language cannot exist among humans who continue to think and to perceive. With such an assumed language, one could only compare the language admixtures that would result from the association of peoples of quite different nations and the dialects that would arise here and there, especially in seaports, such as the lingua franca of the Mediterranean coasts. In addition, the individual viewpoint and emotion always maintain their rights. Indeed, it is very probable that the first use of language, were it possible to retrace development to that point, was a mere expression of sensation. I have already expressed myself against the explanation that language originated from the helplessness of the individual (see p. 40). Not even the urge or drive toward gregarious association originates from helplessness. The most powerful beast, the elephant, is at the same time the most social or gregarious. Everywhere in nature, life and activity develop from innate freedom, whose primordial source is vainly sought in the area of phenomena. However, in every language, even in the most highly cultured, the usage here mentioned occurs in isolated instances. Whosoever orders a tree to be felled thinks of nothing when using the word except the trunk designated; it is quite different, however, when this item, even without adjective and additional elucidation, appears in a portrayal of nature or in a poem. The variation of the conceptual mode imparts to the same phonemes a value varyingly enhanced, and it is as if in every expression something not absolutely determined by it spills over.

This distinction is obviously dependent on whether the language is used with reference to the inner totality of the thought association and sensation, or whether it is employed unilaterally for an isolated spiritual activity with a conclusive purpose. From this approach, it is even more intensively restricted by mere scientific use, if the latter is not subject to the guiding influence of higher ideas, than it is by the mundane requirements of life, since in the latter both perception and passion are admixed. Neither in its ideas nor in language itself does anything exist in isolation. Associations, however, only increase to the status of ideas when the spirit is active as an inherent unit, when complete subjectivity is joined by complete objectivity. Then no aspect to which the object may react is neglected, and each of these reactions leaves behind a slight trace in the language. When in the soul the emotion is truly awakened, language is not merely a medium of exchange for mutual understanding but is a true realm which the intellect places between itself and the objects via the internal operation of its power; in this case, language is upon the road to incorporating increasingly more in it.

Where such an interaction of the language, which is confined to definite phonemes, and of the innate conception, which is expanding continually according to its nature, is alive, the intellect considers the language not as a closed entity but as engaged in eternal creation, striving incessantly to add new material which, incorporated in it, in turn reacts upon it. This presumes two things: a feeling that there is something which the language does not directly contain but which the intellect, excited by language, must complement; and the drive, in turn, to associate everything that the soul perceives with the phoneme. Both spring from the conviction that the essence of human premonition governs an area which transcends language but which is actually restricted by language. However, human premonition is cognizant of being the sole medium for researching and fructifying this region, and it is cognizant also that by technical and intellectual perfection it is capable of transforming an ever greater part thereof for its own advantage. This attitude is the basis of character expression in languages. The more this attitude moves in the twofold direction, that is, toward the perceptible form of language and toward the profundity of the mind, the more clearly does the peculiarity in language become evident. It gains, so to speak, in transparency and permits us to gaze into the inner recesses of the speaker.

Thus, that which becomes apparent through language in this manner cannot be something isolated, objective, and qualitatively indicative. For every language would be able to indicate everything if the people to which it belongs had traversed all stages of its culture. Each language has a portion which is either still concealed or, if it has perished earlier, remains eternally hidden. Each is, as man himself, an infinite quantum gradually developing in time. Every radiant factor is therefore something that modifies all indications subjectively and, even more so, quantitatively. This factor appears in language not as an effect, but as the effective force which is expressed directly as such; therefore, in an inherent manner difficult to recognize, it appears to encompass the effects with its breath, so to speak. Man always compares himself to the universe in unity. He always conceives and treats objects in the same way and according to the same goal and the same scale of motion. Upon this unity is based his individuality. In this unity repose two properties, although they are mutually determinative; these are the property of the effective force and that of its activity as in the corporeal universe the moving body is distinguished from the impulse which determines the intensity, velocity, and duration of its motion. We have the first in mind when we ascribe to a nation more virile plasticity, more creative imagination, more inclination toward abstract ideas, or a more definite practical direction; we have the latter in mind when we describe a nation as more intense, variable, and rapid in its ideological trend and more persistent in its perception than others. In both, therefore, we distinguish being from action and oppose the former, as the invisible cause, to the thinking, perception, and action which become manifest. However, in this case I am not referring to this or that isolated existence of the individual, but to the general existence that appears determinatively in every single one. Every exhaustive character portrayal must keep this existence in view as the end point of its research.

Now, if we pursue the total internal and external activity of man to its simplest terminal points, we discover it in the way he relates to reality as an object he picks up or as material which he molds, or even how he plots courses for himself independently thereof. How deeply and in what way man becomes rooted in reality is the original characteristic mark of his individuality. The various types of the foregoing association may be innumerable, depending upon whether man attempts to separate the reality and the mentality, neither of which is capable of getting along entirely without the other, or whether he combines them in various degrees and directions.

Such a scale is applicable not merely to nations already intellectually cultured. In the expressions of joy of a troup of savages we will be able to learn whether such cries represent mere satisfaction of sensual appetites or lust, or whether they are a divine spark of truly human sensation which will at some time glow in song and poetry. If the character of a nation is revealed by everything truly peculiar to it, which we cannot doubt, it is especially apparent in its language. Because it becomes fused with all the expressions of the spirit, it brings back more often the ever constant individual features. And because it is associated with individuality by such tender and intimate bonds, it must repeatedly fasten the very same bonds to the mind and spirit of the auditor in order to be completely understood. The entire individuality of the speaker is therefore transferred to the other, not to displace his own but to construct from the foreign one and his own a new, fruitful contrast.

The distinction between the material which the soul absorbs and produces, and the power motivating and attuning this twofold activity—that is, the distinction between the effect and the effective being, or the correct and relative evaluation of both and the more or less clear presence of what is uppermost in our consciousness—does not pervade every national peculiarity equally. If the reason for this difference is investigated more profoundly, it is found to lie in the more or less clearly perceived necessity of the association between all ideas and sensations of the individual throughout his entire existence and of a similar association divined and required in nature. This is but a fraction of what the soul is capable of bringing forth. Moreover, the more motile and vigorous its activity, the more everything related in various gradations to the product produced is stimulated. Thus, above and beyond the individual detail, there is always an excess to be expressed less definitely; or, rather, to the detail is appended the requirement for further presentation and development which is not directly present in it. Hence the requirement proceeds through an expression in the language into another expression which is, let us say, invited to complement in its concept the given factor with the lacking one. Where the sense for this process is alive, the language appears deficient and insufficient for complete expression since, in the opposite case, the premonition scarcely arises that something over and beyond what has been given could be lacking. Between these two extremes is found an innumerable quantity of intermediate stages. The prevailing direction of these is either toward the intimacy of the mind or toward external reality.

The Greeks furnish the most instructive example in this entire area. Under song they combined in their poetry in general, but particularly in their lyric poetry, instrumental music, dance rhythms, and dramatic gestures. That they did not do this merely to augment and multiply the sensual effect is clearly evident from the fact that they imparted an additional, uniform character to all of these individual operations or actions. Music, terpsichorean art, and dialectal speech had to be subjected to one and the same original, national peculiarity, that is, Doric or Aeolic, or they had to be of a different tonality and in a different dialect. In this way, they sought out the motivating and modulating factors in the soul in order to maintain the ideas in the song in a given direction and to animate and intensify them by the stimulus of their dispositions, which is not valid as an idea. In poetry and song, the words and ideological content predominate, and the accompanying mood and emotion are secondary. In music it is just the opposite. The mind is stimulated with enthusiasm to produce ideas, perceptions, and actions. These must proceed freely from the heart of this inspiration, and the musical tones simply determine them to the extent that only certain ones can develop in the directions in which they guide the stimulation. Since the power which includes all activity of the soul can only be a definite one, and since it can operate only in such a direction, the feeling of motivation and modulation in the mind is always necessary; this is evident in the case of the Greeks in a feeling of existing or required individuality.

Hence, when I was speaking in the foregoing exposition of something beyond the expression, and lacking in it moreover, I did not imply something indeterminate. It is rather the most highly determined factor of all because it completes and perfects the final traits of individuality; the word, owing to its dependence on the object and the general validity required of it, becomes ever less individualized and is incapable of doing this alone. Therefore, if an emotion presumes a more inherent mood, not restricted to reality, it does not revert for this reason from a lively and vivid notion to remote and abstract cogitation. Rather, as it emanates from its own individuality, it awakens the demand of the highest individualization of the object, which is attainable only by the penetration of the sensory conception into all details and by the maximum vividness of presentation. Once again, this is shown by the Greeks. Their thought proceeded especially toward what things are and how they appear, not unilaterally toward the use to which they could be put in the realm of reality. Its direction was therefore originally internal and intellectual.

Their entire private and public life confirms this, since everything in it was treated in part ethically and in part artistically. Moreover, for the most part the ethical factor was interwoven into their art. Thus, in the case of the Greeks, almost every external configuration reminds us of an internal one, often at great risk and even at real disadvantage to its practical value. For this reason, they terminated all their intellectual activities in the concept and representation of character, always with the feeling, however, that only complete penetration into perception permitted recognition and delineation of character, and that the totality thereof may originate only from a correct association of details, regulated by a tactful effort toward the foregoing unity. This makes their earlier poetry, especially the Homeric verse, so thoroughly plastic. Nature as it is—even the most diminutive action such as the gradual donning of armor—is brought before our eyes; from the depiction, the character of the action always proceeds without ever being reduced to a mere narration of events. This is effected not only by the choice of the material portrayed but by the fact that the tremendous power of the poet, endowed with the feeling of individuality and striving toward individualization, pervades his poetry and is imparted to the listener. By virtue of this intellectual peculiarity, the Greeks were led into the entire living multiplicity of the material world, and from the latter, since they were seeking something in it that can pertain only to the realm of ideas, they were forced back to intellectuality. For their target was always character, not simply the characteristic, and the divination of the former is completely different from pursuit of the latter. Their thought, directed toward true, individual character, then immediately proceeded to the idealistic, since the collaboration of individualities at the most elevated stage of conception leads to the effort to annihilate the individual factor as a limitation and to maintain only a tacit outline of definite form. From this arose the perfection of Greek art— the organic imitation of nature in every instance, succeeding, moreover, as a result of the artist's striving for the highest union of the ideal and inspired by a most complete view of reality.

In the historical development of the Greek race, there was something that especially stimulated them to develop and cultivate the characteristic element. This was the division of various ethnic groups into individual dialectic and psychological groups, together with the many migrations and the inherent motility that resulted in the geographical mixing of peoples. All were included homogeneously in the general Hellenic group, and Hellenism placed its peculiar imprint on every tribe and on the activities of each individual; it was evident, for example, in the constitution of the state as well as in the pitch of the flute player. Historically, there was associated to the foregoing the additional favorable circumstance that none of these clans suppressed the others; rather, all flourished in a certain equality of effort. None of the individual dialects of the language became reduced to a mere vernacular, and none became elevated to a general prestige dialect. Furthermore, this equal growth of individuality was strongest and most decisive in the period of the most vigorous and powerful formation of the language and the nation. Owing to the foregoing factors, the Greek mind, trained in every respect toward achieving the highest attainable from the most individual factors, produced something that is not discernible to a like degree in any other people. The Greek mind treated these original ethnic peculiarities as categories of art and in this way introduced them into architecture, music, and poetry, and into the more elegant use of language.[1] The mere popular character was removed from these categories; phonemes and morphemes were purified in the dialects and subjected to feeling for beauty and harmony. Thus ennobled, the phonemes and morphemes became elevated to the point of possessing a personal character of style and poetry, and they became capable of collaborating in their mutually complementary antitheses. I scarcely need to mention that here, insofar as poetry and the dialects are concerned, I am speaking only of the use of various pitches and dialects in lyric poetry and of the distinction between the choruses and the dialogue in Greek tragedy, and not of those instances in Greek comedy where various dialects are spoken by the protagonists and actors. The latter cases have nothing at all in common with the former and are encountered probably more or less in the literatures of all peoples.

Among the Romans, though their peculiarity as a nation is also represented in their language and literature, there is revealed much less the feeling for the necessity of providing to the expressions of their mind the direct influence of its motivating and attenuating force. Their perfection and greatness were developed in another, more homogeneous way—by the imprint which they made upon their external destinies. In contrast, this emotion is perhaps not less intensively pronounced in the German mentality than it is in the case of the Greeks, but the latter were more inclined toward individualizing external contemplation, while we, the Germans, tend more toward individualizing intimate sensations.

I have the feeling that everything being produced in the mind, as the efflux of a single power, constitutes a great totality. Moreover, I believe that the individual detail, as the breath of the foregoing power, must bear characteristics of its relationship with this totality, which up to now has been observed more in its influence upon the individual utterances. This totality does not, however, exert a less significant reaction upon the manner in which the power mentioned, as a primary cause of all intellectual productions, attains consciousness of itself. The image of this original power may appear to the human being only as a striving along a definite course. However, this presumes a goal, which can be nothing but a human ideal. In this mirror, we catch sight of the manner in which nations view themselves. Now, the first proof of their higher intellectuality and of their more profoundly penetrating internal nature is evident when they do not enclose this ideal within the limits of suitability for definite purposes, but regard this factor as something whose purpose can be sought only in its own perfection, as a gradual flowering to a never-ending development, whence inner freedom and versatility arise. However, even if we assume this initial condition in all its purity, varying phenomena originate from the differences in the individual direction of the sensual attitude, the innate perception, and the abstract thought. In each of the foregoing, the human, ambient world, perceived by man from a different vantage point, is reflected by him in a different form. Just to pick out one such trait, everything in external nature produces simultaneously a continuous series of images for the eye, following one upon the other in the unravelling of the circumstances from one another. This is just as true in the plastic arts. In the case of the Greeks, to whom was bestowed the ability of always drawing the fullest and tenderest meaning from external, sensual perception, perhaps their most characteristic trait, insofar as their intellectual activity is concerned, was their reserve and reticence with respect to all excessiveness and exaggeration. In other words, with all of their alert activity and the freedom of their imaginative power, with all of their apparent unrestraint of sentiment, with all of their variability of mental attitudes, and with all of their flexibility in proceeding from one resolve to another—in short, with everything which took form in them, it was their innate inclination to remain always within the bounds of moderation and harmony. They possessed, to a higher degree than any other people, tact and taste. Moreover, these qualities, manifest in all their works, are further emphasized by the fact that injury to the tenderness of feeling is never avoided at the cost of its intensity or with respect to natural truths. Inner perception permits, even without deviating from the proper course, sharper contrasts, more abrupt transitions, and the splitting of moods into chasms which cannot be bridged. All these phenomena, therefore—and this already begins with the Romans—are manifest in the younger cultures.

The variation of intellectual peculiarity is of immeasurable extent and of unfathomable depth. The course of the present observations did not permit me to leave it entirely untouched. It may appear, however, that I have sought the character of nations too greatly in the intimate humor of the mind, particularly since it is revealed more vividly and manifestly in reality. It is pronounced, if language and its products are excepted, in physiognomy, body structure, dress, customs, domestic and civilian behavioral patterns, and, above all, in the stamp which peoples over several centuries impress upon their products and deeds. This living image appears to be transformed into a shadow if the character pattern is sought in the state of mind forming the basis for these virile expressions. To show its effect on the language, however, it did not seem possible to the author to avoid this method. Language cannot be brought directly into connection with the foregoing factual expressions everywhere. The medium in which these two factors meet and, originating from a single source, pursue their differing paths must be found. This is obviously accomplished in the innermost recesses of the mind.

Just as difficult as delimiting intellectual individuality is finding an explanation of how it takes root in languages, and how character is associated with languages and in which of its parts it can be recognized. The intellectual peculiarity of nations, because nations make use of languages, becomes visible in all stages of the existence of languages. The influence of nations modifies the languages of various races, several of the same race, dialects of a single language, and indeed the same externally constant dialect in accordance with the differences in eras and in writers. The character of the language then becomes admixed with that of its style, but the character always remains peculiar to the language, since only certain types of style are easy and natural to each tongue. If a distinction is made between the cases noted here, as to whether the phonemes are different in the words and inflected forms, as can be shown in the descending degrees of the languages of various origin down to the dialects, or whether the influence lies only in the usage of words and combinations, since the external form stays completely or essentially the same, then in the latter case the effect of the intellect is more obvious, but more refined, since the language in this instance must have arrived at a high, intellectual state of development. In the former case it is more powerful but less obvious, since the relationship of the phonemes to the intellect can be recognized and described definitely and clearly only in few cases. Yet, even in dialects, minor modifications of individual vowels, producing but little change in the language as a whole, may be justifiably related to the mental reaction patterns of the people, as indeed the Greek grammarians observed of the masculine Doric *a* in contrast to the more effeminate Ionic *ae* (η).

We must consign the languages of various ethnic groups which cannot e derived from each other to the period of original linguistic structure. At hat point in time there prevails too strong an effort to construct language s an intellectual product, the creation of its own technology, as it were, lastically present to one's own consciousness and comprehensible to the istener, in order to avoid obscuring to some extent the effect of the ntellectual attitude of the individual which permeates later usage more almly and clearly. But the original disposition of the people certainly vorks toward this goal most powerfully and influentially. That becomes vident to us immediately at two points, which determine many others imultaneously since they characterize the total intellectual disposition. he various methods mentioned above by which languages connect lauses constitute the most important component of their technique. It is recisely in this factor that the clarity of the logical arrangement is nitially revealed. This arrangement alone accords a secure basis to the reedom of flow of thought and, at the same time, furnishes principles and xtension of intellectuality; it also brings to light the more or less apparent eed for sensual wealth and harmony, as well as the requirement of the nind to express externally what is inherently perceived and felt. How-ver, there certainly must rest in this technical format of languages proof f other and more special intellectual individualities of nations, even if hey can be less surely derived from them. Should not, for example, the ne distinction between numerous vocalic modifications and vowel ositions and the meaningful use thereof, combined with the restriction of his process and the disinclination toward compounding, betray and romote a preponderance of sagacious and subtle reason among the eoples of the Semitic race, particularly the Arabs? To be sure, the realth of imagery in the Arabic language seems to contradict the fore-oing. However, if it does not in itself represent a subtle division of ideas, would say that this wealth of imagery reposes in the words once coined.)n the other hand, the language itself, compared in this respect to anskrit and Greek, contains a far smaller stock of media permitting terature of every kind to flow forth from it continuously. It seems certain o me at least that the stage of a language in which it, as a faithful picture f such a period, contains many poetically constituted elements must be istinguished from that stage in which indestructible seeds of eternally prouting poetry are implanted into its phonemes, morphemes, free ombinations, and close-knit phrases. In the former, the form once coined bates little by little, and its poetic content is no longer felt to be inspira-onal. In the latter, the poetical form of the language is continually able o appropriate to itself new and fresh material which is produced in ccordance with the intellectual culture of the age and the genius of its

poets. We can also verify here what was said previously about the inflectional system. The true advantage of a language consists in attuning the
intellect, in accordance with the complete sequence of its development
and its individual capacities, to a disciplined activity; or, to express i
from the approach of intellectual effect, the advantage consists of the
language bearing within itself the stamp of such a pure, principled, anc
vigorous energy.

However, even where the morphological system of several languages is
identical on the whole, as in Sanskrit, Greek, Latin, and German
in all of which inflection, produced rarely by vowel change and more
generally by affixation, prevails, there may exist important differences ir
the application of this system owing to intellectual peculiarity. One of the
most important differences is the more or less visible predominance of
correct and complete grammatical concepts and the distribution of the
various phonetic forms among them. Depending directly on whether this
factor becomes dominant among a people in the more elevated treatment
of its language, attention turns from the perceptible plentitude of
phonemes and the multiplicity of forms to the fineness of their usage. This
can, therefore, be found in the same language at various times. Such a
meticulous relationship of morphological material to grammatical concepts is consistently revealed by Greek; and if consideration is accorded
to the difference between a few of its dialects, it betrays at the same time
a tendency to rid itself of the voluptuous phonemic repleteness of the overly
sonorous forms, to contract them or to replace them by shorter ones. The
youthful surge of development in the physical aspect of the language is
concentrated more upon its suitability for intimate ideological expression
Time contributes to this factor in two ways: on the one hand the intellec
in its progressive development inclines ever more toward mental activity
and on the other hand the language suffers phonetic decay in the course
of its use and becomes simplified where intellectual peculiarity does no
preserve intact all the originally significant phonemes. In Greek, as
compared to Sanskrit, the latter direction is already evident, but not to
the degree that an adequate explanation could be found in this fact
alone. If in the Greek morphological usage there lies in fact a more highly
matured intellectual tendency, which seems to me to be the case, it
originates in truth from the innate sense of the nation for rapid, delicate
and clear development of ideas. Higher German culture, in contrast
found our [German] language already at a point where significant phonemes were wearing away, so in our case a lesser inclination to sensory clarity
and a greater retreat toward perception certainly may have had their
basis in these facts too. In the Latin language a very luxuriant phonemic

plentitude and a great freedom of phantasy were never expended on its morphology. The more masculine and serious sense of the people, directed much more toward material reality and the directly valid intellectual component in it, probably did not allow such an exuberant and free phonemic growth. Greater facility, flexibility, and a more pleasing grace in comparison to the remaining members of the group can probably be ascribed to Greek grammatical forms as a consequence of the great mobility of Greek phantasy and the tenderness of their aesthetic sense.

The extent to which nations make use of the technical media in their languages also differs in accordance with their varying intellectual peculiarity. I remind the reader here merely of the structure of compound words. Sanskrit exploits this factor within the broadest limits which a language can allow itself, whereas the Greeks do so to a much more limited extent determined by the difference in dialect and style. In Roman literature, compounding is found especially among the older writers and is excluded more from the progressive culture of the language.

The varying philosophy of a people contained in the value of its words is found only upon more exact reflection, but it then appears distinctly. In the foregoing (see pp. 130, 134, 135), I have expounded the fact that any word is not easily accepted into their conceptual patterns by various individuals in the same way, unless it is merely used at a given moment as a material sign of its idea. It may therefore be quite definitely stated that in each word there reposes something not again to be distinguished by words, and that the words of numerous languages, even if they designate the same ideas on the whole, are never true synonyms. Strictly speaking, one definition cannot include them, and often it is possible only to indicate more or less the position they occupy in the area to which they belong. I have also mentioned in what way this is the case even for the designation of corporeal objects. The true area of differing lexical validity, however, is the designation of intellectual concepts. Here a word rarely expresses the same idea as that of another language, in spite of the fact that evident distinctions are lacking. Where we do not have any idea of the finer shades of meaning of words in the languages of rude and uncultured peoples, the opposite appears to be true. However, attention directed toward other, more highly cultured languages prevents us from taking such a premature viewpoint. Furthermore, a fruitful comparison of the expressions pertaining to the same category, drawn from a synonymic dictionary of several languages, could be profitably compiled. For nations of great intellectual activity, this validity, if pursued to its finest gradations, remains in a state of uninterrupted flux. In every era, every independent writer involuntarily adds material or modifies existing vocabulary, since he cannot avoid qualifying his language with his individuality, and the language in turn conveys a different necessity of expression back to him. In these cases it will be informative to undertake a double comparison, namely one relative to the words used in several languages for a concept identical on the whole, and another one relative to those of the same language which belong to the same category. In the latter comparison is delineated the intellectual peculiarity in its unity and uniformity; that which becomes admixed with objective concepts is always the same. In the former comparison we recognize how the same concept, for example that of the soul, is conceived from different approaches, and, as a result of this historical comparison, we become acquainted with the scope of human conceptual patterns. These patterns may be expanded by individual languages and, indeed, by individual writers. In both cases the result arises partially from the variously stressed and collaborative intellectual activity, and partially from the multifarious associations into which the intellect (in which nothing ever exists in isolation) brings the concepts involved. For we are speaking here of the expression that flows forth from the plenitude of intellectual life, not of the configuration imparted to ideas by school which restricts them to their necessary earmarks. From this systematically precise limitation and establishment of concepts and their signs originates the scientific terminology that we find developed in Sanskrit in all epochs of philosophization and in all areas of knowledge; the Hindu intellect, it seems, proceeded especially toward the sifting and enumeration of concepts. The double comparison to which allusion was made above clearly brings out the definite yet subtle separation of the subjective and objective factors. It shows, moreover, how both of these factors always interact with each other, and how the elevation and refinement of the creative force keep pace with the harmonious integration of knowledge.

Erroneous or deficient interpretations of concepts have been excluded from the viewpoint I have developed here. I have been speaking only of the regulated and vigorous pursuit of the expression of ideas and of the conception of same in their reflection in the intellectual individuality, seen from limitless aspects. Naturally, however, hunting up the intellectual peculiarities in language is above all a matter of considering the correct classification of ideas. If, for example, two ideas, though not necessarily this number, are combined and expressed by the same word in a language, a pure expression for each of them alone may at the same time be lacking. Examples are found in several languages in the expressions for "wanting," "wishing," and "becoming." It is scarcely necessary to make special mention at this point of the intellectual influence of the concepts on the type of designation; this influence depends on the degree of their relationship, which produces similarity of sound, and on the metaphors employed.

To a greater extent than is true for individual words, the intellectual differences between nations are distinguished in the speech patterns—in the scope and range these patterns are capable of imparting to clauses and sentences as well as in the multifariousness attainable within these limits. Herein lies the true picture of the course of ideas, with which speech is incapable of truly associating unless the language possesses the appropriate wealth and the inspiring freedom of word order. Everything that the labor of the intellect is per se, according to its form, appears here in the language and in turn reacts upon the inner personality. The gradations here are innumerable, and the detail produced by the interaction cannot always be presented exactly in words. However, the spirit transformed by this interaction hovers as a gentle breath over the whole.

Up to now I have touched upon the individual points relative to the mutual influence of the character of nations and of languages. There are however two phenomena in languages in which all points most definitely coalesce, and in which the effect of the totality is revealed to such an extent that even the concept of the individual vanishes from them. These are poetry and prose. They must be called phenomena of the language, since even the original predisposition of language gives preferential direction to the one or the other; where the form of the language is truly sublime, it allows an equal development of both in accordance with a regular relationship. In fact, however, poetry and prose are primarily developments of intellectuality itself and must, if their basis is not deficient and if their course of evolution suffers no confusion, necessarily originate from it. They require, therefore, the most careful study not only in their relationship to each other but also with respect to their time of origin.

If we consider poetry and prose simultaneously from that aspect within them which is most concrete and ideal, we see that they embark upon differing courses for a similar purpose. Both move from reality to something not belonging to it. Poetry conceives of reality in its sensual aspect, as it is perceived internally and externally, but it is unconcerned with that feature which makes it reality and intentionally rejects its character. It then combines the sensual aspect with its imaginative power and proceeds to the contemplation of an artistic and idealistic whole. Prose seeks in reality the roots which nourish it and the threads of its connections with existence. Prose thereupon intellectually associates fact with fact and concept with concept, striving toward an objective connection in an idea. The difference between poetry and prose as depicted here lies in the way that each finds expression in the intellect according to its true nature. If we simply look at the possible phenomenon in the language, and even here only at a simple aspect of the language, highly powerful combination but alone an almost unimportant aspect, then the inner prosaic direction can be executed in poetic discourse and the poetic direction in prosaic discourse. For the most part, however, this may be achieved only at the expense of both, with the result that poetically expressed prose material evinces neither the character of prose nor that of poetry. The same is true of poetry clothed in a prose format. Poetic content forcibly engenders poetic raiment, and there is no lack of examples which reveal that writers under the feeling of this power have concluded in verse works begun in prose. To return to their true nature, the tension and the scope of the spiritual forces, which the combination of the complete penetration of reality and the attainment of an ideal association of infinite variety requires, and the focusing of the mind upon the consistent pursuit of a given course are common to both. Yet this course must in turn be so conceived that the pursuit of the opposite course in the intellect of the nation is not excluded but promoted by it. The poetic and prose dispositions must complement each other to produce a common factor, namely the establishment by man of strong and deep roots in reality; in turn, these roots will allow man to ascend into a freer element. The poesy of a people has not reached its highest peak unless in its versatility and in the unfettered suppleness of its ardor it proclaims the possibility of a corresponding development in prose. Inasmuch as the human intellect, conceived in power and freedom, must attain the establishment of both poetry and prose, the one is recognized by the other just as one may ascertain from a fragment of a statue or sculptured work whether it was a part of a group of statuary.

Prose can stop, however, with the mere representation of reality and to a certain extent can become a mere chronicle of things and events rather than the stimulus of ideas or emotions. In such a case, it does not deviate from ordinary speech and fails to achieve the potential of its actual nature. It therefore cannot be termed an intellectual development, and it will have no formal but only material relationships. Where it follows a higher path, it requires, in order to gain its aims, means which engage the mind more profoundly. It is then elevated to that level of refined speech which alone is worthy of mention, and it can be regarded as the companion of poesy. In this case, it demands with all the united powers of the mind the comprehension of its object; at the same time a course of action originates which reveals the mind emitting rays in all of the directions upon which it can exert an effect. Discriminating reason is not the only active power. The remaining powers collaborate with it and fashion the conception which in more elevated language is termed a highly intelligent one. In this unified way the intellect not only comprehends the object but also carries over the impression of its own mood into speech. Language, elevated by the sweep of ideas, makes its advantages felt but subordinates them to the governing purpose. The ethical and emotional tenor is imparted to the language, and the soul radiates from the style. Through subordination and juxtaposition of clauses and sentences, prose reveals in its own peculiar manner the logical eurhythmus, corresponding to the development of ideas, which is tendered to prose discourse in its general elevation by its special purpose. If the poet devotes too much of his attention to the elevation, he turns poesy into something similar to rhetorical prose. Owing to the fact that everything mentioned here works together in spirited and intelligent prose, there is revealed in it the whole vivid birth of the idea, the struggle of the intellect with its subject matter. Where the subject matter permits, the idea is formulated as a free and direct inspiration and imitates in the realm of truth the independent beauty of poetry.

From all this it is evident that poetry and prose are determined by the same general requirements. In both an impetus originating from within must elevate and bear the intellect. Man in all his peculiarity must move with his ideas toward the external and internal cosmos and, in comprehending individual detail, must permit it the form which connects it to the whole. In their directions, however, and in the media of their operation, poetry and prose differ and can actually never be intermingled. We must also note that poetry in its true nature is inseparable from music, whereas prose is exclusively committed to language. We all know how precisely Greek poetry was associated with instrumental music, and the same is true of the lyric poetry of the Hebrews. The effect of the various melodic patterns upon poetry has been discussed above. No matter how poetical ideas and language may be, we do not feel we are in the true realm of poetry if the musical element is absent. This is the source of the natural alliance between great poets and composers, although the inclination of music to develop in unrestricted independence probably helps it to intentionally overshadow poetry.

Strictly speaking, we can never state that prose proceeds from poetry. Even where this appears to be the case, as in Greek literature,[2] this can be explained by the fact that prose originated from a most genuine and most varied poetry that was intellectually nurtured for centuries and from a language also cultivated in this manner. Poetry and prose are essentially different, however. The germ of Greek prose, as well as that of poetry, reposed originally in the Greek intellect; because of the individuality of this intellect, poetry and prose correspond to each other in their peculiar casts.

Greek poetry reveals a broad and free intellectual flight, which brings forth the need of prose. The development of both was completely in accordance with their common origin and sprang also from an all-embracing intellectual urge whose perfect development could have been hindered only by external circumstances. Literary prose can be explained even less as originating from an admixture of poetic elements, no matter how far it is removed from the definite purpose of speech or how fine its taste. Naturally, the essential differences of poetry and prose exert their effect on the language, and poetic diction and prose diction have their peculiarities with regard to expressions, grammatical forms, and syntactic patterns. They are kept apart to a far greater extent, however, by the tone of the whole rooted in their abstruse nature. No matter how infinite and inexhaustible it is in its innermost being, the sphere of poetry remains a closed entity; it does not absorb everything, and it does not permit what has been absorbed to retain its original nature. The idea, unfettered by an external form, can move freely in its development, both in the conception of detail as well as in the compilation of the general idea. To this extent, the requirement for the cultivation of prose lies in the wealth and freedom of intellectuality, and this in turn makes prose peculiar to certain periods of intellectual development. Prose has still another aspect by which it excites and by which it insinuates itself into the mind: its close relationship with the conditions of ordinary life, which can be intensified by the refinement of intellectuality without thereby sacrificing truth and natural simplicity. From this approach even poetry may select prose raiment to portray emotion in all its purity and truth. A man who may be averse to language itself as restricting the mind and distorting its pure expressions and who may yearn for a perception and reflection devoid of such a medium of expression, is able by divesting language of all its adornment—even in the highest poetic mood—to take refuge in the simplicity of prose. In accordance with its nature, poetry is always clothed in an external artistic form. However, there can exist in the soul an inclination toward nature in contrast to art, with the result that the entire ideal content of poetry is preserved for the feeling of nature. This appears in fact to be native to more recently cultured peoples. Certainly—and this is true of the less material form of our language of comparable depth—this lies in our German way of thinking. The poet can then remain intentionally close to the conditions of actual life, and, if the power of his genius suffices, he can produce a genuine poetic work in prose vestments. Here I need only remind the reader of Goethe's *Werther*; I am sure that every reader will feel how the external form is related to the inner content. I mention this merely to show how attitudes of prose and poetry with respect to each other and to the association of their inner and outer natures can originate from quite different spiritual moods, all of which influence the character of language but all of which in turn undergo a reflex action, a factor that is even more evident to us.

Poetry and prose themselves obtain, each for itself, a peculiar coloration. In Greek poetry the external artistic form predominated above all others in accordance with its general intellectual peculiarity. This sprang from its animated and thorough association with music, but also from the fact that this people understood how to ponder and evaluate the innate effects of poetry upon the mind. Thus ancient Greek comedy was clothed in the richest and most varied rhythmic dress. The more deeply it descended in its portrayals and expressions to the common levels, the more it felt the necessity of gaining its bearing and inspiration through the constraint of the external form. The combination of the highly poetic tone with the solid, old-fashioned virtues of the content-laden *parabases*, which we feel vividly in reading Aristophanes, grips the mind in antithesis which fundamentally resolves itself. For the Greeks the admixture of prose into poetry was decidedly foreign, as it was to the Hindus and to Shakespeare. The need to approximate colloquial speech on the stage and the correct feeling, so that even the most detailed narrative, placed in the mouth of an actor, would have to differ from the epic recitation of the rhapsodist (although be vividly reminiscent of it), brought forth unique metrical forms for these parts of the drama; they were mediators, as it were, between the art form of poetry and the natural simplicity of prose. But the latter was also affected by the same general mood and received from it an externally more artistic mold. The national peculiarity is revealed particularly in the critical attitude and judgment of the great prose writers. Although we would take a quite different approach, the cause of their excellence is to be sought in the artistic figures of speech and in the external features of structure. The collaborative effect of the whole, the intuitive perception of thought development, of which style is only a reflection, appears to us to vanish completely on reading such works as those of Dionysius of Halicarnassus. We cannot deny that, disallowing biases and sophistries, the beauty of the foregoing great models is based partially upon these details. More exact study of this viewpoint leads us at the same time more deeply into the peculiarity of the Greek intellect. The works of genius exert their effect only in the manner that they are comprehended by nations in any case. Moreover, it is precisely the effect upon languages with which we are here concerned and which depends especially upon this conception.

Progressive cultivation of the intellect culminates at a stage where, more or less ceasing to divine and to conjecture, it strives to establish cognition and to summarize its substance in unity. This is the era of the origin of science and its resultant scholarship. This moment, moreover, can be nothing other than the most highly influential upon the language. I have already spoken of the formation of a specialized, technical language (see p. 146). The general influence of this epoch should be mentioned at this point, since science, strictly speaking, demands a prose style, and a poetic one can accrue to it only accidentally. In this field of thought the intellect is concerned exclusively with objective material. It is concerned with subjective material only insofar as necessity requires. The intellect here seeks the truth and the elimination of all external and internal pretense. Not until this period, then, does language achieve its ultimate acuity in sifting and establishing concepts, and the evaluation of the sentences and their components gravitates toward a single goal. As a consequence of the scientific form of the cognitional structure and the establishment of the conditions governing the latter, something quite new is disclosed to the cognitional capacity of the intellect, which surpasses everything in its eminence and grandeur. This factor acts immediately upon the language and gives to it a character of greater seriousness and a strength elevating ideas to their greatest clarity. But, on the other hand, its use in this region requires a coldness and sobriety, as well as an avoidance in syntax of all artificial intricacy which is harmful to the ease of understanding and inappropriate to the simple purpose of presenting the object. The tone of such prose is hence quite different from that delineated previously. Without making its own independence felt, the language should associate itself with the concept as closely as possible, accompany it, and represent it. In the course of development of the human intellect within our purview, Aristotle may justifiably be termed the founder of science and of the cognizant mental faculties. Although efforts in this direction naturally began much earlier, progress was gradual and science did not become a complete concept until the contribution of the great Stagirite. As if the concept had suddenly burst forth in him in a hitherto unknown clarity, there is revealed between his lectures and the methodology of his investigations and those of his most immediate predecessors a definite gap, one that cannot be negotiated by degrees. He searched after facts, collected them, and strove to deduce general ideas from them. He checked systems erected before him, revealed their untenableness, and expended effort to impart to his own system a basis founded on a more profound exploration of man's cognitional capacity. At the same time he brought all knowledge which his gigantic intellect comprehended into a relationship that was arranged according to concepts. From such a profoundly searching and extensively comprehensive method, which was directed with equal rigor to both the matter and form of knowledge, and in which the search for truth was emphasized by a sharp dissociation from all seductive sham, a language had to develop; in his case, it constituted a striking contrast to that of his direct predecessor and contemporary, Plato. In fact, the two cannot be relegated to the same developmental period. Platonic diction must be regarded as the pinnacle of an epoch subsequently not repeated, whereas Aristotelian diction must be considered as the beginning of a new epoch. But here we see a striking example of the peculiar effect of philosophical cognition. We would certainly be very much in error were we to ascribe to Aristotle a speech that is divested of grace, without adornment, and often hard in its natural somberness and its inadequacy of intellect. Music and poetry had occupied a great part of his studies. Their effect had, as is evident from the few remaining judgments made by him in this area, penetrated deeply into his nature, and only an inborn inclination could have led him to this branch of literature. We still have preserved from his legacy a hymn replete with poetic ardor. Furthermore, if his esoteric writings, particularly his dialogues, had come down to us, our judgment of the scope of his style would probably be quite different. Individual passages of his preserved writings, especially in his ethics, reveal to what a height he could rise. Truly profound and abstruse philosophy also has its own ways to attain the lofty peak of great diction. Where theory proceeds from a genuinely creative intellect, the intrinsic quality and even the conclusiveness of the concepts involved impart to language a loftiness suitably corresponding to inner profundity.

A configuration of philosophical style of quite peculiar beauty is also found in the pursuit of abstract concepts in Fichte's and Schelling's writings; in isolated but truly gripping instances, it is found in the writings of Kant as well. Factually scientific investigations are especially capable of producing an imposing prose style because they result in an elaborated, more profound, and more general consideration of nature as a whole. Moreover, such a prose style promotes scientific investigation itself by stimulating the intellect, which alone in this area can lead to great discoveries. If at this point I mention pertinent works by my brother, Alexander von Humboldt, I believe that I am only stating a general and often repeated judgment.

All points of the field of knowledge can coalesce to form a universality. In fact, this resultant eminence and the most precise and complete treatment of the factual fundamentals are intimately related. Only where erudition and the effort toward its expansion are not permeated by genuine intellect does language suffer. This is then one of the ways in which prose is threatened, just as it is threatened by the decline of cultured, resourceful conversation. Linguistic words can flourish only so long as the surge of the spirit directed toward the expansive development of language and the association of the cosmos with its essence carry them along to lofty heights. This twofold inspirational impetus appears in countless gradations and shapes, but it always strives, even where man is individually unconscious of the impetus as a result of his own innate drive, toward the foregoing grandiose association. Where the intellectual peculiarity of the nation is not raised with sufficient force to this height, or where the language is deserted by the intellect owing to the intellectual decline of a cultured people, to whom it owes its power and flourishing existence, a sublime prose never originates or, if the creative labor of the intellect reverts to mere shallow scholarly collection and compilation, it disintegrates.

Poetry can only belong to individual moments of life and to individual moods of the intellect. Prose accompanies man continuously and is evident in all expressions of his intellectual activity. It clings closely to every idea and to every sensation. If in a language it has developed, through clarity, supple flexibility, euphony, and harmony, the ability to rise to the freest effort and, at the same time, to a quality of fine tact wherever and to whatever extent this elevation is possible, it betrays and promotes an equally free, facile, and judiciously progressive intellectual process. This is the highest pinnacle which language is capable of attaining in the development of its character, and which therefore from the first sprouting of its external form requires the broadest and most secure foundations.

Given such a prose format, poetry cannot have remained behind, since both flow from a common source. It can, however, attain a high degree of excellence without a concomitant and equal development taking place in the prose of the language. The circle becomes complete only when both develop simultaneously. In this respect Greek literature offers us, even if with great and regrettable gaps, a more complete and purer example of the course of language than appears anywhere else. Without recognizable influence of foreign works, which, however, does not preclude that of foreign ideas, it develops in all the phases of its career, from Homer down to the Byzantine writers, from its own elements and from all of the transformations of the national intellect caused by internal and external historical upheavals. The individuality of the Greek tribes consisted in their mobility and in their struggle for freedom and supremacy, which, for the most part, readily gave the impression of a struggle for freedom to subject peoples. Like the waves of the enclosed sea surrounding them, this constant motion brought about incessant changes within the same moderate boundaries, including those of abode, political size, and rule; thus it steadily furnished to the intellect new nourishment and the impulse to indulge in every type of activity. Wherever the Greeks extended their operations to distant shores, as they did in the establishment of colonial settlements, the same spirit prevailed. As long as this condition predominated, this innate national principle permeated their language and their works. During this period we sense in a vital way the inborn progressive interrelation of all their intellectual products, the vigorous meshing of poetry and prose, and of all the genera of both. Even when the Greek language and literature had been spread afar through conquest since the time of Alexander and later, even when the Greeks were a conquered people, and their language and literature became combined with the world-dominating tongue of the victors, there still arose excellent minds and poetic talents, but the soul-giving principle had died out, and with it the vigorous creative power that sprang from the fullness of its own energy. Information and knowledge of a large part of the earth were now for the first time truly disclosed. Scientific observation and systematic treatment of the entire field of knowledge had in a true cosmic historical connection become clear to the intellect through the efforts of an exceptional man, rich in ideas—that is, through the doctrine and example of Aristotle. The world of physical objects was opposed with overwhelming might to subjective creativity. And the latter was suppressed even further by the earlier literature which, inasmuch as its inspiring principle had disappeared along with the freedom from which it welled, suddenly had to appear as a power against which, even though numerous imitations were attempted, no real competition was to be dared. Therefore, from this epoch on, we see a gradual decline in the Greek language and its literature. However, scientific activity now turned to the treatment of both—they had been preserved in the purest state of their golden age— so that there have come down to us not only a great portion of the works dating from the best epochs but also indications of the way in which these works, although they were seen through the external vicissitudes of a suppressed people, always resemble one another, even as seen through the eyes of people in subsequent generations.

With respect to Sanskrit, we cannot judge with certainty on the basis of our knowledge of its literature to what degree and scope prose was developed in that tongue. The conditions of plebeian and social life in India, however, hardly offered the same inducements to this type of cultural development. More than was true perhaps for any nation, the Greek intellect and character proceeded toward unifications in which conversation constituted the principal spice, if not the sole purpose. Legal transactions before courts of law and in the popular assembly demanded convincing oratory and eloquence to sway and guide the minds of men. The explanation may then lie in these and similar causes if in the future among the residua of Hindu literature nothing is discovered that can be compared to the style of Greek historians, orators, and philosophers. A rich, pliant language, Sanskrit is provided with all the media through which speech achieves solidity, dignity, and grace, and it visibly preserves all the nascent sources therefor in itself; it would have developed quite different characteristics than those with which we are now familiar given a more elevated prose treatment. Even the simple, graceful, and attractive tone of the *Hitôpadeśa* story, which is characterized by faithful and neat portrayal and by a unique keenness of understanding, proves this.

  Latin prose stood in an entirely different relationship to poetry than did the Greek. In this respect the imitation of the Greek models by the Romans contributed radiant originality; the Romans, however, possessed their own originality as well, for they quite obviously impressed upon their language and style their national and international political development. When they transplanted their literature into entirely different times, they were unable to achieve an original and natural development such as we find in Greek literature from the Homeric age onward, particularly in the enduring influence of those earliest songs. The great, original Latin prose springs directly from the mind and character of the Romans, from their masculine seriousness, from their rigorous morality, and from their all-exclusive love of country; sometimes this is intrinsic and sometimes it is in contrast to their later moral depravity. It has far less mere intellectual shading than Greek prose and hence, for all the above reasons taken together, necessarily lacks the naïve grace of some Greek writers; in the case of the Romans, this grace appears only in a poetic mood, inasmuch as poetry is capable of causing the mind to shift into any and all states. In fact, in almost all comparisons which can be made between the Greek and Latin writers, the former appear less solemn and ceremonious, simpler and more natural. This results in a powerful difference between the prose of these two nations. Moreover, it is scarcely credible that a writer such as Tacitus would have been perceived as veracious by the Greeks of his time. That is all the more reason why such a prose had to have a quite different effect upon the language, since Greek and Latin both received the same impulse from the same national peculiarity. A more or less unrestricted suppleness, yielding to every idea, pursuing every intellectual direction with equal facility, and finding its true character in this universality and motility which did not reject anything, could not originate from such prose nor, by the same token, engender it. A glance at the prose of newer nations would lead to even more complex considerations. Though not original themselves, these nations could not avoid being attracted in different ways by the Romans and by the Greeks. At the same time, however, they created entirely new relationships and even a previously unknown originality.

Ever since the masterful investigations by F. A. Wolf concerning the origin of the Homeric poems, it is probably generally recognized that the poetry of a people may remain unrecorded for a long time after the invention of writing and that by no means must both epochs necessarily coincide. Written to glorify an occasion of the moment or to cooperate in the celebration of ceremonial affairs, poetry in earliest times was too intimately associated with life and proceeded too voluntarily from the imaginative power of the poet and from the comprehension of his auditors for the intention of cold recording not to have remained foreign to them. It flowed freely from the lips of the poet or from the singing school which had assimilated his poems. It was a lively recitation, accompanied by song and instrumental music. The words only constituted a part of the latter and were inseparably combined with it. This entire recitation was handed down in subsequent times, and it did not enter the minds of the people to want to change what was so firmly interlaced. The idea of writing things down did not occur because of the manner in which poetry became rooted in the popular intellectual life during this period. This would presuppose on the one hand reflection which always originates with the art as it is practiced naturally for a period of time, and on the other, development of those conditions in bourgeois life which quicken the desire to sort out activities and to permit their successful aspects continual interaction. Only then could the connection of poetry with recitation and immediate *joie de vivre* become more relaxed. The necessity of poetic word order and the meter also made it largely superfluous to resort to writing to aid transmission to posterity.

In the case of prose, the situation was quite different. The principal difficulty cannot, I am convinced, be sought in the impossibility of committing long segments of nonmetric speech to memory. Among peoples there is certainly nationalistic prose that is preserved by oral tradition in which the garb and the expression are not accidental. We encounter in the stories of nations which do not possess any manner of writing a use of language, a kind of style, from which it is evident that they were handed down with only minor changes from one narrator to the next. In repeating stories they have heard, even children conscientiously utilize the selfsame expression as a general rule. In this connection I need merely remind the reader of the story of Tangaloa on the Tonga Islands.[3] Among the

Basques, such unrecorded stories continue to be circulated today. According to the natives, they lose all of their fascination and natural charm when translated into Spanish. This is visible proof that the external form is also accorded special attention. The people are so devoted to these stories that they are divided into various classes according to content. I personally heard one story told that bore quite a resemblance to our tale of the Pied Piper of Hamelin. Other stories, merely changed in various ways, relate myths of Hercules, and one quite localized tale, pertaining to a small off-shore island,[4] tells the story of Hero and Leander, but it is changed to deal with a monk and his beloved. Nonetheless, the written recording, the idea of which does not arise at all in earliest poetry, is necessary and immediate for prose in its original purpose, even before it becomes elevated to the truly artistic plane. Facts are to be researched or presented, concepts must be developed and associated, and something objective must be ascertained. The mood which this tends to produce is a sober one, directed toward research, separating truth from sham, and conveying to our reason the conduct of the business at hand. It immediately rejects metric form, not exactly owing to its limitations, but because the need for it cannot be inherent and because a linguistic form which restricts the universality of the rational mind researching and associating in all directions is found unsuitable. Written recording of knowledge for this reason is found desirable and even indispensable throughout the entire research enterprise. What has been determined by research and even the course of research must in all details stand forth solidly and securely. The purpose itself is the greatest possible unification: history should preserve what otherwise evaporates in the lapse of time, furnish precepts for further development, and connect one generation to the next. Prose also establishes the particular emergence of individuals from the mass in the field of intellectual production, since research carries with it personal inquiries, visits to foreign lands, and personally selected methods of combining data. Truth, particularly in times where other proofs are lacking, requires an authority, and the historian, unlike the poet, cannot derive his substantiation from Mount Olympus. The disposition toward prose composition developing in a nation must therefore seek facility in the area of literary media, and may be stimulated by those already extant.

Two different types of poetry,[5] distinguished specifically by the use of writing in one case and by its absence in the other, originate from the natural growth of culture among peoples. One, as it were, is especially natural, flowing from inspiration without intention and consciousness of art; the other develops later and is more artistic, yet for this reason it is no less a part of the most profound and genuine poetic spirit. In the field of prose, such development cannot possibly take place in the same way and still less in the same periods. However, in another way the same thing is true for it as well. If, for instance, in the case of a people fortunately organized with respect to both poetry and prose, opportunities evolve in life which require free-flowing eloquence, we find an association of prose with the life of the people which is similar to but different in orientation from that established above with reference to poetry. So long as it persists unconscious of artistic intent, this prose style rejects the qualities of a lifeless and cold chronicle. This was certainly the case in Athens during the great era between the Persian War and the Peloponnesian Wars and even later.[6] Orators such as Themistocles, Pericles, and Alcibiades developed great oratorical talents. This is especially true of the latter two. Nevertheless, none of their actual speeches have come down to us, since the ones in the histories naturally derive from the historians. Moreover, antiquity does not appear to have any writings which could with certainty be attributed to them. At the time of Alcibiades, there were speeches written beforehand as well as speeches intended to be given by others than their authors. It was inherent in all the conditions of political life of that period that these men, who were really leaders guiding the destinies of the state, found no occasion to write down their speeches, either before or after delivery. Still, this natural eloquence surely preserves, as did the poetry mentioned of earlier times, the seed of eloquence and is in many segments the unrivalled prototype of the more artistic, later literary product. Here, however, where discussion pertains to the effect of both categories on the language, a more detailed consideration of this situation cannot be overlooked. The language of later orators was handed down to them from a time when great and splendid material in plastic and literary arts had excited the genius of orators and cultivated the people's taste; the language handed down, then, was in an entirely different state of repletion and refinement than it could boast of having previously attained. The animated discussions in the schools of philosophy must have presented a similar situation.

CHAPTER EIGHTEEN

The Independent Synthesis in Languages

IT IS MARVELOUS to see what a long series of languages of equally fortunate structure and of equally stimulating effect upon the intellect Sanskrit produced. If we are to assume in each ethnic group a primitive or mother tongue, we must place this language at the apex of the Sanskritic family. To enumerate at this point only the features of closest resemblance, we first discover Zend and Sanskrit to be closely related. However, they are found also to differ strikingly, but both their similarities and their differences are permeated by the most virile principles of fruitfulness and regularity in lexical and morphological structure. There emerged from this linguistic group the two languages of our classical scholarship[1] and, even if of a more recent scientific development, the entire Germanic branch of related dialects. Finally, when the Latin tongue degenerated owing to moral depravity and mutilation, the Romance languages (to which our contemporary culture owes so very much) blossomed forth from these Romanic substrata with renewed vigor. The foregoing primitive language preserved, therefore, a virile principle in itself by which for three millennia at least the thread of the intellectual development of the human race was capable of spinning itself forth, and which possessed the power of generating new linguistic structure from decayed, deteriorated, and dispersed linguistic material.

In the history of peoples and nations, the question may well be raised concerning what would have transpired had Carthage conquered Rome and dominated Occidental Europe. With equal justification we may also ask in what condition our present-day culture would be if the Arabs had remained the sole possessors of scientific knowledge (as they indeed were over a period of time) and had spread their dominion over the Occident. In both instances, a less favorable measure of success does not seem doubtful to the author. We owe the mighty influence of Roman world dominion upon our civilian establishments, laws, and culture to the same elements that produced Roman world domination—that is, to the Roman intellect and character, and not to external, accidental turns of fate. Owing to an inclination toward this culture and to an intimate ethnic relationship, we became truly receptive to the Greek intellect and language, whereas the Arabs clung for the most part only to the scientific findings of Greek research. Even upon a base of the same antiquity, however, they would have been incapable of erecting the scientific and artistic structures, on which we may justifiably pride ourselves.

Now, if this be accepted as correct, we may ask whether this precedence of the people belonging to the Sanskrit group is to be sought in their intellectual capacities, in their language, or in their more favorable historical destinies. It is manifest that none of these causative factors may be regarded as solely effective. Language and intellectual capacities cannot be distinguished or separated in their interaction. Furthermore, historical destinies even if the relationship does not become immediately evident to us in all its implications, ought not to be so very independent from the innate nature of peoples and individuals. Yet, the foregoing superiority must be recognizable in some feature of language. Therefore, using the Sanskrit linguistic group as a point of departure, we must investigate why one language above others possesses a stronger and more various self-creative virility factor. The cause is to be traced to the fact that it is a related family of languages of which we are speaking in this case and not an individual tongue, and to the individual quality of its linguistic structure per se. I shall first discuss the latter, inasmuch as I cannot deal with the particular conditions relative to dialects forming a linguistically related group until a later point.

It is self-evident that a language whose structure is most extensively suited to the intellect and which most intensively stimulates its activity must also possess the most enduring power to produce from its reservoir of linguistic materials new conformations, brought forth by the lapse of time and the destinies of peoples. An answer that makes reference to the entire linguistic form is far too general, however, and, taken rigorously, only reiterates the same question differently stated. We need an answer that leads to particulars, and such an answer seems possible to me. In the individual word as well as in connected discourse, language is an action, a truly creative operation of the intellect. This action is an individual one in every language, proceeding in a definite manner. Concept and phoneme, combined in a way commensurate with their true nature which is recognizable only in the fact itself, are uttered as word and speech. As a result, something different from both is created between the external ambient and the intellect. The perfection of the language in all of its individual advantages—no matter what they be termed—depends upon the intensity and the regularity of the principle governing this act. Hence the vital principle responsible for further creative effort is based on such perfection also. It is not even necessary to mention the regularity of this action, for the latter is inherent in the concept of intensity. The full power develops only upon the correct course of development. Every incorrect procedure produces limitations that impede a perfect and complete development. Now, if the Sanskritic tongues have for at least three millennia given proof of their productive capacity, this is simply an effect of the intensity of the creative linguistic action in the peoples to which they belonged.

In the previous exposition (see Chapter 9), I discussed the juncture of the intimate ideological form with the phoneme, and in this combination we recognized a synthesis which, as is possible only via a truly creative act of the intellect, produces from the two elements to be combined a third in which the individual nature of the participant factors vanishes. It is the intensity or strength of this synthesis with which we are here concerned. That race which brings about this synthesis with the greatest vigor and undiminished power will in the linguistic creativity of nations wrest the victory. In all nations having more imperfectly developed languages, this synthesis is by nature weak, or it is impeded and crippled by some intrusive circumstance. However, even these statements are still too general to show what is determined in the languages themselves and what can be demonstrated as fact.

There are points in the grammatical structure of languages in which this synthesis and to some extent the power producing it appear more directly, and with which the entire remaining linguistic structure necessarily stands in the most intimate relationship. Since the synthesis is not a property or an action but a true, always instantaneous, and transitory operation, there can be no particular sign indicating it in the words taken individually. Furthermore, the effort to find such a sign would give evidence in itself of the lack of true intensity owing to a failure to recognize its nature. The actual presence of this synthesis must be, so to speak, immaterially revealed in the language. We must become aware of the fact that the synthesis, like a bolt of lightning, has illuminated the language and fused the materials to be combined like a glowing spark from unknown regions. This point is too important not to require an illustrative example. When in a language a root is turned into a substantive by the addition of a suffix, the appended suffix is the material sign of the relationship of the concept to the category of the substance. The synthetic act by which, directly at enunciation of the word, this displacement in the intellect actually proceeds does not have any individual sign or symbol in the word. Yet its existence is revealed by the unity and interdependency in which the suffix and root are fused, that is, by a varying, indirect designation ensuing from this effort mentioned.

This act can generally be termed, as I have done here in this individual case, the act of independent establishment by summarization (synthesis). It is most distinctly and obviously detected in sentence structure, then in words derived by inflection or by affixes, and finally in all associations of concept with phoneme in general. In each of these cases something new is created by combination and is truly established as something (ideal) existing in its own right. The intellect produces, but stands in contrast to, the created item via the selfsame act and allows it as the object to react upon itself in turn. Thus from the cosmos reflected in man originates between him and it, the cosmos, the language which associates him with his environment and which, through his effort, reacts fruitfully upon the latter. In this way, it becomes clear how the life of a given language inspiringly depends on the intensity of this act.

If with respect to the historical evaluation and investigation of languages, from which I never stray in this particular investigation, research is carried out to ascertain in what way the intensity of this act is detectable in the structure of a language, there are revealed three points especially to which it is associated and in which the deficiency of its original intensity can be discovered by an effort to replace it by another approach. For here is expressed what I have already reiterated several times, namely that the correct requirement of the language (for example, in Chinese the demarcation of the parts of speech) is always present in the mind, although it is not always so vitally pervasive that it should again be represented in the phoneme. There arises then in the external grammatical structure a lacuna which must be bridged intellectually or replaced by inadequate analogs. Essentially, this amounts to finding a synthetic process in linguistic structure which not only proves intellectual effectiveness but forms a genuine transition to the phonemic construction. These three points are the verb, the conjunction, and the relative pronoun. A bit of special comment must be devoted to each of these three items.

The verb (to speak first of it alone) is distinguished from the noun and from the other parts of speech possibly occurring in the simple sentence by the fact that to it alone is imparted the act of synthetic establishment as a grammatical function. It originated, just as the declined noun did, in the fusion of its elements with the root word by such an act. It has, however, also obtained the incumbency or obligation of performing this act itself

in the intent of the sentence. Therefore, there is a difference between it
and the remaining words of the simple sentence which forbids enumerating them with it in the same category. All remaining words of the sentence
are, so to speak, dead material to be associated; the verb alone is the midpoint which contains and propagates life to the remainder. By one and the
same synthetic act, the verb joins the predicate with the subject through its
being. But this is done in such a way that the being, which is transformed
with an energetic predicate into an action, is in turn attributed to the
subject itself. Thus that which was conceived as combinable actually
becomes so in reality. One does not merely conceive of lightning striking;
it is the lightning itself which descends. One does not merely bring together the intellect and the imperishable as combinable factors; it is the
intellect which is imperishable. The idea, if I may be permitted to express
myself so materially, abandons through the verb its internal dwelling
place and steps forth into the realm of reality.

Now, if herein lie the differing nature and the peculiar function of the
verb, the grammatical conformation of the verb in every individual
language must make known whether and in what way its characteristic
function in the language is indicated. It is probably customary, in order
to give an idea of the attributes and the differences in languages, to cite
how many tenses, moods, and conjugations the verb has, to enumerate the
various types of verbs, and so forth. All the points mentioned here are of
indisputable importance. However, concerning the true nature of the
verb, insofar as it is the nerve center of the entire language, they do not
give us any information. What mood factor is really involved is whether
and how in the verb of a language is expressed its synthetic force, the
function by which it is duly a verb.[2] This point is all too frequently left
untouched. As a result, we do not go far enough into the true internal
efforts devoted to linguistic formation, but rather remain in the external
reaches of linguistic structure without considering that the latter attain
significance only when in their connections with the aforesaid more profound directions of development are revealed.

In Sanskrit, the indication of the summarizing power of the verb rests
solely in the grammatical treatment of this part of speech and, as it completely follows its own natural proclivities, it leaves nothing else to say on
the subject. Just as the verb is distinguished with respect to the point under
discussion from all remaining parts of speech of a simple sentence in
accordance with its nature, so too it has in Sanskrit absolutely nothing in
common with the noun; both of them exist in pure and separate states. In
certain cases, however, verbs can be derived from the morphologically
complete noun. This is nothing more than the noun being treated as a

root word without consideration for its special nature. Its ending, that is, its grammatically designative component, in such case undergoes numerous changes. Generally, in addition to the verbal treatment reposing in the inflection, there is included a syllable or a letter [representing a phoneme] which adds to the idea of the noun a second concept, that of an action. This is directly and clearly evident in the syllable काम्य्, *kâmy*, from काम, *kâma*, 'desire.' However, were the remaining infixes of another type, such as *y*, *sy*, and so forth, to have no real meaning, they would still express their verbal relationships formally by the fact that they come about, if an investigation of individual cases is made, in a very analogous way among primitive verbs that originate from true roots. It is very rare that nouns are converted into verbs without such an additive element. At any rate, the older language made use of this entire process of conversion of nouns into verbs only very sparingly.

Second, inasmuch as the verb in the function considered here is never in a resting, substantive-like state, but always appears in a state of action, the language as well does not grant it any repose. It does not first construct a basic form to which it appends relationships, as it does in the case of the noun. Even its infinitive is not of verbal nature but is a noun derived from the root itself and not from a part of the verb. To be sure, this is to be termed a deficiency in the language, which the completely peculiar nature of the infinitive seems not to recognize. But it just proves all the more how carefully the language endeavors to eliminate any semblance of nominal quality from the verb. The noun is an entity, and as such can enter into relationships and assume their signs or insignia. The verb, as a momentary, fleeting action, is nothing but an aggregate of relationships. In fact, the language presents it thus. I scarcely need to remark at this point that it could hardly occur to anyone to consider the class syllables of the special tenses of the Sanskrit verb as basic forms of the noun. If the fourth- and tenth-class verbs are excepted (they will be discussed shortly), there are left only vowels with or without nasal infixes; hence all that is visible are phonetic addenda to the root, which is transformed into the verbal form.

Third, regardless of how the inner conformation of a part of speech without an overt phonetic symbol is indicated by the symbolic phonemic unit of the grammatical form, it may be claimed that this unit is included much more rigidly in Sanskrit verb forms than in nominal forms. I have already pointed out that a noun in its inflection never increases a stem vowel by gunation as verbs so frequently do. The language in this respect appears to tolerate a cleavage of the stem from the suffix in the case of the noun but not in the case of the verb. With the exception of the pronominal suffixes in the personal endings, the significance of the not merely phonetic elements of verbal constructions is much more difficult to disclose than is that of at least some elements of nominal constructions. If as the partition separating those languages which are based on the concept of grammatical forms (i.e., inflectional) from the imperfect tongues striving in this direction (i.e., agglutinating) we establish the twofold principle that the former construct from the form a single, entirely incomprehensible sign whereas the latter merely attach two significant concepts to each other, then in the entire Sanskrit language the verbal forms are identified most distinctly with the former. As a consequence of this procedure, the designations of each individual relationship are not the same but are analogically uniform; the individual case is treated particularly, with only the general analogy preserved, according to the phonemes of the medium of designation and the stem. Therefore, the individual designational media have differing idiomatic peculiarities, only to be applied to definite cases, as I have already mentioned in the discussion of the augment and reduplication (see pp. 99–101). The simplicity of the media with which the language produces such an uncommonly great number of verb forms is truly marvelous. Distinction between the verb forms, however, is possible only by the fact that all modifications of the phonemes, whether merely phonetic or designative, are accomplished in varying ways. Moreover, the particular one among these multiple combinations stamps the individual inflectional case, which thereupon remains designative merely because it occupies precisely this position in the conjugational scheme, even when time has abraded away its significant phonemes. Personal endings, symbolic designations produced by augment and reduplication, and perhaps sound-related phonemes, whose insertion indicates the verbal class, are the principal elements of which the verb forms are constructed. In addition to the foregoing, there are only two phonemes, *i* and *s*, which, where not of simple phonetic origin, must hold as true designations of classes, tenses, and moods of the verb. I shall devote a bit more attention to these, since they seem to contain a particularly refined and meaningful usage of words grammatically marked, though originally significant in themselves.

F. Bopp was the first to verify with great acumen and indisputable certainty that the first future and one of the formations of the multiform augment preterite were combined from a root word and the verb अस्, *as*, 'to be.' Sir G. C. Haughton believes he has discovered in an equally erudite manner in the syllable *ya* of the passive the verb "to go," इ, *i* or या, *yá*. Also, where *s* or *sy* appear without the presence of the verb *as* evident in its own inflection as it is in the tenses mentioned above, these phonemes can be regarded as from *as*. In fact, this finding also has already been in part accomplished by F. Bopp. If one weighs this fact and at the same time puts together all cases in which the root *i* or phonemes deriving from it seem significant in the verbal forms, there is revealed in the verb something similar to that found in the noun in the above discussion. Just as the pronoun produces inflectional cases of various configuration, two verbs of the most general meaning do the same in this instance. In accordance with this meaning as well as with the phoneme, the language betrays by this choice its intention of exploiting composition. Its purpose is not a true combination of two definite verbal concepts, which is the case in other languages when they indicate the verbal nature by addition of the concept "do" or "make"; rather, it is to make use of its phoneme as a mere indicative agent stipulating into which category of the verb the individual form in question is to be placed, an indication that depends only slightly upon the inherent meaning of the appended verb. "To go" could be applied to an indeterminable quantity of concept relationships. Motion toward a thing can be regarded, from the approach of its cause, as arbitrary or as involuntary, as an active desire or as a passive happening; from the aspect of effect, it may be regarded as a production, an attainment, and so forth. From a phonetic approach, however, the *i* vowel was the most suitable to serve essentially as a suffix and to play this hybrid part intermediate between significance and symbolization such that in the process the former was entirely put in the shade, even if the phoneme emerged from it. Moreover, it already serves frequently in the verb per se as an intermediate sound, and its euphonic changes into *y* and *ay* increase the multiplicity of the phonemes constituting the forms. The phoneme *a* did not accord this advantage, and *u* has a too peculiarly heavy sound to serve so frequently for immaterial or abstract symbolization. We cannot say the same thing of the *s* of the verb *as* ['to be'] as we did of *i*, although similar statements can be made with respect to it since it is also in part used phonetically and its phoneme changes in accordance with the quality of the vowel preceding it.[3]

In languages one development always proceeds from another so that the earlier language determines the successor. This is strikingly verified in Sanskrit, especially by the passive voice, where the thread of these developments can be spun forth principally from the phonetic forms. According to correct grammatical concepts, this verbal category is always simply a correlative of the active and, moreover, an actual reversal thereof. However, because in accordance with the meaning the acting party becomes the passive one and vice versa, with respect to the grammatical form the passive party should still be the subject of the verb and the acting one should be governed by the verb. Grammatical construction in Sanskrit did not conceive the passive from this, the only correct approach, as is most distinctly evident in those cases where the passive infinitive is expressed. At the same time, the passive designates something proceeding with the person, that is, something inherently referring to the person exclusive of his activity. Now, since Sanskrit had already separated the effect in external direction from intimate, internal experience in inflection, it conceived the passive morphologically from this approach. This was probably why that class of verbs which especially followed the foregoing internal type of conjugation also gave rise to the characteristic syllable identifying the passive. If it is difficult to conceive of the passive in its correct usage, which is the union of an unresolved contradiction between meaning and form, as it were, then it cannot be conceived adequately as an alliance with the action confined to the subject itself and can scarcely be kept uncontaminated by secondary concepts. In the former respect we can see how some languages, the Malayan for example, and among the latter the Tagalog most ingeniously, strive with great effort to produce a sort of passive voice. In the latter respect, it becomes clear that the pure concept which the later Sanskrit correctly conceived, as manifested by its literature, did not borrow at all from the earlier linguistic formation. For instead of imparting to the passive an expression that uniformly or analogously extends through all tenses, it associates this construction with the fourth-class verbs and permits its characteristic syllable to terminate its function within the limits of this class; beyond these limits, it is satisfied with deficient designation of forms.

In Sanskrit, therefore, to return to our principal object of consideration, the feeling for the summarizing power of the verb has completely penetrated the language. It has created in the verb not merely a decisive expression, but one which is suitable and congenial to this language alone; moreover, it is a purely symbolic expression, all of which is proof of Sanskrit's strength and vitality. I have already remarked in these pages that, where the linguistic form exists clearly and vitally in the intellect, it becomes enmeshed in the development of the external linguistic structural process. In such case, it makes its influence felt and, in the mere spinning forth of started threads, does not permit substitutes or makeshifts to be produced in place of pure forms. Sanskrit gives us fitting examples of success and failure in this respect. The function of the verb is expressed purely and definitively, but in the designation of the passive the language allows itself to be led astray in the pursuit of an external path.

One of the most natural and most general consequences of inner misconstruction, or rather of the incomplete recognition of the verbal function, is the obfuscation of the boundaries between noun and verb. The same word can be used as both parts of speech; every noun can be recoined as a verb. The identifying characteristics of the verb modify its concept more than they characterize its function. The tenses and moods accompany the verb in its independence, and the association of the pronoun is so loose that one is forced in one's mind to supply the verb "to be" between it and the alleged verb, which is really a nominal form with a verbal meaning. From the foregoing, it naturally arises that true verbal relationships are attracted toward nominal ones, and both intermingle in the most multifarious manner. All that is said here is evident perhaps nowhere to such a high degree as in the Malayan family of languages. On the one hand, this family, with few exceptions, suffers from the Chinese lack of inflection; on the other hand, unlike the Chinese, it does not reject grammatical structure with disdainful resignation, but rather searches for the latter, attains it in a one-sided way, and in this one-sidedness wondrously multiplies it. Constructions carried through entire conjugations completed by the grammarians may be proved distinctly to be true nominal forms. And although the verb cannot be lacking in any language, still, he who looks for the true expression of this part of speech in the Malayan languages is struck to some extent by a feeling of its absence. This holds not merely for the language of Malacca [the Malay Peninsula], whose structure is in any case of still greater simplicity than that of the remaining, but also for Tagalog [Tagalic] which in the Malayan manner is very rich morphologically. It is remarkable that in Javanese by the mere change of the initial character into another of the same class nominal and verbal forms are alternately merged with each other. At first glance, this seems a truly symbolic designation. I have, however, shown in the second book of my treatise on the Kawi language that this change of alphabetical characters is owing only to the wearing down of a prefix in the course of time.[4] I shall not elaborate on this point in greater detail here, since it is thoroughly discussed in the third book of the work mentioned.

In languages where the verb possesses no characteristics of its true function or only very defective ones, it more or less automatically coincides with the attribute, that is, with a noun, and the actual indication of physical placement of the concept must be supplied to the subject and to this attribute in the form of the verb "to be." Such an omission of the verb where a property is merely to be attributed to a thing is not foreign even to the most highly cultivated languages. Indeed, it is encountered frequently in Sanskrit and Latin, and more rarely in Greek. It has nothing to do with the characterization of the verb but is merely a kind of sentence structure. Conversely, some of the languages which in their structure attain verbal expression only with effort accord a particular form to these constructions and thereby to some extent draw them into the structure of the verb. Thus, in the Mexican Indian tongue the verbal form "I love" can be expressed by *ni-tlazotla* as well as by *ni-tlazotla-ni*. The former is the combination of the verbal pronoun with the stem of the verb; the latter is the same but with the participle. At any rate, this is true to the extent that certain Mexican verbal adjectives can still be called participles with a view to whether they are active, passive, or reflective, whether or not they contain the concept of the sequence of action (the element from which the actual tense originates by means of the combination with the three stages of time).[5] A. de Vetancurt in his Mexican grammar[6] makes of the second of the above Mexican forms a tense denoting a custom. This is an obviously erroneous viewpoint, inasmuch as such a form of the verb cannot be a tense; if it were, it would have to be inflected throughout the tenses, which is not the case. It is evident from A. de Vetancurt's more exact definition of the expression that it is nothing but the combination of a pronoun and a noun with omission of the verb "to be." "I love" possesses pure verbal expression; "I am a loving one" (i.e., "I am accustomed to love") is, taken exactly, not a verbal form but a clause. The language, however, to a certain extent stamps this construction as a verb, since it permits in it only the use of the verbal pronoun. It therefore also treats the attributive as a verb by appending to it the words it governs: *ni-te-tla-namaca-ni*, 'I (am) one selling something to someone,' that is, 'I am accustomed to sell, I am a merchant.'

The Mixteca language, which also belongs to New Spain [Mexico],[7] distinguishes between the case where the attributive, as an appendant to the substantive, designates, and where it is only imputed to it by the verbal expression, that is, by the position of the two parts of speech. In the former the attributive must follow the substantive, in the latter it must precede: *naha quadza*, 'the wicked woman,' versus *quadza naha*, 'the woman is wicked.'[8]

The impossibility of placing the expression of the collective verb "to be" directly within the verb form, which in the just-mentioned cases totally eschews this expression, can also lead, conversely, to its inclusion quite materially where in accordance with this speech pattern it should not appear. This occurs when to a truly attributive verb (he goes, he flies) the *being* is drawn upon as an actual auxiliary verb (he is going, he is flying). Yet this informative medium does not really remedy the dilemma of the creative linguistic intellect. Inasmuch as the auxiliary verb itself must have the form of a verb, and yet since what we really have is only the amalgamation of being with an energetic attributive, the same problem repeatedly arises. The difference is simply that, while the same combination recurs for every verb, in this instance it is contained in one unit only. Also, the feeling for the necessity of such an auxiliary verb shows that the idea thereof was present in the linguistic structure and development, even if they did not possess the power of creating a proper expression for the true function of the verb. It would be useless to cite examples for a matter that frequently occurs in languages, sometimes in the entire verbal construction and sometimes only in individual conjugations. In contrast, I shall dwell for a few moments on a more interesting and rarer case, namely that where the function of the auxiliary verb (the addition of *being*) is allotted to a different part of speech than to the verb itself, specifically to the pronoun and, moreover, in a quite similar way.

In the Yarura tongue,[9] spoken by an Indian tribe dwelling on the Casanare and lower Orinoco rivers, the entire conjugation is constructed in the simplest way by the union of the pronoun with the tense particles. These combinations produce in themselves the verb "to be," and when suffixed to a word they constitute the inflectional or conjugational syllables thereof. An indigenous root phoneme, which would not belong to the pronoun or to the tense particles, is entirely lacking in the verb "to be"; and since the present has no particle of its own, its persons consist simply of the persons of the pronoun itself, which are distinguished from the independent pronoun only as abbreviations.[10] Therefore, the three persons of the singular of the verb "to be" are *que, mé,* and *di,* and in literal translation denote simply 'I,' 'thou,' and 'he.'[11] In the imperfect, the syllable *ri* is prefixed to the foregoing monosyllables as follows: *ri-que,* 'I was'; and it is combined with a noun as follows: *ui ri-di,* 'water was (present).' As a true verb, however, we have *jure-ri-di,* 'he ate,' 'he was eating.' Accordingly, the monosyllable *que* thus denoted 'I am,' and this form of the pronoun actually expressed the function of the verb. Still, this amalgamation of the pronoun with the temporal particles could never be used alone in its own right, but only in such a fashion that by means of another word, which could be any part of speech, a clause or sentence was constructed. The monosyllables *que* and *di* never mean 'I am' and 'he is' by themselves alone, but we find *ui di,* 'it is water,' and *jura-n-di* which, with an euphonic or transitional nasal phoneme, means 'he eats.' If we look at this matter carefully, we can see that the grammatical form of these idiomatic expressions is not what I am talking about here, namely an incorporation of the concept of being into the pronoun, but it involves omission and restoration or complementation of the verb "to be" in the association of the pronoun with another word. The time particle *ri* is, by the way, nothing but a word indicating remoteness. It may be contrasted to the particle *re*, which is stated to be the characteristic identifying the subjunctive. This particle *re* is, however, simply the preposition 'in,' and it has a similar application in a number of American Indian dialects. It is used to construct an analog to the gerund: *jura-re*, 'in eating' (in Latin, *edendo*). This gerund is then converted into the subjunctive or optative moods by prefixing the independent pronoun: "if I ate," or "that I ate." Here the concept of being is united with the characteristic of the subjunctive, and therefore the verbal suffixes of the persons otherwise invariably associated to it drop out when the independent pronoun is prefixed. J. Forneri actually includes *re* and *ri-re* as gerunds of the present and past in his verb paradigm and translates them as follows: 'if I were,' 'if I had been.'

Thus the language determines a form of the pronoun of its own with which the idea of being is persistently and exclusively associated; however, the concept of the pronoun itself being incorporated was not extant in its pure state. The same is true, but in a different way, in the Huasteca tongue,[12] another dialect spoken in New Spain [Mexico]. In it also the pronouns are combined. However, this applies only to the independent ones which are united with a time particle and in this way then constitute the verb "to be." They approximate the verb "to be" in its true concept to a high degree, since these combinations—unlike those in the Yarura dialect—can stand quite alone: *nânâ-itz*, 'I was,' *tâtâ-itz*, 'thou wast (wert),' and so forth. In the attributive verb, the persons are indicated by other pronominal forms which very closely approach the possessive pronoun. However, the origin of the particle associated with the pronoun is too little known to permit deciding whether it contains its own verb root. It serves in the language certainly as a past-tense characteristic, invariably for the imperfect but, according to special rules, for the other tenses as well. The mountain dwellers, who have most likely preserved the oldest forms of speech, are reputed to make more general use of this syllable and to add it also to the present and future tenses. Occasionally, it is appended to a verb to indicate intensity of action. In this sense, as an intensification (as in so many languages reduplication accompanies the perfect tense as an intensifying element), it could probably little by little have become the exclusive characteristic of past tenses.[13]

The case being discussed here is encountered in its pure and perfect state in the Mayan dialect, spoken on the Yucatan Peninsula.[14] It possesses a pronoun which, used alone, constitutes a substitute for the verb "to be"; this attests to a most remarkable care always to indicate the true function of the verb by an element of its own designed for this purpose. The pronoun is twofold: one type bears the concept of being inherently;

the other does not possess this property but is also combined with the verb. The former of these two types is in turn subdivided into two sub-types. One of these provides the meaning of being only in combination with another word, whereas the other contains this significance directly in itself. The second subtype produces the verb "to be" completely, since it is combined also with the tense particles (which, however, are lacking in the language for the present and perfect). In the first-person singular and plural, these pronouns are *Pedro en,* 'I am Peter,' and analogically they continue: *ech, on,* and *ex.* On the other hand, we have *ten,* 'I am,' *tech,* 'thou art,' *toon,* 'we are,' and *teex,* 'you are.' With the exception of the three types mentioned here, there is no independent pronoun. However, the form *ten* is used for this purpose and simultaneously serves as the verb "to be." The form not having the concept of being inherently is always affixed, and *en* has no other use than that cited. Where the verb dispenses with the first type of pronoun, it is regularly combined with the second. Then, however, an element (*cah* or *ah,* alternating according to definite rules) is found in its forms. This element is left over when the verb is analyzed, that is, when all of the elements generally accompanying the verb (person, tense, or time, mood, and so forth) are abstracted. The forms *en, ten, cah,* and *ah* appear therefore in all verbal forms. However, they are always used in such a way that one of these syllables excludes the remaining. From the foregoing, it is self-evident that all are expressions of the verbal functions; at least one must be present, but the use of this one makes use of the others superfluous. Their application is subject to definite rules. The particle *en* is used simply for intransitive verbs, and in such case not in the present and imperfect tenses but only in the remaining ones. The mono-syllable *ah* appears in the same tenses of the transitive verbs, and *cah* is used in intransitive and transitive verbs without distinction, but only in the present and imperfect tenses. The particle *ten* is found merely in an allegedly anomalous conjugation. If the latter is examined more closely, it is found to have the meaning of a custom or of an enduring state, and, when *cah* and *ah* are discarded, the form becomes provided with endings which in part form the so-called gerunds. In this case, a transformation of a verbal form into a nominal form takes place, and this nominal form then requires the true verb "to be" to become again a verb. To this extent, these forms agree entirely with the above-mentioned Mexican custom tense. I must note additionally that, in this manner of conception, transi-tive verbs are restricted to those which actually govern an object external to themselves. Verbs used indefinitely, true active verbs, such as "to love" or "to kill," and verbs containing the governed object in themselves, such as the Greek οἰκοδομέω, are treated as intransitive.

The reader will already have noticed that the two subtypes of the first pronominal category differ simply by a prefixed *t*. As this dental is found in that pronoun which in its own right has verbal meaning, the natural conjecture is that it constitutes the root phoneme of a verb, so that it is not a pronoun that is used in the language as the verb "to be," but rather it is a verb that is used as a pronoun. In this case, the inseparable union of existence and the person would remain the same, but the viewpoint would be different. That *ten* and the remaining forms dependent upon it are truly used as independent pronouns is evident from the Lord's Prayer in the Mayan tongue.[15] In fact, I hold this *t* to be a stem phoneme not of a verb but of the pronoun itself. The expression valid for the third person supports this contention. This expression is entirely different from the two first discussed, and in the singular for both types expressing the verb "to be" it is *lai-lo*; in the plural for the type not serving as a verb it is *ob*, and for the other type it is *loob*. Now if *t* were the root phoneme of a verb, these expressions could not be explained in any way. Since a number of languages encounter difficulty in conceiving the third person in its pure concept and in separating it from the demonstrative pronoun, it is not striking that the two first persons have a stem phoneme peculiar to them alone. Actually, in the Mayan language, an alleged relative pronoun *lai* is cited, and other American Indian languages are provided with stem phonemes that proceed through all the persons of the pronoun. In the language of the Maipure Indians,[16] the third person is found again in the two first only with differing addendum; it seems more or less that the third person perhaps originally meant "human being," and that the two first persons signified "I-human being" and "thou-human being." In the language of the Achaguas,[17] all three persons of the pronoun have the same final syllable. Both of these tribes inhabit the region between the Rio Negro and the upper Orinoco. Between the two main types of the Mayan pronoun, there is only in some persons a similarity of phonemes; in others there prevails great difference. The dental *t* is found nowhere in the affixed pronoun. The *ex* and *ob* of the second- and third-persons plural of the pronoun associated with the idea of being have merged entirely into the same persons of the other pronoun not having this inherent meaning. As these syllables, however, are only appended to the second and third persons of the singular as endings, we can recognize that they (perhaps derived from the foregoing, and perhaps older, pronoun) serve the other one merely as a sign of the plural.

The forms *cah* and *ah* differ from one another only by the added consonant *c*. This consonant appears to me to be a true verbal root phoneme which, when combined with *ah*, forms an auxiliary verb "to be." Where the syllable *cah* is enduringly incorporated into a verb, it carries in itself the idea of violence. This may be the reason why the language came to make use of it to designate all action, since force and movement are part and parcel of every action. With truly fine tact, the monosyllable *cah* has been preserved to indicate only the vitality of the continuous action, that is, the present and imperfect. That *cah* is actually treated as a verbal stem is evidenced by the difference in the position of the affixed pronoun in the forms constructed with *cah* and *ah*. In the forms constructed with *cah*, the pronoun always appears directly before the syllable *cah*; in those constructed with *ah*, the pronoun appears not before the *ah* but before the attributive verb. The fact that *ah* is always prefixed only to a root word, that is, to a noun or verb, proves distinctly that in these forms the syllable *ah* is neither a noun nor a verb, that, compared to *cah*, it has a different function. Thus, of the verb *canan*, 'to guard' or 'watch over,' the first person of the present singular is *canan-in-cah*. Contrastingly, the same person of the perfect tense is *in-canan-t-ah*. The monosyllable *in* is the first-person singular pronoun, the interpolated *t* is a euphonic glide consonant. As a prefix, *ah* has multiple uses in the language: it is the characteristic sign identifying the male sex, it identifies local inhabitants, and it identifies nouns derived from active verbs. Therefore, it may have made the transition from a substantive to a demonstrative pronoun, finally becoming an affix. Since, in accordance with its origin, it is less suited to indicate intensive motion of the verb, it is used for the designation of tenses that are more remote from the immediate phenomenon. These tenses of intransitive verbs require that even more of the motionless concept of being enter into the verb, and therefore they find it sufficient to combine with that pronoun for which this idea of being is always supplied mentally. Thus the language designates the various degrees of the liveliness of the phenomena, and, as a result, its conjugational forms are constructed in a more artistic way than are those of even highly cultivated languages. However, these forms are not constructed in a simple and natural manner that delimits the functions of the various parts of speech correctly, and thus the structure of the verb is always faulty. Still the feeling for the true function of the verb, as well as an anxious effort to avoid a lack of an appropriate expression for it, is obvious.

The affixed pronoun of the second principal type serves also as a possessive pronoun for substantives. A complete failure to recognize the difference between the noun and verb is betrayed by assigning a possessive pronoun to the verb, that is, by exchanging "our eating" for "we eat." In languages guilty of this, however, it appears to me to be attributable to a deficiency in properly distinguishing the various pronominal categories from one another. For, obviously, the misconception becomes of smaller magnitude if the idea of the possessive pronoun itself is not conceived in its actual trenchancy. I feel this to be the case here. In almost all American Indian languages, understanding of their structure proceeds from the pronoun, and the latter encompasses in two great branches as a possessive pronoun the noun, governing or governed, and the verb, and both parts of speech in most cases always remain united with the possessive pronoun. Generally the language also possesses for this purpose differing pronominal forms. Where this is not the case, the concept of the person is indeterminately combined with the noun and the verb. The difference between the two situations is probably felt, but not with the formal precision and definiteness that are required by the transition to the phonemic designation. At times, however, the feeling for the distinction is indicated in a way other than by the exact separation of a double pronoun. In the Betoyan dialect, spoken by the Indians of the Betoya tribe[18] who dwell in the vicinity of the Casanare and lower Orinoco rivers, the pronoun, when combined as governing agent with a verb, occupies a position different from that of the possessive pronoun combined with the noun. The possessive pronoun is attached to the noun initially, whereas that accompanying the person of the verb is appended finally. The variation in the phonemes consists only in an abbreviation produced by attachment. Thus, for example, *rau tucu* denotes 'my house,' but *humasoi-rrù* means 'a human am I,' and the expression *ajoi-rrù* signifies 'I am.' In the latter word, the meaning of the root syllable is unknown to me. This suffixation of the pronoun takes place, however, only where it is combined aoristically with another word and without special temporal determination. The pronoun then forms with this word a single morpheme, and in truth a verbal form, a semanteme, originates. In these cases, the accent shifts from the combined word to the pronoun. This is more or less a symbolic sign of the mobility of the action, which is the case also in English where the same disyllabic word may be used both as noun and verb, and where, moreover, the oxytonesis denotes the verbal form.[19]

The designation of the transition from noun to verb and vice versa through accent shift is certainly found in Chinese. However, this does not occur with a symbolic relationship to the nature of the verb, inasmuch as the same accent unchanged expresses the twofold transition and indicates only that the word is changed to the opposite part of speech in comparison to its natural meaning and its ordinary usage.[20]

I did not wish to interrupt the exposition by mentioning an exception in the Mayan dialect, which I will briefly make up for at this point. The future in this tongue is entirely distinct in its structure from the remaining tenses. To be sure, it combines its characteristic syllables with *ten*, but it never includes either *cah* or *ah*; it possesses its own suffixes, yet in certain modifications of its form it dispenses with all of them. It is especially averse to the syllable *ah*, for it drops this syllable even where it is actually the termination of the root verb. It would lead us too far afield were I to enter into a detailed investigation of this feature to determine whether these deviations originate from the nature of the peculiar future suffix or from other causes. However, this exception refutes nothing of what has been said above. Rather, this aversion toward the particle *ah* confirms the meaning assigned to it above, since the uncertainty of the future does not call forth the vitality of a pronoun and contrasts with the vitality of a phenomenon that has actually transpired.

Where languages choose to indicate the function of the verb symbolically by the intimate association of its ever-changing modifications with the root, this is a sign of their correct feeling for the verb even if they do not completely reach this goal. This is particularly true when the closeness of this tie is produced by the pronoun. More and more they then approach the transformation of the pronoun into the person, and they thus approach the true verbal form in which the formal indication of the persons (which is not attained by mere introductory placement of the independent pronoun) is the most essential point. All remaining modifications of the verb (with exception of the moods, which belong more to sentence structure) are capable of characterizing that part of the verb which is more similar to the noun and which is to be set in motion only by the verbal function. In this feature lies the explanation for the Malayan languages, which have a certain resemblance to the Chinese, but in which the verbal nature is so little prominent, whereas the definite inclination of the American Indian languages to affix the pronoun in one way or another guides them in this respect along a more correct course of development. If all verb modifications are actually associated with the root syllable, the perfection of the verbal form is then based only on the closeness of the connection, that is, upon whether the power of allocation latent in the verb is more energetically inflectional or more inertially agglutinative.

To the same degree as the verb, the correct and adequate formation of conjunctions in languages is based upon the operation of the creative linguistic intellect. Conjunctions, taken in the true sense of the term, reveal the relationship of two clauses. Therefore a twofold summarization, a more complex synthesis, is inherent in them. Every clause must be taken as a unit. These units must in turn be connected to produce a larger one, and the preceding clause must be kept hovering in the mind until the subsequent one imparts the complete determination to the entire statement.

Rudimentary structure in such case expands to the sentence, and conjunctions are divided into two groups—those which only connect and separate clauses and those which make one clause dependent upon another. The Greek grammarians had already allocated the symbols that distinguish the simpler from the more artistically elevated style in the so-called straightforward or involved periodic flow. Sentences whose clauses are merely connected continue in an indeterminate sequence and do not take the form of a totality whose beginning and end relate to each other. Other clauses, which are truly united in periodic construction, support and secure each other like the stones of a vault.[21] Less cultured languages are generally lacking in conjunctions, or make use for this purpose of forms that are only indirectly suitable, that is, of words not exclusively devoted to such use, and often allow clauses to follow each other without connection. Also, those clauses depending on each other are converted, insofar as possible, into directly sequential clauses. Even cultivated languages preserve traces of this feature. When we say, for example, "I see that you are ready," this certainly means, "I see that; you are ready." In later times, correct grammatical feeling has led us to indicate the dependency of the result clause symbolically by the transposition of the verb [i.e., in German].

Most difficult for grammatical conception is the synthetic allocation that occurs in the case of the relative pronoun. Two sentences are to be connected such that the one constitutes a mere expression of the attributes of a noun contained in the other. The word by which this is effected must therefore be at the same time a pronoun and a conjunction, and it must further represent the noun and govern a clause. Its nature is immediately lost if the two parts of speech combined in it and modifying each other are not conceived as indivisibly linked. The relationship of the two clauses to each other finally requires that the conjunction-pronoun (the relative) take the case requisite to the relative clause and, no matter what case this may be, that it govern the clause at the beginning of which it stands. Here the difficulties obviously mount up, and a clause containing a relative pronoun can be completely understood only in terms of the other to which it is connected. Only those languages in which the noun is declinable can fully correspond to the idea in this pronoun. But even without this requirement, it becomes impossible for most less cultivated languages to find a true expression for this clause designation. They actually lack relative pronouns, and they circumvent as much as possible their use. Where such circumvention is entirely impossible, they utilize in a more or less suitable way substitute constructions.

Such a substitute, though in fact an ingenious one, is found in the

Quechua tongue, the general Peruvian Indian dialect.[22] In this tongue, the sequence of the clauses is reversed: the relative precedes as an independent and simple statement, and the main clause follows it. In the relative, however, the word to which reference is made is omitted, and this word, along with the demonstrative pronoun that introduces it, is placed at the beginning of the principal clause in the case governed by the verb concerned. Thus, instead of saying "The human being who trusts in God's grace attains it; that which you now believe you will in future see revealed in Heaven; I shall walk the path upon which you lead me," the Quechuas say, "He trusts in God's grace, this person attains it; you believe now, this you will in future see revealed in Heaven; you are leading me, this path shall I walk." In these constructions, the essential characteristic of the relative clauses, namely that a word is to be conceived only as determined by the relative clause usage, not only is preserved but is to some extent expressed symbolically. The relative clause, toward which attention is first to be drawn, precedes, and the noun determined by it is placed at the head of the main clause, even if construction of this clause would otherwise allot a different position to it. Moreover, all grammatical difficulties of word order are circumvented, and the dependency of both clauses is evident without expression. The artificial method of always having the relative clause governed by the pronoun, even if this clause is actually governed by its verb, disappears completely. There is absolutely no relative pronoun in these syntactical arrangements. However, the common and easily comprehended demonstrative pronoun is allotted to the noun, so that the language visibly feels the interrelationship of the two pronouns but indicates it from the easier approach. The Mexican Indian language operated with greater brevity in this case, but not in a manner that approached the true significance of the relative clause. It places the word "in" in front of the relative clause, which represents the position both of the demonstrative pronoun and of the article, and in this configuration unites the relative clause to the independent clause.

If a people preserves in its language the power of synthetic placement to the degree of allocating to it in the realm of linguistic structure a sufficient and precisely fitting expression, an immediately happy organizational pattern, remaining constant in all parts, follows. If the verb is correctly construed, the remaining parts of speech must also be correctly construed in accordance with the way the verb governs the clause or sentence. The same power which places ideas and expression in their correct and most fruitful relationship penetrates the language in all of its parts. Moreover, it can not fail in the easier areas of interest if it has surmounted the greater difficulty of synthesis involved in the construction of clause and sentence. The true expression of synthesis can, therefore, be native only to genuinely inflected languages and, among the latter, only to those which are so to a high degree. Factual expression and relationship must be stated in proper proportion, word unity must under the influence of rhythm possess the greatest strength, and the sentence, in contrast, must still reveal the separation of the individual words that assures its freedom. This entire fortunate organization is produced in the language by the power of synthesis.

This same power induces the perfect agreement of the germinating idea with its accompanying language in the inner recesses of the soul. Since thinking and speaking always alternatively complement each other, the correct course of both operates in a manner that attests to uninterrupted progress. If left to its own devices, language, insofar as it is material and depends at the same time on external effects, puts difficulties in the way which react upon its internal form, or, in case such difficulties do not attain prevalence, it slinks away in its constructions toward analogies peculiar to it. However, where permeated by an energetic inner power, it feels itself borne by such analogies, and it arises joyously and reacts through its material independence. It is precisely here that its lasting and independent nature becomes beneficial, that is, when it—as is manifestly the case for a fortunate type of organization—serves oncoming generations as an inspiring implement. In addition to the intimate national foundations and the quality of the language, success of intellectual activity in science and literature is based upon manifold external influences, which are sometimes present and sometimes absent. However, since the structure of the language persists independent of such influences, a fortunate stimulation is required to permit the people to whom the language belongs to recognize that in it they possess an implement suited to an entirely different mental inspiration. National capacities are aroused, and through their interaction and collaboration with the language a new period blossoms for the nation. If we compare the history of peoples, we will certainly find that it is rare for a nation to have experienced two different and unconnected golden ages in its literature. But in another respect, it seems to me that we cannot get around attributing the development of peoples to a higher level of intellectual activity to a condition, both in their intellectual foundations as well as in their language itself, in which the germs of this powerful development were not lying dormant in a somnolent and preformed state. Even if we were to assume entire ages of poets and singers prior to Homer, we would also have to assume that the Greek language was only developed, but not originally constructed, by them. Its fortunate organization, its genuine inflectional structure, and its synthetic power, in a word all that constitutes the foundation and the main nerve of its structure, were surely present in it for an indeterminable number of centuries. On the other hand, we see peoples in possession of the noblest languages who, to our knowledge, have never developed a commensurate literature. This can be attributed to deficient stimulus or impeding circumstances. I remind the reader in this regard of the Lithuanian tongue, which has remained more faithful to the Sanskritic group of dialects than have her sister languages. If I term the retarding and promoting influences "external" and "accidental," or, even better, "historical," these expressions are completely correct owing to the actual power these influences, by their presence or absence, exert. In the matter itself, however, the effect can only originate from within. A spark must be fanned into a flame; a bond which, so to speak, prevents the spirit from expanding must be broken. This can occur at a moment's notice, without slow preparatory efforts. The true origin of this phenomenon, which will always remain incomprehensible, does not become more explicit by postponing its first moment.

The harmony of linguistic structure with the totality of ideological development, the sign of which in concrete linguistic structure is the suitable expression of synthetic composition, leads to that intellectual activity which alone is creative from the intimate sources outward. If we consider successful linguistic structure simply as retrogressively operative, and forget for the moment that what it bestows to the intellect it originally received from it, we then find that it grants intellectual power, clarity of logical arrangement, a feeling for something deeper than that which can be attained through mere psychological analysis and the desire to discover its nature, suspicion of an interrelationship of the intellectual and sensual factors, and finally a rhythmical treatment of melodic sounds with reference to general artistic conception; or we find that it promotes all this where it is already present inherently. Through the proper effort of intellectual powers, there arises therefore, just as any glowing coal shoots forth sparks when fanned, a development of pure intellectual thought. And thus a linguistic structure which is lively and fortunately oriented produces by its very nature philosophy and literature. The flourishing success of these, however, permits reverse conclusions to be drawn with respect to the vitality of the foregoing effect of the language. Language which is conscious of itself prefers to operate where it deems itself dominant. Moreover, its intellectual activity expresses its great application of effort, and the language attains its maximum satisfaction where, in intellectual consideration or in an autonomously created culture, it draws upon its own plenitude or ties together the threads of scientific research. In this region, however, intellectual individuality emerges most vitally. Hence, at the same time that a highly perfected linguistic structure, having originated from propitious foundations which continuously nourish and stimulate it, is securing the vital principle of the language, it is also giving rise to and promoting the multiplicity of the directions that are revealed in the above-considered character variations of languages belonging to the same linguistic group.

How can the claim made above that the fruitful vital principle of languages is based chiefly upon their inflectional structure be reconciled with the fact that the wealth of inflection is always greatest during the youthful period of languages and gradually declines in the course of time? It appears strange, to say the least, that a declining principle should also be the maintaining principle. The wearing away of inflection is an undeniable fact. The formative linguistic sense allows it for different stages of development to drop off indifferently, or it discards it intentionally. It is, in fact, more correct to express the phenomenon in this way than it is to place the blame exclusively on time. In the formations pertaining to declension and conjugation, which have certainly experienced numerous accretions, visibly characteristic phonemes are increasingly discarded the more the concept of the total scheme, which ascribes to each individual case its position, becomes established. Sacrifice to euphony becomes more bold, and where the form is already secure from confusion with others, the accumulation of characteristic signs is avoided. If my perceptions do not deceive me, the latter phonetic changes, which are generally ascribed to time, take place less frequently in the allegedly ruder languages than they do in the cultured ones. This phenomenon can probably be explained in a very natural way. Among all factors reacting upon language, the most highly motile is the human intellect itself. Furthermore, most of the modifications that language undergoes are owing to the lively activity of the intellect. However, the human intellect, in keeping with its great strides forward and influenced by an increasing confidence in the integrity of its own internal view, finds it appropriate to regard as superfluous a too careful modification of the phonemes of a language. As a result of this very principle, a change, which gravely affects their nature, threatens the inflected languages at a very much later linguistic period. The more mature the intellect regards itself, the more boldly it operates within its own confines, and the more confidently it abandons the bridges which language has built for the understanding. To this mood becomes readily associated a lack of feeling for poetic charm based on a feeling for sounds. Poetry then prepares for itself inner paths upon which it can dispense with the foregoing advantage less hazardously. It is, thus, a transition from a more sensual or physical set of mind to one more purely intellectual by which the language is transformed. Yet the primary causes are not always of noble nature. Ruder organs less suited for a pure and refined distinction of phonemes, such an ear less sensitive by nature and untrained musically, lay the groundwork for indifference to the tonal principle in language. Similarly, an inclination toward practicality can impress upon language abbreviations, omissions of relative terms (relative pronouns and adverbs), and elliptical expressions of all types, for when man is merely intent upon being understood, he scorns everything not directly requisite thereto.

In any case, the effect of the popular mind on the language must be entirely different when the language is in the period of its initial formation on the one hand, and when the already molded tongue is busy serving the needs of daily life on the other. So long as the elements, including their origin, pertaining to the earlier period remain clearly in mind, and so long as the mind is occupied in connecting these elements, the mind finds this constructive activity pleasurable. During this time, nothing that can be retained in the expression of any shading of emotion is cast by the wayside. In the subsequent period, the purpose of comprehension predominates. The meaning of the element becomes more obscure, and custom based on usage takes precedence over the details of structure and over the exact preservation of its phonemes. In place of the joy derived from ingeniously combining characteristics with a fully sonorous, syllabic rhythm arises the factor of convenient understanding, which ultimately resolves the forms into auxiliary verbs and prepositions. This objective elevates clarity above the remaining advantages of the language, inasmuch as this analytical method certainly diminishes mental exertion; moreover, in those individual cases where this factor is attained only with great difficulty through the synthetic approach, it increases definiteness. During the time that these auxiliary words are used, however, inflection becomes more dispensable and gradually loses its weightiness in the linguistic sense.

Whatever the cause might be, it is certain that in this way genuine inflectional languages become poorer in forms, frequently substituting grammatical words for them, and they may approach in individual features those languages which differ from their group by a quite distinct and less highly developed principle. Our contemporary German and the English language contain frequent examples of this, with the English language containing by far more than the German. Insofar as I can ascertain, the mixture of English with Latin and Romance material does not appear to be responsible for this condition, inasmuch as this admixture seems to have had little or no effect upon its structure. But still, I do not believe that an objection to the fruitful effect of inflectional nature, even to its most protracted existence in languages, may be raised from the fore-going statements. Even if there were a Sanskrit language which had approximated the Chinese habit of dispensing with the referential signs of the parts of speech in this manner, the causes for this would be entirely different in the two languages. No matter how you explain it, apparently there is an imperfection in the linguistic structure of the Chinese language; this is probably an indigenous custom of isolating the phonemes, combined with a linguistic sense too weak to demand combination and mediation. In a similar Sanskrit dialect, in contrast, the most genuine inflectional character or nature, with all of its beneficial influences, would have become firmly established over an indeterminable number of generations and would have given its configuration to the linguistic sense. In its true nature, therefore, such a language would always have remained Sanskritic. It would differ from other Sanskrit languages merely in those individual features which would be unable to eradicate the characteristic stamp which the inflectional nature of the rest of the language had impressed upon it. The nation would bear the same fundamental features inherently as other Sanskrit nations, since it would belong to the same linguistic group to which the more refined linguistic structure owed its origin, and it would conceive its language with the same intellect and meaning even if it were to correspond externally to this linguistic spirit to a lesser extent in isolated instances. Also, as is specifically the case in English conjugation, isolated genuine inflections would be residually preserved, and they would not allow the intellect to go astray with respect to the true origin and actual nature of the language. A lesser morphological wealth and a simpler structure that originate in this way do not in any manner render languages incapable of attaining high advantages, as we have just seen in the case of the English and German, but merely endow them with a different charac-ter. As a result, their poetry, to be sure, is deprived of the complete force-fulness of one of its chief elements, but if, in such a nation, poetry were actually to decline or were to diminish in its fruitfulness, this condition would derive certainly from deeper, internal causes and would not be any fault of the language itself.

The derivative Romance languages owe their pure grammatical structure to the firm, indeed we can probably say ineradicable, adherence of the genuine organism to the languages, once it became peculiar to them. It appears to me a principal requisite for the correct evaluation of the remarkable phenomenon of their origin to emphasize the fact that in the reconstruction of the ruined Latin tongue, if we consider only the formal grammatical structure of Latin, no foreign material operated in any essential way in this process. The primordial, that is, the original,

languages of the countries in which these new dialects blossomed forth do
not appear to have played any part in this development. With respect to
the Basque, this is certain. But it is also highly probable with respect to the
languages originally prevailing in Gaul. The foreign immigrant tribes,
belonging for the most part to Germanic or related peoples, contributed a
great number of words to the conversion of the Latinic tongue. However,
in the grammatical components it is difficult to detect any significant
traces of their dialects. Peoples do not easily permit metamorphosis of the
mold into which they are accustomed to pour their thought. The foundation
from which the grammar of the new idioms proceeded was therefore
essentially and principally that of the ruined tongue itself. However, the
causes of the ruination and the decay must be sought much earlier than in
the period in which the ruination and the decay themselves became manifest. During the height of the Empire, the Latin language was already
being spoken differently in the provinces than in Latium and in the capital
city of Rome. Even in the nation's original places of residence, the popular
language (the vulgar tongue) certainly contained peculiarities which did
not come to the surface until a later period, subsequent to the decline of
the prestige language. There arose naturally deviations in the pronunciation, solecisms in the constructions, and probably facilitations in the forms
through ancillary words which the cultivated language permitted not at
all or only in quite isolated instances. The popular peculiarities became
preponderant, since the cultivated language, owing to the decay of the
commonweal, no longer felt itself borne to an elevated position by literature and public usage.[23] The looser the bonds which attached the provinces
to the whole of the Roman Empire became, the more widespread this
provincial degeneration became.

Finally, the foreign intrusions of immigrant peoples increased this
distintegration. It was now no longer a question of a mere degeneration of
the language formerly predominant; rather, it was a casting off and
smashing up of its essential forms, often accompanied by a true misunderstanding of them but always involving a substitution of new media in order
to maintain the unity of speech. This material, though drawn from the
existing linguistic inventory, was often connected in a manner contrary to
common sense. In the midst of all these changes, the basic principle of the
declining language—the distinction between the objective and relative
concepts and the need of creating for both an expression peculiar to them
—persisted, as did the feeling therefore in the people, having been strongly
established by the custom of centuries. This principle was imprinted upon
every fragment of the language. It could not have been extirpated even if
the peoples involved had failed to recognize it, for it was inherent in them

to seek it out, to puzzle it out, and to apply it to linguistic reconstruction. The explanation for the phenomenon that the procedure in the Romance languages in mutually quite remote regions of Europe has remained so constant, often occasioning surprise by sporadic coincidence, must be sought in this uniformity of the reconstruction. It originated from the universal nature of linguistic sense itself, combined with the grammatically unadulterated mother tongue. Forms sank into oblivion, but the essence of form did not; it pervaded the new transformations with its time-honored spirit.

For, if in these newer languages a preposition replaces a case, the situation is not identical to that in which a word indicates the case simply by attaching particles. If the original factual significance of the word has also been lost, it does not purely express a relationship as such. This is because this method of expression is not peculiar to the entire Romance group; its structure did not flow forth from the inner linguistic attitude which neatly and energetically insists upon a sharp demarcation between parts of speech; and the spirit of the nation does not absorb its structures from this standpoint. In the Latin language, this situation was precisely and completely the case. The prepositions formed a totality of such relationships. Each required according to its meaning a case suitable to it, and only in conjunction with this case did it designate the relationship. The degenerated Romance languages, in accordance with their origin, did not absorb this fine grammatical agreement. However, the feeling for the recognition of the preposition as a distinct part of speech, for its true significance, did not disappear. This, moreover, is not an arbitrary assumption. It is unmistakably evident in the structural pattern of this entire group, which does have a number of gaps in the individual forms but on the whole retains a formal structure and in principle is no less inflectional than its parent. The same thing is encountered in the use of the verb. No matter how deficient its forms may be, the synthetic determinative power of the verb is still the same, for this group bears its differentiation from the noun in its basic structure. The pronoun, which is used in innumerable cases where the mother tongue does not express it independently, also corresponds emotionally to the true idea of this part of speech. When the pronoun is placed as an objective idea ahead of the verb in languages that lack designations for the persons in the verb itself, it represents in the derivative Latin dialects only the detached and differently placed person. The inseparability of the verb and person derived from the parent tongue is securely incorporated in these dialects and is attested by individual final sounds that are residual in the daughter languages. As in all inflected languages, the representative function of the pronoun becomes more pronounced in the daughter languages. And since this culminates in the pure conception of the relative pronoun, these languages are thereby led to the correct use of the latter. Everywhere, therefore, the same phenomenon recurs. The demolished morpheme is reconstructed in a quite different way, but its spirit still hovers in the neologistic construction, confirming the great indestructability of the vital principle of genuine, grammatically constructed linguistic families.

Despite all the uniformity in the treatment of the reconstructed material, which the daughter dialects of Latin manifest on the whole, an individual principle in the conception of each is basic. As I have repeatedly indicated in the foregoing, the innumerable details which the use of the language necessitates must be drawn together to form a unit, regardless of how speech is to be practised. And this unit cannot be other than an individual one, inasmuch as the language sinks its roots into all the fibres of the human intellect. Only by the fact that a change in the unity principle takes place—a new conception is embarked upon by the spirit of a people —does a new language become a reality. Where a nation experiences tremendous revolutionary changes affecting its language, it must by new morphological treatment embrace the new or modified elements. Previously we have spoken of the moment in the life of a nation when the possibility becomes clear to it of turning its language, independent of external use, toward building up a totality of thoughts and feelings. Even if literary origins, which in a sense we have been specifying as to their actual nature and from the standpoint of their ultimate perfection, proceed in fact but gradually and from obscurely perceived drives, their inception is always the result of a unique impulse. This consists of a compulsion, emanating from within, toward an interaction of the form of the language and the individuality of the intellect, in which the genuine and pure nature of both is reflected and which has no purpose other than this reflection. The way in which this compulsion develops determines the ideological course which the nation traverses to the time its language distintegrates. This is a second and a more or less higher association of language to unity. How this association relates to the cultivation of the external, technical form has been discussed in greater detail above in the chapter devoted to the character of languages.

This twofold treatment of languages is clearly distinguishable in the transition of the Latin language into its derivatives. Two of these derivative dialects, Rhaeto-Romansh and Daco-Rumanian, have not shared in the scientific effort of the others. This is not to be construed as implying that their technical form is inferior to that of the rest. The Daco-Rumanian has preserved to the greatest extent the inflections of the mother tongue and, moreover, approximates the Italian in its treatment of them. Thus, the deficiency is to be imputed to external conditions, to a lack of events and situations giving rise to the impulse to use the language for loftier purposes.

If we take up a similar case, we can see that this same lack of favorable events was indisputably the reason why a new, salient tongue with its own peculiar structure did not arise from the collapse of the Greek language. In many respects, with the exception of peculiarity, the structure of the Neo-Greek tongue is very similar to that of the Romance languages. Since these reconstructions are to a large extent the result of the natural development of the languages, and since both parent tongues have the same grammatical character, this similarity is readily explicable. However, it makes the difference in the final results even more striking. Greece, as the province of a declining empire that was often subjected to devastations by foreign migratory tribes, was unable to achieve the uplifting power that fresh internal and external conditions produced in the Occident. With the new social patterns, accompanied by the complete cessation of association with a disintegrating state and the accretion of powerful and courageous immigrant stocks, the emerging nations of the Occident were forced to follow new paths in all activities of the intellect and of the character. The new configuration thus created was coupled with a religious, warlike, and poetic sense, which exerted the most fortunate and decisive effect upon the language. In these nations a new, poetically creative youth blossomed, and the condition of these nations became to some extent similar to one which is separated from us by the obscurity of the dawn of history.

As surely as the development of the new Occidental languages and literatures to a peculiar state in which they were capable of competing with the parent mother tongue must be ascribed to this external historical turn of events, it seems to me that a second factor, discussed previously in passing (see p. 185), participated significantly. The evaluation of this second cause, since it concerns language particularly, belongs quite definitely within the scope of these considerations. The conversion which the Latin language suffered was incomparably more profound, more powerful, more penetrating, and more sudden than that experienced by Greek. It was equivalent to a true demolition, whereas that of the Greek remained restricted to individual mutilations and morphological dissolutions. In this example, we may recognize that there are two possible ways in which a language having a wealth of morphological material may be transformed into one less richly endowed; these possibilities are confirmed moreover by other examples in linguistic history. According to one of these possibilities, the artistic structure decays and is recreated, though on a less perfect level. With respect to the other possibility, mere superficial wounds are made in the declining language; these then heal, but remain detectable by their scars. There is no new or pure creation; the obsolescent language persists, but in a deplorable and pitiable state of disfigurement. Because the Byzantine Greek Empire, in spite of its weakness and decreptitude, continued to endure for a long time, the old language continued to persist as well, standing as a treasure house from which the peoples could always draw or as a canonical authority to which they could always refer. Nothing proves so convincingly the difference between the Neo-Greek and the Romance languages with respect to this point than the fact that the method through which individuals have attempted to elevate and purify the former in most recent times has always been characterized by the greatest possible approximation to the Old Greek. Not even a Spaniard or an Italian could conceive of such a possibility. The Romance nations truly spun off into new paths of development, and the feeling that this was imperative endowed them with the courage to pursue new directions commensurate with their individual intellect, inasmuch as a reversion was impossible. Regarded from another aspect, however, the Neo-Greek is found by this difference to be in a more favorable position. A mighty difference prevails between those languages which, as related members developing from the same parental source, diverge in the course of their development and these tongues which arise from the decomposition and upon the wreckage of others, that is, by the effect of external conditions. In the former languages, which are undisturbed by powerful revolutions and by significant admixtures with foreign dialects, it is possible more or less to retrace the steps of every expression, word, or form back to a depth which cannot be fathomed. For the most part, these languages preserve the bases for the forms within themselves and can boast of being self-sufficient and verifiably consistent within their boundaries. The daughter languages (such as the Romance derivatives) obviously do not find themselves in this position. They are based on the one hand upon a language no longer extant, and on the other upon foreign languages. Therefore all expressions, no matter how they are traced to their origin, for the most part lead through an entire series of intermediary morphemes and finally reach a foreign area unknown to the people. Even in the grammatical portion, which is little or not at all adulterated by foreign elements, the consistency of structure, insofar as it is actually present, can be revealed in every case only by reference to the foreign tongue of origin. A more profound understanding of these languages, even of the impression which each language gives through the harmonious relationship of all elements, can be achieved only in part and requires for its completion material inaccessible to the people speaking it. In both types of languages we can be forced to take recourse to the earlier tongue. However, the difference in the manner in which this is accomplished is clearly felt if we see that the inadequacy of explanation in Latin leads to Sanskrit foundations, whereas in French it leads back to Latin. Apparently, in the transformation of French there is a greater admixture of arbitrariness resulting from external influence, and even the natural, analogical process which establishes itself again in this instance depends on the presumption of that external influence. In contrast to the Romance languages, Neo-Greek does not find itself at all in this condition, or at least to an infinitely lesser degree, because it did not actually become a really new language. In the course of time, it can be liberated from admixture with foreign words, since these with few exceptions have not penetrated as deeply into the structure as they have in the Romance dialects. Its true parent, the Old Greek, cannot even appear foreign to the people. Even if the people are now incapable of comprehending the totality of its ingenious structure, they still must recognize its elements as belonging in great part to their language also.

With respect to the nature of the language itself, the difference mentioned here is certainly noteworthy. Whether it also exerts a significant influence on the spirit and character of the nation may appear rather dubious. The objection may be justifiably raised that every consideration transcending the contemporary state of the language at a given time is foreign to the people, that therefore the inherent explicability of organically close-knit languages is unfruitful for the people, and that consequently, regardless of origin, every language which has survived centuries of progressive culture attains a consistency that is completely adequate in its effect on the nation. It can in fact be conceived that languages like the Romance dialects could have originated and could appear to us as parent tongues, although a careful analysis would likely soon reveal to us their inexplicability outside their own region. Undeniably, however, there lies in the secret obscurity of the soul structure and of the continued inheritance of intellectual individuality a powerful connection between the tonal fabric of the language and the totality of ideas and emotions. It can, therefore, not possibly be a matter of indifference whether sensation and perception were cast in an unbroken chain into the same phonemes and permeated them with their content and warmth, or whether this autonomous series of causes and effects undergoes powerful disturbances. To be sure, a new consequence is established here, and time has in the area of languages more than in the human soul a power to heal wounds. It should not be forgotten, however, that this consistency is only gradually restored, and that before it becomes solidly established living generations enter the lists as causative agents. Hence it does not appear to me at all ineffectual upon the profundity of the intellectuality, upon the intimacy of perception, and upon the power of sentiment whether a people speaks a language based upon its own devices or one proceeding from an organizational, progressive development. Therefore, in the portrayal of nations whose language is in the latter category, investigation should be made to determine whether and in what way their equilibrium disturbed by the influence of their language has been restored in some other way, and indeed whether and how from this undeniable imperfection a new advantage may have been won.

CHAPTER NINETEEN

A Review of the Present Investigation

WE HAVE NOW reached one of the points to which the present investigation has been designed to lead us. The entire viewpoint of language that has been advanced here is based essentially on the fact that language is both the foundation of the perfection of thinking and a natural development that designates man as such. This development, however, is not that of an instinct which could be simply explained physiologically. Without being an act of direct consciousness, indeed without being one of instant spontaneity and freedom, it can nonetheless belong only to a being endowed with consciousness and freedom. Moreover, in such a being it proceeds from the unfathomable depth of his individuality and from the activity of his innate powers. It depends, therefore, absolutely upon the energy with which and the form in which, unconscious of his own intellectual individuality, man imparts the motivating impulse (see pp. 2, 3, 21, 24, 25). Through this relationship with an individual reality, as well as from other accessory causes, language is at the same time subject to conditions that surround man in the universe and that even exert an effect upon his freedom. Thus, in language, insofar as it actually appears with respect to man, we may distinguish two constitutive principles: the intimate linguistic sense (by which, with reference to the culture and the use of language, I do not mean a particular power but the entire intellectual capacity) and the phoneme insofar as it depends upon the quality of the organs and upon what has already been handed down. The intimate linguistic sense dominates the language from the interior and outward direction; it is the principle that everywhere supplies the guiding impulse. The phoneme would in itself be equivalent to passive material being molded. However, owing to the penetration of the linguistic sense, it is converted into articulation, thereby encompassing in itself in inseparable unity and constant interaction an intellectual and sensory power; it thus becomes the truly creative principle in the language, and is characterized by its steady and apparently independent symbolizing activity. Inasmuch as it is absolutely a law of the existence of man that he cannot release anything from himself that does not react upon him and determine his further creative effort, the phoneme in turn modifies both the viewpoint and the procedures of the intimate linguistic sense. Therefore, all creation does not proceed in the simple direction of the original power, but its course changes, being affected by what was created earlier.

Since the natural inclination to language is universal to man, and since all men must carry the key to the understanding of all languages in their minds, it follows automatically that the form of all languages must be fundamentally identical and must always achieve a common objective. The variety among languages can lie only in the media and the limits permitted the attainment of the objective. The variety is, however, multifariously present in languages, and not only in the simple phonemes, such that the same things would merely be otherwise designated, but also in the use which the linguistic sense intentionally makes of the phonemes in the morphology of the language and, indeed, in its own attitude toward this morphology. Insofar as languages are simply formal, only uniformity should be able to originate in them through this linguistic sense. For this linguistic sense requires in all tongues a correct and principled structure, which cannot be other than one and the same for all languages. In reality, however, matters are otherwise, owing partially to the retroactive effect of the phoneme, and partially to the individuality of the intimate meaning in the phenomenon. It is a matter of the energy of the force with which the linguistic sense acts upon the phoneme, transforming it into the living expression of the idea; the latter encompasses all shades of meaning, including even the finest nuances. This energy cannot be everywhere constant; nor does it reveal everywhere equal intensity, vitality, and legitimacy. Hence, it is not always supported by the same symbolic treatment of the idea and by the same aesthetic pleasure in phonetic wealth and harmony. Still, the effort pertinent to the intimate linguistic sense is always directed toward conformity in languages, and its dominant power seeks in one way or another to lead digressing forms back to their proper course. On the other hand, the phoneme is truly the principle that augments diversity. For it depends upon the quality of the organs which are chiefly trained by the alphabet, and the alphabet in turn, as proper analysis proves, is the foundation of every language. Moreover, the articulated sound has its own peculiar laws and customs, which are founded in part on facility and in part on euphony of pronunciation, and which, to be sure, again incorporate uniformity but produce variations in the particular application. Finally, inasmuch as we are at no point concerned with an isolated language at its very birth, the phoneme must always be associated with a predecessor or with a foreign one. In all of these factors taken together, then, repose the reasons for the variation in human linguistic structure. Languages cannot contain the selfsame factor in themselves because the nations speaking them differ and have an existence that is determined by different situations.

In the consideration of language per se, a form must become manifest, which among all conceivable forms coincides to the greatest extent with the objectives of the language, and we must be able to judge the advantages and deficiencies of those forms available according to the degree to which they approximate this single form. Following this procedure, we found that this form is that which is most congenial to the general course of the human intellect, which promotes its growth by a most highly regulated activity, and which not only facilitates the relative accord of all its directions but by a reactive stimulus produces them in a lively way. Intellectual activity, however, does not have merely its own inner elevation as its purpose, for in the pursuit of this end it is necessarily driven outward to erect a scientific structure of a cosmic concept, and from this standpoint also to operate creatively. This, too, we have taken into consideration, and we have seen unmistakably that this broadening of the human point of view flourishes best, or rather only, by following the guideline of the most perfected linguistic form. We have, therefore, gone into the latter in great detail, and I have tried to establish the properties of this form in which the processes of language converge toward the immediate attainment of their ultimate objectives. The question of how language proceeds to represent an idea in a simple sentence, as well as in a longer one in which many clauses are interwoven, appeared here to offer the simplest solution to the task involved in the evaluation of language with respect both to its internal and its external purposes. By this method, it was possible to revert immediately to the structure of the individual elements. That an extant linguistic family or simply an individual language of such a family coincides completely with the perfect linguistic form cannot be expected, and we have not encountered one within the scope of our experience. However, the Sanskritic languages approach this form to the highest degree and are also those in which the intellectual progress of the human race has developed through the longest series of progressions and in the most fortunate manner. Thus, we can regard them as a fixed point of comparison for all remaining tongues.

The latter cannot be portrayed with equal simplicity. Inasmuch as they strive toward the same terminal points as the purely principled languages do, but do not reach the goal to the same degree or by the proper procedure, no such clearly evident consistency can prevail in their structure. To analyze the factor of sentence structure we have established, with the exception of Chinese which is devoid of all grammatical forms, three possible language patterns: the inflectional, the agglutinating, and the incorporating. All languages bear one or more of these patterns or forms in themselves. Hence, for an evaluation of their relative advantages, it is a matter of ascertaining how they have absorbed the foregoing abstract forms into their concrete ones, or rather what is the principle of this assumption or mixture. I flatter myself that this distinction between possible abstract linguistic forms and concrete ones that are actually present will contribute to reducing the curious impression that is produced by raising a few languages to a position of preeminence, which automatically then marks the others as less perfected. The fact that among the abstract type the inflectional tongues can alone be termed correct might not be easily disputed. The judgment resultantly made of the other ones does not, however, apply in equal measure to the concrete extant languages in which there is not exclusively a single one of such forms prevailing, but in which, in contrast, there is always alive a visible striving toward the correct form. This point is in need of a more precise justification.

For those having knowledge of a number of languages, in all probability their general feeling might be that, insofar as these latter tongues are found to be upon the same cultural level, peculiar advantages deservedly accrue to each in question without our being able to assign a decisive advantage to any one over the others. However, the viewpoint established in the present considerations is in direct antithesis to this; moreover, this viewpoint might seem highly repugnant to many, because the effort made in the present considerations is especially directed toward proving, that there is an animated and indivisible connection between languages and the intellectual capacity of nations. Therefore, the same rejective judgment relative to languages appears to apply also to peoples. In this respect, however, a more precise differentiation is requisite. In the foregoing discussion, I have remarked that the advantages of languages generally depend upon the energy of the intellectual activity, but still further upon the peculiar inclination of the latter toward the cultivation of ideas through the phoneme in particular. A more imperfect language hence proves immediately the lesser drive of the nation developing it, but I have made no other decisions regarding the nation's other intellectual advantages. In all cases, we began first with the structure of the language, and adhered to it in the formulation of a judgment thereof. Impartial scholars could deny only with difficulty that this structure is in degree more excellent in the one tongue than in another, that it is better, for example, in Sanskrit than in Chinese or better in Greek than in Arabic. No matter how we tried to balance advantage against advantage, we would always have to admit that a fruitful principle of intellectual development inspires one bracket of these languages more than the other. Now, if we did not wish to extend the various conclusions to be drawn from this to the reactive effect of these languages and to the intellectuality of the peoples who created them (to the extent that this is at all within human power), we would fail to recognize all the relationships that exist between the intellect and language. From this approach, therefore, the viewpoint established is completely justified. However, the objection may still be raised, that individual advantages of language are capable of developing individual intellectual aspects, and, further, that the intellectual foundations of nations themselves differ far more in their mixture and quality than we can measure off on a graduated scale. Both statements are undeniably correct, but the true advantage of languages must still be sought in their universal and harmoniously effective power. Languages are tools which intellectual activity needs, they are the roadways upon which such activity rolls forward. Therefore, they are truly beneficial only when they facilitate this intellectual activity and accompany it inspiringly, placing it in the center so that each of its categories may develop harmoniously. Hence, even though we are willing to admit that the form of the Chinese tongue more than perhaps any other brings out the power of the pure idea and directs the soul toward it more exclusively and precisely because it lops off all small disturbing connecting phonemes, and even if reading of but a few Chinese texts increases this conviction to a state of admiration, the most resolute defendants of this language could scarcely claim that it guides intellectual activity to the true central point from which poetry, philosophy, scientific research, and eloquent recitation blossom forth.

No matter from which aspect of the matter I begin, therefore, I still cannot avoid establishing an absolute antithesis between languages of a purely principled form and those clearly deviating from such a pure principle. According to my most profound conviction, an undeniable fact is thereby expressed. However, the excellence of digressive languages, which preserve such individual advantages as the genius and artistry of their technical structure, is neither mistaken nor derogated herein. I am denying only their capacity, when compared to principled languages, to affect the intellect with the same universality and harmony. Nobody could be farther from condemning any language, even the rudest or primitive peoples, than the present writer. Not only would I consider such a condemnation as degrading to humanity in its most private and peculiar foundations, but I would also deem it incompatible with all correct viewpoints relative to language that have accrued from reflection and experience. Every language remains a likeness of the original predisposition responsible for language, and, to be capable of achieving the simplest objectives which every language must necessarily attain, an artistic structure is always required such that its study necessarily attracts research without consideration of the fact that every language, in addition to its already developed component, possesses an indeterminate capacity for flexibility and for the incorporation of increasingly rich and lofty ideas. In all that has been stated herein, I have presumed the nations as restricted to their own devices. However, they attract foreign culture also, and as a result their intellectual activity is enriched by an increment not derived from its own language but which serves to expand its peculiar operational periphery. For every language possesses the pliancy to absorb everything and is capable in turn of imparting its own expression to everything. Under no condition can it become an absolute restriction to man. The difference between languages is only whether the point of departure for the power increase and ideological expansion lies within its very self or is of foreign extraction. In other words, the problem resolves itself as to whether the language is inspired or whether it remains more or less passive and resignedly collaborative.

If such a distinction between languages is at hand, we may ask by what signs it can be recognized. That I have sought it precisely in the grammatical method of sentence structure may appear one-sided and incommensurate with the plentitude of the concept. But it has certainly not been my intention to restrict consideration to this factor alone, inasmuch as this difference is equally active in every element and in every syntactic component. I have, however, deliberately returned to that which more or less constitutes the foundations of the language, and which immediately has a quite decisive effect upon the development of ideas. The logical arrangement of sentence structure, its clear distinction, and the definite portrayal of its interrelationships—these constitute the indispensable foundation of all, even the highest expressions of intellectual activity, but they depend essentially upon the foregoing differing linguistic methods, as must be obvious to everyone. In keeping with the proper method, moreover, correct thinking proceeds easily and naturally, whereas in other languages it encounters difficulties to overcome or does not at least enjoy as much help on the part of language. The same intellectual attitude from which the foregoing three variant methods originate extends also to the formation

of all of the remaining elements of language and is only especially
recognized in sentence structure. Finally, these peculiarities are suited to
be illustrated factually in the linguistic structure, a circumstance that is
especially important in an investigation aimed particularly toward finding in the factual, historically recognizable components of languages the
form which they impart to the intellect or in which they are innately
represented to it.

CHAPTER TWENTY

Less Developed Linguistic Structure:
The Semitic and Delaware Indian Languages

THE PATHS DEVIATING from the course prescribed by pure principles can
be of an infinite number, and languages which do deviate cannot be
classified and exhaustively analyzed through the application of pure
principles. They can at best only be compared according to similarities in
their most basic structural components. If it is right, however, that the
natural structure depends on the one hand on fixed word unity and on the
other on the appropriate separation of the sentence components, all
languages of which we are here speaking must narrow down either the
factor of word unity or that of freedom in connecting ideas, or, finally,
combine both of these disadvantages. In the comparison of even the most
divergent languages, a general scale for their relationship to intellectual
development will always be found within the restriction. A search for the
reasons of such digressions from the natural course of development is
fraught with peculiar difficulties. Whereas the natural course can be
traced via the concepts involved, the deviation is based upon individualities which, owing to the obscurity into which the earlier history of
every language withdraws, can only be suspected and divined. Where the
imperfect organization is simply to be explained by the fact that the innate
linguistic sense has been unable in all cases to produce a meaningful
expression in the phoneme, and hence that the formative power has
languished prior to the attainment of complete morphological con-
ventionality, this difficulty certainly appears to a lesser extent inasmuch
as the basis of this imperfection is to be found in this weakness itself. However, these cases seldom appear so simple, and there are others, precisely
the most remarkable, which cannot be at all explained merely in this way.
Yet the investigation must be pursued indefatigably even to this point,

unless we wish to give up the disclosure of linguistic structure in its primary foundations so to speak, that is, where it takes root in the speech organs and in the intellect. It would be impossible for me to go into this material exhaustively in any way. Therefore, I shall satisfy myself to tarry only a few moments with a discussion of two examples. For the first I have selected the Semitic languages, especially the Hebrew tongue.

This linguistic family obviously belongs to the inflectional group. Indeed, it has already been noted that inflection in the truest sense of the word is indigenous to Hebrew in contrast to significant agglutination. The Hebrew and Arabic languages have also recorded the innate excellence of their structure, the former in works of the highest poetic inspiration, and the latter in a rich, comprehensive scientific literature as well as in a poetic one. Regarded from a merely technical standpoint, the organization of these languages, with respect to rigorous consistency, artistic simplicity, and meaningful adaptation of the phoneme to the idea, is not only not inferior to any other but perhaps excels them all. Yet these languages have two inherent peculiarities which do not lie in their natural requirements; indeed, we may add with certainty that they are scarcely within the permissible range of the language. In their present configuration at least, they definitely require three consonants in each word stem. Furthermore, consonant and vowel do not together contain the meaning of the words, but meaning and relationship are exclusively assigned to one and the other factor—that is, the meaning is assigned to the consonant, whereas the relationship falls to the vowel. From the first of these peculiarities arises a constraint for the morphology of the word, to which honestly may be preferred the freedom of other languages, especially those of the Sanskritic group. From the second of the foregoing peculiarities disadvantages accrue with respect to inflection by the attachment of properly subordinate phonemes. Therefore, I am convinced that from this approach the Semitic languages must be counted among those deviating from the most suitable course of development. If we attempt, however, to trace the reasons for this phenomenon and its connection with national linguistic foundations, it would be difficult for us to arrive at satisfactory results. It immediately appears dubious which of the foregoing two peculiarities is to be regarded as the determinative basis of the other. Obviously the two are most intimately connected. The syllabic range possible for three consonants invited the development, so to speak, of indicating the multifarious relationships of words by vowel change. And if it had been desired to restrict the vowels exclusively to this purpose, the requisite semantic wealth could have been attained only through the use of several consonants in the same word. The interaction depicted here is more suited, however, to elucidate the inner associations of the language in its present-day formation than it is to serve as the basis for the origin of such a structure. The indication of the grammatical relationships by mere vowels cannot be reasonably assumed to be the primary determinative basis, since everywhere in languages the meaning naturally precedes and therefore the exclusion of the vowels from it would be explained. To be sure, the vowels must be considered from a twofold standpoint. They serve first only as sound without which the consonant could not be pronounced. In addition, however, the variation of the phonetic sound confronts us, which the vowels assume in the vocalic series. In the first respect, there are no vowels but only one, a universal vowel sound, or, if you will, there is actually no true vowel at all but an indistinct schwa phoneme still undeveloped in detail [allophones]. Something similar is encountered with respect to consonants in their combination with vowels. However, to become audible, the vowel also requires consonantal breath. Insofar as the latter includes only the property requisite for this determination, it differs from the tones in the consonantal series distinguished from each other by sound.[1] From the foregoing it follows automatically that the vowels in the expression of ideas merely become associated to the consonants and, as the most profound comparative linguists have already recognized,[2] serve mainly for the more exact determination of the word configured by the consonants. It lies also in the phonetic nature of vowels that they indicate something finer, more penetrating, and more intimate than do the consonants and are, so to speak, less corporeal and more spiritual. For this reason, to which is to be added the facility of producing their sound and their capability of association, they are more adapted to grammatical indication. In any case their exclusively grammatical exploitation in the Semitic languages is still very different from all of this. This usage, I believe, is a unique phenomenon in linguistic history and therefore is in need of special explanation. If, to find the reasons responsible, we start from the disyllabic root structure, we are confronted by the circumstance that this type of root structure was probably still not really the original one, even though it was constitutive for the state of these languages familiar to us. Rather, as I shall subsequently discuss in more detail, it is apparent to a greater extent than is presently assumed, that monosyllabic roots constituted the basis in these tongues. The peculiarity being discussed here may perhaps be derived from this and from the transition to disyllabic morphemes to which we are lead by a comparison of the disyllabic ones with each other. These monosyllabic forms contained two consonants with a vowel between them. Perhaps the vowel thus enclosed and drowned out by the consonantal sounds lost the capacity for an independent development and therefore did not participate in the expression of the meaning. The necessity for grammatical designation which later became evident perhaps triggered this development, and then, to accord greater operational scope to grammatical inflections, produced the addition of a second syllable. There must always have been some additional reason which did not permit the vowels to be pronounced freely in final position. This reason is probably to be sought in the quality of the organs involved and in the peculiarity of pronunciation rather than in the innate linguistic viewpoints involved.

In contrast, it seems more certain to me than what has been discussed to this point, and more important for determination of the relationship of the Semitic languages to intellectual development, that the intimate linguistic sense in the case of these peoples was still lacking the necessary acuteness and clarity of distinction with respect to the material meaning and to the relationship of words. The foregoing was true in part with regard to the general forms of speaking and thinking and in part with regard to sentence structure, so that as a result even the purity of discrimination between consonantal and vocalic determination was endangered. First, I must call attention to the particular nature of those phonemic clusters which are termed roots in the Semitic languages but which differ essentially from the root phonemes of other languages. Since the vowels are excluded from material significance, the three consonants making up the root, taken rigorously, must be nonvocalic, that is, merely accompanied by the sound requisite for their utterance. In this state, however, they lack the necessary phonetic or phonemic form for occurrence in speech since the Semitic languages do not countenance several, directly successive consonants connected simply by schwa. With added vowels, they express this or that definite relationship and cease to be nonreferential or nonrelational roots. Therefore, where roots really appear in the language, they are already true word forms [semantemes]. But even in their actual root format, they still lack an important component necessary to complete their morphological configuration in speech, and, owing to this, inflection in the Semitic languages becomes endowed with a different meaning than this concept has in the remaining languages, where the root —free of all relationship and audibly perceptible—appears at least as a word component in speech. Inflected words in the Semitic languages do not contain inflectional modifications of original tones; rather they contain complementations that produce the true phonetic form. Now, since the original root morpheme cannot become, in addition to the inflected one, perceptible to the ear in connected speech, the animate distinction between semantic and relational expression suffers. To be sure, the connection between the two becomes resultantly even more intimate, and the application of the phonemes, in accordance with H. von Ewald's correct and astute remark, becomes more suitable than in any other language, since to the readily motile vowels is imparted the more intellectual factor, and to the consonants, the more material one. The feeling for the necessary unity of the word, encompassing both meaning and relationship, is greater and more energetic if the amalgamated elements can be separated into their purely independent states. This is fitting to the purpose of the language, which eternally divides and combines, and to the nature of thinking as well. However, even in the investigation of the individual types of semantic and relational expression, the language is not found to be free of a certain mixture of both. By the deficiency of inseparable prepositions, it loses an entire class of relational designations which constitute a totality and which can be portrayed in a completely schematic way. In the Semitic languages this shortcoming is obviated in part by the fact that there are special words for expressing those verbal concepts that are prepositionally modified. This, however, cannot guarantee completeness, and even less is this apparent wealth capable of indemnifying for the disadvantage that, as the one extreme becomes less palpably represented, even the totality does not become clearly visible. Hence speakers lose the possibility of a facile and certain linguistic expansion via individual applications previously untried.

I cannot skip over at this point a distinction in the various types of relationships which appears important to me. The indication of the cases of the noun, insofar as they permit expression and are not distinguished simply by position, is effected by the addition of prepositions, whereas the distinction between persons of the verb is made by the addition of pronouns. By these two additions, the meaning of the words is in no wise affected. They are simply expressions of pure and generally applicable relationships. The grammatical medium, however, is attachment, specifically of alphabetical characters or syllables which the language recognizes as independent but which it combines with the words to a certain degree of solidity. To the extent that vowel change occurs in the process, it is a consequence of the foregoing increments, whose attachment cannot remain without having some effect upon the lexical morphology of a language which possesses highly fixed rules for word structure. The remaining referential expressions, whether consisting of pure vowel change, of the addition of consonants (as in the *hifil*, *nifal*, and so forth), or of the gemination of one of the consonants of the word itself, as is the case in most of the comparative forms, have a closer relationship with the material meaning of the word. The language affixes these elements, changing them more or less completely, as if precisely from the stem "great" the verb "to educate" is produced by such a form. Originally and principally they designate actual grammatical relationships—the distinction between noun and verb, and between transitive and intransitive, or reflexive and causative verbs, and so forth. The change in the original meaning through which concepts derived from stems arise is a natural consequence of these forms themselves, without any attendant necessity for an admixture of the relational and semantic expression. The same phenomenon in the Sanskritic languages confirms this. However, the entire difference between the foregoing two classes (on the one hand the pronominal and case affixes, on the other that of internal verbal inflections) and their designations is striking in itself. To be sure, in this distinction reposes a certain fitness with respect to the variation of the cases. In those instances where the idea undergoes no change, the relationship is designated merely externally; in contrast, it is designated internally in the stem itself, where the grammatical form extending to the individual word affixes the meaning. In the latter case, the vowel receives the precise delineating, more closely modifying component discussed above. In fact, all cases of the second class are of this type and can be applied to the simple participles, if we restrict consideration to the verb without concern for the actual verbal force itself.

In the Barmanic [Burmese] language this actually occurs, and the verbal prefixes in the Malayan dialects form approximately the same pattern as do those of the Semitic in this type of designation. All cases thereof can be related to something modifying the idea itself. This holds even for the indication of the tenses, insofar as they are produced by inflection and not syntactically. For in the former manner the language distinguishes merely the reality and not the uncertainty that is still to be definitely determined. It seems strange that precisely those relationships which to the greatest extent only place the unmodified idea into another state of relationship, as do the cases, and those relationships which form most basically the verbal nature, as do the persons, are less formally designated, indeed almost incline away from the concept of inflection and toward agglutination, while those modifying the idea itself assume the most formal expression. The linguistic sense of the nation appears here not to have made a sharp distinction between relationship and meaning, but rather to have derived the ideas flowing forth from the original meaning in an ordered way—that is, in accordance with systematic grammatical classification with respect to the various nuances of the ideas in question. Otherwise the common nature of all grammatical relationships would not have been to some extent obliterated by treatment in a twofold method of expression. If this reasoning is correct and appears in agreement with facts, this case thus proves how a people can treat its language with admirable acumen and with a rare feeling for the reciprocal requirements of concept and phoneme, and yet lose the thread which in such a language is the most naturally suited. The disinclination of the Semitic languages toward compounding is readily explicable by their entire form, here only delineated in its main outlines. Even if the difficulty of imparting to poly-syllabic words the lexical form firmly rooted in the language could be overcome, as compound proper names prove it could be, compounding still had to be avoided owing to the fact that the people were accustomed to a shorter, rigidly segmented lexical form which permitted the internal structure of the word to be readily surveyed.

In the Delaware Indian dialect of North America there prevails perhaps more than any other the custom of constructing new words through com-pounding. The elements of these compounds, however, seldom contain the entire original word; only parts of the latter, indeed only individual phonemes, go over into the compound. From an example cited by S. du Ponceau[3] we must even conclude that it depends on the speaker to com-bine such words or entire phrases which are reduced to the status of words more or less from fragments of words. From the words *ki*, 'thou' or 'you,' *wulit*, 'good,' 'pretty,' or 'cute,' *wichgat*, 'paw,' and *schis* (a word used in a diminutive sense as an ending) is constructed the expression *k-uli-gat-schis*, 'thy cute little paw,' which is used in addressing a small kitten. In the same way, idiomatic phrases are turned into verbs and are then com-pletely conjugated. *Nad-hol-ineen*, from *naten*, 'to fetch,' *amochol*, 'boat,' and the concluding governed pronoun of the first-person plural, means 'fetch (or carry) us with the boat,' specifically, 'across the river.' It is already evident from these examples that the changes undergone by the words forming compounds are very significant. For instance, in the above example *wulit* becomes *uli*; in other cases, where no consonant precedes in the compound, *wul* alone or with a preceding consonant becomes *ola*.[4] At times, the abbreviations are very powerful. In order to construct the word "horse," only the syllables *es* of the word *awesis*, 'animal,' is incorporated into the compound. Since the word fragments come into combination with other phonemes, euphonic changes occur at the same time which make the fragments even less recognizable. Save for the ending *es*, only *nayundam*, 'bearing a burden upon the back,' lies at the basis of the word just men-tioned for "horse," *nanyung-es*. The guttural *g* has been inserted, and the intensification produced by the doubling of the first syllable is applied only to the compound. A simple initial *m* of the word *machit*, 'bad,' or from the word *medhick*, 'evil,' or 'wicked,' imparts to the word a pejorative, that is, a bad, base, or vile, meaning.[5] This word mutilation has been very strongly criticized as a barbaric crudity. However, a deeper knowledge of the Delaware tongue and its word relationships would be necessary to decide whether in these abbreviated words the stem syllables are destroyed or preserved. That the latter is true in some cases is illustrated by a remarkable example. The word *lenape* means 'man' or 'human being.' The term *lenni*, which with the foregoing word constitutes the name of the main tribe of the Delaware Indians (Lenni Lenape), has the meaning of 'something original, pure, or unadmixed,' or the meaning of 'belonging to the country from way back'; therefore, it also denotes 'common,' 'ordinary,' or 'usual.' In the latter sense, it serves as the expression for designating everything indigenous, everything given to the land by the great and good spirit, in contrast to everything brought from foreign shores more recently by the white man. The monosyllable *ape* signifies 'to walk erect.'[6] In the word *lenape* then, the identifying characteristics of the erect-walking aborigine are quite correctly contained. That the word serves generally for 'human being,' and that in becoming a proper name it combines in itself the concept of originality, are readily explainable phenomena. In the word *pilape*, 'youth,' is compounded the word *pilsit*, 'chaste,' or 'innocent,' with that portion of *lenape* which designates the property characterizing man. Since the words united in compounding are largely polysyllabic and are themselves already compounds, everything depends upon which of their components is used as the element of the new compound. More detailed information concerning this feature could be obtained only from a complete dictionary. Also, it is probably self-evident that linguistic usage will have subjected these abbreviations to definite rules. This is already seen from the fact that the modified word in the examples given is always the last element in the compound, following the modifying terms. The process involved in this apparent word mutilation might therefore deserve a milder judgment, and might not be as destructive to etymology as one might fear from a superficial scrutiny. It is related to the tendency already cited herein as distinctive of American Indian tongues to combine the pronoun in abbreviated or in still more divergent form with the verb and noun. What has just been said of the Delaware dialect confirms an even more general effort toward combining several ideas in the same word. If several of the languages which indicate grammatical relationships without inflection via particles are compared with each other, some of them, such as the Barmanic [Burmese], the majority of the dialects of the South Sea Islands, and even the Manchu and Mongolian, tend to keep the particles and the words determined by them apart, while, in contrast, the American Indian tongues are inclined to combine them. The latter trend emerges naturally from the incorporative process already outlined herein (see Chapter 14). In the foregoing, I have described this as a limitation of sentence structure, and have explained it as owing to the anxiety of the linguistic sense to tie the parts of the sentence quite closely together for purposes of comprehension.

From the process of Delaware word formation considered here, however, we can derive yet another aspect. There is in this Indian tongue a noticeable inclination to present to the intellect in a package the ideas combined in the concept, instead of individually, and at the same time to associate them phonemically. It is a picturesque treatment of the language, associated with its evidently figurative treatment of concepts that reflects all their designations. The acorn is called *wu-nach-quim*, 'the nut of the leaf hand' (from *wumpach*, 'leaf,' *nach*, 'hand,' and *quim*, 'the nut'), because the lively imaginative power of the people compared the lobed oak leaf to the human hand. We should also note the twofold agreement with the above-mentioned principle concerning the position of the elements, first that of the latter, then that of the former two; the hand formed from a leaf, so to speak, follows this word and not the reverse. It is obviously of great importance to note how much a language includes in a single word instead of paraphrasing with several. The good writer practises careful distinction in this respect, where his language permits him free choice. The proper equilibrium which the Greek language observes in this matter certainly contributes to its great beauty. What has been combined into a single word is represented more as a unit to the soul, since words in a language are what individuals are in reality. As a unit, the single word arouses the imaginative power more animatedly than does a group of words imparted to it individually. Therefore, the inclusion of several concepts in a single word is more a thing of imaginative power, while their separation is more a thing of reason. Both can even confront each other and behave in such case according to their own rules, whose variance is betrayed in a distinct example in the language. Reason requires of the word that it call up the concept completely and purely defined, but that at the same time it indicate the logical relationship in which it appears in language and speech. The Delaware language satisfies these rational requirements in its own way, but does not meet the demands of the more elevated linguistic sense. Conversely, this language becomes the living symbol of imaginative power connecting images serially, and in this respect it preserves a very peculiar beauty. In Sanskrit, the so-called indeclinable participles, which so often serve as the expression of parenthetical clauses, contribute essentially to the virile representation of the concept whose components they more nearly simultaneously bring to mind. However, since they possess grammatical designation, in them is united the rigorousness of the comprehensional requirement with the free outpouring of imaginative power. This is their praiseworthy aspect. However, they also reveal an opposite aspect when, through clumsiness, they apply fetters to the freedom of sentence structure and when their incorporative process brings to mind a deficiency in the multiplicity of media necessary to expand the sentence properly.

It does not seem surprising to me that this bold and figurative association of words belongs to a North American Indian language. However, I should not desire to draw any rigorous conclusions respecting the character of these people in contrast to that of their southerly neighbors, since for this purpose more data respecting both peoples and their early history would be requisite. It is certain, though, that in the speeches and transactions of these North American stocks a greater elevation of the spirit and a bolder flight of imagination can be recognized than exist to our knowledge in southerly America. Nature, climate, and the hunting culture more peculiar to this part of America, requiring wide-ranging expeditions through the most solitary forests, may have contributed to these developments. It also seems inherently correct that the great despotic governments —particularly the priest-dominated Peruvian theocracy which suppressed the free development of individuality—exerted a very deleterious effect, whereas the foregoing hunting races, so far as we know, always lived in a free association. Following their conquest by Europeans, moreover, both of these racial groups suffered, precisely in the respect here being discussed, very different but basically decisive fates. The foreign settlers along the North American coasts pressed the natives back and deprived them probably unjustly of their property; they did not, however, subject them because their missionaries, endowed with the freer and gentler spirit of Protestantism, found a tyrannical, monkish regime, such as that which the Spaniards and Portuguese systematically introduced, foreign to their natures.

We may also ask whether in the rich imaginative power of which such languages as the Delaware Indian tongue bear a visible stamp, there is also a sign that we have found a more youthful linguistic configuration. This is a difficult question to answer since it is not possible to separate very many of the factors pertaining to time and to the intellectual bent of the nation. In this respect, I merely remark that this compounding of words, of which in our present-day state of the language often only individual characters [or sounds] have perhaps remained, is readily encountered in the most beautiful and most highly cultured languages also. This is to be expected, since it lies in the nature of things to ascend from the simple level. Moreover, in the lapse of so many millennia during which the language has propagated in the mouth of the people, the meanings of the primordial phonemes have naturally been lost.

CHAPTER TWENTY-ONE

Less Developed Linguistic Structure:
The Chinese and Burmese Languages

AMONG ALL THE known languages, those that are found to be in a state of greatest antithesis are Chinese and Sanskrit. Whereas the former has referred all grammatical form of the language to the operation of the intellect, the latter has striven to incorporate it even into the finest nuances of the phoneme. Obviously the distinction between the two languages lies in their manner of designation, which is deficient for Chinese and visibly brilliant for Sanskrit. With exception of the use of a few particles, which, as I will show later, can be dispensed with to a high degree, Chinese indicates all grammatical form by position, that is, by the use of words fixed once and for all in a given pattern and by their logical context, thus simply by media whose application demands intellectual effort. Sanskrit, in contrast, imparts to the phonemes themselves not merely the sense of the grammatical form, but also its more intellectual configuration, its relationship to the material meaning.

Accordingly, at first glance the Chinese language ought to be deemed the one most greatly digressing from the natural requirement of language, that is, the most imperfect of all. This viewpoint vanishes, however, upon closer inspection, for Chinese possesses a high degree of excellence and exerts a mighty—even if one-sided—effect upon intellectual capacity. The basis for this could be sought in its early scientific treatment and its literary wealth. Yet, obviously the language itself has participated to a great degree as a challenge and as an aid in such cultural progress. To begin with, the great consistency of its structure cannot be disputed. All other noninflected languages, even though they betray a great striving toward inflection, stop underway without attaining this goal. Chinese carries its fundamental principle to a logical conclusion by abandoning this course completely. Then nature impelled all the media applied for the comprehension of all formal material—without support of significant phonemes—toward the objective of more rigorously noting the various formal relationships and ordering them systematically. Finally, the difference between material meaning and formal relationship becomes so much the clearer to the intellect because the language as perceived by the ear merely contains the significant phonemes, whereas expression of the formal relationships, although it depends on the phonemes, does so only proportionately with respect to position and subordination. By this almost consistent nonphonetic designation of formal relationships, the Chinese language, insofar as the general coincidence of all languages admits variation within a single inner form, differs from all others known. This is most distinctly recognized if we attempt to force any of its parts into the form of inflectional languages, as one of its greatest scholars, J. P. Abel Rémusat, tried to do. This great authority on the Chinese tongue compiled a complete Chinese declension.[1] Naturally, there must exist in every language media for distinguishing the various relationships of the noun. However, the latter may not always be considered as cases in the true sense of the word, and the Chinese language does not at all profit from such a viewpoint. Its characteristic advantage lies conversely, as J. P. Abel Rémusat has very succinctly remarked in the reference cited, in its system that deviates from that of other languages, even if precisely by this system it does without numerous advantages and as a language and intellectual implement lags behind the Sanskritic and Semitic tongues. The lack of a phonemic designation of formal relationships in the Chinese language, however, must not be studied in isolation. Simultaneously, and moreover principally, we must consider the retroaction which this deficiency necessarily exerts upon the intellect by compelling it to combine these relationships in a more refined way with the words, while still not actually incorporating them in these associations but truly discovering them as resident in them. No matter how paradoxical this may sound, I still deem it to be definite that the apparent absence in Chinese of any and all grammar increases the sharpness of the mind in the nation with respect to the recognition of the formal concatenation of speech; in contrast, languages revealing an attempted but unsuccessful designation of grammatical relationships are inclined to induce intellectual somnolence and to obfuscate the grammatical sense by admixing materially and formally significant factors.

I suspect that this odd Chinese linguistic structure stems indisputably from the phonemic peculiarity of the people in earliest times, from their custom of keeping syllables rigorously apart in pronunciation, and from a deficiency in the motility with which one tone acts to modify another. This sensory peculiarity must be assumed as the basis if the intellectual idiosyncrasy of the internal linguistic morphology is to be explained, since every tongue can start out only from the uncultivated popular vernacular. Now, if a philosophic and scientific treatment of the language originated through the brooding and inventive sense of the nation, and through its acute and lively sense of phantasy which was dominated by reason, the language could pursue only the path disclosed by the older style. That is, it had to retain the isolation of the tones existing in the speech of the people, but at the same time it could establish everything and distinguish precisely what was required in the more elevated use of the language for the clear presentation of an idea, even though it would be divested of accent and attitude or gesture. That such a treatment began very early is historically confirmed and is revealed also in the slight but unmistakable traces of pictorial representation in Chinese writing. It can probably be generally maintained that, when the intellect commences to elevate itself to scientific thinking and such a trend enters into the treatment of the language, pictographic writing cannot survive long. For the Chinese, this must have been doubly true. Like all other peoples, they would have been led to an alphabetical script by the distinctions in the articulation of the phoneme. But it is explicable that the invention of writing did not follow this route in their case. Inasmuch as the spoken language never entangled the tones, their individual designation was less requisite. Because the ear perceived monograms [pictographic outlines] of the phoneme, the writing was modeled upon reproduction of these monograms. Using pictographic script as a point of departure, and without approaching alphabetical notation, the people devised an artistic, arbitrarily produced system of signs; this system is not without relationship between the individual symbols, but this relationship is always only in an ideal, never a phonetic context. Because the bent of understanding prevailed in the nation and in the language over the pleasure in phonetic change, these signs became indications of concepts more than of phonemes, save that to each sign there still corresponds a definite word since the concept attains fulfillment only through the word.

In this way, the Chinese and Sanskrit languages constitute in the entire linguistic area familiar to us two extremes, unequal to each other in fitness for intellectual development, but certainly equal in inner consistency and thorough application of their system. The Semitic languages cannot be regarded as lying between them. They belong, in accordance with their definite inflectional bent, in one and the same class with the Sanskritic dialects. However, all of the remaining languages may be considered as

ccupying a medial position between the foregoing extremes, inasmuch as
ll must approach either the Chinese isolation of words from their grammatical relationships or the fixed association of phonemes designating
uch grammatical functions. Even incorporative languages, such as the
Mexican Indian dialects, fall into this category, for incorporation cannot
ndicate all relationships, and where this feature falls short particles must
e used which are attached or which may remain separated. However,
hese multifarious languages differ from one another and have nothing in
ommon beyond the facts that these negative properties do not dispense
with all grammatical designation and these languages possess no inflec-
ion. Hence, they can be put into the same class only in a very indefinite
manner.

Accordingly, we may ask whether in linguistic structure (not merely in
he same linguistic family but generally) there ought not be stepwise
levations to an ever increasing level of perfection. This question can, in
act, be approached from the actual origin of language, as if in the various
pochs of the human race there had been only successive linguistic
tructures, differing with respect to origin and preconditioning. In such
ase, Chinese would be the oldest language while Sanskrit would be the
oungest, for time could have preserved for us forms deriving from varying
pochs. I have already outlined above, and this constitutes a principal
oint in my linguistic views, that the more perfect language, when the
uestion is merely considered from a conceptual viewpoint, need not also
e the more recent. Historically, nothing can be decided on this point;
till, in one of the following sections—in my discussion of the effective
rigin and admixture of languages—I shall attempt to determine this
oint more precisely. Nonetheless, without consideration for what has
ctually prevailed, we may inquire whether the languages occupying the
nedial position relate to each other structurally with respect to such
radational elevations or whether their differences do not permit their
neasurement by such a simple scale unit. On the one hand, the former
ctually seems to be the case. For example, whereas the Burmese language
ossesses for most grammatical relationships true phonemic designations in
articles, but does not interlace or incorporate them with each other or
with nouns by phonetic changes, the American Indian languages, as I
ave shown, combine abbreviated elements and impart to the word thus
riginating a certain phonetic unity. It appears that the latter method
pproaches true inflection more closely. But, if in turn we compare the
urmese with the actual Malayan, we observe that the former certainly
esignates many more relationships while the latter retains the Chinese
ondesignational character; in contrast, however, the Malayan treats the

agglutinative syllables with careful attention both to their own and to the noun phonemes. Thus, it becomes perplexing to decide to which of these two languages the preference should be accorded, although by evaluation from a different approach the preference indubitably accrues to the Malayan language.

It is evident, therefore, that it would be one-sided to determine in this way and in accordance with such criteria stages of linguistic development. This is, moreover, completely understandable. If the previous observations justifiably recognize one linguistic form as the only principled type, this preference is based only on the fact that, by a happy coincidence of a rich and delicate origin with an animate power of the linguistic sense, the entire foundation with which man is physically and intellectually endowed with respect to language develops completely and unadulteratedly in the phoneme. A linguistic structure developing under such favorable conditions then appears to have sprung from a correct and energetic intuition of the relationship of speech to thought and of all the components of the language to each other. In fact, a truly principled linguistic structure is possible only where such an intuition, similar to an animating flame, pervades the structure with its luminous glow. Without such an inner principle, which operates mechanically but effectively, such a structure remains unattainable. However, even if such favourable circumstances do not everywhere concur, all peoples in their linguistic development have always but one and the same tendency. All of them desire what is right in conformity with nature—the optimum. The language developing in and about them produces this automatically, without additional aid on their part. Moreover, it is inconceivable that a nation would more or less intentionally designate, for example, only the material meaning and grammatical relationships and would dispense with phonemic designation. However, since language, which man develops and in whose circumstances of development, moreover, he discovers a personal pleasure, is restricted in its effort, it does not achieve the same goal everywhere, but rather senses its own insufficiency owing to a limitation not inherent in itself. But, regardless of the foregoing, the necessity of always satisfying its general purpose impels language in some way or another to break this limitation and to achieve an appropriate configuration. Thus originate the concrete form of various human tongues, and it therefore contains insofar as it deviates from the structural principle, a negative component designating the limit of creation, as well as a positive component channeling the imperfectly attained state toward its general objective. In this negative bracket, we probably could conceive of a gradational elevation in accordance with the degree to which the creative power of the language proved effective. The positive factor, however, in which even in less perfect languages the often very artistic, individual structure is found to exist, does not by far always permit such determinations. Because in such cases a greater or lesser agreement with the principled structure and lack thereof are simultaneously present, we often satisfy ourselves by balancing the advantages and deficiencies against each other. In this anomalous type of linguistic creation, if I may be permitted to use this expression, an individual linguistic component with a certain preference over others often develops. Herein, moreover, frequently reposes the characteristic trait of individual languages. Naturally, in such cases the true purity of the correct principle cannot become pronounced in any component, for this requires equivalent treatment of all and would automatically extend its effect to the other components, were it possible for it to truly permeate one of them. Therefore, deficiency of true internal consistency is a common characteristic of all of these languages. Even the Chinese cannot attain such a consistency completely since in a few cases, although not many, it must take recourse to the principle of word order through the aid of particles.

If less perfect languages are lacking the true unity of a principle uniformly permeating them from the interior outward, the process here described does give each of them a unity nonetheless. This may not always proceed from the nature of the language generally, but rather from its particular individuality. Without unity of form, no language would be conceivable; and as people speak, they necessarily embrace their language with such a unity. This occurs for each internal and external increment accruing to the language. For, according to its innermost nature, language constitutes a continuous texture or fabric of analogies in which the foreign element can be secured only by its own association with the language.

The observations made here reveal what a multiplicity of varying linguistic structures man is capable of creating, and they consequently permit us to despair of the possibility of formulating an exhaustive classification of languages. Such a classification can probably be established for specific purposes if individual features of the language are accepted as classification criteria; on the other hand, it encounters insoluble difficulties if, owing to more penetrating research, the classification is also to include the essential nature of languages and their intimate relationship with the intellectual individuality of nations. However, even without the difficulties just mentioned, the establishment of a system of relationships and differences of any completeness would still be impossible given the present state of linguistic knowledge. A not insignificant number of researches which have not as yet been undertaken would, of necessity, have to precede such a labor, for the correct insight into the nature of a language requires much more persevering and profound investigations than have to date been dedicated to most languages.

Nonetheless, there are found between nonrelated languages, and in areas most distinctly associated with the intellectual bent, differences which appear to separate languages into various classes. At an earlier point in this treatise (see Chapter 18), I spoke of the importance of according to the verb a designation formally characterizing its true function. In this peculiarity, languages which otherwise seem to stand upon the same level differ. For example, "particle languages," a term applicable to those which designate grammatical relationships by syllables or words but attach such particles only loosely and inter-changeably or not at all, do not establish any fundamental difference between noun and verb. Even if they do designate a few isolated categories of the noun, this is done only with reference to definite concepts and in certain cases and not consistently in the sense of grammatical isolation. Therefore, it is not rare that in them every word, without distinction, may be stamped as a verb, whereas, in contrast, every verb inflection may likely serve simultaneously as a participle. However, languages which in this respect are equivalent to one another, may differ in turn by the fact that some do not provide the verb with any expression characterizing its peculiar function in sentence connection, whereas others do this at least by pronouns attached either as abbreviations or modifications, and thus maintaining the distinction between pronoun and person of the verb frequently touched upon in the previous discussion. The Burmese language, for instance, follows the former process insofar as I am able to judge; the Siamese, the Manchu, and the Mongolian do also insofar as they do not abbreviate the pronouns to mere affixes; so, too, do the languages of the South Sea Islands and to a major extent the remaining Malayan dialects of the western archipelago. The latter process is true of the Mexican, the Delaware, and other American Indian tongues. Inasmuch as the Mexican Indian language provides the verb with the governing and governed pronouns, sometimes in a concrete form and then again in a general significance, it truly expresses in a more ingenious way the unique function of the verb by directing it toward the remaining principal sentence components. In the first of these two methods, the subject and predicate can be connected only by indicating the verbal force through the addition of the verb "to be." For the most part, however, this verb is merely understood; what is termed a verb in languages employing this process is only a participle or a verbal noun, but it can, if the genus of the verb, time, and mood are also expressed by it, be used as a verb solely in this form. In terms of mood, however, these languages understand only the cases where the ideas of wishing, fear, capability, compulsion, and so forth find application. As a rule, the pure subjunctive is foreign to them. The uncertain and dependent assignment expressed by the subjunctive without addition of a material subordinate idea cannot be suitably designated in languages in which simple and actual assignment finds no formal expression. This formal aspect of the alleged verb is then more or less carefully treated and is fused into a word unity. The difference depicted here is exactly the same as when the verb is broken down periphrastically, or when it is used in its vital unity. The former is more a logically ordered method, while the latter is a sensory, pictorial process; absorbed in the peculiarity of these languages, one imagines what must take place in the intellect of the peoples for whom only the analytic process of resolution is peculiar. The other languages, including those of principled structure, utilize both of these methods in accordance with the prevailing circumstances. According to its nature, language may not sacrifice the sensory, pictorial expression of the verbal function without great disadvantage. Even for languages which suffer from the actual absence of the true verb, the disadvantage is actually reduced by the fact that for a great part of the verbs the verbal nature lies in the meaning itself and therefore the formal deficiency is materially compensated. Now if in addition (as is true in Chinese) it is found that words which could assume both functions, that of the noun and of the verb, become stamped by usage into a single entity, or that they are capable of indicating their validity by accent, the language in another way becomes still more established in its rights.

Among all the languages with which I am acquainted, none is as greatly lacking in the formal designation of the verbal function as is the Burmese.[2] F. Carey remarks emphatically in his grammar that in the Burmese language verbs are scarcely used other than in participial forms, and he adds that this is because they suffice to indicate every concept to be expressed by a verb. At another point, he categorically denies the existence of all verbs in the Burmese language.[3] This peculiarity becomes entirely understandable only if it is studied in connection with the remaining structure of the language.

Burmese root words undergo no modification by the attachment of grammatical syllables. The only changes in characters [phonemes] in the language are the conversion of the first aspirated letter [sound] into an unaspirated one where an aspirated sound is geminated; and in the combination of two monosyllabic root words into a single word, or in the repetition of the single word, the transition of the mute initial consonant of the second word into a nonaspirated voiced counterpart. Also in Tamil [Tamul, Tamulic], the phonemes *k*, *t* (both the lingual as well as the dental), and *p* medially in words become *g*, *d*, and *b*.[4] The difference is only that in Tamil the consonant remains voiceless if it occurs geminated medially, whereas in Burmese the change also takes place when the first of two root words terminates in a consonant. Therefore, the Burmese achieves in each case a greater unity of the word by the greater fluidity of the consonant added.[5]

Burmese word structure (with the exception of the pronoun and grammatical particles) is based on monosyllabic root words and compounds made from them. Two classes of root words can be distinguished. One type indicates actions and properties, and hence refers to several objects. The other type includes names of individual objects, living creatures, or inanimate items. Thus, in this case the verb, adjective, and substantive lie within the meaning of the root words. Also the distinction just mentioned between these words is only in their meaning, not in their morphological makeup; for example, *ê* 'to be cool,' or 'to become cold,' *kû*, 'to surround, combine, or help,' and *mâ* 'hard,' 'strong,' or 'to be healthy' are not formed differently than are *lê* 'the wind,' *rê* (pronounced *yê*),[6] 'the water,' and *lû*, 'the human being.' F. Carey has enumerated the root words denoting properties and actions in a special alphabetical index, appended to his grammar, and he has treated them entirely as the roots of the Sanskrit tongue. On the one hand, they may in fact be compared with them. They belong in their original form to no single part of speech, and appear in speech only with the grammatical particles which provide their determination in the spoken language. Moreover, a great number of words are derived from them, which emanate naturally from the type of concepts designated by them. However, considered exactly, they are of an entirely different nature than the Sanskrit roots, for the grammatical treatment of the language only strings together root words and grammatical particles, does not construct any fused word entities, and, precisely for this reason, does not combine simple derivational syllables with root phonemes. Hence, the root words in speech appear not as inseparable parts of combined word morphemes but actually in their completely pristine state, and there is no need for any artificial separation of them from larger fused lexical forms. Derivation from them is also not true derivation but simple compounding. Finally, the substantives have for the most part nothing that distinguishes them from the root words and for the most part cannot be derived from them. With few exceptions, in Sanskrit the form of the noun differs from the root form, even if it may justifiably be termed inadmissible to derive all nouns through the use of *unâdi* suffixes from the roots. Thus, the alleged Burmese roots behave actually as Chinese words, but, when taken with the remaining structure of the language, they do betray a certain approximation to Sanskritic roots. Very often the alleged root—without any change whatever—has the meaning of a substantive in which its actual verbal semanteme more or less clearly emerges. Thus, the word *mai* means 'to be black,' 'to threaten,' and 'the indigo plant,' while *nê* denotes 'to remain,' 'to continue,' and 'the sun,' and *pauñ* signifies 'for strengthening or adding,' hence 'to pawn or pledge,' as well as 'the loin or haunch of animals.' Only in one case do I find that the grammatical category is modified and designated by a derivational syllable from the root; at least to all appearances this instance is distinct from the customary compound. According to G. H. Hough,[7] substantives and adjectives are constructed from roots by prefixing *a*: *a-châ*, 'food,' or 'nutritional medium,' from *châ*, 'to eat'; *a-myak* (*amyet*, H.), 'anger,' from *myak*, 'to be or to get angry'; *a-pan*, 'a wearying business,' from *pan*, 'to breathe with difficulty'; and *a-chang*, 'order' or 'method,' from *chang* (*chî*), 'to place in an unbroken row or series.' This prefixed *a* is dropped, however, when the substantive appears as one of the final components of a compound. This loss also takes place in other cases, as will be seen further on with respect to *ama*, where the *a* is definitely not a derivative syllable of a root. There are substantives, too, which without change of meaning sometimes include and sometimes dispense with this prefix. For example, the above-cited word *pauñ*, 'loin,' is at times written *apauñ*. Consequently, this *a* cannot be equated to any true derivational syllable.

Combined with such a root in compounds are two attributive or action words (F. Carey's roots), two nouns, or one noun. The first case is often applied in place of a mood of a verb, the optative for example, by the combination of some verbal concept with "to wish." However, the two roots are combined simply to modify the sense, and the final one at times adds scarcely more than a small nuance. Indeed, sometimes the reason for the compounding cannot be divined from the meaning of the individual roots involved. For instance, *pan*, *pan-krâ*, and *pan-kwâ* signify 'to request permission, to ask'; *krâ*: (*kyâ*:) denotes 'to receive and impart information,' but it also means 'to be separated'; *kwâ* means 'to separate itself,' and following a previous combination it means 'to be separated or divided.' In other compounds the composition is more explicable. For example, *prach-hmâ*: means 'to sin against something, to overstep'; it comes from *prach* (*prîch*), which denotes 'to hurl at something,' and from *hmâ*: which means 'to err, to be on the wrong course,' and hence in its own right 'to sin.' Thus, through compounding an intensification of the idea is attained.

Similar cases are encountered rather frequently in the language, and they show distinctly that it possesses the peculiarity of constructing, in addition to a simple and therefore monosyllabic root, a disyllabic verb consisting of two roots. These disyllabic verbs are constructed in such a way that the additional root either repeats the idea of the other one in a somewhat different way, simply repeats it unchanged, or appends a quite general concept.[8] I shall come back to this phenomenon, which is generally important for the linguistic structure, at a later point. A number of roots, even when they are the first component of a compound, are never used individually. Of this type is the word *tuṅ·*, which always occurs with *wap* (*wet*), although both roots include the meaning 'to bow with respect,' and this is what the compound also means. However, when this combination is used in the reverse as *wap-tuṅ·*, the meaning of the compound is intensified and is as follows: 'to creep upon the ground, to lie prostrate before persons of high rank or caste.' At times, the roots also serve to form compounds to which only a part of their meaning is transferred, and no attention is paid to the fact that the residuum thereof is contradictory to the other member of the compound. For example, according to A. Judson's remark, the word *hchwat*, 'to be very white,' is also used as an intensification with words that denote other colors. How powerfully compounding affects an individual word is in the final analysis evident from the fact that A. Judson notes with respect to the above-mentioned word *hchauñ* [*hchwat*] that at times owing to the combination in which it appears it assumes a specific meaning.

Where nouns are united with roots the latter generally follow the former: *lak-tat* (*let-tat*, H.), 'an artist, manufacturer, or maker,' from *lak* (*let*, H.) 'the hand,' and *tat*, 'to be skilled in something, to understand something.' These compounds thus agree with their Sanskrit counterparts where, as in धर्मविद्, *dharmavid*, a root is joined as the final component to a noun. Often, however, in these compounds the root is also taken simply in the sense of an adjective, and a compound then originates only insofar as the Burmese language always considers an adjective combined with its substantive a compound: *nwâ:-kauñ*, 'cow good' (precisely: 'to be good). A compound of this type in the more restricted sense of the word is *lû-chu*, 'a mass of people,' made up of *lû*, 'man,' or 'human being,' and *chu*, 'to convene, gather, or meet.' In the compounding of nouns with each other are found cases where that noun serving as the final member becomes so remote from its original meaning that it turns into a suffix of general meaning. For example, when *ama*, 'woman, mother,'[9] is abbreviated to *ma* and compounded with a noun, it adds to the first member of the compound the meaning of 'the great, most noble, or important': *tak* (*tet*), 'the oar,' combines with *ma* to form *tak-ma*, 'the main or most important oar, the steering oar.'

Between the noun and the verb there is no original difference in the language. This difference is determined only in speech by the particles attached to the word; however, it is not possible in Burmese as it is in Sanskrit to recognize the noun by definite derivational syllables, and the concept of a basic form standing between the root and the inflected noun is totally absent in Burmese. The only possible exceptions are the previously mentioned substantives constructed by prefixing *a*. All grammatical construction of substantives and adjectives consists of a distinct composition in which the final member adds a more general concept to that of the first, unless the first is a root or a noun. In the former case, nouns originate from the roots, whereas in the latter case several nouns are collected in a single concept or put into a single class to so speak. It is clear that the last member of these compounds cannot actually be termed an affix, although in Burmese grammar it bears this name. The true affix indicates by phonetic treatment in the word unit that it is shifting the meaningful portion of the word into a definite category without adding something material to it. Where, as in this instance, such a phonetic treatment is lacking, this shift has not symbolically gone over into the phoneme, but rather the speaker must change the word with the special significance derived from the meaning of the alleged affix or from the accepted linguistic usage. This distinction must be kept firmly in mind for an evaluation of the entire Burmese language, for Burmese expresses everything, or at least most of that which can be indicated, by inflection. But in all cases this language lacks the pure symbolic expression by which the form goes over into the language and from which it reverts to the soul [mind]. Hence in F. Carey's grammar, under the heading "the formation of nouns," the most varied cases are lumped together—derived nouns, pure compound nouns, gerunds, participles, and so forth. Moreover, it would be difficult to fault this compilation, since in all of these cases words are listed under a single concept by means of an alleged suffix and, to the extent that the language possesses word unity, even under a single word. It cannot be denied that the continuously recurring use of these compounds brings their final members closer to the status of true affixes. This is especially so if, as is actually the case in Burmese, the so-called affixes have no meaning for themselves alone that may be stated; those possessing an independent meaning may also approach the status of affixes if, when they are affixed, this meaning cannot be traced at all or but very remotely. A look at the dictionary will reveal that both cases occur not infrequently in the language, although the latter cannot always be evaluated with complete certainty because the combinations of ideas may be so multifarious. This inclination toward compounding of the forms of affixation is confirmed also by the fact that, as I have already shown above, a significant number of roots and nouns are never used independently beyond the state of compounding, a situation which is encountered in other languages as well, particularly Sanskrit. A widely used affix, which consistently produces the conversion of a root, hence of a verb, into a noun, is *hkyañ:*.[10] It brings forth the abstract concept of the state which the verb contains, and the action conceived as a thing: *chê*, 'to send,' *chê-hkyañ:* (*che-gyeñ:*), 'a sending, a transmission.' As an independent verb, *hkyañ:* denotes 'to bore, perforate, or penetrate.' Between this meaning and its meaning as an affix no connection can be discovered. Indisputably, however, long lost general meanings lie at the base of these present-day concrete ones. All the remaining affixes used to construct nouns, insofar as I have been able to survey them, are of a more particularized nature.

The treatment of the adjective is to be explained solely from the approach to compounding, and it proves quite apparently how the language always keeps this medium in view for grammatical structure. Per se, the adjective can be nothing other than the root itself. Its grammatical quality is attained only in composition with a substantive, or, when it is used absolutely, where it is provided with a suffixed *a*, as are the nouns. In combination with the substantive, it can precede the latter or follow it, but when it precedes the substantive it must be associated with it by a connecting particle (*thang* or *thau*). I believe the reason for this difference is found in the nature of the compounding. In a compound, the final member must be of general nature and must be capable of absorbing the first member in its greater scope. In the association of an adjective with a substantive, however, the adjective has the greater scope and hence, to attach itself to the substantive, requires an addendum suitable to its nature. These combinatory particles, which will be discussed more fully at a later point, satisfy this purpose; and the compound or combination then means, for example, not only "a good man" but also "a good being one" or "a man who is good." In Burmese, however, these ideas follow each other in reverse ("good, which, man"). The alleged adjective is in this way treated completely as a verb; for, if *kauñ:-thang-lû* denotes 'the good man or person,' the two first elements of this compound standing by themselves would mean 'he is good.' The fact that in quite the same way a complete verb—instead of a simple adjective—even provided with the words it governs, may be placed ahead of a substantive makes this all the more evident. In Burmese word order, the expression "the bird flying in the air" is stated: "air space in flying (connecting particle) bird." In the case of the postpositional adjective, the placement of the concepts agrees with the compound; when a root occurs as the final member, such as "to possess," "to ponder," or "to be worthy," it forms, together with other words, nouns which are modified by the meaning of these words.

In connected speech, the relationship of words to each other is indicated by particles. It is therefore comprehensible that these particles differ for the noun and verb. Still, this is not always the case, and noun and verb thus fall to an even greater extent into one and the same category. The combinatory particle *thang* is the true nominative sign and, at the same time, it forms the indicative of the verb. In these two functions it is found to appear twice in the brief expression for 'I do,' *ña-thang pru-thang.* It is obvious that a different viewpoint lies at the basis of the use of this word, and we shall search out this attitude at a later point in this exposition. The same particle, however, is cited as the instrumental and is used in this way in the following expression: *lû-tat-thang hchauk-thang-im,* 'the house built by a skilled man.' The first of these two words contains the compound consisting of 'man' and 'skilled,' upon which follows the ostensible sign of the instrumental case. In the second is found the root 'build,' here in the sense of 'to be built,' prefixed as an adjective in the manner previously mentioned, that is, by means of the combinatory particle *thang,* to the substantive *im* (*ieng,* H.), 'house.' I do not know whether the concept of the instrumental really lies originally in the particle *thang,* or whether at some later date grammatical opinion supplied it, for in the first of the foregoing words only the idea of the skilled man originally reposed, and it was left to the hearer to furnish the relationship of this compound to the second word. In a similar way, the particle *thang* is cited as a sign of the genitive. If the great number of particles which allegedly express as cases the relationships of the noun are taken together, it is seen clearly that Pali grammarians, to whom the Burmese language owes its scientific arrangement and terminology, expended effort to distribute them through the eight cases of Sanskrit and their language in order to construct a declensional system. But in a precise sense, such a declensional system is foreign to Burmese which employs the alleged case endings with respect merely to the meaning of the particles and not at all with respect to the noun phonemes. To each case are allotted several endings, each of which, however, expresses individual nuances of the relational idea. To the listing of his declensional system, F. Carey added a few more endings separately. To some of these case signs are associated, sometimes before and sometimes behind, other signs which determine the sense of the relationship more exactly. Furthermore, these case signs always follow the noun; and between the latter and them, when they are present, appear the designations of gender and those of the plural. The plural designations serve, as do all case signs, for the pronoun also, and there are no actual pronouns for "we," "you," and "they." The language thus distinguishes everything according to significance, unites nothing via phonemes, and hence visibly rejects the natural endeavor of the linguistic sense to produce from gender, number, and case combined phonemic modifications of the materially important word. Hence, the original meaning of case signs can be ascertained only in a few instances. This is true even of the plural sign *tô*. (*do*, H.), whose meaning we can learn only when we undertake to derive it, ignoring the accent, from *tô:*, 'to increase or add to.' The personal pronouns always appear only in independent form and never serve either abbreviated or modified as affixes.

The verb, if the simple root word is considered, is distinguishable solely by its material meaning. The governing pronoun always stands before it, thus indicating that it does not belong to the form of the verb because it is separated entirely from the verbal particles that always follow the root word. What the language possesses of verbal forms is based exclusively upon the latter particles which, if present, designate the plural, the mood, and the tense. Such a verbal form is the same for all three persons; hence, the simple observation of the complete verb or of the sentence structure reveals that the root word with its verbal form constitutes a participle, which is combined with the subject standing quite independently of it through an imagined verb, that is, one supplied mentally. To be sure, the latter is explicitly present in the language, but it is rarely taken as an aid for ordinary verbal expression.

Now, if we revert to the verbal form, we find that the plural expression clings directly to the root word, or to that part of the root word which is regarded together with the root as comprising one and the very same totality. It is noteworthy, however, and in this factor reposes a recognitional medium of the verb, that the plural sign of the conjugation is completely different from that of declension. The never absent, monosyllabic plural sign *kra* (*kya*) is generally followed, though not always, by a second sign, *kun*, which is related to *akun*, 'whole, entire, or complete';[11] the language in this case gives evidence of a double peculiarity—the designation of the grammatical relationship by compounding and, in the latter expression, the intensification of this relationship by the addition of another word even where one would suffice. Yet here we find the remarkable case that to a word which has lost its original meaning and become an affix is added one of known meaning.

As I have already mentioned, the moods are based for the major part on the combination of roots of general meaning with concrete ones. In this way, being directed simply toward material significance, they transcend entirely the logical periphery of this verbal form, and their number becomes to a certain extent indeterminable. The tense signs follow them and, save for a few exceptions, are attached to the actual verb. The plural sign, however, adjusts itself according to the rigidity with which the root indicating the mood is considered as combined with the concrete root. There appear to be two differing viewpoints concerning the plural sign in the popular linguistic sense. In a few isolated cases the plural sign seems to be inserted between the two roots, whereas for the most part it follows the concrete one. It is obvious that in the former case the roots indicating the mood are accompanied by an obscure feeling for the grammatical form, while in the latter case both roots in the unification of their meanings are held more or less to be one and the same root word. Under the heading here termed "mood by combination of roots" occur forms of quite differing grammatical significance. These include, for example, the causative verbs, constructed by addition of the root "to send, enjoin, or command," and verbs whose meanings are modified by inseparable prepositional prefixes in other languages.

With respect to tense particles, F. Carey cites five of the present, three that are simultaneously of the present and the past, two that pertain exclusively to the past, and a few serving for the future. He terms the verbal conjugations or declensions constructed with them forms of the verb, without stating the difference in usage of those designating identical time. That a distinction is made between them is revealed by his opportune remark that two of those which he has discussed differ but little in meaning from each other. A. Judson notes that the particle *thê :* indicates that action in the present moment has not ceased to continue. In addition to those cited, there are still others which are reserved for entirely completed past time. Actually, these tense signs pertain to the indicative insofar as they do not inherently indicate any other mood; a few of them, however, serve also for designating the imperative, but this tense has its own particles or is indicated by the bare root. A. Judson calls some of these particles simply euphonic or fillers. If they are traced through the dictionary, we find that most of them are actual roots, even if only in a remotely related sense of the word. Thus, here again, the *modus operandi* of the language is meaningful compounding. In accordance with the intent of the language, these particles with the root obviously constitute a single word, and the complete form must be regarded as a compound. However, this unity is not indicated by written change, except for the fact that in the pronunciation of the above-stated cases the mute characters are changed to their unaspirated voiced counterparts. This is not noted explicitly by F. Carey;

however, it seems to follow from the universality of his rule and from G. H. Hough's orthography. G. H. Hough applies this conversion for all words used in this way as particles; for example, he writes the sign of completed action as *prî:* and, in accordance with its pronunciation, as *byî:*. I have also found in the future tense of causative verbs a contraction of the vowels of two such monosyllabic words actually occurring in the written language. The causal sign *chê* (the root 'to command') and the particle *aṅ·* of the future fuse to form *chim·*.[12] The same situation appears to exist with the composite particle of the future, *lim·-mang*, where the particle *lê* is contracted with *aṅ·* to produce *lim·*, and then another particle for the future, *mang*, is added. The language may certainly reveal other similar cases, yet they cannot possibly be plentiful because they would otherwise be encountered often. The verbal forms portrayed here can in turn be declined by the addition of case signs, which are attached either directly to the root or to the particle accompanying it. Now, although this may coincide with the nature of gerunds and participles in other languages, I will show later that Burmese continues to treat verbs and verbal clauses in a quite peculiar manner.

There is another particle which must be distinguished from the particles of moods and tenses mentioned here, for it exerts upon the construction of verbal forms a most essential influence; it also belongs to the noun and plays an important part in the grammar of the entire language. One can guess from the foregoing that I am referring to the monosyllable *thang*, which has already been mentioned as the sign of the nominative. F. Carey, too, felt that this particle was used in differing ways. For, although he immediately cites *thang* as the first of the particles used in constructing the present forms of the verb, he nevertheless separately treats it under the name "combinatory particle" (connective increment). Unlike the other particles, the particle *thang* does not add a modification to the verb; rather it is nonessential to its meaning.[13] It indicates, however, in what grammatical sense the word to which it becomes associated is to be taken and restricts—if the expression be permitted—its grammatical forms. Therefore, with respect to the verb it belongs not to the significant words but to those that lead toward an understanding of the connected elements of speech, and coincides entirely with the concept of the words termed "empty" or "hollow" in Chinese. Where the particle *thang* accompanies the verb, it assumes a place directly behind the root, or, if other particles are present, it follows these. In both positions it can be inflected by the attachment of case signs. However, the notable difference is revealed here that in the declension of the noun *thang* is merely the nominative sign. Moreover, upon attachment of the remaining cases it does not appear further, while for the participle (only the verb can be taken for such an entity in this instance) it retains its position. This appears to prove that its determination in the latter instance is to indicate the belonging together of the particles and the root, and consequently the limitation of the participial form. Its regular usage is found only in the indicative. It is completely excluded from both the subjunctive and imperative moods; it also drops out in a few additional constructions. According to F. Carey, it serves to unite the participial forms with the following word. This observation agrees with my contention to the extent that the particle is seen as separating the participial forms from those following them. If we consider all that has been said about this particle, including its use with the noun, it is soon felt that we cannot explain it in conformity with the theory of the parts of speech but that we must revert to its original meaning, which is also the case with Chinese particles. In its original meaning, *thang* expresses the idea of 'this,' or 'thus' and is, in fact, termed by both F. Carey and A. Judson (who do not connect this meaning with the use of the word as a particle) a demonstrative pronoun and adverb. As both of these, it is used to construct a number of compounds of which it is the first member. Even in combination with verbal roots, where one of more general meaning modifies the sense of the others, F. Carey cites *thang* in a sense related to its adverbial meaning: 'correspond or agree' (thus, 'be just the same'). He did not include it in his list of roots, however, and unfortunately does not cite any example of this meaning.[14] It appears to me that it is used in the same sense as a medium for understanding. When a speaker wishes to emphasize a few words so that they will be taken together, or when he wishes to stress in particular the substantives and verbs, he has them followed by a 'this!' or 'thus!,' thereby directing the attention of the hearer to what has been said in order to unite it with what follows or, when *thang* is the last word of the sentence, to conclude the speech. F. Carey's explanation of *thang* as a particle combining preceding and following elements does not fit this case. This may be the source of his assertion that the root or verbal form combined with *thang* has the force of a verb if it is situated at the conclusion of a sentence.[15] In the midst of speech, the verbal form associated with *thang* is, according to him, a participle or at least a construction in which it is possible only with effort to recognize the true verb, while at the end of a sentence it is actually an inflected verb. To me this distinction appears unfounded, for at the end of a sentence the form discussed here is still only a participle or, to be more precise, only a form modified like a participle. In both positions, the actual verbal force must be supplied in the mind.

To actually express this verbal power, however, the language possesses another medium. Neither F. Carey nor A. Judson offers a complete explanation of its true properties, but the force of this linguistic element has a great similarity to that of an added auxiliary verb. When we desire to conclude a sentence with a verb that is actually inflected and sever all connection with what follows, we place after the root or the verbal form the particle *éng* (*î*, H.), which is used in place of *thang*.

In this way, all misunderstanding which could arise from the combinatory nature of *thang* is prevented, and the series of interconnected participles is really concluded; *pru-êng* actually means 'I do,' not 'I am doing'; and *pru-prî: -êng* means 'I have done,' not 'I have been doing.' The actual meaning of this little word is expressed by neither F. Carey nor A. Judson. The latter merely avers that it is equivalent to *hri* (*shi*), 'to be,' yet it seems strange that it is used only for conjugation of this verb. According to F. Carey and G. H. Hough, it is also the case sign for the genitive: *lû-êng*, 'of the human being.' A. Judson does not list this meaning.[16] F. Carey assures us, however, that this final sign is really used in conversation and that in writing it is found chiefly in translations from Pali; these observations can be explained on the one hand by the inclination of Burmese to hook the clauses of speech to one another and on the other by the uniform periodic structure of a daughter language of Sanskrit. I believe I have found a more intimate reason why this auxiliary word is found in particular in translations from Pali. This is because the Pali tongue combines participles with the verb "to be" to indicate several tenses and then always has the auxiliary verb with some phonetic change follow.[17] The Burmese translators, wanting to keep exactly to the words, sought an equivalent for this auxiliary verb and selected *éng* for the purpose. In spite of this, however, the word is no less a genuine Burmese one; it is not a loan word borrowed from Pali. A true translation of the Pali auxiliary form was impossible in any event simply because the Burmese verb does not include the designation of the persons. It is a peculiarity of the language that this terminal word is used after all particles except those of the future. Moreover, the Pali construction mentioned appears to be found especially in past tenses. The reason can scarcely be sought in the nature of the future particles, inasmuch as they permit the use of *thang* without any difficulty. F. Carey, who directs his praiseworthy attention toward differentiating the participial forms from the inflected verb, observes that the command and the question forms of the verb are the only ones in the language which bear any resemblance to the inflected verb.[18] But this apparent exception can be explained by the fact that the forms mentioned cannot be connected to case designators with which the particles peculiar to them would not combine. For these

particles close the form, and, in the case of the question verbs, the combining *thang* stands in front of them in order to connect them to the tense
particles.

The connective particle *thau* behaves in ways very similar to those of
thang. But since I am concerned only with indicating the character of the
language as a whole, I shall skip the individual points of their agreements
and divergence. There are still other connective particles which are also
attached to the verb form without adding anything to the sense and
which thereupon displace *thang* and *thau* from their position. But on other
occasions some of these are used as designations of the subjunctive, and
only the context of the speech betrays their purpose.

The sequence of the parts of the sentence is first the subject, then the
object, and finally the verb: "God the earth created"; "the king to his
generals spoke"; "he to me gave." The position of the verb in this construction is apparently not the natural one since this part of speech inter-
poses itself in the sequence of the ideas between subject and object. In
Burmese, however, the position of the verb is explained by the fact that the
verb is actually only a participle which does not expect its final clause until
later, and which even contains within itself a particle whose destiny is to
combine with something following. This verbal form, without forming the
sentence in the way that a true verb would, absorbs within itself everything that has gone on before and carries it over into that which follows.
F. Carey observes that by virtue of these forms, the language can weave
sentences together without arriving at a conclusion, and he adds that this
is generally the case in all purely Burmese works. The further the key
point of the full argument, which is made up of loosely joined sentences, is
extended, the more careful the language must be always to conclude the
individual sentences with a subordinate final word. The language remains
true to this form, and it always allows the designation to precede that
which is to be designated. It does not say, for example, "the fish is in the
water," "the shepherd walks with the cows," and "I eat cooked rice with
butter"; rather, it says, "in the water the fish is," "with the cows the
shepherd walks," and "I with rice cooked butter eat." Thus, a word is
always placed at the end of each intermediate sentence which does not
expect a modification after itself. On the contrary, the broader modification regularly precedes the narrower one. This becomes especially clear in
translations from other languages. Whereas it says in the English Bible in
the Book of St. John (21:2), "and Nathanael of Cana in Galilee," the
Burmese translation turns the phrase around and says, "Galilee of the
district Cana of the city descendant Nathanaël."

Another means of connecting many sentences with one another is to transform them into parts of a composite so that each individual sentence forms an adjective preceding the substantive. In the phrase, 'I praise the Lord who has created all things, who is free of sin, . . .'' each of these ever-so-numerous sentences is connected to the substantive by *thau*; we have already observed *thau* in this function, but in this case it follows only after the last sentence. These individual relative sentences therefore precede the substantive and together with it are regarded as a composite word; the verb ("I praise") concludes the sentence. As an aid to understanding, Burmese script separates each individual element of the long composite by a punctuation mark. The regularity of this construction actually makes it easy to follow, for one needs only to proceed from the end toward the beginning in sentences of this type. But one must listen with rapt attention in order to discover at whom the endless predicates are aimed. Presumably everyday speech avoids these innumerable figures of speech. It is not at all common for the Burmese language to arrange the individual parts of a construction so that the governed sentence follows the governing one. Rather, it attempts to assimilate the former within the latter, so that the governed sentence must then naturally precede the governing one. As a result, in such a construction complete sentences are treated like individual nouns. In order to say, for example, "I have heard that you have sold your books," the language turns the phrase around. It permits "your books" to go first, lets the perfect form of the verb "to sell" follow, and then adds to this the sign of the accusative, to which "I have heard" is joined in final position.

If the analysis attempted here has been successful in discovering the correct path by which the Burmese language strives to summarize thought and speech, then one sees indeed that on the one hand it is far removed from a complete lack of grammatical form but that on the other it does not even attain the development of these forms. To this extent, it is centrally located between the two extreme types of language structure previously discussed. Its original word construction prevents the Burmese language from attaining truly grammatical forms since it is one of the monosyllabic languages belonging to the ethnic groups living between China and India. To be sure, even though each concept is contained in individual, closely bound sounds, this peculiarity of word formation does not affect the more basic structure of these languages. But since the monosyllabicity in these languages arose not by chance but was fixed intentionally by the organs and was also a product of the individual direction of these languages, the discrete enunciation of every syllable is related to it. This, in turn, because of the impossibility of coalescing suffixes that indicate relational concepts with the materially significant words, extends to the innermost depths of the language structure. The Indo-Chinese nations, says J. Leyden,[19] have adopted many Pali words, but they adapt all of them to their peculiar pronunciation by treating every single syllable as an individual word. One must therefore regard this property as the characteristic peculiarity of these languages, just as it is of the Chinese, and in the investigations of their structure one keep it firmly in mind, if not start with it as a basis, since all languages originate from the sound.

Along with this first peculiarity, there is a second characteristic, which is found in every language to a much lesser degree. This is the diversification and the increase in the wealth of vocabulary by means of the various accents accorded the words. The Chinese accents are known; however, several Indo-Chinese languages, including Siamese and Annamese, possess such a large quantity of them that it is almost impossible for our ear to differentiate them correctly. As a result, speech becomes a kind of song or recitative, and J. Low compares Siamese to a musical scale.[20] These accents result in even greater and more numerous dialect differences than do the letters themselves; and we are told that with respect to Annamese every locality of any significance at all has its own dialect, and that neighboring ones in order to be understood must at times take refuge in the written language.[21] The Burmese language possesses two such accents: the long, soft one, which in Burmese writing is designated by a colon at the end of the word; and the short, broken-off one, which is indicated by a dot set below the word [although von Humboldt replaces this system with a dot placed after the word about halfway up]. If, in addition to these, we count the accentless pronunciation, then we can find in the language the same word appearing in three forms with more or less different meanings: *pô*, 'to stop,' 'to pour out,' 'to fill to overflowing,' 'a long, oval basket'; *pô:*, 'to fasten or bind to one another,' 'to hang up,' 'an insect or worm'; *pô.*, 'to carry,' 'to fetch,' 'to teach or instruct,' 'to offer (a wish, or a blessing),' 'to be thrown in or on something.' Similarly, *ñâ* designates 'I,' and *ñâ:* means 'five' or 'fish.' Not every word is capable of this varying accentuation. Several final vowels take neither of the two accents while others take only one, and it is always true that they can attach themselves only to words which end with a vowel or a nasal consonant. The latter proves clearly that they are modifications of the vowels and are inseparably bound to them. If two Burmese monosyllabic words occur together as a composite, the first one does not lose its accent; hence, we can probably conclude that even in composites the pronunciation treats the syllables separately, just like discrete words. We are accustomed to ascribe these accents to the necessity of monosyllabic languages to increase the number of possible sound combinations. But such an intentional procedure is hardly conceivable. On the contrary, it seems much more likely that these various modifications of the pronunciation arose first and primarily in the organs and the speech habits of the peoples. In order to pronounce the syllables clearly, the peoples meted them out individually and with small pauses between them. This habit did not contribute to the formation of the polysyllabic words.

Therefore, without presupposing any kind of historical relationship between them, we may say that the monosyllabic Indo-Chinese languages have several characteristics in common both with one another and with the Chinese. However, at this point I will stick to the Burmese since I do not have at my command reference works for the others which would furnish sufficient data for investigations like the present one.[22] One must first admit of Burmese that it never modifies the sound of the stems as an expression of their relationships and never makes the grammatical categories the basis of its syntax. Indeed, we have seen above that it does not differentiate between them originally in the words but parcels out the same word to several of them; we have also seen that it fails to recognize the nature of the verb and, in fact, uses the same particle with the verb and the noun to such a degree that only the meaning of the word or, where even that is not sufficient, the context of the speech allows us to ascertain which of the two categories is intended. The principle of their syntax is to indicate which word in the speech modifies the other one. In this respect, it agrees completely with Chinese.[23] Like the latter, it has among its particles used to introduce the subject one which serves simultaneously as a separating and combining element in the ordering of the construction; the similarity between *thang* and the Chinese *tchî* in their use in such constructions is too striking to be overlooked.[24] On the other hand, Burmese deviates very significantly from the Chinese both in the sense in which it receives modification and in its means of indication. The modification here mentioned encompasses two cases between which we must make a careful distinction: these are the government of one word by the other one and the completion of a concept which has remained unmodified in certain aspects. The word must be delimited qualitatively in accordance with its scope and its nature, and relatively in accordance with its causality, that is, whether it is dependent on something else or whether it is leading something else.[25] The Chinese language differentiates between these cases in its construction and uses each one where it truly belongs. It allows the governing word to precede the governed—it places the subject before the verb, the latter before its direct object, and this latter before its indirect object if one is present. Here it cannot really be said that the preceding word completes the concept; rather, the verb is completed in its

concept both by the subject and by the object, between which it is standing, and the concept of direct object is similarly completed by the indirect
one. On the other hand, the language always allows the completing word
to precede the one still unmodified from the point of view of its concept,
that is, the adjective is placed before the substantive, the adverb before the
verb, and the genitive before the nominative. By this means, the language
follows to a certain extent an opposite procedure from that outlined in the
preceding, for this still unmodified postpositional word is the governing
one and if placed in accordance with the procedure of the previous case, it
would have to precede. The Chinese construction rests therefore on two
broad, general, but in themselves varying laws and obviously does well in
indicating by a special position the relationship of the verb to its object.
This is significant since in a much more important sense than any other
word in the sentence the verb is governing. Thus, the first procedure is
concerned with the chief articulation of the sentence, and the second with
its subordinate parts. If it had modeled the latter on the former so that the
adjective, the adverb, and the genitive were permitted to follow the substantive, the verb, and the nominative, then the concinnity of the sentence
structure, which arises from the contrast developed here, would surely
suffer from this. For example, the position of the adverb after the verb
would not permit a clear differentiation between the adverb and the
object; no advantage would accrue by such a procedure to the simple
arrangement of the sentence itself, and the agreement between its course
and the essence of the language sense would in no way be enhanced. The
essential task is to determine the concept of governing correctly, and, with
the exception of a few deviations from the usual rule of word order which
in all languages are more or less justified, the Chinese construction does
this well. The Burmese language hardly differentiates between these two
cases at all. Rather, it actually preserves only one law of construction and
ignores the more important of the two. Thus, although it allows the subject to precede the verb and the object, it also permits the verb to follow
the object. This inversion makes it more than doubtful whether placing
the subject first really represents it as governing rather than as a completion of the following sentence parts. The governed object is apparently
regarded as a completing modification of the verb which, unmodified in
itself, follows all of the modifications by its subject and object and concludes the sentence. The fact that the subject and object attach themselves
to the front of the completing secondary modifications is self-evident from
the examples cited in the preceding.

This difference between the Burmese and Chinese construction
obviously arises from the correct view of the verb prevailing in Chinese

and from the deficient one in the Burmese language. The Chinese construction betrays a feeling for the true and proper function of the verb. It expresses this by placing the verb in the middle of the sentence between subject and object; the verb thus dominates and is the soul of the whole speech configuration. Even when divested of sound modifications, the verb by virtue of its position extends to the sentence the life and the movement which arise from it, and actually establishes the sense of the speech or at least betrays its inner spirit. In Burmese, all of this is completely different. The verbal forms vacillate between inflected verbs and participles; according to the material sense, they are actually the latter, and they cannot attain a formal sense since the language possesses no form for the verb itself. Not only does the actual function of the verb find no expression in the language, but the peculiar formation of the ostensible verb forms and their obvious similarity to the noun prove that the speakers themselves lack the feeling for the true power of the verb. If we consider that the Burmese language characterizes the verb through the use of particles so much more than does the Chinese, and also differentiates it from the noun, it then appears all the more strange that it displaces it from its true category.

Although this is undeniably the case, it can be explained by the fact that the language designates the verb simply in accordance with modifications which can be taken materially without betraying even a suspicion of the simply formal element in the verb. Chinese rarely uses this material indication. It usually avoids it completely, but in the correct position of the words the language recognizes a form that clings invisibly to the speech. One might even say that the less Chinese uses external grammar, the more inner grammar it possesses. Moreover, wherever a grammatical aspect penetrates Chinese, it is the logically correct one. A grammatical aspect imparted the first arrangement to Chinese, and then the language developed through the use of such a correctly tuned instrument in the spirit of the people. One can object that it is not at all unusual for even the inflected languages to place the verb after its object and that Burmese, as we know, retains the cases of the noun through the use of their own particles. But since the language shows clearly at many other points that it has no clear concept of the parts of speech, and that, on the contrary, in its constructions it follows the modification of the words only through one another, it cannot in fact be absolved of the charge that it fails to recognize the true nature of sentence formation. It also proves this by inviolably placing its ostensible verb at the end of the sentence. The second reason for placing the verb at the end, namely so that the language may attach a new sentence to this form, makes it even clearer that the language is driven neither by the actual nature of the periodic construction nor by the power of the verb at work in it. It has an obvious lack of particles which, like our conjunctions, furnish life and variety to the sentences. Chinese, which here too observes the general law of its word order by allowing, as it did in the case of the genitive and the nominative, the more closely modifying and completing sentence to precede the one modified by it, is far superior in this respect. In Burmese, the sentences seem to run past one another in a straight line. Moreover, they are rarely arranged serially through the use of coordinate conjunctions which like our "and" retain their independence. They join together in a manner which more or less closely unites the material content. This is evident from the particle *thang*, which is usually used at the end of each of such continuous sentences, and which by summarizing that which precedes always applies it to the understanding of that which immediately follows. It is obvious that this procedure will produce a certain clumsiness, and an enervating uniformity seems unavoidable.

Chinese and Burmese indicate the word sequence in the same way to the extent that they both use position and special particles. Burmese actually does not need laws as strict as those of Chinese since the large number of particles indicating the relationships assures understanding. Nonetheless, it conscientiously keeps the words in the same position, and only in one respect is it not quite consistent in their arrangement—it permits placing the adjective before and after the substantive. However, since placing the adjective before the substantive always requires the addition of particles in order to determine the word sequence, we see that the second position is looked upon as the natural one. One must probably view this as a consequence of the fact that adjective and substantive together make up a compound in which, when the adjective precedes, the case inflection is always lacking; that is, the adjective simply belongs to the substantive, which is modified in its meaning by the adjective. With its composites of the nouns as well as of the verbs, the language usually permits the word which serves as the type concept to precede in the first segment, and the specifying, more general one (insofar as it can find applicability to several types) follows in the second segment. Thus, the language forms modes of the verbs; nouns might be formed, for example, with the word "fish" preceding and with a large number of fish names following. If in other cases it seems to take the opposite path and forms words denoting craftsmen by means of the general construction, in which the craftsmen stand as the second member behind the names of their tools, one remains doubtful whether in these cases the language is really following a different method or whether it only has a different view of what is the type concept. Similarly, in combinations with postpositional adjectives, the language treats the adjective as a specifying type concept. Here, too, Chinese remains true to its general law: the word to which a more special meaning is supposed to accrue is the final member in the composite. If the verb "to see" is used in a somewhat less than natural manner in the formation of, or rather in place of, the passive, it precedes the main concept: "see kill," that is, "to be killed." Since so many things can be seen, then "kill" should really go first. However, the reverse position shows that here "see" is supposed to be regarded as a modification of the following word and to indicate the condition of "kill." Although the expression is somewhat strange, this is a fine and sensible manner in which to indicate the grammatical relationship. In similar fashion are formed such words as "lands men," book house," and so forth.

Both Burmese and Chinese solve their problems of speech configuration and word order through the use of particles. They are also similar to each other in that they use several of these particles merely as an indication of the construction—these particles add nothing to the material meaning. However, it is precisely in the use of these particles that Burmese forsakes the character of Chinese and takes on its own. The care which the language takes to designate by means of intermediate concepts the relationship in which a word is supposed to be regarded vis-à-vis another word increases the number of these particles and produces in them a certain completeness, although, to be sure, not a wholly systematic one. The language also shows a desire to bring these particles into a closer proximity with the stems rather than with the rest of the words in the sentence. To be sure, true word unity cannot take place in a pronunciation that separates syllables and in view of the complete spirit of the language. But still, we have seen that in some cases the effect of a word produces a consonant change in the one directly attached to it; and in the verb forms, the particles *thang* and *éng* follow the verb particles and with the stems form a unit. Indeed, in one single case two syllables are drawn together to form one. In Chinese writing this could be represented only phonetically, that is, as a foreign element. A feeling for the true nature of the suffixes is evident in the fact that even those particles which could be regarded as modifying adjectives, such as the plural signs, never precede the root words but always follow them. In Chinese, both of these positions are customary, depending on the variety of the plural particles.

To the same degree to which Burmese is remote from Chinese it approaches Sanskrit. However, it would be superfluous to depict in detail what a genuine gap separates it from the latter. The difference lies not simply in the more or less narrow juncture of the particles with the noun.

It becomes especially evident from a comparison of these particles with the suffixes of the Indic language. These particles of Indic are just as important as all the others of the language even though the meaning, to be sure, is for the most part extinguished in the memory of the people. They are largely subjective sounds, suitable only for the innermost relationships. Even though Burmese seems to stand in the middle between the two other languages, one cannot regard it as representing in any way a transition from one to the other. The life of each language rests on the inner attitude of the people concerning the manner of expressing thought in sound. In the three language groups compared here, this is absolutely at variance. Even though the number of the particles and the frequency of their usage betray a gradual increase in grammatical indication beginning with the old style of Chinese through the newer one up to Burmese, still the latter of these languages is completely different from both styles of the former in its basic attitude, which remains essentially the same in the old and newer styles of Chinese. Chinese is based solely on word order and on the stamp of the grammatical form in the innermost spirit. Burmese in its speech configuration does not rest on word order, although it clings with great vigor to that which befits the Burmese manner of thinking. It transmits the concepts by new ones which are added, and it is forcibly led to this ploy as a result of its own peculiar position, which is open to ambiguity without this crutch. Since the intermediate concepts are expressions of the grammatical forms, the latter, to be sure, also appear in the language. The notion of these, however, is not immediately clear and definite as it is in Chinese and Sanskrit; Burmese is unlike the former because it possesses mediating concepts which lessen the necessity of true concentration in the linguistic sense; it is unlike Sanskrit because it does not dominate the sounds of the language and never achieves the formation of genuine word unity and forms. On the other hand, one cannot place Burmese among the agglutinating languages since in the pronunciation it conscientiously keeps the syllables apart from one another. It is more consistent in its system than those languages even though it is therefore more distant from all inflection. However, even in the agglutinating languages, inflection does not derive from the proper sources but is only an accidental phenomenon.

Sanskrit and the dialects descending from it have joined themselves more or less to the languages of all the peoples surrounding India; and it is fascinating to see how the various languages relate to one another through ties that arise more from the spirit of religion and of science than from political relationships and living conditions. In the remote part of India, Pali, an inflected language whose forms have lost many sound differentiations, has joined the languages which agree to a significant degree with Chinese, that is where the contrast between rich grammatical allusion and the almost complete lack of the same is at its greatest. I cannot agree with the view that the Burmese language in its genuine form and insofar as it belongs to the nation itself has been significantly transformed by Pali. The polysyllabic words in it have arisen from its peculiar proclivity for agglutination, and it did not need the example of Pali; likewise, the manner in which the particle is used with these forms belongs to this language alone. The speakers of Burmese who are also knowledgeable in Pali have simply clothed Burmese externally with its grammatical garment. One sees this in the multiplicity of the case indications and in the classes of the composite words. That which they equate with the Sanskrit *Karmadhâraya* is completely different from it since the initial Burmese adjective always needs a joining particle. To judge from F. Carey's grammar, they seem not to have dared even once to apply their terminology to the verb. Still the possibility is not to be denied that through continued study of Pali the style and to some extent also the character of the Burmese language as an approach to Pali can be changed and might still be changed more. The truly physical form of languages dependent on the sounds permits such an effect only within very measured limits. On the other hand, the inner aspect of the form is easily accessible to such an effect; and the grammatical views, indeed even the strength and vigor of the linguistic sense, are corrected and elevated through intimacy with more complete languages. This then has a retroactive effect upon the language insofar as it permits usage and dominance over itself. In Burmese this retroaction would be advantageously strong since chief parts of its construction already approach Sanskrit; primarily, they lack only being taken in the correct sense, and the language itself is not capable of leading to this since it has not arisen from this sense. In this respect, the outside point of view would be of help to it. To this end, one might gradually assimilate the aggregate particles of the definite grammatical forms, though rejecting some of them, and use the present auxiliary verb more frequently in the construction. However, even with the most careful efforts of this type no one will ever succeed in erasing the fact that a quite different form is peculiar to the language; and the creations of such a procedure would always sound non-Burmese since, to stress just this one point, the several particles present for the same form do not find application indifferently but in accordance with fine nuances present in the linguistic usage. One would therefore always recognize that something strange to it had been injected into the language.

According to all the evidence, historical relationship between Burmese and Chinese does not seem to be present. Both languages are said to have only few words in common. Still I do not know whether this point might not need a more careful evaluation. The great similarity between the sound of some of the words taken right out of the class of the grammatical ones is striking. I will put these down here for the better students of the two languages. The Burmese plural signs of the nouns and verbs are *tô.* and *kra* (pronounced *kya*), and *toû* and *kiâi* are the Chinese plural signs in the old and new style; *thang* (pronounced *thi*, H.) corresponds, as we have already seen above, to *ti* of the newer and *tchî* of the older style; *hri* (pronounced *shi*) is the verb "to be," and in Chinese, according to J. P. Abel Rémusat, it is *chi*. In accordance with the English manner, R. Morrison and G. H. Hough write both words as *she*. The Chinese word is at the same time a pronoun and an affirmative particle, so its verbal meaning has probably been taken from Burmese. However, this origin would add nothing to the relationship between *hri* and *chi*. Finally, the general expression used in both languages for the indication of numbered objects, in this respect similar to our word "piece," is pronounced in Burmese *hku* and in Chinese *ko*.[26] Even if the number of these words is slight, they belong to the parts of the structure which betray the relationship of both languages to the greatest extent; and the differences between Chinese and Burmese grammar, although reaching broadly and deeply into the linguistic structure, are not of the type that make relationship impossible, as do the differences between Burmese and Tagalic for example.

CHAPTER TWENTY-TWO

The Origin of Polysyllabic Linguistic Structure

CLOSELY RELATED TO the investigations just begun is the question whether the difference between mono- and polysyllabic languages is absolute or relative, and whether the form of the words significantly shapes the character of the language or whether monosyllabicity is simply a condition out of which polysyllabic languages have gradually developed.

During earlier stages of language study, people declared Chinese and several Southeast Asian languages to be monosyllabic. Later they became somewhat doubtful about this, and J. P. Abel Rémusat expressly denied this assertion with reference to Chinese.[1] However this view seemed to quarrel too much with the facts lying before our eyes, and one can rightfully maintain that we have now returned to the earlier assumption, and not incorrectly so. At the base of this quarrel lie several misunderstandings; and therefore we first need an adequate explanation of what we call monosyllabic word form and of the sense in which we differentiate mono- and polysyllabic languages. All the examples of polysyllabicity in Chinese cited by J. P. Abel Rémusat amount to compounds; and there can certainly be no doubt that compounding is completely different from original polysyllabicity. In the compound, even the concept that is regarded as quite simple arises from two or more concepts connected with one another. The word which results from this is therefore never a simple one, and for this reason a language with compound words does not cease to be monosyllabic. Obviously, polysyllabicity is a matter of simple words in which no elementary concepts forming a longer concept can be differentiated but in which the sounds of two or more syllables meaningless in themselves make up the concept symbol. Even when we find words in which this is apparently the case, a more precise investigation is always necessary to find out whether it might not be true that each individual syllable originally possessed a meaning peculiar to it which has simply become lost. A correct example of polysyllabicity would have to bear the proof within itself that all sounds of the word are meaningful only in conjunction with one another and together, and not separately. J. P. Abel Rémusat has definitely not seen this clearly enough, and therefore in his essay cited above he failed to recognize the original formation of Chinese.[2] From another aspect, however, J. P. Abel Rémusat's opinion was indeed founded on something correctly observed. Although he remained with the division of languages into mono- and polysyllabic, his keen vision did not fail to note that this, as it is usually understood, is not to be taken too precisely. I have already mentioned that such a division cannot rest on the simple fact that mono- or polysyllabic words predominate but that two much more essential conditions lie at its root, namely a lack of affixes and a peculiarity of the pronunciation to keep the syllable sounds separate even where the spirit combines the concepts. The reason for the lack of the affixes lies truly in the spirit, for if the spirit feels the dependency of the affix upon the chief concept in a vital manner, the tongue cannot possibly render an equal sound value to the affix in a proper word. A direct consequence of this feeling is the coalescense of two different elements into the unity of the word. Therefore, J. P. Abel Rémusat seems to me to have made a mistake in that he attacked the monosyllabicity of Chinese rather than trying to show that even other languages proceed from a monosyllabic root construction and approach polysyllabicity in part by way of affixation peculiar to them and in part by compounding which is not strange to Chinese, but that they really attain this goal only when the above-mentioned hindrances do not stand in their way as they did in the case of Chinese. This is the direction I now want to strike out in and follow through the actual investigation of several languages.

Although it is difficult and sometimes impossible to trace words back to their true origin, a careful analysis leads us back in most languages to monosyllabic stems. Individual cases of polysyllabic stems cannot be regarded as proof of original polysyllabicity since these phenomena can probably be attributed to an analysis which has not gone far enough back. If one studies the question simply from ideas, one will probably not go too far in generally assuming that every concept was originally designated by one syllable. The concept in language invention is the impression which an object, external or internal, makes on man. Sound enticed from the breast by the vitality of this impression is the word. Two sounds cannot easily correspond to a single impression. If two sounds, following directly upon one another, were to arise, they would prove to be two impressions of the same object, and at its birth the word would already form a compound without the principle of monosyllabicity being seriously damaged. In fact, this is the case in gemination, which takes place in all languages but especially in the more uncultivated ones. Each of the repeated sounds expresses the whole object, but by means of the repetition one nuance more is added to the expression; this is either simple intensification indicating the great vitality of the experience or it is the expression of a repeating object. Gemination takes place especially in adjectives because it is especially characteristic of a property that it appears ubiquitously in space, not as an individual body but as a surface, so to speak. In several languages, of which I will cite here only those of the South Sea Islands, gemination really belongs preferably, indeed almost exclusively, to the adjectives and the substantives formed from them, which are originally felt as adjectives. To be sure, if one conceives of the original language designation as an intentional distribution of sounds among the objects, then the matter is far different. The care not to give completely identical signs to various concepts could then be the most probable reason why a second and third syllable would have been added to a single syllable, irrespective of new meaningfulness. But this manner of thinking, in which one completely forgets that language is not a dead mechanism but a living creation and that the first speaking human beings were by far more sensitive and excitable than we, who are dulled by culture and knowledge that are dependent on foreign experience, is apparently false. All languages undoubtedly contain words which can create ambiguity by virtue of the fact that completely identical sounds have very different meanings. However, the fact that this is rare and that as a rule a differently intoned sound corresponds to each concept did not arise from intentional comparison of the words already present, which could not even be present for the speaker, but from the fact that the impression of the object, as well as the sound elicited, was always individual and no individuality agrees completely with another. From another point of view, the word supply was also expanded by an increase in the individual designations present. As man came to know more objects and the individual ones more precisely, he came to see special variety in the general similarity. This new impression naturally produced a new sound which, joined to the previous one, became the polysyllabic word. But here, too, there are related concepts with related sounds, which are really designations of one and the same object. As far as the original designation is concerned, one might at best consider it possible that the voice could have added quite meaningless sounds merely because of sensual pleasure derived from murmuring the tones or that merely exhaled puffs of air among the more regulated pronunciation could have become true syllables. I would not like to deny that sounds without any significance in a language do indeed maintain themselves on a purely sensual basis. But this is the case only because their meaningfulness has become lost. Originally the breast expels no articulated sound which a feeling has not awakened.

In the course of time, matters become quite different with respect to polysyllabicity. One cannot deny that it exists in the cultured languages. One questions it only in the roots. Outside of this sphere, it rests on compounding for its origin, which is to be accepted as a whole and very often can be proved in detail, thus losing as a result its peculiar nature. But even though a compound appears meaningless to us because the meaning of the individual word elements is lacking, there is often something positive at the base of the phenomenon. At first the language combines concepts which really modify one another. Then it connects one chief concept to another, but this is done metaphorically or with only a part of their meaning remaining valid; such is the case when the Chinese use the word "son" in compound relationship names in order to distinguish between an older and a younger one—that is, they use it to indicate relationships in which neither direct descendancy nor sex but simply chronological sequence in age is important. If several such concepts became word elements designating specific relationships, the language probably grew accustomed to using them also for a relationship that is quite distant and hardly traceable or where one must freely admit that there is no real relationship at all; as a result, the significance disappears into nothingness. This phenomenon, whereby a language, following a general analogy, applies sounds appropriate to specific cases to other cases to which they are strange can also be found in other parts of its operation. For example, it is not to be denied that in several inflections of the Sanskrit declension pronominal stems are concealed, and, moreover, that in several of these cases no reason can really be found why precisely this and no other root is given a specific case; indeed, it cannot even be explained how a pronominal stem can make up the expression of this definite case relationship. In those cases which seem the most striking to us, there may be quite individual, finely conceived connections between the concept and the sound. But for general purposes these no longer have any function and, although it is no accident, they are recognizable just from the historical standpoint so that for us even their existence is wasted. I have intentionally not mentioned here the incorporation of foreign polysyllabic words from one language into another since, if the assertion I have made is correct, the polysyllabicity of such words is never original and the meaninglessness of their individual elements for the language into which they are incorporated remains merely relative.

In the languages which are not monosyllabic there is, in varying degrees, a striving toward pure polysyllabicity; this arises from concurrent internal and external circumstances without regard to the origin of polysyllabicity in compounding, whether known or shrouded in darkness. The language then demands phonemic scope for the expression of individual concepts and allows the elementary ideas united in them to dissolve within this scope. The designation of one concept by several syllables arises then in this twofold way. Whereas the Chinese language struggles against polysyllabicity and whereas its writing which has obviously originated from this opposition confirms it, other languages have the opposite inclination. Through pleasure in beautiful sound and through a striving toward rhythmic proportions they gradually form larger word units and, while responding to an inner feeling, differentiate further between bare compounding that arises simply through speech and that which can be confused with the expression of a simple concept by several syllables whose individual meaning is no longer known or is no longer relevant. But, since everything in language is connected internally, this striving, which at first appears to be only sensual, rests on a broader and firmer basis. Indeed, the spirit which is naturally inclined to combine the concept and its relations in the unity of the same word obviously works along with it toward this goal. The language may really reach this goal, as a truly inflected one does, or it may stop halfway, as an agglutinating one does. The creative power of the language itself which drives out of the root all that which belongs to the inner and external formation of the word, is here the truly effective power. The farther this creation extends, the larger it becomes. The earlier it tires, the lesser is the degree of striving. But the phonemic scope of the word arising out of that striving is limited by the laws of good sound. Languages that are less fortunate in uniting syllables join a greater number of them together unrhythmically, whereas perfect striving for unity results in a smaller number joined together harmoniously. The internal and external success are here in close agreement with each other. However, through the concepts themselves an effort is made in many cases to join several of them together merely in order to give a proper sign to a simple one, without wanting to maintain the meaning connected to the individual ones. From this there naturally arises true polysyllabicity, for the concept compounded merely makes its simplicity valid.

Among the cases about which we are speaking, two classes in particular stand out. In one class the concept indicated by a sound is supposed to be determined more definitely or explained by the joining of a second one; that is, on the whole uncertainty and lack of clarity are supposed to be avoided. To this end, languages often combine identical concepts or concepts that differ only very slightly; they also join general ones to special ones and to other general ones that originated out of special ones. In Chinese, for example, the concept of "striking" almost goes over into that of "doing" in these compounds. In the other class belong those cases where a third concept is really formed out of two different concepts; for example, the "sun" is called the "eye of the day"; "milk" the "water of the breast," and so forth. In the first class of combinations there lies either a distrust in the clarity of the expression used or a lively haste to increase their number. They are rarely found in very cultured languages but occur frequently in those which are conscious of a certain indefiniteness. In cases of the second class, the two concepts to be combined are the direct illustration of the impression received; that is, they represent the actual word in its special meaning. Actually, they would form two concepts. But since they designate only one thing, comprehension demands their closest union in the speech form. As their power over the language grows and the original concept disappears in the language, the most beautiful metaphors of this type lose their historical influence and disappear from the consciousness of the speakers, no matter how clearly their origin may be proved. Both classes can also be found in the monosyllabic languages, but in them the inner need for the combination of the concepts is unable to conquer the claim to the separation of syllables.

It is in this manner, I believe, that the phenomena of mono- and polysyllabicity must be conceived of and judged in languages. I will now attempt to document this general reasoning, which I have not wanted to interrupt by enumerating facts, with several examples.

The newer style of Chinese possesses a not insignificant number of words consisting of two elements whose compounding has had as its purpose only the formation of a third simple concept. In several of them it is apparent that the addition of the second element, which adds nothing to the sense, has only as a result of truly significant cases become habitual. The expansion of concepts and of languages must lead to designating new objects by comparing them with other, already known ones and hence to a transformation in the procedure whereby the intellect forms concepts in the language. This method gradually takes over in place of the earlier one and reproduces the impression symbolically through the analogy present in the articulated sounds. But at a late stage of development, even this method disappears among peoples with great imagination and a keen sensual outlook, and therefore languages still in the formative stages possess for the most part a great number of picturesque woɪds that represent the nature of the objects. In modern Chinese, however, a malformation belonging in fact to a later culture reveals itself in this respect. Descriptions of objects, which are more playfully witty than truly poetic, and in which the objects like puzzles often lie concealed, frequently form words consisting of two elements. One class of these words appears very strange at first glance, namely those in which two opposed concepts expɪess a general concept that embraces both of them. This is the case, for example, when "the younger and older brotheɪs" or "the high and low mountains" is used to refer to "the brothers" or "the mountains" in general. The universality contained in the definite article is suggested in these cases visually, that is, through opposite extremes which permit no exceptions. Actually, even this type of word is more a rhetorical figure of speech than a formational method of the language. But in a language where an expression which is otherwise simply grammatical must so often be placed materially into the content of the speech, it is not unjust to call this procedure a formational method. Such compounds can be found in all languages. In Sanskrit they remind one of the स्थावरजङ्गमम्, *sthâwara-jangamam*, which occurs frequently in philosophical poems. But in Chinese there is the additional fact that the language possesses no word at all in several cases even for the general concept and must necessarily avail itself of these circumlocutions. The condition of age, for example, cannot be separated from the word "brother," and one can only say "older and younger brothers" and not just "brothers." This may originate from an early lack of culture. The desire to represent this object visually, with its properties in the word, and the lack of abstraction cause the general expression, which embraces several varieties within itself, to be neglected. The individual, sensual concept thus precedes the general one in the understanding. Even in the American languages this phenomenon is frequent. However, as a result of this aɪtificial method of understanding, this type of word structure in Chinese stands out even more. This is because the symmetric arrangement of the concepts which stand in a definite relationship to one another is regarded as an advantage and an adornment of the style, on which even the nature of the writing, which incorporates every concept into one symbol, has influence. One seeks therefore to weave such concepts intentionally into the speech, and Chinese rhetoric has made a business out of counting the contrasting concepts in the language since no relationship is as definite as one of pure contrast.[4] The older Chinese style makes no use of compound words; this may be because in earlier times, as is very understandable, one had not yet arrived at this procedure, or because this more severe style, which to a certain extent scorned coming to the aid of the understanding by means of language, excluded it from its circle.

I can omit the Burmese language here since I have already shown in the general description of its construction how it forms polysyllabic stems by joining together monosyllabic stems of like meaning or monosyllabic stems that modify one another. In the Malayan languages, even after the removal of the affixes, there remains very frequently, indeed one can well say usually, a disyllabic root which is not further divisible. Even where the stem is monosyllabic, it is frequently geminated, particularly in the Tagalic language. One finds therefore that the disyllabic construction of these languages is often mentioned. Up until now, so far as I know, an analysis of these word stems has never been undertaken. I have tried it; and even though I have not yet succeeded in accounting for the nature of all of the elements in these words, I have convinced myself that in very many cases each of the two joined syllables can be shown to be a monosyllabic stem and that the cause of the combination is understandable. If this is the case even with our incomplete aids and our faulty knowledge, we can probably assume a greater extension of this principle and hence the original monosyllabicity of these languages. The words which end in mere vowel sounds, such as the Tagalic *lisà* and *lisay*, from the root *lis* (see below), create more difficulty to be sure. Still, these two will presumably be explicable after future investigation. Indeed, it is already apparent that in the majority of the cases one may not regard the final syllables of the Malayan disyllabic stems as suffixes joined to meaningful words; on the contrary, real roots, exactly like those forming the first syllable, can be recognized in them, for they can be found sometimes as the first syllables of compounds and sometimes quite separately in the language. But for the most part one must seek the monosyllabic stems in their geminations.

From this quality of the disyllabic words, which seems simple at first glance and yet leads back to monosyllabicity, there arises an inclination in the speech toward polysyllabicity which, as one sees from the frequency of the gemination, is in part phonetic and not merely intellectual. The uniting syllables, however, become one word to a greater extent than they do in Burmese since the accent binds them together. In Burmese, every monosyllabic word carries its own accent with itself and brings it into the compound. That the resultant word would possess an accent holding its syllables together is impossible with pronunciation that audibly separates the syllables. In Tagalic, the polysyllabic word always has an accent which stresses the penultimate syllable or lets it fall. Changes in letters, however, are simply not related to the compounding.

I have started my researches on this subject with the Tagalic and New

Zealand languages. In my estimation, the former illustrates the Malayan linguistic structure in its greatest circumference. It was important to include the South Sea languages in the investigation because their structure seems to be even more primeval or at least to contain a greater number of such elements. In the examples taken from the Tagalic, I have adhered almost exclusively to those cases where the monosyllabic stem, at least in the gemination, belongs as such to the language. Naturally the number of disyllabic words whose monosyllabic stems merely appear in compounds is far greater. Moreover, these monosyllabic stems are recognizable in these compounds by their ever identical meaning. These cases, however, are not so convincing for there are usually other words in which this identity seems to be less or not at all present; such apparent exceptions, however, can very easily arise for the simple reason that one does not guess a more remote connection of the ideas. It is understandable that I was constantly seeking the proof of two syllables since the opposite procedure could offer only doubtful indication as to the nature of these word constructions. Naturally, attention must also be paid to words which have their original root not in the same but in another language; this is true of several words in Tagalic which have come over from Sanskrit or even from the South Sea languages.

Examples from the Tagalic Language

Bag-sàc, 'to throw something with force on the ground' or 'to press up against something'; *bag-bàg,* 'to land on the beach' or 'to dig up a grain field' (used to indicate powerful thrusting or throwing); *sac-sàc,* 'to place something in firmly, to penetrate, to stop up, to throw into something' (*apretar embutiendo algo, atestar, hincar*). *Lab-sàc,* 'to throw something in the mud or outhouse,' from the word already cited and from *lab-làb,* 'swamp, refuse heap, outhouse.' From this word and *as-às* is formed *lab-às, semen suis ipsius manibus elicere. Sac-àl,* 'to press someone's neck, hand, or foot,' probably belongs here also, although the meaning of the second element, *al-àl,* 'to file down the teeth with a little stone,' does not fit here very well. *Sac-yòr,* 'to catch grasshoppers,' could also belong here, but I do not know how to explain its second element. On the other hand, one cannot figure in here *sacsì,* 'witness,' since the word is unquestionably the Sanskrit साक्षिन्, *sâkshin,* and may have come into the language as a legal term with Indic culture. The same word with the same meaning can also be found in the actual Malayan language.

Bac-às, 'footsteps, tracks of men and animals, the remaining physical signs of tears, beatings,' and so forth; *bac-bàc*, 'to take off the rind or to lose'; *ás-as*, 'to rub' (used of clothes and other things).

Bac-làs, 'wound' (particularly those which come from scratching) from the just cited *bac-bàc* and from *las-làs*, 'to take off leaves or roof tiles' (also used to refer to the destruction of twigs and roofs by the wind). The word is also rendered *bac-lìs*, from *lis-lìs*, 'to weed, tear out grass' (see below).

Ás-al, 'usage, accepted custom,' from the above-cited *ás-as* and *al-àl*, that is, from the combination of the concepts of 'to use up' and 'to file off.'

It-ìt, 'to suck in,' and *im-ìm*, 'to close up' (used when referring to the mouth). From these two *it-ìm*, 'black' (Malayan, *ētam*), has presumably arisen, since this color is very easily compared with something sucked in and closed up.

Tac-lìs, 'to whet, sharpen' (particularly to sharpen one knife with another). *Tac* means 'the emptying of the body, the execution of the bowel movement.' The geminated *tac-tàc* denotes 'a large spade, a hoe' (*azadon*), and as a verb it means 'to work, to hollow out with this tool.' It becomes clear that this latter concept is actually the basic meaning even of the simple root. *Lis-lìs* will occur again below, but it unites in itself the concepts of 'destruction' and 'the small or the making small.' Both fit very well with the grinding down of whetting.

Lis-pìs, with the prefix *pa*, 'to clean the grain for seed,' originates from the above-mentioned *lis-lìs* and from *pis-pìs*, 'to sweep out, to brush off' (used especially when referring to bread crumbs).

Lá-bay, 'a bundle of silk, yarn, or cotton' (*madeja*), and, as a verb, 'to wind on a reel'; *lá-la*, 'to weave rugs'; *bay-bay̆*, 'to go' (along the coast of the sea). *Bay-bay̆* thus denotes travel in a definite direction, which fits very well with the motion of reeling.

Tú-lis, 'to point, sharpen,' used when referring to large wooden nails (*estacas*); in Javanese and Malayan it is applied to the concept of writing.[5] *Lis-lìs*, 'to destroy bad, useless growths, to tear out,' has already appeared above. The concept is actually 'to make small,' and therefore it goes well with the idea of scraping off in order to produce a point; *lisà* means 'the little eggs of the lice,' and from this concept of the small or of the dust comes the application of the word to the concept of 'cleaning out, sweeping out,' as in *ua-lìs*, the general word for this work. I do not find the first element of *tú-lis* in Tagalic in either simple or geminated form. On the other hand I do find it in the South Sea languages: in the Tongic *tu* (W. Mariner writes it *too*),[6] 'to cut, to get up, to stand upright'; and in New Zealandic, where it has this latter meaning as well as that of 'to strike.'

Tó-bo, 'to come forth, to sprout,' used of plants (*nacer*), from *bo-bò*, 'to empty something out' and *tó-to*. In Tagalic *tó-to* has only metaphorical meanings: 'to form a friendship, to be in agreement, to attain one's intent in speech or action.' But in New Zealandic, *to* is 'life, vivacity,' and from this comes *toto*, 'flood.' In Tongic, *tubu* (W. Mariner writes it *tooboo*) has the same sprouting meaning as the Tagalic *tóbo*, but it also means 'to spring up.' *Bu* is found in Tongic as *bubula*, 'to swell'; *tu* means 'to cut, to separate, to stand.' The New Zealandic *tupu* corresponds to the Tongic *tubu*, both in meaning as well as in derivation. For *tu* is 'to stand, to stand up,' and in *pu* lies the concept of a body which has become round through swelling since it means 'a pregnant woman.' The meanings 'cylinder, flint, and tube' which S. Lee[7] places first are only derivatives. The fact that the concept of breaking open through swelling up is already present in *pu* is proved by the compound *pu-ao*, 'daybreak.'

Examples from the New Zealandic Language

The Tagalic dictionary of D. de los Santos[8] is intended, like most missionary works of this type and especially the older ones, simply as an introduction to the writing and preaching in the language. Therefore, it always gives the most concrete meanings of the words, which have been evolved through linguistic usage, and rarely goes back to the original, general terms. Even quite simple terms, which belong in fact to the roots of the language, very often contain concepts of definite objects; for example, *pay-pày* means 'shoulder blade, fan, and sunshade,' all of which embrace the larger concept of stretching out. One sees this also in *sam-pày*, 'to hang laundry or other things in the air on a line or a stick' (*tender*), in *cá-pay*, 'to row with the arms lacking oars, to wave the hands in calling,' and in other compounds. It is absolutely different in the New Zealandic dictionary, which has been very perceptively assembled by Professor S. Lee in Cambridge. He worked with the materials of T. Kendall and was assisted by two natives. The simplest sounds have the extremely common meanings of motion, space, and so forth, an observation that can be ascertained from a comparison of the articles on the vowel sounds.[9] As a result, one becomes embarrassed at times concerning the special application, and one is tempted to ask whether this conceptual scope in fact is present in the spoken language or whether it has not perhaps just been added to it. S. Lee has undoubtedly derived this from the indications of the natives; and it cannot be denied that this is of great help in the derivation of the New Zealandic words.

Ora, 'health, increase, restoring of the same,' from *o*, 'motion' and particularly 'refreshment,' and from *ra*, 'strength, health, the sun.' *Ka-ha* means 'strength, a rising flame, to burn, enlivenment' (both as a process and as a vigorous effect); *ha* denotes 'the breathing out.'

Mara, 'a place exposed to the warmth of the sun,' as well as 'a person standing opposite the speaker' (probably used when referring to the shining of the countenance and therefore as a form of address), from *ma*, 'clear, white in color,' and *ra*, the word just mentioned for 'sun'; *marama* is 'the light, the moon.'

Pono, 'true, truth,' from *po*, 'night, the region of darkness,' and *noa*, 'free, unbound.' If this derivation is really correct, then the compounding of the concepts is strangely sensible.

Mutu, 'the end, to end,' from *mu*, used as a particle, 'the last, finally,' and *tu*, 'to stand.'

Examples from the Tongic Language

Fachi, 'to break, to wrench,' from *fa*, 'capable, to be something or to do something,' and *chi*, 'small' (the New Zealandic *iti*).

Loto means 'the center, the middle point, that which is locked within,' and unquestionably from this it has the metaphorical meaning of 'attitude, temperament, thought, opinion.' The word is identical in meaning to the New Zealandic *roto*, which, however, has only the physical and not the figurative meaning; that is, *roto* means just 'the inmost,' and as a preposition it means 'in.' I believe that I can derive both words correctly from both languages. The first element seems to me to be the New Zealandic *roro*, 'brain.' The simple *ro* is translated in S. Lee's dictionary merely by the ambiguous 'matter, material,' which one must probably take here as 'pus, ulcerous matter,' and which perhaps means more generally 'all enclosed sticky material.' I have already spoken about the second element, the New Zealandic word *to*, and I note here only that it is also used of pregnancy, that is, of the inwardly, vitally enclosed. In Tongic I know it up to now as the name of the tree whose berries have a sticky flesh and which are used for sticking things together Thus, the concept of hanging on to something else is present even in this meaning. The expression for 'brain' in Tongic, however, is only partially present in *loto/roto*. The word for 'brain' is *uto* (W. Mariner writes it *ooto*). I consider the last member of this word to be the word *to*, about which we just spoke, since the concept of stickiness is quite suitable for the brain mass. The first syllable is not less expressive for a description of the brain since *u* is 'a bundle, a package.' I think I also find this word in the Tagalic *ótac* and the Malayan *ūtak*, and hence I do not seek the roots for these words in these languages. As in other Malayan words, it is quite possible that the final *k* in *ūtak* is not radical. Both words, *ótac* and *ūtac*, mean 'marrow' and 'brain,' apparently because of the identity of the material, and, as a result, are differentiated often, or in fact usually, by the addition of 'head' or 'bone.' According to E. de Flacourt, the word for 'marrow' in Madecassic is *oteche*, and the word for 'brain' is *otechendoha*, 'marrow of the head'; he writes the word *loha*, 'head,' with the customary metathesis of letters and connects it to the other word by a nasal. In Challan, the expression for 'brain' is *tso ondola*, and 'marrow' the *tsoc*, or *tsoco*. It is difficult to decide whether *ondola* is supposed to belong to *tso*. Presumably, however, only the differentiating mark has been left out; for in the Madecassic-French part of the dictionary, only the word *ondola* is found for 'brain,' which I have not been able to explain. In the manuscript word list by E. Jacquet, 'brain' is given as *tsokou loha*, and E. Jacquet notes that he finds no corresponding word in the other dialects.[10] But I consider *tsokou* and the variants in Challan simply a distortion of the Malayan *ūtak*; that is, the initial vowel has been discarded, and the *t* has been given a hissing pronunciation. Consequently, it has the same meaning as E. de Flacourt's *oteche*, which reminds one even more of the Tagalic *ótac*. J. Chapelier's manuscript dictionary, which I owe to the kindness of Mr. A. Lesson, has *tsoudoa* for 'brain'; once again, the final *doa*, 'head,' stands for *loa*. I regret very much not knowing the word for "brain" in the form used by the English missionaries today. But the word "brain" occurs in the Latin Vulgate Bible only in two passages of the Book of the Judges, and the English Bible, from which the missionaries translate, has "skull" for this.

The disyllabicity of the Semitic stems (to skip the slight number of those containing more or fewer syllables) is entirely different from that studied up to now since it is to a greater extent inseparably imbedded in the lexical and grammatical structure. It forms an essential part of the character of these languages and cannot be disregarded so long as we are speaking about the origin and development of culture and its influence on the speech. Yet one can accept it as an established fact that even this multisyllable system is founded on an originally monosyllabic one that is still clearly recognizable in the modern language. This has been pointed out by several scholars of the Semitic languages, by D. Michaelis in particular and by others even before him, and it has been more closely studied by F. H. W. Gesenius and H. von Ewald.[11] There are, says F. H. W. Gesenius, whole series of root verbs which have only the first two root consonants in common and have quite different ones for the third but which still agree in meaning, at least in the chief concept. He thought it exaggerated that C. Neumann, who died at the beginning of the previous century in Breslau, wanted to trace all disyllabic roots back to monosyllabic ones. In the cases mentioned here, monosyllabic roots consisting of two consonants enclosing a vowel form the basis for the modern disyllabic root words. The disyllabic root words arose in a later writing down of the language when a third consonant, as well as a second vowel, was added. H. J. von Klaproth has also recognized this and in an essay has listed a number of the series indicated by F. H. W. Gesenius.[12] In this he shows in a strange but clever manner how the monosyllabic roots, freed of their third consonant, very frequently agree completely or for the most part with Sanskritic roots in sound and meaning. H. von Ewald observes that a carefully arranged comparison of the stems would lead to many new results, but he adds that by using such etymology one goes beyond the age of the Semitic language proper. In the latter I agree with him completely since it is my conviction that a new language begins in fact with every essentially new form which the dialect of a tribe acquires in the course of time.

In considering the scope of the origin of disyllabic roots from monosyllabic ones, we would first have to establish precisely how far the etymological analysis would be able to go in this matter. If there were no cases left which could be traced back, then the fault would most likely lie in the lack of members which would show the series completely. But even on the basis of general reasons, it seems necessary to me to assume that a mixture of mono- and disyllabic word stems, and not just monosyllabic ones, preceded the extension of all roots to two syllables. One must never imagine changes in the language so powerful that a new educational principle for which there were no examples might be thrust on the people (for that does mean the language). There must certainly be such cases, and in some quantity, if certain sound characteristics are supposed to be made general by grammatical law-making, but this is certainly more powerful in the eradication of present forms than in the introduction of new ones. I would not like to deny the possibility of an original disyllabic root simply because of the general pronouncement that a root must always be monosyllabic. I have explained my thoughts on this matter in the foregoing. But if I trace the disyllabicity back to compounding, so that two syllables are the combined representation of two impressions, then the compounding can already be present in the spirit of that person who speaks the word for the first time. This is all the more possible here than it is with a tribe endowed with a sense of inflection. In the Semitic languages, however, there is an even more important circumstance.

Although the nullification of the law of disyllabicity displaces us into a time previous to the present linguistic structure, this structure still contains two other characteristics which indicate that the root syllable to which the analysis of present stems leads was always closed by a consonant and that the vowel was regarded as indifferent insofar as the significance of the concept was concerned. For, if the medial vowels had really possessed conceptual importance, it would have been impossible to tear it away from them. I have already discussed the relationship of the vowels to the consonants in those monosyllabic roots (see pp. 199–202). On the other hand, the earlier language formation could have been traced to the expression of a double feeling in two connected syllables. The inflectional sense allowed the word to be regarded as a whole which embraced various things within itself; and the tendency to place the grammatical implication into the heart of the word itself lead to investing it with greater scope. As a matter of fact, the existence of disyllabic roots could be defended for the most part by the reasons developed here, which to me do not seem forced in any way. The uniform meaning of the first syllable of several would only prove the equality of the main impression of various objects. Nonetheless, it seems more natural to me to accept the existence of monosyllabic roots, though not for the purpose of excluding disyllabic ones. It is regrettable that the investigations known to me do not examine the meaning of the third consonant joined to the two preceding consonants. Only this admittedly very difficult analysis would shed complete light on this material. But if one regards all disyllabic Semitic word stems as compounded, then one sees at first glance that this compounding is quite different from that in the languages we have examined here. In these other languages, each member of the compound makes up an independent word. Even though it frequently happens, at least in Burmese and Malayan, that these independent words do not appear by themselves but merely in such compounds, this is after all simply a consequence of language usage. Nothing in them contradicts their independence. In fact, they have definitely existed as independent words formerly, and they have simply dropped out of fashion as such because their meaning was unusually suitable for designating modifications in compounds. However, the second syllable added to the Semitic word stems could not exist alone since it did not possess at all independently the legitimate form of nouns and verbs when it occurred, preceded by a vowel and followed by a consonant. One can see clearly from this that the procedure which lies at the root of this formation of disyllabic word stems is totally different from that in Chinese and in the languages similar to it in this part of its structure. Two words are not compounded, but, on the contrary, with an unmistakable view toward word unity one is expanded. Even in this respect the Semitic branch preserves its nobler form which corresponds to a greater extent to the demands of the linguistic sense and which more surely and freely advances the progress of thinking.

According to the theory of the Indian grammarians, the few polysyllabic roots of Sanskrit can be traced back to monosyllabic ones, and all other words in the language arise from these. Hence, Sanskrit knows no other polysyllabicity than that produced by grammatical addition or apparent composition. But it has already been mentioned above (see p. 77) that the grammarians often go too far in this respect so that among the words of uncertain origin, which can be derived from the roots only in an unnatural manner, there are disyllabic ones whose origin remains in doubt to the extent that neither derivation nor composition is perceptible in them. Probably, however, they do contain the latter within themselves, and it could be that not only the original meaning of the individual elements was lost in the memory of the people but also that their sound has gradually undergone a sloughing action making them similar to mere suffixes. Even the principle of uninterrupted derivation established by the grammarians had to lead gradually to both of these positions.

In several, the composition is really recognizable. For example, F. Bopp regards शरद्, *śarad*, 'fall, rainy season,' as a composite from शर, *śara*, 'water,' and द, *da*, 'giving,' and he regards other *unâdi* words as similar compounds.[13] The meaning of the words which have gone over to a *unâdi* word may have become so changed in its application whenever this form was introduced that the original was no longer to be recognized in it. The spirit of formation through affixes generally predominant in the language might lead to the same treatment of these forms. In several cases, *unâdi* suffixes assume the form of substantives and are independently present in the language. Of this type are आण्ड, *aṇḍa*, and अङ्ग, *aṅga*. According to the laws of the language, substantives would not allow themselves to be joined with a root as the final members of a composite, and hence the nature of the above formations remains puzzling. However, a more precise observation of all individual cases would certainly resolve the confusion. In those cases where, according to natural derivation, the word can be attributed neither to the indicated root nor to another one, the difficulty resolves itself since no root is present in the word. In other cases, one can assume that the root was first transformed by the *krit* suffix *a* into a noun. Finally, however, there seem to be several among the *unâdi* suffixes which one would more properly attribute to the *krit* suffixes. In fact, the difference between the two categories is difficult to determine, and I could cite no other than that the *krit* suffixes are applicable to whole categories of words because of a general concept in them which expresses itself clearly. To be sure, even this distinction often remains at variance in the individual application. On the other hand, the *unâdi* suffixes create only individual words whose formation cannot be explained from concepts. Basically the *unâdi* words are nothing other than those which one has tried to trace back in an anomalous manner to roots since they did not permit the application of the usual suffixes of the language. Wherever this tracing back takes place naturally and whenever the frequency of the suffix appearing there occasions it, there seems to be no reason for not adding it to the *krit* suffixes. Therefore, F. Bopp, in his Latin grammar as well as in his abbreviated German one, has followed the method of arranging those most common *unâdi* suffixes, which are used mostly as suffixes, in alphabetical order, but these are mixed with the *krit* suffixes.

अाण्ड, *aṇḍa*, 'egg,' itself a *unâdi* word, from the root अण्, *aṇ*, 'to breathe,' and the suffix ड, *ḍa*, was at least originally probably one and the same word with the *unâdi* suffix of identical sound. The concept of nourishment taken from the concept of the egg and that of round form are more or less suitable for words formed from this suffix, even though these words do not make one think of an egg itself. In the case of *waraṇḍa*, in its meaning of 'an open portico,' the same concept is present, perhaps because of the configuration or decoration of these structures. The concepts of 'roundness' and of 'covering,' indicated by both elements of *waraṇḍa*, are revealed most clearly in the meaning of 'a skin disease consisting of pimples on the face,' which this word likewise has. These same concepts have gone over in part individually and in part jointly into the other meanings of *waraṇḍa*: 'the throng,' 'that which is covered on top,' and 'at the sides of an open portico.'[14] On the basis of the examples known to me, it appears that the *unâdi* suffix अाण्ड, *aṇḍa*, combines only with roots whose final sound is the vocalic *r*, and that it then always assumes *guna*. One could therefore regard the first syllable of *waraṇḍa* (*war*) as a noun formed from the root. The fact that the final *a* from this does not form a long *a*

with the initial *a* from *aṇḍa* admittedly contradicts this explanation. However, the fact that it does not do so seems natural since this formation,
even though this may have been true originally, was treated in the later
language not as a compound but as a derivation. Moreover, it is always
difficult to assume that these identically sounding words, that is, the
word for 'egg' and this *unâdi* suffix, were supposed to be completely
different. It is much easier to understand this construction if we assume
that our suffix has been gradually formed in meaning and grammatical
treatment from the substantive.

We may make, indeed perhaps with greater correctness, approximately
the same observations about the *unâdi* suffix अङ्ग, *anga*, since the substantive अङ्ग, *anga*, which denotes 'a body walking or moving,' has
another meaning more suitable for the formation of the suffix. Such a
suffix might easily be compared with our German *thum*, *heit*, and so forth.
F. Bopp has taken this suffix apart in a manner so ingenious and so
marvelously applicable to all of the words of this type known to me by
making the first syllable into the accusative ending of the noun and
deriving the last from गा, *gâ*, that I would not like to insist on its reconstruction in contradiction to him. Still, *anga* is used in Sanskrit in a fashion
so strikingly similar to the way it is used in the Kawi language and also in
several modern Malayan languages that I cannot avoid mentioning it
here. In the *Brata Yuddha*, the Kawi poem which my treatise on the Kawi
language treats extensively, Sanskrit substantives of the first declension
occur with the additional endings *anga* and *angana*: for example, there is
sura (1, a), 'hero' (शूर, *sûra*) and *suranga* (97, a); there is also *rana* (82, d),
'battle' (रण, *rana*) and *rananga* (83, d) as well as *ranangana* (86, b). These
additions seem to have no influence at all on the meaning since the manuscript paraphrase explains both the simple and the lengthened words by
the same modern Javanese word. In fact, the Kawi language as a poetic
language permits the abbreviation as well as the addition of completely
meaningless syllables. However, the agreement of these additions with the
Sanskrit substantives अङ्ग, *anga*, and अङ्गन, *angana*, the latter of which
also has a very common meaning, is too striking for one not to think of this
language. These substantives and the identically sounding *unâdi* suffix
were able to produce endings which were harmonious with the sound of
the syllables. I would not know where to point them out in the usual
modern Javanese language. On the other hand, *anga* is found in it but
with slight change as a substantive, and it is found in the New Zealandic
and Tongic quite unchanged as a substantive and as an ending; this leads
one to suspect that even here we should think of a Sanskrit origin. In
Javanese, *anga* is *hanggê*, which means 'the art and manner in which

something takes place'; the fact that this word belongs to the aristocratic language points to India as its source of derivation. In Tongic, *anga* means 'mood of the spirit, custom, usage, the place where something takes place.' In New Zealandic, the word, as one sees from the compounds, has this latter meaning, but its primary meaning is that of 'doing,' especially 'doing communal work.' To be sure, these meanings agree only with the concept of motion in the Sanskrit word, but even this has the meaning of soul and spirit. The true similarity seems to me to lie in the breadth of the concept which can be conceived of in various manners. In New Zealandic, the usage of *anga* as the last member of a compound is so frequent that it almost becomes a grammatical ending for abstract substantives: *udi*, 'to turn oneself around, to roll over,' also used of the year, and *udinga*, 'a rolling over'; *rongo*, 'to hear,' and *ronganga*, 'the action or time of hearing'; *tono*, 'to order,' and *tononga*, 'an order'; *tao*, 'a long spear,' and *taonga*, 'property gained with the spear'; *toa*, 'a hearty, bold man,' and *toanga*, 'the forcing, the overcoming'; *tui*, 'to sew, to designate, to write,' and *tuinga*, 'the writing, the tablet on which one writes'; *tu*, 'to stand,' and *tunga*, 'the place where one stands, the anchor place of a ship'; *toi*, 'to dive in the water,' and *toinga*, 'diving in'; *tupu*, 'a shoot, to sprout forth,' and *tupunga*, 'the forefathers, the place at which something has grown'; *ngaki*, 'to till the field,' and *ngakinga*, 'a farm.' On the basis of these examples, one might believe that *nga*, as well as *anga*, would be an ending. However, the initial *a* is merely sloughed off because of the preceding vowel, and S. Lee has observed that one always says *udi anga* instead of *udinga*. The Tongic language permits the *a* to exist even after vowels. This can be seen, for example, in *maanga*, 'a bite,' from *ma*, 'to chew'; in *taanga*, 'the chopping down of trees,' but also (figuratively, presumably from the tempo of the striking) 'song, verse, poetry,' from *ta*, 'to strike' (in sound and meaning this agrees with the Chinese word); and *nofoanga*, 'dwelling,' from *nofo*, 'to dwell, demonstrate.' To what extent the Madecassian *manghe*, 'to do,' is related to these words requires an investigation of its own. But this would very probably lead to some relationship since the initial *m* in this word even when it is used as an auxiliary and a prefix could very easily be a verbal prefix which can be released from it. E. Froberville[15] derives *magne*, as he writes it, from *maha aigne*, and cites several sound changes of this word. Since *manganou* is also among these forms, the Javanese *mangun*, 'to build, bring about,' probably also belongs here.[16] Thus, if one raises the question as to whether there are polysyllabic words in Sanskrit after the dissolution of all affixes, one must answer it in the affirmative since words whose last member cannot be regarded with certainty as a suffix attached to a root do occur. Meanwhile the simplicity of these words is, to be sure, only apparent. They are unquestionably compounds in which the meaning of one element has been lost.

Aside from this apparent polysyllabicity, there is a question whether there is not a form of concealed polysyllabicity present in Sanskrit. It might, after all, be possible that the roots beginning with a double consonant and especially those ending in consonants have become monosyllabic from originally disyllabic words. The former would have done this through contraction, whereas the latter would have sloughed off the final vowel. In an earlier writing,[17] I expressed this thought with reference to the Burmese language. The simple syllabic structure with a final vowel. to which several languages of Eastern Asia have remained true for the most part, seems in fact to be the most natural one; consequently, the roots which now seem monosyllabic to us could easily be disyllabic roots of a language preceding the one known to us or a reflection of the more primitive condition of the present language. In this case, the final end consonant would actually be the initial consonant of a new syllable. For this last member of the present-day roots would, according to the various genius of the languages, be either a more definite development of a chief concept through a closer modification or the second element of a real compound consisting of two independent words. In the Burmese language, for example, an obvious compound would rise on the basis of one now no longer recognized. Closest to this are the initial and final roots that have the same consonant and that have a simple vowel situated between them. In Sanskrit, if one excludes दद्, *dad*, which can very easily have a different relationship, these roots have a meaning suitable for designating, by means of reduplication, violent motion, as in कक्, जज्, शश् (*kak, jaj,* and *śaś*), or desire, as in लल्, *lal*, or sleep, a condition that extends itself uniformly, as in सस्, *sas*. In its original form, one can hardly imagine that कक्क्, खकख्, घघ् (*kakk, khakkh,* or *ghaggh*), which imitates the sound of laughing, did not repeat the full syllable. I would doubt, however, whether one could get very much farther in an analysis of this type. Indeed, such a final consonant could very easily have been just that originally. In Chinese, for example, although the Mandarin book language has no genuine consonants in final position, the provincial dialects very frequently add them to words ending in a vowel.

The disyllabicity of all Sanskrit roots ending in consonants has been quite recently maintained by R. Lepsius.[18] This assertion is derived from the logical and clever system established in his writing to the effect that in Sanskrit syllabic division predominates and that the indivisible syllable cannot generate from itself a single letter in the further development of the root but only another indivisible syllable. The author insists on regarding the inflected vowels only as organic developments of the root, not as involuntary infixes or additions. The question therefore is whether in बोधामि, *bôdhâmi*, for example, one is to regard *â* as the final vowel of बुध, *budha*, or as a vowel externally added to the root बुध्, *budh*, simply in the conjugation. From our point of view, the answer depends on the meaning of the apparent or genuine final consonant. But since the author expounds only on the vocalism in his article, he does not discuss this point at all. Hence I simply observe that although one does not speak, even figuratively, of the root further developing itself but speaks instead of addition and infixing, for this very reason, if we look at it correctly, every bit of whimsy is excluded since even the addition or infixing always takes place in accordance with organic laws and by virtue of them.

We have already seen in the foregoing that at times in languages a generic concept is added to a concrete one. Since this is one of the chief ways in which disyllabic words can arise in monosyllabic languages, I must now return to this point. Among natural objects, such as plants, animals, and so forth, which very obviously fall into separate classes, frequent examples of this are found in all languages. But in some languages we meet two concepts that are combined in a manner strange to us, and this is what I intend to talk about here. In such combinations, the true concept of the concrete object is not joined to another concept. Rather, concepts are joined together because they share some kind of general similarity. For example, the concept of extended length is connected with such words as "knife," "sword," "lance," "bread," "rope," and "cord," with the result that the most varied objects are placed in the same class simply because they have a property in common. If on the one hand these word combinations bear witness to a sense of logical arrangement, on the other they are fine illustrations of a lively imagination. This can be seen in Burmese where the hand, for example, serves as the generic concept for all types of tools, including both fire arms and the chisel. On the whole, this type of expression depicts the objects sometimes for the purpose of aiding the understanding and sometimes for the purpose of increasing the pictorial qualities. In individual cases, however, there may have been a genuine necessity for clarification, even though it is no longer apparent to us. In any event, we are remote from the basic meaning of the words. That which in all languages is called "air," "fire," "water," "man," and so forth is for us, with few exceptions, simply a conventional sound. What caused this remains foreign to us; that is, we do not know the original view of the peoples of the objects for which they were determining the word symbols. But right at this point the necessity for clarification by the addition of a generic concept can lie. For example, if we grant that the

Chinese *ji*, 'sun and day,' originally meant 'the warming, the illuminating,' then we can see why it was necessary to add to it *tseoû*, a word for 'a material, ball-shaped object,' in order to make it clear that one was referring not to the warmth or brightness scattered in the air but to the warming and illuminating heavenly body. It is for similar reasons that 'the day' with the addition of *tseù* could be called in another metaphor 'the son of the warmth and of the light.' It is very strange that this expression belongs only to the newer and not to the old style Chinese since the kind of imagination contained in it seems to be the more original one. This favors the opinion that expressions like these have been formed with the intention of avoiding misunderstandings which could arise from the use of the same word for several concepts or for several written symbols. But should the language still be metaphorically imitative even at a later time and should it not perhaps have applied similar means for the mere purpose of understanding and hence have differentiated the day in some way other than by a relationship concept?

At this point, I cannot suppress a doubt which I have often entertained concerning the comparison of the old and new styles. We know the old one only from writings and for the most part just from philosophical writings. We know nothing of the spoken language of that time. Is it then not possible that much, indeed perhaps a great deal, of what we now ascribe to the modern style was already in vogue in the old style as spoken language? One fact really seems to speak for this. The older style *koù wên* contains a moderate number of particles, if one discounts the agglutinations of several, while the newer style *kouân hoá* contains a much larger number, especially of those which determine grammatical relationships more precisely. One must regard the historical form, *wên tchang*, as a third one inasmuch as it is substantially different from the other two; and this one makes only sparing use of the particles, indeed dispenses with them almost completely. However, the historical style begins later than the old style, although its origin is still about two hundred years before our time calculations. According to the usual formative course of languages, this variant treatment of a part of speech, particularly one as important in Chinese as the particles, is inexplicable. On the other hand, if one assumes that the three styles are only three versions of the same language, with each version being used for a different purpose, then this becomes understandable. The greater frequency of the particles would naturally belong to the spoken language, since it is always desirous of making itself more intelligible through new additions and does not even reject that which really seems useless. The older style, already strained owing to the matter treated by it, scorned the use of particles for the purpose of clarification but did find in them a splendid means of lending the lecture a symmetrical arrangement; that is, by differentiating between the concepts and the sentences, they allowed the expression to correspond to the inner, logical order of the thoughts. The historical style has the same reason for rejecting the frequency of the particles, but it does not have the same calling to draw them again into its circle for another purpose. It wrote for serious readers, but its narrative was relatively simple and its subjects easily understandable. The fact that historical writings dispense with the use of the usual concluding particle (*ye*) in transitions from one subject matter to another may stem from this difference. The newer style, used for works of the theater, novels, and the later forms of poetry, had to assume the whole garment of the language and hence a complete supply of particles; this is because it represented the society and its relationships and introduced the people to a spoken language.[19]

After this digression, I return now to dissyllabic words in monosyllabic languages, which apparently originated through the addition of a generic expression. To the extent that one conceives of these words as expressions for simple concepts in the designation of which the individual syllables share in consonance, the dissyllabic words can originate in two ways: either as relative to the subsequent understanding or for their own sake. The origin of the generic expression can disappear from the memory of the nation, and the expression itself hence becomes a meaningless addition. Then the concept of the whole word really depends on both syllables. However, this is only relative for us in that the word can no longer be composed of the meanings of the individual concepts. Moreover, a generic expression in a known meaning can be added to objects thoughtlessly, with the result that it stands in no relationship to the object and becomes meaningless in the combination. Then the concept of the whole word truly lies in the combination of both syllables, but it is an absolute property of the word that its meaning does not derive from the combination of the sense of the individual syllables. The fact that both of these types of disyllabicity can easily arise through the transferring of a word from one language to another is self-evident. In addition, the linguistic usage of some languages burdens speech with a special type of these configurations which are in part explicable and in part inexplicable, and which arise whenever numbers are combined with concrete objects. I am familiar with four languages in which this frequently occurs: Chinese, Burmese, Siamese, and Mexican. To be sure, there are several others, and individual examples can be found in all languages, particularly in our own German. It seems to me two causes underlie this usage: one is the general addition of a generic concept, about which I have just spoken; the second is the special nature of certain objects that are gathered under one number. In instances where a genuine measure is not indicated for the entities to be counted, such a measure must first be artificially created as in the expression "four heads of cabbage for one bundle of hay" [that is, the measures "heads" and "bundle" must be artificially created]. Sometimes objects are gathered under a general number as in the expression "four heads of cattle, cows and steers included." Of the four languages mentioned, Burmese extends this usage further than the others. Aside from a large number of definite classes of truly established expressions, the speaker can use for this purpose every word of the language which indicates a similarity embracing several objects; moreover, there is a general word (*hku*) that is applicable to objects of every kind. The compound is formed in such a way, that regardless of differences dependent on the order of numerical magnitude, the concrete expression constitutes the first member, the numerical expression the middle member, and the generic expression the final member. If the concrete object is known to the listener at all, the generic word is used alone. Such expanded compounds must occur very frequently, especially in conversation, since the mere usage of the numerical concept embodied in the indefinite article evokes them.[20] Since several of the generic concepts are expressed by words which appear to have no relationship at all to the concrete objects or by those which have become quite meaningless except for this usage, these numerical words are also called particles in the grammars. Originally, however, they are all substantives.

From the foregoing, it is clear that if one regards the Chinese and Sanskrit languages as extreme and opposite points in language development, in terms of the indication of grammatical relationships by special sounds and the syllabic scope of the words, then one can say that the languages lying between, including those which separate the syllables from one another as well as those which strive incompletely for their combination, exhibit a gradually increasing inclination toward more obvious grammatical indication and freer syllabic scope. Without drawing conclusions from this observation concerning historical progress, I am satisfied that I have shown this relationship as a whole and that I have presented individual examples of it.

Notes

TRANSLITERATION OF FOREIGN ALPHABETS

1. *Translator's note*—This term apparently refers to the Tagalog variants; insofar as the alphabets are concerned, the chief Malayan examples are the Battak of central Sumatra, the Rejang and the Lampong in southeastern Sumatra, the Bugi and the Makasar in Celebes, and the Tagala and Visaya of the Philippines.

OBJECTIVE OF THE PRESENT TREATISE

1. *Translator's note*—As a philosopher, von Humboldt approaches language from an ontological viewpoint, as F. A. Raven has pointed out ([67], p. 166).

CHAPTER ONE

1. Emphasis supplied by translator.
2. *Translator's note*—This concept is obviously borrowed from J. G. Herder [37].
3. *Translator's note*—Von Humboldt is groping here to express the idea that language is a sociopsychological vehicle of communication.
4. *Translator's note*—In other words, intellectual growth is not merely diachronic or cumulative, which accounts for the rapid advances of some cultures and the retardation of others. The Greeks entered into the Early Bronze Age around 2800 B.C. (see J. Chadwick [21], p. 7), whereas the African Negro tribes were still in a Stone Age culture two centuries ago, never having domesticated a single animal. The aborigines of Australia were even more primitive.
5. *Translator's note*—For a thorough discussion of the causal chain in linguistic evolution, see O. Jespersen [49], particularly Chapter XIV, "The Causes of Change."
6. *Translator's note*—See L. Bloomfield [10], pp. 1–20.
7. *Translator's note*—These "requirements" could only be communication. As culture expands, innovations are linguistically taken care of by analogy, semantic change, borrowing, spontaneous invention, acronyms, compounding, and onomatopoeia. The ideas generally grow faster than the language, which tends to be conservative.
8. See my treatise on the objective of the historian ([39], p. 322).

9. *Translator's note*—See the critique of von Humboldt in H. Steinthal ([78], pp. 58–81 and 104–132). The idea of human speech originating in Biblical ages was promulgated in the eighteenth century by J. G. Hamann, J. G. Herder, and others. The tongues of the earth were divided into Semitic, Hamitic, and Japhetic, after Sem, Ham, and Japhet. After Sir W. Jones discovered in 1786 that Sanskrit was related to Greek and Latin, the term "Indo-Japhetic" arose, which is equivalent to the present-day "Indo-European."

Chapter Two

1. *Translator's note*—Von Humboldt here employs the German term *Laut* (sound, sonic quantum), which is apparently equivalent to the later term, *Sprachlaut* (phoneme).

2. *Translator's note*—Such borrowing from higher cultures by ruder ones is axiomatic, as witnessed by the many weak English verbs derived from Latin supine stems, the mass of loan translations from the same tongue into Old High German, similar borrowings into Middle High German from Provençal, and, more recently, the borrowing of technical vocabulary into Russian.

3. *Translator's note*—Von Humboldt is probably referring to Quechua, the language of the Quechuan tribe. These people were far more numerous than the Inca, who came south from the desert of Atacama and conquered them.

4. *Translator's note*—Von Humboldt is obviously referring here to the operation of the substratum theory. For example, English, a Germanic language, has coined a vast number of weak verbs from Latin supine stems, and all weak verbs currently added are constructed according to this pattern: to telegraph, to bowdlerize, to camouflage, to escalate, to sauté, and so forth.

5. *Translator's note*—This lack of communication and the social rigidity of the classical civilizations were largely responsible for their collapse. Von Humboldt was one of the first to note the deficiencies of classical cultures when compared to the experimental empiricism of the nineteenth century.

6. *Translator's note*—Here von Humboldt delineates even more clearly the effect of cultural and linguistic substrata.

7. *Translator's note*—Von Humboldt is referring to the Greek colonies of southern Italy (Graeca Magna), Sicily, and Spain. The city of Nice in southern France was another such colony.

8. *Translator's note*—Apparently von Humboldt is referring to the Malay Archipelago.

Chapter Three

1. *Translator's note*—Here von Humboldt expresses a strong argument against the "cult of the contemporaneous," the doctrine of existentialism, and similar self-defeating philosophical trends.

2. *Translator's note*—Von Humboldt is referring to the development of Romance from the Vulgar and Classical Latin dialects. This unpreserved, *spoken* idiom, together with substratal and intrusive loan elements, produced Italian dialects, Spanish, Catalán, Portuguese, French, Provençal, Rhaeto-Romansch, and Roumanian.

CHAPTER FIVE

1. *Translator's note*—Evidently von Humboldt here means significant communication, i.e., meaningful transmission of signals or semantic association.

2. *Translator's note*—Von Humboldt pertinently points out, though somewhat obliquely, that such logical categories were derived inductively by such grammarians as Dionysios Thrax and are in reality abstract, mechanical devices designed to make the study of languages easier and not to become rigid objectives in themselves.

3. *Translator's note*—Evidently the author is thinking of metalinguistics or perhaps even of acoustic phonetics.

4. *Translator's note*—The creation of weak verb infinitives from Latin supine stems or the German infinitives terminating in *-ieren* are pertinent examples.

5. *Translator's note*—According to H.-E. Hengstenberg ([36], pp. 93 ff.), the linguistic word (*Sprachwort*) in its origin, i.e., when uttered, is materially a series of sounds produced by physical and physiological causes. The sequence of these sounds is temporal. However, such words contain a meaning imparted by our intellect in a manner transcending time (*überzeitlich*), and are hence ontological. The reality of this impartation becomes evident if we consider that in such case it is not merely a question of the abstract meaning the word "inherently" possesses and which is completely immaterial with respect to the accidental subject just happening to think it and to the actual circumstances prevalent when it is thought. It is rather a matter of the real significance which is here and now relegated to the linguistic word (as opposed to a word reproduced by a parrot or a tape recorder, or one pertaining to an artificial tongue such as Novial or Esperanto) upon emission; that is to say, whenever a unique person indicates, i.e., communicates, to a unique fellow human being in a unique situation a given state of affairs. In its use the word has in each instance *kairos* (i.e., an instant at which a decision is made) and hence a real and unique significance, distinguished but not divorced from the constant abstract meaning. A real order is effected in the sequence of phonemes which cannot be derived from physical-physiological sources, for the physics of sound are just as well satisfied when the order is meaningless as when it is meaningful. Hence a determination of reality is assigned to the sounds of linguistic words which can only emanate from the intellect. This phenomenon of expression persists as long as speech is practised, and it does not consist of component parts in temporal sequence because each new sound is *ab origine* provided with meaning and order.

6. *Translator's note*—The characters of the alphabet continue to preserve the external morphology long after the phonemic structure has changed in a written language. Hence this statement must be restricted to those tongues which have evolved (or borrowed) the art of writing. It must be recalled that only a few years earlier, in 1816 [13] and in 1833 [16], F. Bopp had put comparative Indo-European linguistics on a scientific basis, though this early research was largely graphic rather than phonemic.

7. *Translator's note*—Here von Humboldt points out a fact that remained ignored until the advent of E. Sapir, L. Bloomfield, and A. L. Kroeber. Of course, the enormity of the task of working out the linguistic relationships of the Indo-European precluded any digression on the part of any linguist and led

simultaneously to positivism, especially in Germany during the nineteenth century.

8. *Translator's note*—Kawi or Kavi is the ancient language of Java (about 800 to 1400 A.D.) and is the parent of Javanese. It contains many borrowings from Sanskrit and employs an old Pali alphabet, which was introduced into Java by Buddhist missionaries (see [83], p. 1354). In Javanese, *kawi* means 'poem' or 'poetic' (language); in Sanskrit, *kavi* means 'poet' or 'learned,' whereas *kavya* means 'poem' or 'poetic.'

9. *Translator's note*—Insofar as ideas prevail, all people will have the same language. However, where an idea does not exist, the language will fail to comprehend and express it. For example, early Christian missionaries in Polynesia were unable to communicate the idea of the Virgin Mary to the natives; however, as a result of their efforts the word "Mary" came to signify "woman." With respect to the second portion of his statement, von Humboldt is quite correct. Every individual, family, or neighborhood has a special vocabulary, as well as special prestige vocabularies that are used in school and church and with other more formal groups.

10. *Translator's note*—Perhaps the closest approximation of the Indo-European consonantism is found in the morphology of Sanskrit, which also preserves the original number of Indo-European cases in the nominal declensions, the three numbers, and voices; Greek and Old Lithuanian, on the other hand, retained its original vocalic structure more closely.

CHAPTER SIX

1. *Translator's note*—Von Humboldt here anticipates modern speech communication and auditory theories.

2. *Translator's note*—Von Humboldt here recognizes that speech consists of much more than vocalization of words, a feature which punctuation but faintly reproduces in written language. M. Heidegger ([35], p. 51) makes some pertinent remarks concerning the human hand and the differences between the human body and those of animals. See also H.-E. Hengstenberg ([36], pp. 98–102) and C. Morris ([63], pp. 35 ff.).

3. *Translator's note*—This interesting phenomenon is treated in detail by G. von Békésy [7].

4. *Translator's note*—In *Loom of Language* ([11], pp. 449–518), F. Bodmer, a firm believer in "one world" and world socialism, touches upon the social aspects of language and discusses artificial languages and language planning for a new order. We feel constrained to point out that such mathematically constructed languages, though well-meant, are doomed to failure. Their proponents visualize an era such as the Middle Ages and the Renaissance in which Medieval and Neo-Latin furnished the scholarly world with an international medium of communication. We have often heard it said that an international language would lead to world understanding and avert war. This statement is absurd. Many of the bloodiest wars in history—the French Revolution, the American Civil War, and the Spanish Civil War—were fought by people speaking the same language but harboring radically different ideas.

5. *Translator's note*—Apparently von Humboldt means that the significance of unknown words emerges more or less per force from the context, a phenomenon

generally but not invariably true. A meaning may emerge in many instances, but not by any means will it necessarily be the correct one.

6. *Translator's note*—This *Stammanlage* is apparently the structural substratum handed down in the linguistic community.

7. *Translator's note*—Here von Humboldt appears to anticipate J. Schmidt's Wave Theory. See J. Schrijen ([76], pp. 64 ff.) and J. Schmidt ([74] and [75]).

8. *Translator's note*—It may be recalled that scientific historical linguistics dates from F. Bopp ([13] and [16]).

9. *Translator's note*—The author says literally: "Die Sprache hat diese anfangs— und endlose Unendlichkeit für uns . . ." ("Language has for us this beginningless and endless infinity . . ."). This is certainly tautological for any concept of infinity, whether positive or negative.

10. *Translator's note*—It is obvious that von Humboldt neglects accretion and loss or change of phonemic structure as negligible detail.

11. *Translator's note*—This change in phonemic structure, morphology, syntax, semantics, tempo, vocabulary, and accentuation has been termed elsewhere "linguistic flux" by the translator.

12. *Translator's note*—Von Humboldt here recognizes that every individual possess his own peculiar language, distinct from his family, church, regional, and national ties.

CHAPTER SEVEN

1. *Translator's note*—Although phonemes can be analyzed by sound (spectroscopy), the coincidence of sound and significance cannot.

2. *Translator's note*—Here von Humboldt anticipates contemporary phonemic theory, i.e., a gradual variation of allophones from one phoneme to the next.

3. *Translator's note*—This statement reflects the German emphasis on a prestige dialect (*hochsprache*), which dates from the speech societies of the seventeenth and eighteenth centuries.

4. *Translator's note*—From the approach of physics, the speech mechanism consists of two resonators, a large one coupled with a smaller one with the vocal cords medially situated.

5. *Translator's note*—As is so frequently true in the nineteenth and twentieth centuries, there is a confusion here of symbol with phoneme. However, the contention that every consonant—whether voiced or unvoiced—requires vocalic support is true, although it is stated somewhat obliquely. This idea is well illustrated by the Hebrew and Arabic alphabets in which vowels are either omitted completely or indicated by vowel signs, and by the Sanskrit *devanagari*, a derivative of Hebrew, where, when no vowel appears, a short *a* is inserted.

6. *Translator's note*—Apparently von Humboldt is referring to the glottal stop so apparent in the pronunciation of accented initial vowels in German and otherwise present.

7. *Translator's note*—This refers to such marks as those indicating the *spiritus lenis* (') and the *spiritus asper* (ι)—the "smooth" and "rough" breathings of Classical Greek orthography.

8. *Translator's note*—Von Humboldt terms this process simply a progressive voicing: *Verhärtung*, 'hardening' or 'induration.'

9. *Translator's note*—Evidently von Humboldt is referring to continuous

allophones of a phoneme. E. Sievers pointed out around the end of the nineteenth century that every sound in a sequence is modified in coalescence.

10. *Translator's note*—Von Humboldt is referring to the phenomenon of chemical change, still held at that time to be a function of the affinity of substances for each other.

11. *Translator's note*—For example, the Sanskrit grammarians were wont to construct complete paradigms of transitive conjugations for inherently intransitive verbs. They appear to have been under a compulsion (*Systemzwang*) to make their paradigms uniform.

12. From this fact it is also explicable why no consideration is accorded the principles of euphony in the form of Sanskrit roots. The catalogues of roots which have been handed down to us bear in all respects the impression of being a labor of the grammarians per se, and quite a number of roots may owe their existence merely to their abstraction. A. F. Pott's excellent researches [65] have already clarified a great deal in this area, and their continuation appears to promise much more.

13. *Translator's note*—Simply because a language does not readily reveal such derivational features is not sufficient reason to presume their nonexistence, for the language may not have been recorded early enough. Such statements reveal the growing positivism of nineteenth-century comparative Indo-European linguistics, particularly in Germany.

14. *Translator's note*—The absence of such Indo-European features in Chinese is owing to "linguistic decay" (as nineteenth-century philologians termed it), resulting in a language consisting entirely of monosyllables. These are distinguished by the progressive development of pitch accent in several keys, depending on the dialect.

15. *Translator's note*—Von Humboldt here again confuses symbols with phonemes.

16. Several especially remarkable examples of this type are found in my treatise on the origin of grammatical forms ([41], p. 413).

17. *Translator's note*—Von Humboldt has failed to realize that all nations are continuously constructing language as long as they speak, read, or write.

18. The influence of the disyllabic character of Semitic root words not only has been noted by H. von Ewald ([25], pp. 144, 165) but has been illustrated masterfully throughout the entire linguistic field with respect to the spirit inherent therein. That the Semitic languages have developed a peculiar character unique to them by virtue of the fact that they construct their word forms and in part their word declension almost exclusively by modification in the heart of the words themselves has been elucidated by F. Bopp in detail and has been applied to the classification of languages by him in a new and sagacious manner ([16], Vol. I, pp. 107–113).

CHAPTER EIGHT

1. F. Bopp ([48], Vol. II, p. 465) first noticed that the ordinary usage of the potential mood consists in expressing general categorical contentions separately and independently of any particular temporal determination. The correctness of this observation is confirmed by a quantity of examples, especially in the moral apothegms of the *Hitôpadeśa*. However, if one reflects more exactly upon the

reason for this use of this tense, which appears striking at first glance, it is found that it is used in its basic sense in such cases as the subjunctive. But in this case, the entire idiomatic expression must be explained elliptically. Instead of saying, "the wise man never acts differently," we say, "the wise man would act thusly," and the omitted words, "under all conditions and at any time," are understood. Therefore, I should not care to term the potential mood a necessity mood on account of this usage. Rather, it appears to me in this instance to be the quite pure and simple subjunctive, isolated from all material, secondary concepts of being able, of inclination or desiring, of intention, and so forth. The peculiarity of this usage lies in the ellipsis mentally added, and only to the extent in the so-called potential that the potential is motivated by the ellipsis, especially preceding the indicative. For it cannot be denied that the use of the subjunctive, by the severance of all other possibilities so to speak, here becomes more intensive than the simple indicative of statement. I mention this expressly, because it is not unimportant to retain and to protect the pure and ordinary meaning of grammatical forms to the extent that we are not inevitably compelled to do the opposite.

2. I have treated this interchange of one grammatical form for another in greater detail in my treatise on the origin of grammatical forms ([41], pp. 404–407).

Chapter Ten

1. See my treatise on the relationship of adverbs of place to the pronoun in several languages ([45], pp. 1–6); see also my treatise on the dual ([40], pp. 182–185).

Chapter Eleven

1. *Translator's note*—Von Humboldt apparently ignores the fact that the ω (omega) in Greek and the final long *o* in Latin are the vestigial portions of the first-person singular subject pronoun *ego.* and that the remaining verb endings are of identical pronominal origin.

2. *Translator's note*—Von Humboldt fails to realize that agglutination results from the gradual incorporation of originally but loosely attached components.

Chapter Twelve

1. *Translator's note*—What von Humboldt here terms "rhythm segments" (*Rhythmus-Abschnitte*) are apparently simply breath groups.

2. *Translator's note*—Von Humboldt here means the sounds conveyed by the alphabetical symbols.

3. I have borrowed the individual items of Sanskrit linguistic structure mentioned in this treatise, even where I do not cite the source, from F. Bopp's grammar [14], and I am pleased to confess that I owe my clearer insight into them solely to this classical work; none of the earlier linguistic theories permits this to a like degree, no matter how meritorious some of them may be in another respect. F. Bopp's Sanskrit grammar in its various editions and his later comparative grammar [16], as well as his individual academic treatises, contain a fruitful and talented comparison of Sanskrit with its related languages; they will always remain true models of profound and intellectual penetration, indeed often of bold and intuitive

perception of the analogy of the grammatical forms. To them linguistic study owes the most important progress achieved upon a partially new course of development. As early as 1816, F. Bopp laid the foundation for his investigations into the conjugational system of the Hindus, which, fortunately, he subsequently pursued with great consistency.

4. *Translator's note*—Telingic refers to the Dravidian people of eastern India called the Telinga. Their language is termed Telugu and was rather contemptuously call "Heathen Tongue" (*Gentoo*) by early travelers. This language is spoken along the east coast of the Dekhan from Orissa southward almost as far as Madras. In the 1930s, it was spoken by approximately twenty-four million people. Its peculiar alphabet was derived from the older Sanskrit, and its literature, which dates at least from the twelfth century B.C. and which is not unimportant but not widely known, consists of translations of and commentaries on Sanskrit works. See *Mayer's Konversations-Lexikon* ([62], Vol. XV, pp. 576, 579), and L. Bloomfield ([10], pp. 44, 70).

5. See F. Bopp ([47], p. 281). He makes this comment only with respect to directly agglutinated derivatives. The law appears to me, however, to be generally applicable. Even the most apparently valid objection to it, the change of the liquid vowel *r* into *ur* in the non-*guna* inflections of the verb, कृ *kri* (कुरुतस्, *kurutas*), can be explained otherwise.

6. R. Lepsius explains this analogical phonemic development in a very ingenious manner: *ar* and *âr* are diphthongs of the *r* vowel. For more information on this matter, consult his treatise ([55], pp. 46–49), which points out a new direction for linguistic research and is replete with incisively erudite elucidation.

7. F. Bopp defends the former of these viewpoints ([12], Section 33). However, if I may be permitted to differ with this thorough researcher, I should like to declare myself in favor of the latter. In F. Bopp's assumption, the close connection of the *guna* and *vriddhi* can scarcely be preserved in view of the general phonetic laws of the language, as dissimilar simple vowels—irrespective of their length— always change into the admittedly weaker *guna* diphthongs. Since the nature of the diphthong lies essentially in the inequality of the tones, it is understandable that the length and shortness of the new sound are swallowed up without residual distinction. Not until a new inequality comes into play does a strengthening of the diphthong occur. Therefore, I do not believe that the *guna* diphthongs originally fuse from short vowels. That they, in comparison to the *vriddhi* type, assimilate in their resolution a short *a* (*ay*, *aw* compared to *ây*, *âw*) can be explained in this way: since the difference between the two phonemic expansions could not be made distinguishable by the semivowel, it had to fall into the quantity of the vowel of the new syllable. The same holds for the liquid vowel *r*.

8. This has perhaps contributed in stimulating F. Schlegel to formulate his theory for the classification of all languages ([73], p. 50), although this is a theory which we cannot accept. It is, however, noteworthy, and it seems to me too little recognized, that this profound thinker and highly intellectual writer was the first German who called our attention to the remarkable phenomenon of Sanskrit; he had already made significant progress in it at a time when the many present-day aids for learning the language were lacking. His treatise, for example, appeared in the same year as Sir C. Wilkins' grammar [84].

9. In a paper read by me in 1828 at the French Institute on the relationship of the Greek pluperfect, the reduplicated aorists, and the Attic Greek perfects to a

Sanskrit tense formation, I discussed in detail the similarity and differences of the two languages with respect to these forms and attempted to derive them from their sources.

10. *Translator's note*—Von Humboldt is referring here to the fact that the temporal augment and the *alpha privatum* in Sanskrit and Greek are identical.

11. I have drawn the material here concerning the form of the preterite of causative verbs from a treatise worked up many years ago on these tense forms. In this study, I investigated all the roots of the language as treated in H. P. Forster's grammar [27], an excellent text for the purpose. Furthermore, I attempted to trace the various constructions to their foundations and also noted the individual exceptions. This paper remained unprinted, however, because it seemed to me that an exposition of such a specialized type, treating very rarely occurring forms, would interest but very few readers.

CHAPTER THIRTEEN

1. The so-called nonaccented words of Greek do not appear to me to contradict this contention. However, it would lead me too far afield from my principal topic were I to attempt to show here how for the most part as syllables preceding the accent of the following word they associate with it. Those examples of word order which do not admit of such an explanation (such as οὐκ in Sophocles, *Oedipus Rex* [77], verses 334–336) likely had in pronunciation a weak but undesignated accentuation. The Latin grammarians state expressly that every word can have but one main accent: *natura, quasi modularetur hominum orationem, in omni verbo posuit acutam vocem, nec una plus* (Cicero, *Oratio*, 18). The Greek grammarians treat accentuation more as a property of the syllable than of the word. I know of nothing in their works which expresses the accent unity of the latter as a general canon or rule. Perhaps they were led astray by those cases where a word was provided with two accent marks owing to two enclitic syllables. Probably, however, that accent pertaining to the association always constituted merely a secondary accent. Yet for them also there is no lack of definite indication of the foregoing requisite unity. Thus Arcadius says ([6], p. 190) of Aristophanes: τὸν μὲν ὀξὺν τόνον ἐν ἅπαντι μέρει καθαρῷ τόνου ἅπαξ ἐμφαίνεσθαι δοκιμάσας.

2. E. Buschmann has treated accentuation, an interesting yet most difficult part of English pronunciation, in detail and creatively in his English pronunciation text [19]. For this feature, he states essentially three directions of development: accentuation of the stem or first syllable (paragraphs 2–15, 26, 27, and 33); the retention of foreign accentuation (paragraphs 16–22); and a remarkable attraction of the stress by the endings (paragraphs 23–25). In paragraphs 28–32 and 34, E. Buschmann points out that the language in the realm of its non-Germanic vocabulary is often perplexed by these three types of accentuation, not knowing which to use. E. Buschmann (paragraphs 75–78) attempts to establish for the English language the secondary accent, which I have touched upon in the foregoing exposition, according to a syllabic interval (of two and, for reasons of original significance, occasionally of three syllables).

3. The Greek grammarians termed this awakening the slumbering or dormant tone of the syllable. They also used the expression "rejection of the tone" (ἀναβιβάζειν τὸν τόνον). This latter metaphor is less fortunate, however, for

Greek accent theory shows that what is going on in this case is what I have described above.

4. See, for example, *Iliad*, I, verse 178: θεός που σοὶ τόγ' ἔδωκεν.

CHAPTER FOURTEEN

1. I shall permit myself a remark here concerning the pronunciation of the name Mexico. If we give the *x* in this word the usual sound in German, we are palpably incorrect. We would, however, deviate even further from the true indigenous pronunciation were we to follow the most recent and even more reproachable Spanish spelling *Mejico*, in which the *x* (*ks*) is rendered by the guttural *ch* in accordance with the indigenous pronunciation. The third letter of the name of the god of war, *Mexitli*, and of the name of the city of Mexico derived therefrom, is an intensive sibilant, even if we cannot state exactly to what degree it approximates the German *sch*. My attention was first directed to this by the fact that *Castile* in Mexican is pronounced *Caxtil*, and in the related Cora language the Spanish word *pesar*, 'weigh,' is written *pexuvi*. I found my surmise confirmed even more distinctly by F. S. Gilij's method of transliterating the Mexican *x* in Italian by *sc* ([31], Vol. III, p. 343). I found this phoneme or a similar sibilant written by Spanish language teachers in several other languages as well by an *x*, and I explained this unusual feature to myself by the lack of the German *sch* phoneme in Spanish. Because the Spanish grammarians found no corresponding phoneme among their own alphabetic symbols, they selected the *x*, which is ambiguous and even foreign to their own tongue. Later I found the same explanation of this interchange in the writings of the ex-Jesuit J. Camaño, who compares the phoneme represented by *x* with the German *sch* and the French *ch*. This observation is found in a very systematic and complete hand-written Chiquitin grammar, which I owe to the generosity of State Counsellor A. L. von Schlözer, who gave it to me as a present from his father's estate. That the *x* of the Spaniards represents such a phoneme in the American Indian languages was last expressly verified for me by E. Buschmann from on-the-spot observations made by him. Moreover, he has extended the range of the idea as follows: the Spaniards designate by this letter the allophones lying between the German *sch* and the equally unfamiliar French *j*, as well as both of these phonemes. To stay close to the indigenous pronunciation, the capital of New Spain [Mexico] would have to be pronounced approximately as the Italians pronounce it, but it should be more exact so that the phoneme involved would come between *Messico* and *Meschico*.

2. The final phoneme of this word, which by its frequent recurrence becomes to some extent the characteristic of the Mexican language, is consistently written *tl* by the Spanish language teachers. C. de Tapia Zenteno ([79], pp. 2–3) remarks only that the two consonants would certainly be pronounced initially and medially in words as they are in Spanish. In contrast, in final position they represent but a single phoneme that is very difficult to master. After having indistinctly described this phoneme, he finds fault with the pronunciation of *tlatlacolli*, 'sin,' and *tlamantli*, 'stratum,' as *claclacolli* and *clamancli*, respectively. However, when through the kind offices of my brother I questioned by mail Mr. W. Alaman and Mr. Castorena, a native Mexican, concerning this point, I received in reply the statement that the present-day pronunciation of the *tl* in all cases is that of *cl*. To this fact also attests the quite common word *claco*, which has been borrowed by

Spanish; the term *claco* refers to a copper coin, worth one-half of a *quartillo*, i.e., the eighth part of a *real*. The Cora language lacks the phoneme *l*, and therefore in Mexican words it absorbs only the first letter of the combination *tl*. However, the Spanish grammarians of this language always set a *t* in such cases (never a *c*), so that *tlatoani*, 'governor,' is pronounced *tatoani*. E. Buschmann informs me that this same substitution of *t* for the Mexican *tl* is found also in the Cahita tongue, which shows a remarkable relationship to the Mexican and which is spoken in the Mexican province of Sinaloa. To the present I have not found the name of this language which was first called to my attention by E. Buschmann, mentioned anywhere. In this idiom, for example, the above cited word for 'sin,' *tlatlacolli*, has the form *tatacoli* ([58], p. 36). I wrote once more to Mr. L. Alaman and to Mr. Castorena and acquainted them with the opposition arising from the Cora tongue. The answer remained the same as before, however. Hence, there is no doubt about the contemporary pronunciation. We are simply uncertain whether to assume that the pronunciation has changed with time, i.e., that it has made the transition from *t* to *k*; or whether the cause may be found in the fact that the phoneme preceding the *l* is an obscure sound fluctuating between *t* and *k*. I have checked personally that in the pronunciation of native Tahitians and Hawaiian Kanakas these phonemes are scarcely distinguished from one another. I deem the latter explanation to be the correct one. The Spaniards, who first seriously concerned themselves with the language, likely conceived the obscure phoneme as a *t*. Moreover, inasmuch as they adopted it in this way into their orthography, matters probably stopped at this point. From C. de Tapia Zenteno's statement, a certain indecision respecting this phoneme appears to be evident: he does not wish it to degnerate into a distinct *cl* enunciated in accordance with Spanish speech habits.

3. See J. Eliot [24]; see also D. Zeisberger [85] and J. Edwards [23].

CHAPTER FIFTEEN

1. *Translator's note*—Even though Sir W. Jones had pointed out as early as 1786 that Sanskrit resembles both Greek and Latin too closely to be a matter of chance, and that in his estimation all three likely sprang from a common source perhaps no longer existing, German linguists ignored this observation and regarded Sanskrit as the Indo-European parent until around the middle of the nineteenth century. The Greek past perfect, therefore, and the Sanskrit form mentioned were both derived from a common Indo-European form, and not the one from the other. See L. Bloomfield ([10], p. 12).

CHAPTER SEVENTEEN

1. In his edition of Pindar, A. Boeckh presents a clear and full discussion of the close relationship between the popular national spirit of the various Greek peoples and their poetry, music, dance, and dramatic arts, and even their architecture. He is not content simply to depict the character of the pitches in general terms; rather, he goes into the individual metric and musical points associated with them. This has never been accomplished in a such thorough manner, historically and scientifically speaking. It would be highly desirable if this philologist, who combines the most extensive knowledge of the language with a

rare and incisive insight into Greek antiquity in all of its parts and ramifications, were very soon to carry out his resolution to devote a separate volume to the influence of the character and customs of the individual Greek peoples upon their music, poetry, and art. See his remarks concerning such an objective in his edition of Pindar ([64], Vol. I, pp. 252 and 279).

2. In the introduction to his scientific syntax of Greek [9], G. Bernhardi gives a very intelligent survey of the course of Greek literature with respect to word order, syntax, and style.

3. See W. Mariner [59], Vol. II, p. 377.

4. Izaro, in the Bay of Bermeo.

5. Incomparably perceived and expressed with a personal poetic sentiment is the exposition of A. W. von Schlegel relative to the earliest poetry of the Greeks and Hindus, which appears in the preface of his edition of the *Râmâyana* [71]. What a gain it would be for the philosophical and aesthetic evaluation of both these literatures and for the history of prosody, if this writer, who is more highly endowed with the commensurate talents than any other, were inclined to write the literary history of the Hindus, or at least to treat individual portions thereof, especially its dramatic poetry, subjecting it to as happy a critique as that which he dedicated to the theater of other nations.

6. *Translator's note*—The Persian War began in 490 B.C. and was concluded in 480–479 B.C.; the Peloponnesian Wars raged from 431 to 404 B.C. between Athens and her allies and Sparta and her allies.

CHAPTER EIGHTEEN

1. *Translator's note*—Von Humboldt again commits the error of presuming that Sanskrit (or the Indo-Iranian group) is the Indo-European parent.

2. I have attempted to answer this question with respect to the American Indian languages familiar to us in a special treatise which I read at one of the section meetings of the Berlin Academy of Sciences.

3. If I attempt to accord greater space here to Sir G. C. Haughton's contention ([34], Part I, p. 329), I flatter myself that this excellent scholar would perhaps have done this himself if, at the point cited, he had been less interested in this etymological conjecture and had given more attention to the logical determination of the *verbum neutrum* and of the passive construction. For it must be frankly admitted that the concept of "going" does not at all coincide with that of the passive per se, but only to some extent when, in combination with the idea of the neuter verb, it is regarded as an origin or "becomingness." This also appears to be the case, according to Sir G. C. Haughton's exposition, in the Hindustani, where it is contrasted to the verb "to be" or "being." The new languages which are lacking in a transition to the verb "to be" and words that are expressive without metaphor, such as the Greek verb γίνεσθαι, the Latin verb *fieri*, and our German verb *werden*, 'to become,' also take refuge in the figurative expression of "going," but they conceive it more meaningfully as the target of the action of going, that is, as a "coming": *diventare, divenire, devenir*, to become. In Sanskrit, therefore, even if we presume the correctness of the foregoing etymology, the principal force of the passive must always lie in the neutral conjugation (that of the *atmanêpadam*), and the language must designate the combination of the latter with the idea of "going," first taking the idea of "going" with reference to itself as an intimate modification

not to be effected in external direction. In this respect, it is not unremarkable, and could have been quoted by Sir G. C. Haughton as his opinion, that the intensive verbs only assume the intermediate syllable *ya* in the *atmanêpadam*, which betrays a particular relationship between the syllable *ya* and this derivational form. At first glance, it is striking that in the passive as well as in the intensive conjugations the syllable *ya* drops out in the general tenses where the class distinction is ineffective. This appears to me, however, to be a new proof that the passive develops from the neuter verb of the fourth verbal class, and that the language, predominately following the course of the forms, did not care to carry out this characteristic syllable abstracted from the class mentioned beyond its confines. The syllable *sy* of the desiderative verbs, whatever its significance may be, also adheres in those tenses to the forms and does not undergo the restriction of the class tenses, because it is not related to the latter. Much more naturally to the passive than to the denominative verbs is suited the idea of "going" produced by addition of *y*, which denotes a desire, an acquisition, or an imitation of a thing. This concept can also have predominated in the causative verbs. Therefore, the fact that the Hindu grammarians regarded the phoneme *i* as the identifying syllable of these verbs and considered *ay* only as the requisite phonetic extension thereof, might not perhaps be disavowed, but might rather be valid for the recollection of the derivation. (Cf. F. Bopp [12], p. 142, n. 233.) Comparison with the quite uniformly constructed denominatives makes this very probable. In the verbs constructed from nouns by the morpheme काम्य्, *kâmy*, this appended syllable appears to be a compound made up of काम, *kâma*, 'avidity' or 'sensual appetite,' and of इ, *i*, from 'to go,' and hence in itself and in its own right it is a complete denominative verb. If I may be permitted to expand this conjecture further, the syllable *sy* of the desiderative verbs could be explained as a going into the condition, which simultaneously would find application to the etymology of the second future. What F. Bopp ([15], pp. 29–33, 45–50) very brilliantly and correctly first discussed relative to the relationship of the potential optative and with respect to the second future fits in with the present observations very well. The denominatives having the characteristic syllables *sya* and *asya* appear to have been patterned after the desideratives.

4. *Translator's note*—Apparently von Humboldt is referring again to phonemic laws and is confusing symbols with sounds.

5. I am following the theory of the Greek grammarians, which in my estimation has been too often unjustly abandoned. According to this theory, every tense consists of the combination of one of the three time brackets with one of the three stages in the action curve. J. Harris in his *Hermes* [33] and F. W Reitz, [68] in his almost unknown academic essays have illuminated this point brilliantly, but F. A. Wolf has expanded it in his exact determination of the three aorists. The verb becomes the summary of an energetic attribute (not merely of a qualitative one) through the copula, i.e., the verb "to be." In the energetic attribute lie the stages of the action, whereas those of time repose in the verb "to be." G. Bernhardi, I am convinced, correctly established and proved this.

6. A. de Vetancurt ([82], p. 6).

7. *Translator's note*—The Mixteca, Mixtec, or Mixteco are an Indian people of eastern Güerrero and western Oaxaca in Mexico. Their language is classed as Zapotecan (cf. Nahūa). (See [83], p. 1574.)

8. See Fr. A. de los Reyes [69].

9. *Translator's note*—The Yaruran stock of South American Indians is presently situated on the Capanaparo River in southwestern Venezuela. The language of the Yaruros is termed Yarura, Pumé, or Yuapin ([83], p. 2967).

10. The difference between the independent pronoun *coddé*, 'I,' and the corresponding verbal characteristic *que* is apparently greater, to be sure. The independent pronoun in the accusative, however, is *qua*; and from the comparison of *coddé* with the demonstrative pronoun *oddé*, it is clearly seen that the root phoneme of the first person consists only of the velar *k*, but that *coddé* is a composite form.

11. Information and reports on this language have been obtained for us through the diligent efforts of a worthy gentleman named L. Hervas y Panduro. He had the praiseworthy idea of encouraging the Jesuits, who settled in Italy after being banished from America and Spain, to record in their memoirs the languages of the indigenous American peoples, amongst whom they had been active as missionaries. L. Hervas collected their communications and, where necessary, he revised them so that a series of manuscript grammars of languages was produced. For some of these languages, we have no other information. I had this collection copied for myself when I was Ambassador in Rome, and through the aid of the present Prussian Ambassador in Rome, the Honorable Baron C. C. J. von Bunsen, I had my copies meticulously compared with the original manuscripts which, following the death of L. Hervas, were deposited in the Collegio Romano. The communications on the Yarura dialect originate from the labors of the ex-Jesuit J. Forneri, working for L. Hervas.

12. *Translator's note*—The Huastecan are an isolated Mayan tribe dwelling in the northern part of the state of Vera Cruz, Mexico. They were inferior culturally to the other Mayan peoples. In the fifteenth century, they were conquered by the Aztecs and were later Christianized by the Spaniards. However, they retained their Mayan speech. (See [83], p. 1210).

13. C. de Tapia Zenteno ([80], p. 18).

14. What I know of this language has been taken from L. Hervas' handwritten grammar. He compiled this grammar partially from epistolary communications from the ex-Jesuit D. Rodriguez, and partially from the printed grammar by the Franciscan churchman, G. de S. Buenaventura (Mexico, 1684), which he found in the library of the Collegio Romano. I have attempted in vain to find this grammar in the library mentioned, but it appears to have been lost.

15. See J. C. Adelung ([3], Vol. III, Section 3, p. 20). J. S. Vater did not correctly recognize the pronoun and incorrectly related and distributed the German words with respect to the Mayan equivalents.

16. *Translator's note*—The Maipure are Indians of an Arawakan tribe native to the upper Orinoco River in Venezuela. The independent and less civilized remnants of this people are termed Amoruas. (See [83], p. 1484.)

17. *Translator's note*—The Achaguas are Indians belonging to an Arawakan tribe of the upper Orinoco Valley. (See [83], p. 19.)

18. *Translator's note*—The Betoya (or Betoi) are Indians of a Chibchan tribe and reside in the eastern portion of the Republic of Colombia. (See [83], p. 259.)

19. *Translator's note*—Von Humboldt is referring here to the distinction between such doublets as "project" (noun) and "project" (verb), or "reject" (noun) and

"reject" (verb). He investigated this phenomenon but found the exceptions too numerous to permit formulating a definite rule.

20. See W. von Humboldt ([44], p. 23).

21. See Demetrius, *De Elocutione*, sections 11–13.

22. *Translator's note*—The Quechua Indians belong to a tribe that formerly dwelled between the Apurimac and Parnpas rivers in central Peru and now dwell farther south on the headwaters of the Apurimac and Pachachaca rivers. Probably originally of Aymaran stock, they spoke the Quechuan dialect at the time of the Spanish conquest. The Quechuas developed one of the highest civilizations of native America, derived largely from the Aymaras, Nascans, Yuncas, and other pre-Incan peoples of advanced culture, whose arts and sciences they inherited. The language of the Quechuas, which is also called Incan and Runa-simi, was the official tongue of the Inca Empire. It was also the medium of evangelization of the Spanish missionaries and is still spoken by several million peoples in a number of related dialects. (See [83], p. 2037.)

23. In this respect, compare L. Diefenbach's highly readable treatise on the present-day Romance literary dialects [22].

CHAPTER TWENTY

1. These statements were most clearly and satisfactorily presented by R. Lepsius in his paleography [55], as was the distinction between the initial *a* and the *h* in the Sanskrit script. I had recognized in the Bûgi and several related alphabets that the sign which is termed an initial *a* is not really a vowel at all but a weak consonantal breathing, similar to the Greek *spiritus lenis*. All the phonemes verified by me ([42], pp. 489–494) can, however, be better explained by R. Lepsius' exposition concerning the same point in the Sanskrit alphabet. *Translator's note*—The Bûgi are a Malayan people of Celebes and neighboring islands. They speak a distinct tongue which is also termed Bûgi and which is one of the Austronesian language group (see [83], p. 350).

2. J. Grimm expresses this in his fortunately selected and meaningful language as follows: "The consonatism shapes, the vowel determines and illuminates the word" ([32], Vol. II, p. 1).

3. See the Preface to D. Zeisberger ([85], p. 20).

4. See the *Transactions of the Historical and Literary Committee of the American Philosophical Society* [81], Vol. I, pp. 405 ff.

5. D. Zeisberger ([85], p. 20) remarks that the word *mannitto* constitutes an exception to this principle, since by this term is understood 'God Himself, the great and good Spirit.' However, it is very common to find that the religious ideas of uncultured people derive from fear of evil spirits, and the original meaning of this word could very easily therefore have denoted such a spirit. Lacking a Delaware dictionary, I was unable to get any information on the meaning of the rest of the word. Striking, though perhaps quite accidental, is the coincidence of this residuum with the Tagalic word *anito*, 'idol.' See my treatise on the Kawi tongue ([43], Vol. I, p. 75).

6. At any rate, this is the way I interpret J. Heckewelder ([81], Vol. I, p. 411). *Ape* is simply the determination denoting 'upright-walking beings,' just as *chum* signifies 'quadrupeds.'

CHAPTER TWENTY-ONE

1. See J. P. Abel Rémusat [2], Vol. III, p. 283.

2. The name which the Barman people [the Burmese] give to themselves is Mranmâ. However, the word is usually wiitten Mrammâ and pronounced Byammâ (see A. Judson's Burmese dictionary [51]). If I may be permitted to explain this name precisely from the meaning of its elements, it designates a strong and powerful race of men, for *mran* means 'swift' and *mâ* denotes 'being hardy, sound, and healthy.' From this indigenous word, the various common methods of writing the name of the people and of the country no doubt originated, among which Barma and Barman are the correct ones. When F. Carey and A. Judson write Burma and Burman, they mean the same phoneme inherent in the consonant and merely designate the latter by a false method now generally abandoned. See also H. Berghaus ([8], p. 77) and J. Leyden ([56], p. 232).

3. See his *Grammar of the Burman Language* [20], p. 79, §1; p. 181. See especially the Preface, pp. 8, 9. The author of this grammar was Felix Carey, the oldest son of William Carey, who taught several Indic languages at the college in Fort William and to whom we owe a number of grammars of Asiatic languages. Unfortunately, Felix Carey died in 1822 (see *Journal Asiatique*, Vol. III, p. 59). His father followed him in death in 1834.

4. See R. Anderson [5], the Table of Alphabets; see also W. Marsden [60].

5. In both languages, this change in pronunciation does not entail a change in the character in the script, although Burmese, unlike Tamil, possesses symbols for all voiced sounds or characters. In Burmese, the pronunciation frequently digresses from the orthography. In my letter on the Polynesian alphabets to Mr. E. Jacquet ([42], p. 500), I was so bold as to voice the conjecture that with regard to the most important of these digressions in the monsyllabic root words, where, for example, the written syllable *kak* is pronounced *ket*, the retention of the orthography deviating from the pronunciation has an etymological basis, and I am still of the same opinion. It appears to me that the pronunciation digressed little by little from the orthography, but that in writing, in order to retain as recognizable the original morphology of the word, these digressions were not followed. J. Leyden appears to have shared this opinion, inasmuch as he ([56], p. 237) ascribes to the Burmese a softer, less articulated pronunciation which coincides to a lesser extent with the contemporary orthography of the language than is true for the Rukhéng, the inhabitants of Arcan (the Rariñ in A. Judson's treatise [51]). However, it lies in the nature of things that it cannot properly be otherwise. If, the above-quoted example, *kak* had not been formerly enunciated, this ending would not be found in the written language. For it is a definite principle, recently expounded by Mr. R. Lepsius in his treatise on palaeography ([55], pp. 6, 7, 89), which is replete with erudite observations and remarks, that nothing is represented in writing that did not occur at some time or another in pronunciation. Only the reverse of this statement do I hold to be dubious, for there are examples which cannot be readily refuted that writing does not always represent the complete pronunciation. That these phonetic changes arose in Burmese by virtue of a progressively fleeting pronunciation is proved by F. Carey's express remark that the endings of monosyllabic words digressing from the written form are not pronounced purely but in a very obscure manner that is scarcely distinguishable to the ear. In such cases, it is not uncommon for the

palatal nasal phonemes at the end of words to be omitted completely in pronunciation. This is the reason that the syllable written *thang*, which is used in a number of grammatical relationships, is pronounced according to F. Carey ([20], see table after p. 20) sometimes as *theen* (so that *ee* serves as a German long *i*) and sometimes as *thee* (p. 36, 105); G. H. Hough in his English-Burmese dictionary says that *thang* is generally pronounced *the* ([38], p. 14). From these observations, we can see that the degree of shortening appears to vary. From another example it can be historically proved that the orthography preserves the pronunciation of a different and presumably older dialect. The verb "to be" is written *hri* and pronounced *shi* by the Burmese. In Aracan, it is written *hi*. The people of this province are held to be older and to have been civilized earlier than the Burmese. See J. Leyden ([56], pp. 222, 237).

6. This pronunciation follows G. H. Hough. The symbol *r* is sometimes pronounced as *r*, at other times as *y*, and there does not appear to be any fixed rule governing this difference. H. J. von Klaproth ([53], p. 369) writes the word as *jî* in accordance with the French pronunciation, but he does not state the source of his Burmese words. Inasmuch as the pronunciation often diverges from the orthography, I write Burmese words exactly in accordance with the latter, and, as a result of the explanation appearing at the beginning of this treatise respecting the transliteration of the Burmese alphabet, every word quoted by me can be reconverted precisely into Burmese scriptural symbols. In parentheses I cite the pronunciation where it digresses and is definitely known to me. An "H." at such a point indicates that G. H. Hough is the source of the pronunciation. It is difficult to tell whether H. J. von Klaproth in the journal *Asia polyglotta* follows the script or the spoken word. For example, he writes (p. 375) *la* for 'tongue' and *lek* for 'hand.' However, the former word is written *hlyâ* and is pronounced *shyâ*, whereas the latter is written *lak* but is enunciated *let*. The word *ma*, which he cites for 'tongue,' I do not find in my dictionaries.

7. See G. H. Hough ([38], p. 20).

8. F. Carey [20] does not set off this type of compound and does not make special mention of it. However, this bracket emerges automatically if one goes through the Burmese dictionary critically. A. Judson [51] seems to indicate this category of compounding when he remarks that *pan* is used only in composition with words of similar meaning. To establish this fact precisely, I shall enumerate several additional examples of such words.

Chî: and *chî:-nañ:*, 'to ride or journey on something'; *nañ:* (*neñ:*, H.) by itself denotes 'to tread upon something.'

Tup (*tôk*—according to F. Carey, the *o* is pronounced as in the English word "yoke," and according to G. H. Hough, it is enunciated as in the English word "go") and *tup-kwa*, kneel'; *kwa* by itself means 'to be low.'

Nâ and *nâ-hkañ* (*nâ-gañ*), 'to listen, pay attention'; *hkañ* by itself means to take, receive.'

Pañ (*peñ*, H.) and *pañ-pan:*, 'to be fatigued, be exhausted'; *pan:* by itself means the same thing. *Pañ-hrâ:* also has the same meaning; *hrâ:* (*shâ:*) by itself means 'to yield, retreat, or recede,' but it also means 'to be present in a small amount.'

Rang (*yî*) means 'to remember, to collect something, to observe, to reflect about something,' while *rang-hchauñ* has the same meaning but with a more definite aim toward something; *hchauñ* by itself means 'to carry, hold, or contain, to complete. *Rang-pê:* means the same as the foregoing, and *pê:* by itself means 'to give.'

(*Hârshâ*) means 'to seek, look after something,' and *hrâ-kraṅ* (*shâ-gyaṅ*) means the same, *kran* by itself means 'to think, reflect, investigate, intend.'

Kan and *kan-kwak*, 'to impede, stop up, frustrate'; *kwak* (*kwet*) by itself means 'to enclose in a circle, establish boundaries.'

Chang (*chî*) and *chang-kâ:*, 'numerous, present in excess'; *kâ:* by itself means 'to disseminate, broaden, expand, scatter.'

Ram: (*ran*, with the vowel as in the English word "pan") and *ram:-hcha*, 'to guess at something, attempt, experiment, research'; *hcha* by itself means 'to reflect, ponder, be doubtful.' By itself and when combined with *hcha*, *taû* means 'to guess, advise, counsel,' but it is not used alone.

Pa and *pa-tha*, 'to make an offering to an evil spirit, to sacrifice'; by itself, *tha* means 'to renew, make new, fabricate,' as well as 'to bring along, offer up.'

I have taken care in the above examples always to compare words having the same accent. However, if words with differing accents are perhaps etymologically related, a factor not considered in the texts and reference material available to me, there would accrue a great number of additional examples, and occasionally the derivation of roots whose meanings correspond even better to the given compound could be determined.

9. A. Judson [51] gives this word *ama* (see *ma*) only the meaning of 'woman, older sister, or sister.' In his study, the word for 'mother' is *ami*.

10. F. Carey ([20], p. 144, § 8) writes *hkran* and does not provide the word with an accent. I have followed A. Judson's spelling.

11. G. H. Hough writes *a-kun:*. The meaning of this word derives from a meaning of the verb *kun*, 'to come to the end'; *kun*, however, is used to indicate exhaustion.

12. See F. Carey ([20], p. 116, § 112); see A. Judson [51], *chim·*.

13. F. Carey states this explicitly at several points in his grammar ([20], p. 96, § 34; p. 110,§§ 92, 93). We shall see immediately the extent to which his further contention that the word has no meaning in itself is valid.

14. See F. Carey [20], p. 115, § 110. See also p. 67; p. 74, § 75; p. 162, § 4; p. 169, § 24; p. 170, § 25; and p. 173.

15. See F. Carey [20], p. 96, § 34.

16. See in the Gospel According to St. John (21.2): *hri-kra-êng* (*shi-gya-î*), 'they are or were.'

17. E. Burnouf and C. Lassen [18], pp. 136, 137.

18. See F. Carey [20], p. 109, § 88.

19. See J. Leyden [56], p. 222.

20. See J. Low [57], pp. 12–19.

21. See J. Leyden [56], pp. 270 ff.

22. To be sure, J. Low does present some highly important conclusions about the Siamese language, but these would be substantially more instructive if one were to compare with them E. Burnouf's outstanding critique ([17], p. 210) of J. Low's paper. Unfortunately, J. Low is too brief concerning most parts of the grammar and is satisfied simply to give examples, without properly analyzing them, instead of rules. On the Annamese language I have before me J. Leyden's estimable treatment, but it is not sufficient for the present status of linguistics ([56], p. 158).

23. See W. von Humboldt ([44], p. 31).

24. *Ibid.*, pp. 31–34.

25. In my letter to J. P. Abel Rémusat ([44], 41, 42), I designated the case of the completion as the restriction of a concept of greater scope to one of smaller scope. Both expressions here, however, amount to the same thing. For the adjective completes the concept of the substantive, and in each of its usages it is restricted from its broad meaning to a single case. That is also true of the adverb and the verb. In the case of the genitive, the situation seems less clear. But even here the words standing in this relationship to one another are regarded as restricted from the many possible relationships among them to one definite one.

26. See my treatise on the Kawi language ([43], Vol. I, p. 253, note 3).

CHAPTER TWENTY-TWO

1. See J. P. Abel Rémusat [2], Vol. III, p. 279.

2. J. J. Ampère, who has felt this correctly [4], reminds us that *Fundgruben des Orients* was written during the first years of J. P. Abel Rémusat's Chinese studies, but J. J. Ampère further observes that even later J. P. Abel Rémusat never entirely abandoned this view. In fact, J. P. Abel Rémusat was probably excessively inclined to consider the Chinese language structure as deviating less from that of other languages than it really does. The adventurous ideas about the Chinese language and about the difficulty in learning it which prevailed when he began his studies might well have led him at first in this direction. But he did not realize to a sufficient degree that, whereas the lack of certain finer grammatical designations is probably harmless at times as far as the sense is concerned, it is never harmless for the more definite shading of the thoughts as a whole. Aside from this, however, it is obvious that J. P. Abel Rémusat has given us the first presentation of the true nature of Chinese, and the value of his grammar became increasingly evident with the publication in 1831 of the very estimable Chinese grammar by Father J. H. de Prémare [66]. Indeed, a comparison of the two works shows what a great contribution the work by J. P. Abel Rémusat has made to this field. In a work of graceful arrangement and great clarity, the reader is able to see the individual nature of the language shining forth. Although the grammar by J. H. de Prémare contains valuable material and certainly embraces all of the peculiarities of the language, it is evident that its author did not have a clear picture of the language as a whole. In any event, he was not successful in communicating this to his reader. Those more familiar with the language may have wished to see many of the gaps in J. P. Abel Rémusat's grammar filled in, but none of us can deny the great service that this splendid man has performed both in presenting the correct view of the language and in having made its study generally accessible for the first time.

3. S. Julien in Paris was the first to draw attention to this device of poetic style. This is a field which demands a thorough investigation of its own, for without such a study one is led into the greatest misunderstandings.

4. In his supplements to Basile's large dictionary, H. J. von Klaproth has given us such a list which is substantially longer than those previously known in Europe. It is distinguished even above the one in J. H. de Prémare's grammar by H. J. von Klaproth's highly valuable observations which shed light on the Chinese philosophical systems.

5. See my letter to E. Jacquet ([42], p. 496). The Tahitian word for 'to write' is *papai* (Apostles, 15.20), and on the Sandwich Islands it is *palapala* (Mark 10.4). In

New Zealandic *tui* means 'to write, to sew, to designate.' From his letters, I know that E. Jacquet has conceived the happy thought that among these peoples the concepts of writing and tattooing are closely related. The New Zealandic language confirms this, for instead of *tuinga*, 'the action of writing,' one also says *tiwinga*; and *tiwana* refers to some of the symbols which are etched in by tattooing and which extend from the eye toward the side of the head.

6. See W. Mariner, *Mariner of the Tonga Islands* [59].

7. See S. Lee's Preface to T. Kendall's *Grammar and Vocabulary of the Language of New Zealand* [52].

8. See D. de los Santos [70].

9. For example, the article on *a* begins as follows: "*A*, signifies universal existence, animation, action, power, light possession, cet., also the present existence, animation, power, light, cet. of a being or thing."

10. See E. de Flacourt [26]; see also E. Jacquet [46], p. 108, No. 13, and p. 126, No. 13.

11. See F. H. W. Gesenius [29], Vol. I, p. 132; Vol. II, "Introduction," p. xiv, and "History of the Hebrew Language," pp. 183 ff. See also H. von Ewald [25], pp. 166, 167.

12. See H. J. von Klaproth, *Observations sur les racines des languages sémitiques.* This essay was appended to A. A. von Merian's *Principes de l'étude comparative des langues*, which appeared directly after his death (on April 25, 1828). As a result of an unfortunate accident, the A. A. von Merian document disappeared from the book trade shortly after its publication. Consequently, the H. J. von Klaproth essay also got into the hands of only a few readers and requires a reprinting.

13. See F. Bopp [12], Paragraph 646, p. 296.

14. See F. Carey [20], p. 613, § 168, and C. Wilkins [84], p. 487, No. 863. A. W. von Schlegel calls ([72], p. 65) *waranda* a Portuguese name for the open verandas customarily found in India, and he says that this is the word which the English have taken into their language. In his dictionary, W. Marsden [61] attributes a Portuguese origin to the Malayan word *barandah*, which has the same meaning. But is this really correct? We cannot deny that *waranda* is a genuine Sanskrit word. It occurs, for example, in the *Amara Kôsha* (Chapter 6, Part II, p. 381). Because the word has several meanings, there could be some doubt as to whether that of a 'columned passageway' is genuinely Sanskritic in origin. H. H. Wilson and H. T. Colebrooke, the latter in his notes to the *Amara Kôsha*, have considered it so. Furthermore, it seems too strange to me that such a long word, in its various meanings and with a complete identity of sounds in Portugal and India, could have been customary. Therefore, I believe that the word came from India to Portugal and that it has gone over into the Portuguese language. According to J. B. Gilchrist ([30], Vol. I, see "Balcony, Gallery, Portico"), in Hindustani the word is rendered *burandu* and *buramudu*. It is possible that the English may have borrowed the name for these buildings from the Portuguese, but S. Johnson, in his dictionary [50], calls it "a word adopted from the East."

15. E. Froberville is the author of the collections on the Madecassian language mentioned by E. Jacquet ([46], p. 102n.).

16. See J. F. C. Gericke's Javanese dictionary [28]. In J. Crawfurd's handwritten dictionary, *mangum* is translated 'to adjust, to put right.'

17. See W. von Humboldt ([42], pp. 500–506).

18. See R. Lepsius [55], pp. 61–74, paragraphs 47–52; pp. 91–93, numbers 25–30; and especially p. 83, note 1.

19. I am happy to be able to add here that Professor H. J. von Klaproth, to whom I owe the data contained in the foregoing, shares my doubt on the relationship of the various Chinese styles. In view of his extensive readings in Chinese, especially of the historical writings, he must have collected a rich treasure of observations on the language. Hopefully, some of these will be included in the new Chinese dictionary which he is now planning. In this case, it would also be desirable to have his general observations on the Chinese language structure, as well as a special introduction.

20. For more information on this see: E. Burnouf ([17], p. 221); J. Low ([57], pp. 21, 66–70); F. Carey ([20], pp. 120–141, §§ 10–56); J. P. Abel Rémusat ([1], p. 50, numbers 113–115, and p. 116, numbers 309–310); and J. Leyden ([56], p. 245). If J. P. Abel Rémusat treats these numerical words in the old style, he has probably cited them for other reasons. They actually belong to the newer style.

Bibliography

[1] Abel Rémusat, J. P. *Éléments de la grammaire chinoise*. Paris, 1822.

[2] Abel Rémusat, J. P. *Fundgruben des Orients*. 6 vols. Vienna, 1809–1818.

[3] Adelung, J. C. *Mithridates, oder allgemeine Sprachenkunde mit dem Vaterunser als Sprachprobe in bey nahe fünfhundert Sprachen und Mundarten* (Fortgesetzt und bearbeitet von J. S. Vater). 4 vols. Berlin, 1806–1817.

[4] Ampère, J. J. "De la Chine et des travaux de M. Abel Rémusat," *Revue des deux mondes*, Vol. VIII (1832), pp. 373–405.

[5] Anderson, R. *Rudiments of Tamul Grammar*. London, 1821.

[6] Arcadius. *De Accentibus*, ed. H. Barker. Leipzig, 1820.

[7] Békésy, G. von. "Das Hören der eigenen Stimme," *Journal of the Acoustical Society of America*, Vol. XXI, No. 3 (1949), pp. 217–232.

[8] Berghaus, H. *Grosser Atlas der aussereuropäischen Erdtheile*. First section: *Atlas von Asia*. Fascicle I, No. 8 (Gotha, 1832), "Hinterindien "

[9] Bernhardi, G. *Wissenschaftliche Syntax der griechischen Sprache*. Berlin, 1829.

[10] Bloomfield, L. *Language*. New York, 1933.

[11] Bodmer, F. *Loom of Language*. New York, 1944.

[12] Bopp, F. *Ausführliches Lehrgebäude der Sanskrita-Sprache*. Berlin, 1827. A Latin edition of this work was published in Berlin in 1832: *Grammatica critica linguae sanscritae*.

[13] Bopp, F. *Frantz Bopp über das Conjugations-System der Sanskritsprache in Vergleichung mit jenem der griechischen, lateinischen, persischen und germanischen Sprache. Nebst Episoden des Ramajan und Mahabharat in genauen metrischen Übersetzungen . . . und einigen Abschnitten aus den Vedas*. Herausgegeben und mit Vorerinnerungen begleitet von Dr. K. J. Windischmann. Frankfurt, 1816.

[14] Bopp, F. *Sanskrit-Grammatik*. See *Ausführliches Lehrgebäude der Sanskrita-Sprache*.

[15] Bopp, F. "Analytical Comparison of the Sanskrit, Greek, Latin, and Teutonic languages, shewing the original identity of their grammatical structure" (partial translation of "Uber das Konjugationsystem der Sanskritsprache,)" *Annals of Oriental Literature*, Vols. I–III (London, 1820–1821), pp. 29–33, 40–45.

[16] Bopp, F. *Vergleichende Grammatik des Sanskrit, Zend, Griechischen, Lateinischen, Litthauischen, Gothischen und Deutschen.* Vol. I; Berlin, 1833. Vol. II; Berlin, 1835. This was a six-volume work—Vol. III (1842), Vol. IV (1847), Vol. V (1849), Vol. VI (1852)—but von Humboldt could have known only the first two volumes.

[17] Burnouf, E. In *Nouveau Journal Asiatique*, Series 2, Vol. IV (1829), pp. 210–228. E. Burnouf's article was a review of J. Low's *A Grammar of the Thai or Siamese Language*, published in Calcutta in 1828.

[18] Burnouf, E. and C. Lassen. *Essai sur le Pali.* Paris, 1826.

[19] Buschmann, E. *Lehrbuch der englischen Aussprache.* Berlin, 1832.

[20] Carey, F. *A Grammar of the Burman Language.* Serampore, 1814.

[21] Chadwick, J. *The Decipherment of Linear B.* Cambridge, England, 1960.

[22] Diefenbach, L. *Über die jetzigen romanischen Schriftsprachen.* Leipzig, 1831.

[23] Edwards, J. *Observations on the Language of the Muhhekaneew Indians*, ed. J. Pickering. Boston, 1823.

[24] Eliot, J. *A Grammar of the Massachusetts Indian Language.* A new edition with notes and observations by S. du Ponceau, and an Introduction and supplementary observations by J. Pickering. As published in the Massachusetts Historical Collection. Boston, 1822.

[25] Ewald, H. von. *Hebräische Grammatik. Kritische Grammatik der hebräischen Sprache ausführlich bearbeitet.* Leipzig, 1827.

[26] Flacourt, E. de. *Dictionnaire de la langue de Madagascar.* 3 vols. Paris, 1658.

[27] Forster, H. P. *An Essay on the Principles of Sanscrit Grammar.* Part I. London, 1810.

[28] Gericke, J. F. C. *Eerste Gronden der Javaansche Taal, benevens Javaansch leeren leesbock, met eene woordenlijst ten gebruike bij het zelve.* Batavia, 1831.

[29] Gesenius, F. H. W. *Hebräisch-Deutsches Handwörterbuch über die Schriften des Alten Testaments. Mit Einschluss der geographischen Nahmen und der chaldäischen Wörter beym Daniel und Esra.* 2 vols. Leipzig, 1810–1812.

[30] Gilchrist, J. B. *Hindoostanee Philology. A Grammar of the Hindoostanee Language; Or, Part Third of Volume First, of a System of Hindoostanee Philology.* Calcutta, 1796.

[31] Gilij, F. S. *Saggio de Storia Americana, ossia Storia naturale, civile, e sacra de regni, e delle provincie Spagnole di Terraferma nell' America Meridionale.* 4 vols. Rome, 1780–1784.

[32] Grimm, J. *Deutsche Grammatik.* 4 vols. Göttingen, 1822–1837.

[33] Harris, J. *Hermes, or a Philosophical Inquiry Concerning Language and Universal Grammar.* London, 1751.

[34] Haughton, Sir G. C., trans. "Manu" ("Manuscript"). This is a translation of a Sanskrit work with commentary by Sir G. C. Haughton. It was published posthumously in 1869, but von Humboldt worked from the manuscript itself.

[35] Heidegger, M. *Was heisst Denken.* Tübingen, 1954.

[36] Hengstenberg, H.-E. *Freiheit und Seinsordnung.* Stuttgart, 1961.

[37] Herder, J. G. "Abhandlung über den Ursprung der Sprache," a paper presented before the Akademie der Wissenschaften of Berlin in 1770. It was later published in *Herder's Werke*, ed. H. Düntzer, Vol. XXI (Cologne, 1878), pp. 17–132.

[38] Hough, G. H. *An English and Burman Vocabulary.* Serampore, 1825.

[39] Humboldt, W. von. "Über die Aufgabe des Geschichtsschreibers," *Abhand-lungen der historisch-philologischen Classe der Berliner Akademie der Wissen-schaften* (1820–1821).

[40] Humboldt, W. von. "Über den Dualis," *Abhandlungen der historisch-philologischen Classe der Berliner Akademie der Wissenschaften* (1827).

[41] Humboldt, W. von. "Über das Entstehen der grammatischen Formen," *Abhandlungen der historisch-philologischen Classe der Berliner Akademie der Wissenschaften* (1822–1823).

[42] Humboldt, W. von. "Extraits d'une lettre de Monsieur le Baron Guillaume de Humboldt à E. Jacquet sur les alphabets de Polynésie asiatique," *Nouveau Journal Asiatique*, Series 2, Vol. IX (June 1832), pp. 484–508.

[43] Humboldt, W. von. *Über die Kawisprache auf der Insel Java, nebst einer Einleitung über die Verschiedenheit des menschlichen Sprachbaues und ihren Einfluss auf die geistige Entwicklung des Menschengeschlechts.* Berlin, 1836. (Actually, all that was printed [Volume I] bears the title "Einleitung" ["Introduction"], so that the promised work on the Kawi language itself never appeared.)

[44] Humboldt, W. von. "Lettre à Monsieur Abel Rémusat."

[45] Humboldt, W. von. "Über die Verwandtschaft der Ortsadverbien mit dem Pronomen in einigen Sprachen," *Abhandlungen der historisch-philologischen Classe der Berliner Akademie der Wissenschaften* (1829).

[46] Jacquet, E. "Mélanges malays, javanais et polynésiens. No. III," *Nouveau Journal Asiatique*, Series 2, Vol. XI (February 1833), pp. 97–159.

[47] *Jahrbücher für wissenschaftliche Kritik.* Stuttgart, 1827.

[48] *Jahrbücher für wissenschaftliche Kritik.* Stuttgart, 1834.

[49] Jespersen, O. *Language, Its Nature, Origin and Development.* New York, 1949.

[50] Johnson, S. *A Dictionary of the English Language.* 2 vols. London, 1755.

[51] Judson, A. *A Dictionary of the Burman Language; with Explanations in English.* Compiled from the manuscripts of A. Judson (F. Carey, J. Coleman) and . . . other missionaries in Burmah [by J. Wade]. Calcutta, 1826.

[52] Kendall, T. *A Grammar and Vocabulary of the Language of New Zealand* [with a Preface by S. Lee]. London, 1820.

[53] Klaproth, H. J. von. In *Asia polyglotta* (1823). This is the title of a journal which was published in Paris.

[54] Klaproth, H. J. von. *Observations sur les racines des langages sémitiques*, appended to A. A. von Merian, *Principes de l'étude comparative des langues.* Paris, 1828.

[55] Lepsius, R. *Paläographie als Mittel für die Sprachforschung zunächst am Sanskrit nachgewiesen.* 2d ed. Leipzig, 1842.

[56] Leyden, J. "On the Languages and Literature of the Indo-Chinese Nations," *Asiatick Researches, or Transactions of the Society, Instituted in Bengal*, Vol. X (1808), pp. 158–289.

[57] Low, J. *A Grammar of the Thai or Siamese Language.* Calcutta, 1828.

[58] *Manual para administrar á los Indios del idioma Cahita los santos sacramentos.* Mexico, 1740.

[59] Mariner, W. *Mariner of the Tonga Islands, An Account of the Natives of the Tonga Islands in the South Pacific Ocean, with an Original Grammar of Their Language.* Compiled from the communications of W. Mariner by J. Martin. 2 vols. London, 1817.

[60] Marsden, W. *Catalogue of Dictionaries, Vocabularies, Grammars, and Alphabets.* London, 1796.

[61] Marsden, W. *A Dictionary of the Malayan Language*. London, 1812.
[62] *Meyer's Konversations-Lexikon*. 4th ed. Leipzig, 1889.
[63] Morris, C. *Signs, Language and Behavior*. New York, 1955.
[64] Pindar. *Carmina quae supersunt*, ed. A. Boeckh. 2 vols. Leipzig, 1811, 1821.
[65] Pott, A. F. *Etymologische Forschungen*. 2 vols. Lemgo, 1833, 1836.
[66] Prémare, J. H. de. *Notitia linguae Sinicae auctore Padre Prémare*. Malaccae, 1831.
[67] Raven, F. A. "Phasenaktionsarten im Althochdeutschen," *Zeitschrift für deutsches Altertum*, Vol. XCII, No. 3 (November 1963).
[68] Reitz, F. W. *De temporibus et modis verbi graeci et latini*. Leipzig, 1766.
[69] Reyes, Fr. A. de los. "Arte Mixteca," MS.
[70] Santos, D. de los. *Vocabulario de la lengua Tagala*. Sampaloc, 1794.
[71] Schlegel, A. W. von. "Aus dem Indischen: Ramayana," in *Sämmtliche Werke*, ed. E. Böcking, Vol. III (Leipzig, 1846), pp. 7–98. This was first published in von Schlegel's journal, *Indische Bibliothek* (1820).
[72] Schlegel, A. W. von. In *Berliner Kalender auf das Jahr 1831*. Berlin. This is an annual, of which eight volumes were published (from 1829 to 1836) by F. Dümmler.
[73] Schlegel, F. *Über die Sprache und Weisheit der Indier. Ein Beitrag zur Begründung der Alterthumskunde*. Heidelberg, 1808.
[74] Schmidt, J. *Die Sprachfamilien und Sprachkreise der Erde*. Heidelberg, 1926.
[75] Schmidt, J. *Die Verwandtschaftsverhältnisse der indogermanischen Sprachen*. Weimar, 1872.
[76] Schrijen, J. *Einführung in das Studium der indogermanischen Sprachwissenschaft*. Heidelberg, 1921.
[77] Sophocles. *Oedipus Tyrannus et Euripedes Orestes*, ed. R. F. P. Brunck. Strassburg, 1779.
[78] Steinthal, H. *Der Ursprung der Sprache*. 4th ed. Berlin, 1888.
[79] Tapia Zenteno, C. de. *Arte novíssima de la lengua Mexicana*. Mexico, 1753.
[80] Tapia Zenteno, C. de. *Noticia de la lengua Huasteca*. Mexico, 1767.
[81] *Transactions of the Historical and Literary Committee of the American Philosophical Society*. Philadelphia, 1819.
[82] Vetancurt, A. de. *Arte de la lengua Mexicana*. Mexico, 1673.
[83] *Webster's New International Dictionary*. 2d ed. Springfield, Mass., 1954.
[84] Wilkins, C. *Sanskrit Grammar*. London (?), 1808.
[85] Zeisberger, D. *A Grammar of the Language of the Lenni Lenape or Delaware Indians*, trans. S. du Ponceau. Philadelphia, 1827. This is the third volume of the new series of *Transactions of the American Philosophical Society*.

Index

Index